PEDALARE! PEDALARE!

JOHN FOOT is Professor of Modern Italian History in the Department of Italian, University College London. He has published many books both in Italy and in the UK and lives in London.

PEDALARE! PEDALARE!

A History of Italian Cycling

JOHN FOOT

BLOOMSBURY
LONDON · BERLIN · NEW YORK · SYDNEY

First published in Great Britain 2011

This paperback edition published 2012

Copyright © by John Foot 2011
Maps by John Gilkes

All photographs reproduced in this book are courtesy of Publifoto/Olycom and
Olympia/Olycom with the following exceptions: the photograph of Enrico Toti
(photographer unknown), the photograph of the Giro of Rebirth (Foto Terreni)
and the poster of the Velodrome Vigorelli (The Lordprice Collection).

Bloomsbury Publishing Plc
50 Bedford Square
London WC1B 3DP

www.bloomsbury.com

Bloomsbury Publishing, London, Berlin, New York and Sydney
A CIP catalogue record for this book is available from the British Library

ISBN 978 1 4088 2219 7

10 9 8 7 6 5 4 3 2 1

Typeset by Hewer Text UK Ltd, Edinburgh
Printed in Great Britain by Clays Ltd, St Ives plc

To Sarah

Contents

PART III: *The Golden Age*

PART IV: *After the Golden Age*

PART V: *The Age of Doping*

Acknowledgements

This book would not have been possible without the generosity and intelligence of a series of sports journalists in Italy. In particular I would like to thank Claudio Gregori, Elio Trifari and Marco Pastonesi of *La Gazzetta dello Sport*. Enzo Pennone provided the perfect setting in Sicily for a series of long discussions about sport, politics, journalism and Italy. Marco Pastonesi introduced me to ex-cyclist Renzo Zanazzi, who rode with Italy's greatest cyclists from the sport's golden age in the 1940s and 1950s, Fausto Coppi and Gino Bartali, and who told me the story of his remarkable life. I am indebted to the work of pioneering sports historians Stefano Pivato and Daniele Marchesini, whose books have been constant companions on my travels to cycling museums and cyclist sites across Italy. Vincenzo Andricciola dug around in the archives in Perugia for me, and found some fascinating and original material. Thanks also to Paolo Pezzino, Salvatore Favuzza, Alessia Salamina and Phil Cooke.

Alberto Brambilla was a treasure trove of information about the literature of cycling, and his own excellent books are the best accounts of the way famous writers have written about this sport. Other people have helped with specific enquiries or simply answered my often naïve questions – Gian Paolo Ormezzano, John Irving, Giovanni Ruffa, Massimiliano Boschi, Paolo Maggioni and Fausto's daughter, Marina Coppi. I also had the honour of meeting, albeit too briefly, the late, great Candido Cannavò. His writings were an inspiration to many at the time, and remain so today. His office is still there at *La Gazzetta dello Sport*, the newspaper that founded and continues to run the Giro d'Italia. On his wall there is a huge photograph of Fausto Coppi and Gino Bartali, the greatest Italian cyclists of all time, who gave birth to one of the most extraordinary sporting duels in history. At a time when cycling itself is still immersed in a crisis largely of its own making, the stature of the stars of the past continues to grow. This book is about the power of that past, about how a sport became a national obsession so dominant that it had the ability to change the course of history itself.

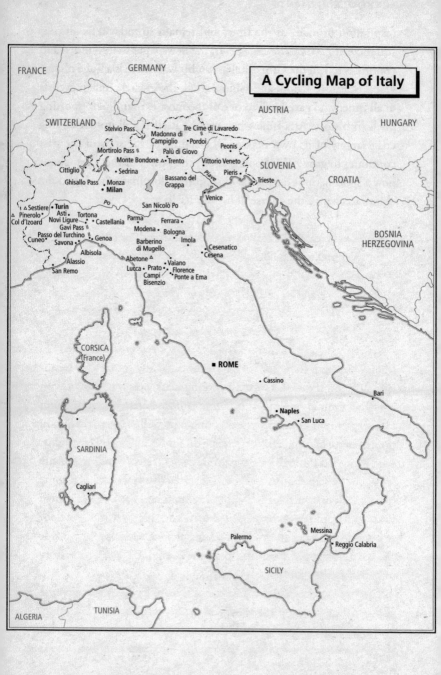

A Cycling Map of Italy

FRANCE
GERMANY
AUSTRIA
HUNGARY
SWITZERLAND
Stelvio Pass
Tre Cime di Lavaredo
Madonna di Campiglio
Pordoi
Peonis
Mortirolo Pass
Palù di Giovo
SLOVENIA
Monte Bondone
△ Trento
Vittorio Veneto
Cittiglio
Pieris
CROATIA
Ghisallo Pass
Sedrina
Trieste
Monza
Bassano del Grappa
Milan
Plave
Venice
△ Sestiere
Turin
Po
San Nicolò Po
Pinerolo
Asti
Tortona
Col d'Izoard
Novi Ligure
Castellania
Parma
Ferrara
BOSNIA
HERZEGOVINA
Gavi Pass
Modena
Cuneo
Passo del Turchino
Bologna
Savona
Genoa
Imola
Albisola
Barberino di Mugello
Cesenatico
Alassio
Abetone △
Vaiano
Cesena
San Remo
Lucca
Prato
Florence
Campi
Ponte a Ema
Bisenzio
CORSICA
(France)
■ ROME
Cassino
Bari
SARDINIA
Naples
San Luca
Cagliari
Palermo
Messina
Reggio Calabria
SICILY
ALGERIA
TUNISIA

Introduction

'And God created the bicycle, so that man could use it as a means
for work and to help him negotiate life's complicated journey . . .'

> – *Translation of the inscription
> at the church of Madonna del
> Ghisallo, the shrine of cyclists, near
> Como, northern Italy*

Milan, northern Italy, 2007. I am in the canal area, one of the trend-
iest parts of the city. Once a working-class neighbourhood with
its own criminal fraternity, this zone is now dominated by fashion
industry employees and by the young and well-off participants in
the city's *movida* who arrive en masse on Friday and Saturday nights.
I am being led through a courtyard by a small, elegant man. He only
looks about sixty but he is, in fact, over eighty years old. We come
to a little door which leads down some stairs. If I hadn't been shown
the way, I would never have been able to find this place. On the door
is a simple inscription. It is not an auspicious entrance, but inside
there is a whole world waiting to be discovered, the *past*, the history
of Italian cycling itself.

The walls downstairs are covered with trophies and photos whose
images range from some of the greatest cyclists ever to anonymous, ordinary riders. To enter this bar, with ex-professional cyclist
Renzo Zanazzi, is to go back in time, to look back into history. As

I walked slowly around it, with its long tables, well-stocked bar and red chairs, Zanazzi showed me all the photos, one by one. He had, after all, ridden with Italian cycling legends Fausto Coppi and Gino Bartali in the 1940s, and he had worn the leader's pink jersey during the country's great national race, the Giro d'Italia. For each image, Zanazzi had a story to tell: of races, falls, secret agreements, missed opportunities, payments and failed payments. In the corner stood a stayer, a strange motorbike once used for track sprinting. On our way out, Zanazzi gave me a bottle of potent grappa, which he had distilled himself. One glass of it, later that evening, was enough to knock me out. I was to return on other occasions to listen to his stories and tape them in his front room. He told me that he still cycled nearly every day, often with *La Gazzetta dello Sport* journalist Marco Pastonesi, whom he described jokingly as *mio gregario* (his cycling support rider, his slave, his worker).

In entering Zanazzi's bar I had come across a lost world, a piece of cycling mythology. It was as if I had stepped out of a time machine. This book will take a similar journey into the past. In these pages I shall tell numerous stories and analyse them, unpick and retell legends and evoke images from a past which lives on in the present. This will not be a complete history of Italian cycling. Zanazzi's bar and its contents represent a very personal albeit extremely diverse collection, and I hope that my journey will be every bit as eclectic. The story of Italian cycling has always been *told* – and this book will not depart from that style.

Professional cycling today bears little relation to the sport in which Zanazzi participated, despite the claims of its contemporary proponents and the organisers of big races. Even Zanazzi's bar is a remnant of that great past, a nostalgic space which is used, as Renzo himself told me, more as a generic meeting place for old people than a site for the discussion of cycling. Zanazzi's bar is a museum piece, radically out of step with the hustle, bustle and pollution of the city above it, out there in the real world. Inside that bar you get a vision of a fascinating, sweaty, grimy and yet glorious past. Outside, it seems as if such a place could not exist. This book will attempt to take the reader into the Italy of Zanazzi's bar, with its smells, tall tales, chiselled faces and arms raised at finish lines. But I shall not try to trick the reader. Let's be clear about this right from the start: Renzo Zanazzi's Italy is gone, *for ever*. It has 'hung up its pedals', as the saying goes, and it will not be making a comeback. But this history still matters in contemporary Italy, and can be seen all over the country, in every nook and cranny, on every mountain top and, sometimes, in the most extraordinary and unexpected places.

If you take the state highway no. 36 out of Milan, passing through the grey, flat, almost endless periphery of the city, you eventually reach the foothills of the mountains around Lake Como. There the landscape quickly becomes spectacular, rising steeply above the Y-shaped lake before plunging down to Bellagio, a small, beautiful town situated at the end of the finger which splits the water into two parts. At the top of this peak, with views stretching over to Switzerland and back to Milan, there is a steep climb – so sharp it is sometimes known as 'a wall' – up to a small church, 750 metres above sea level. Italy is full of drives like this, but this journey should not be taken by car. This is a unique site for Italian cyclists, and a key climb in one of the earliest and most celebrated one-day classic races, the Giro di Lombardia.

In October 1948, in his summer residence at Castel Gandolfo, outside Rome, Pope Pius XII lit a lamp which was called the 'permanent flame of the Ghisallo'.[1] The flame was then taken to Milan by car, and from there to the church on the hill top by numerous cyclists in relay, including Coppi and Bartali. However, other versions of the same event claim that the flame was carried all the way from Rome by bike. In October 1949 the same Pope officially declared that the tiny church known as the Madonna del Ghisallo would become the site of the patroness of Italian cyclists.[2]

Thousands of riders make this climb every year, on what journalist Gianni Brera called 'the poor man's spaceship', to the Madonna del Ghisallo. There they rest and admire the view, but also take in a series of monuments and a museum dedicated to the history of cycling. One memorial depicts a cyclist who has just fallen alongside another triumphant rider. This statue is a testament to the pain and the glory of the sport of cycling, and every year, on 24 December, an annual mass for the cyclists of the past is held here. Inside the tiny church are bicycles (including the one ridden by Fausto Coppi to break the world hour record in 1942, as well as the bikes ridden by Gino Bartali to his 1938 and 1948 Tour victories), shirts and numerous photos of living and dead riders. Next door, looking out over the lake, there are statues of Coppi, Bartali and Giro d'Italia organiser Vincenzo Torriani, alongside Don Ermelindo Viganò, the priest who inspired the link between this church and cycling.

The Madonna del Ghisallo is a living monument to the memory, the popularity, the beauty and the physical effort of bike riding in Italy. A number of famous riders even got married here. The shrine symbolises the sport's continuing hold over the popular imagination and its intimate relationship with landscape and history.

Pedalare! Pedalare! is a history of Italian cycling from the appearance of the first bikes in Italy in the 1880s through to the birth of a mass, popular sport in the 1930s and 1940s and up to the present day. It tells the story by moving between the biographies of individual cyclists, tales of races and an analysis of Italian society. Much of the book is concerned with cycling as a professional sport, but space will also be dedicated to the role of the bicycle in everyday Italian life, from the 'red cyclists' who spread socialist propaganda in the early twentieth century through the cycling commuters of the 1950s and 1960s, right up to the politically inspired, anti-traffic, 'critical mass' riders who have appeared in today's cities. The book will develop chronologically, its chapters set largely around the life stories of riders, and these biographical chapters are interspersed with stories of notable races and incidents. The heroic age of the sport began with the first Giro in 1909 and later saw the bicycle used as a weapon in the First World War. Ottavio Bottecchia, the first Italian to win the Tour de France in the 1920s, had fought in one of his country's special bicycle divisions during the conflict. Cycling became a mass sport in the 1920s and 1930s, a period which saw the emergence of Costante Girardengo, the 'super-champion', Alfredo Binda, the first cycling superstar, and his great rival Learco Guerra. Benito Mussolini was not very interested in cycling himself, but his regime was, and sport became a battleground for the hearts and minds of the people in the 1930s. In that battle, cycling, the most popular sport of all, played a key role.

The golden age of Italian cycling saw a series of epic battles between Gino Bartali and Fausto Coppi – the most celebrated Italian cyclists of all time. As Italy tried to recover from the ravages of the Second World War, in the 1940s and 1950s cycling reached levels of popularity never seen before or since. 'The third man', Fiorenzo Magni, who did battle with both Coppi and Bartali and whose war years continue to excite debate, was also a participant during that golden age. Cycling continued to enjoy great popularity after the end of the golden age, and chapters in this book are dedicated to the two Italians who won the Tour de France in the 1960s, Gastone Nencini and Felice Gimondi, as well as to the revolutionary impact of 'the Cannibal', the great Belgian cyclist Eddy Merckx, in the late 1960s and 1970s.

Cycling was already inextricably entwined with drug-taking and doping by the early 1960s, and by the end of that decade discussions and controversies over testing and test results were beginning to dominate all else. Over the last twenty years, doping scandals have plagued the sport. The tragic odyssey of Marco Pantani was the most potent and unhappy example of this long-term trend. Sadly, it is difficult not to view this period as the age of doping.

Throughout this book, the annual Giro d'Italia will be seen as a key means of understanding changes within Italy as a whole – its culture, its history, its growing sense of national awareness through its geography. *Pedalare! Pedalare!* will take the reader on a historical tour of Italy. Italy's Giro was a powerful creator of national identity, but it also sowed the seeds of (and revealed) a series of local and personal rivalries. If it was a sporting event which created something called 'Italy', it also exacerbated trends that divided Italians. Cycling history was also marked by changes in Italy's relationships with other countries, and international conflict affected and was affected by sporting events. In this respect the connection with France is crucial, as is that with Belgium (home to many great cyclists), the Netherlands, Spain and, latterly, the United States. In the late 1940s and early 1950s, Italian cyclists were subject to verbal and physical attack as they dominated the Tour, yet many also became heroes in France. Foreign riders became stars in Italy, although they were also treated with suspicion and hostility.

Pedalare! Pedalare! will tell the history of cycling as a history of Italy itself. It will link the culture of the country with the traditions of this very particular self-propelled vehicle, which remains today and every day a means of getting around town used by millions of Italians. In a society supposedly dominated by the motor car, the bike has survived in a quite remarkable way in Italy and millions are sold each year. Some towns, especially those in the centre of Italy, seem almost to have been created for the bicycle, and it is difficult to take any trip in the countryside without coming across groups of Italian men, decked out in all the latest body-hugging Lycra kit, riding for hundreds of kilometres across the highways and byways of Italy, often on very expensive bikes. For years, the car supplanted the bike but recently the 'anti-horse' has made something of a come-back. All is not lost.

The biographies and stories of Italian cycling in this book mirror the history and biography of the Italian nation. Developments in this popular sport have always been linked to cultural, economic and social change in Italy as a whole. *Pedalare! Pedalare!* makes no claim to provide a comprehensive history of Italian cycling, and many worthy riders have been omitted from the story altogether. It has been designed to appeal both to experts and non-specialists.

Above all, this book can be seen as a journey, back in time but also across plains, up hills and over mountain passes. As with Renzo Zanazzi's bar in Milan, these pages will try to evoke the past, but they will also question the way that past has been recounted and understood. Cycling history is composed of innumerable anecdotes, myths and stories. This book will endeavour to get behind these stories, not in order to correct them but to try and understand what brought them about. The journey is about to begin. We are in the saddle, out in the open air. It is time to get our legs moving. Time to set off. *Pedalare! Pedalare!*

PART I

The Heroic Age

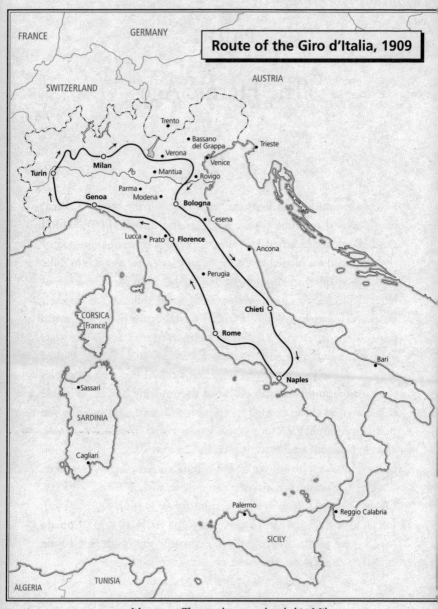

Route of the Giro d'Italia, 1909

13–30 May 1909. The race began and ended in Milan.

The Origins of the Giro d'Italia and the Bicycle Goes to War, 1909–19

It was a revolution, an invention that changed the world, a silent, man-powered machine which went up and down hills and could carry people for hundreds of miles. Moreover, it needed no food or shelter, could be carried quite easily and lasted for years. The bike could be adapted to all kinds of daily tasks, from the delivering of letters and groceries to the transport of small children to school. It was so perfect that nobody could really make it any better, at least in terms of shape. Despite endless tinkering, and over a hundred years of technological progress since then, bicycles in the 1890s looked very similar to those many of us ride today.[1] At first, these vehicles were for the middle classes only, but they quickly became available to the masses, cheap enough for humble peasants, workers and even priests to afford. Italy soon had its own range of bike companies, as well as manufacturers of rubber for the tyres. In Italy bikes soon began to make a lot of money for willing entrepreneurs and riders. Cycles soon acquired their own names, too, such as Bianchi (1885), Olympia (1893), Velo (1894), Maino e Dei (1896), Frera (1897), Lugia (1905), Taurense Legnano (1906), Atala (1907), Torpado (1908) and Ganna (1910).[2] By the turn of the century, a young country was taking to the roads. The Italians had begun to pedal.

In 1909 Italy was engaged in elaborate preparations for the nation's fiftieth birthday, which would be celebrated in 1911. In the north, an industrial revolution was transforming the cities of Milan, Turin and Genoa. Companies as diverse as Pirelli, Campari, Fiat, Beretta and Alfa Romeo had set up factories and were producing goods which would become household names. Successive Liberal governments, under the wise leadership of a low-profile statesman called Giovanni Giolitti, used political reform to modernise the country. Slowly, democracy was becoming a fact of life for a minority of Italians. Yet this was also nation riven by division and social strife. Socialism had taken hold in parts of the country and anarchist revolutionaries preached insurrection. Meanwhile, a radical nationalist movement pushed for imperial conquest.

Above all, there was a vast gap between the relatively wealthy north and the impoverished south of the country. The resolution of this division was the subject of much discussion, and the issue itself became known as the Southern Question. It was perhaps not suprising, then, that cycling took hold in the industrial and rural north. It was in the north and the middle of Italy that bikes could be afforded and where they were first produced by Italian entrepreneurs. Popular sport was also largely concentrated in the north, with the establishing of important football clubs in Genoa, Turin and Milan in the 1890s and early twentieth century.

Did cycling also have its own Southern Question? The sport had many followers in the south, and the great riders, from Girardengo onwards, had big fan bases there. But the south struggled to produce great cyclists in any significant numbers when compared to the north, or to Rome. Why? It could not have been a question of terrain. The *Mezzogiorno* was geographically criss-crossed by good cycling territory – hills, plains and big mountains. But roads, or the lack of them, certainly were a factor, as was the ability of an individual to buy a bike as well as the region's economic backwardness. And perhaps a cycling culture simply never took root in the *Mezzogiorno*. Even today, bikes are rare in, for example, a typically southern city like Naples. Cycling also fed off political and civil associationism, and the political sub-cultures which took root in the centre and north of the country in the late nineteenth and early twentieth centuries. These forms of associationism were weaker in the south. Moreover, cycling was closely linked to industrialisation, which was concentrated in the north. It wasn't, however, merely a question of wealth and poverty. Most of the great Italian cyclists came from extreme poverty. Grinding rural hardship was just as much a fact of life in the north of Italy as it was in the south.

By 1909, sporting culture was blossoming in this young and vibrant nation, and links were made between Italian identity and a healthy, fit body. Gymnastics associations, shooting clubs, mountaineering organisations and cycling groups sprung up all over the country, often with official backing. The idea of a healthy Italian race, hygienic and fit, held great appeal and had strong links with the political right. Sport was seen by many as a heroic activity, linked closely to the fate of the nation. Cyclists were individuals battling against the elements and the limits imposed by their own bodies. They were to be put to the test, and they should be given as little help as possible in their quest. If they were heroic amateurs, so much the better. Sport seen in this way seemed to link up with an individualist ideology, almost as if it was anti-socialist in its very nature. A conflict soon emerged about the purpose and meaning of sport and sporting activity: 'It was in the liberal age that the "triumph" of the ideology of the body took hold.'[3] Yet sport did not always serve the interests of the nation. Both Catholic and socialist sub-cultures quickly began to understand the importance of sporting activity (if not sporting competition) and to promote their own, ideologically inspired societies and associations.[4] It was in this climate that the idea of national competitions took shape, amidst a battle about the very meaning of sport.

Following the success of the Tour de France, various organisations in Italy began to float a proposal for a similar race in Italy. The Italian Touring Club, a tourist association which promoted walking, travel and cycling, was interested in backing such an event, as was the Milanese daily paper *Il Corriere della Sera* alongside the Bianchi bike company. But it was the sports paper *La Gazzetta dello Sport* (founded in Milan in 1896) which won the race to organise the first Giro d'Italia. Armando Cougnet (an Italian born in Nice), the administrative director of the newspaper at the time, had followed the Tour on two occasions and was the brains behind the Giro. Cougnet had started work as a young journalist on the paper in 1898 (at the age of eighteen), riding all the way from Reggio Emilia to Milan by bike. His father was already on the staff of the paper, writing mainly as a fencing correspondent. Armando Cougnet and his colleagues had seen at first hand in France how a month-long cycle race could be used to promote a newspaper (*La Gazzetta* was in deep financial trouble), and at the same time give birth to a genuine national event.[5] In 1908 *La Gazzetta* took its competitors by surprise with an announcement that the first Giro would be run the following year. *La Gazzetta* was already behind the two great one-day classics linked to the start and the end of the cycling season, the Milan–San Remo and the Giro di Lombardia. Nobody could have predicted the extent of the Giro's success, which would forever be linked to the name of its founder. Cougnet remained in overall charge of the Giro d'Italia for nearly fifty years, until after the Second World War.

Since 1909, Milan's pink sports paper and the Giro d'Italia have been inseparable. The paper has always decided on the route, and negotiated the important details of permission and access with villages, towns, cities, the Italian state and occasionally foreign administrations whose paths the race would cross. *La Gazzetta* became, and remains still, the first port of call for cycling fans. For years, on the day before the race started, in Milan, an additional ritual would take place. Riders and teams would turn up in the courtyard of *La Gazzetta* offices in Via Galileo Galilei in order to register their bikes and collect their numbers. This event was known as *la punzonatura*, as the rider number was physically stamped on to their bicycles.[6] Huge crowds would line the roads around the offices as their heroes rode or walked sedately in, dressed in their civilian clothes. During the race itself, the walls outside the courtyard were lined with pages from *La Gazzetta*, and fans would hang around waiting for news from the race and reading reports from the previous day. In later years, *la punzonatura* was held in classic tourist sites in the city, such as the big square in front of the central Castello Sforzesco. Milan, home of *La Gazzetta dello Sport*, was the undisputed Italian capital of cycling. Cycling's northern bias was thus created and reinforced by the way the Giro was born and run. In order not to compete directly with the Tour, the Giro began in May, a tradition which has remained in place ever since.

It was 2.53 in the morning, 13 May 1909, when the first Giro d'Italia set off from Milan.[7] None of the bikes had gears, and everyone had to pedal *all* the time, including when they were riding downhill. One hundred and twenty-seven riders were ready to leave, and forty-nine made it to the finish line. Only five of them were not Italian. It was not an easy start. The first of eight stages which awaited the riders was nearly 400 kilometres long, but afterwards the riders would have two days rest before the next stage. There were early casualties, a pile-up and some cheating. One cyclist was found to have been covering part of the course by train; another fell while eating a chicken leg. Eighteen days later Luigi Ganna rode back into Milan in triumph, in front of tens of thousands of fans. The race was already a great success. One magazine wrote: 'artistic Milan, the Milan of the working class . . . it had all disappeared. Only cycling Milan was left'. Ganna had won thanks to a points system. If the Giro had been measured in terms of time, he would have come third. His prize money was very good, for the time – 5,325 lire – but there would soon be sponsors and many other races. Ganna was a bricklayer and his first comment on winning would become one of the most quoted in the history of cycling. When asked by Cougnet how he felt, he replied, in dialect, 'My arse is killing me.' Ganna was now a star, and although he never won another Giro, his name would forever be associated with the race. In 1947, he turned up as

the starter. The bikes he manufactured were to be ridden to numerous victories right up to the 1950s.

The early days of the Giro and the Milan–San Remo one-day classic
(which began in 1907) were not for the faint-hearted. Without any
of the logistical back-up of modern sport, or help from the mass
media, cyclists often got lost or simply dropped out of the race. In
1910 the Milan–San Remo was hit by torrential rain and 20 centimetres of snow fell on the Turchino Pass, the key climb in the race.
The leading rider, French cyclist Eugène Christophe, was so cold
('my fingers were rigid, my feet numb, my legs stiff and I was shaking continuously', he later wrote) that he stopped to warm up in a
small farmhouse, where he was joined by two other riders. Local
peasants wrapped him in a blanket and gave him some rum. The
Frenchman spoke little Italian and, ignoring the warnings of his
hosts to stay put in such weather, set off again and easily won the
race. The other two riders decided to remain in the farmhouse. Over
an hour after Christophe crossed the finish line, the second-placed
rider, Giovanni Cocchi, finally arrived.

At times Christophe was convinced he had taken the wrong
turning as he rode through empty roads on his way to victory. In
retrospect, this was no great surprise since he finished so far ahead
of the second-placed rider, while many spectators had remained
indoors or given up hope of seeing any racing. The course took
Christophe twelve and a half hours to complete. Only a handful –
seven to be precise – of the sixty-three starters completed the race
and three of these were disqualified. Luigi Ganna had been caught
taking a lift in a car for part of the way. Christophe himself suffered
from frostbite and bad health for some considerable time afterwards. Some stories also recount that the French cyclist donned a
pair of *fustagno* (fustian) trousers in the peasants' farmhouse, which
he then adjusted with a pair of scissors. The travails of the 1910 race
saw the birth of the legend of the Milan–San Remo, which would
develop into the most prestigious of all the one-day Italian classics

and whose history would be made by the greatest cyclists of all time – Costante Girardengo, Alfredo Binda, Coppi, Bartali, Eddy Merckx (who won it seven times), Sean Kelly, Bernard Hinault and the winner in 2009, 'the Manx Missile', Britain's Mark Cavendish.[8]

In Italy, politics and sport quickly became inseparable as, in the early twentieth century, the socialist and union movement began to attract more and more followers. Central Italy, with its subversive traditions and vast landless rural proletariat, was the first part of the country to be won over by the left, and even today it remains Italy's 'reddest' region. Imola, a small town forty minutes from Bologna by train, was the first place in Italy to elect a socialist to parliament, and its walls bear signs of its radical past. In the main street, a plaque marks the birthplace of that first deputy, Andrea Costa, a man described as the 'apostle of socialism'. This was also the region with the highest concentration of bikes in Italy. In 1934 there were nearly 750,000 bikes in Emilia, one for every 4.4 people. In the poorest region of southern Italy, Basilicata, bicycles were a rarity, with, at that time, one bike for every 289 inhabitants and a mere 1,762 altogether.

It was perhaps not surprising, therefore, that the idea of 'red cycling' first took hold in central Italy, and that its first organisations were born in Imola. Socialists and trade unionists saw the opportunities the bicycle provided in terms of activism and mobilisation. In a region dominated by medium-sized towns divided by swathes of countryside, and where the control of space was critical to the success of any mass movement – through strikes, boycotts and protests – the bike offered a crucial advantage. For example, the quick movement of militants to flashpoints could be employed to block the arrival of blackleg labour. Employment – not pay – was the key issue for the rural day labourers of the Po Valley. Their central demand was the right to work for a certain period of the year and to control who worked, and when. The employers resisted this demand with passion and violence. They knew full well that their power lay precisely in the over-supply of labour. In such a delicate situation, 'red cyclists' might well prove decisive in the class struggle. In short, 'the bicycle was not an innocent bystander in the struggle for hegemony [in] Italy'.[9]

In this context, the 'red cycling' movement was born. One of its main aims was to provide cheap bikes 'for the working masses'. Certain companies specialised in this market. In Milan there was even a *pneumatico Carlo Marx* (a 'Karl Marx tyre') – 'the great red brand' – which did business across Italy to 'comrades and cyclists'. *Avanti!* bikes were also produced, complete with red cycling shirts. The bike itself had something left wing about it. To pedal was to work. It was 'the vehicle of the poor', 'the ally of their effort'.[10]

On 24 August 1913, in Imola, the 'red cyclists' held their first national congress and a film cameraman was there to record this unique event for posterity. Socialism in Italy had come around to the idea by then that sporting activity was not necessarily something right wing. As Massimiliano Boschi has written, 'the bicycle was not to be seen as an instrument for the middle classes, but as a means of propaganda . . . it will be at the vanguard of our movement'.[11] One thousand or so 'red cyclists' turned up in Imola, where they met and agreed on a programme with statutes and rules. According to these statutes 'during periods of struggle (elections, agitations, strikes) red cyclists will provide our committees with quick and safe means of communication and correspondence. Our red bicycles are and will be the vanguard of our propaganda and our movement, quick means for our people in every village and every town to remain united . . . both in times of peace and in times of war.'[12] Elaborate rules were produced for comrades demonstrating on their bikes, with trumpeters, flags and a mechanic but also the obligatory presence of someone who could administer first aid. Socialists took cycling very seriously indeed. They had a new weapon in the class struggle.

But the socialists remained, on the whole, firmly critical of sport itself, as opposed to the practice of cycling. The first 'red cycling' convention passed a motion which saw sport as 'a very serious problem . . . a powerful way of diverting the attention of the workers, and of young people in general, from an understanding of social problems and the importance of political and economic organisation'.[13] In a similar vein, in 1912 another socialist condemned 'young people' who were 'more interested in reading *La Gazzetta dello Sport* as opposed to *Avanti!*' (the socialist daily newspaper) and 'only concerned with making love or racing their bikes'. Sport was seen as inspiring 'localistic and militaristic' attitudes. Cycling was good, the sport of cycling was bad. Despite these trenchant statements, the sport soon became immensely popular among peasants and workers all over Italy. If cycling was Italy's 'opium of the people', it was indeed a potent drug.

As the 'red cyclist' movement began to spread, many commentators came to view bikes as dangerous and subversive. The Church, for example, was particularly concerned. At one point priests were banned from cycling in Italy and had to fight for their right to ride a bike. Other writers began to study this new form of transport. At the turn of the century the criminologist Cesare Lombroso dedicated a whole article to the bicycle in which he analysed this new vehicle as a fast track to crime. Lombroso dubbed the bicycle 'the quickest vehicle on the road to criminality, because the passion for pedalling leads people to steal, to fraud, to swindle'. He argued that the bike was both a 'cause and an instrument of criminality'.[14] But Lombroso also understood that bikes could be a force for good. They brought 'the countryside closer to the city', helped increase voter turnout and could be used for trips for the blind, or even for transporting criminals to jail. Moreover, riding a bike was a distraction from the evils of alcohol and the stresses of modern life. In the end, despite the title of his article, 'Cycling and Crime', Lombroso's argument came out decisively in favour of the bike. 'I believe,' he concluded, 'that the cycling people of the twentieth century will be less vulnerable to nervous disorder, and have stronger bodies that the people of the last century.'

In Italy's cities, as more and more bikes turned up on the streets, pedestrians and local councils began to see them as dangerous.

Bikes were banned by a special decree in the wake of street rioting in Milan in May 1898 and licences were later introduced in many cities, as well as punitive fines. Stringent measures applied to the use of bicycles in 1929's highway code although cyclists were allowed, for a while, to ride on the country's first motorways. With time, these restrictions were relaxed. By the 1930s, most Italians, especially those in the industrial north, not only owned a bicycle but it had become their main means of private transport. Despite the legislators, the anti-horse was in the ascendency.[15]

In the meantime, as pro- and anti-cycling debates raged, the sport itself went from strength to strength. Italian cycling quickly produced a series of heroes to rival Ganna, with their own nicknames and fans. Ganna's successor as winner of the Giro was Carlo Galetti. Already, early cyclists were being compared to Greek gods, as in this description by the socialist deputy Ivanoe Bonomi from September 1910, the year of Galetti's victory in the Giro. Bonomi wrote of the masses of cyclists riding on the Po, and of 'spontaneous' races among them, and long discussions about the sport itself. 'Galetti, Ganna, Gerbi, Verri, here are the names on the smiling lips and open mouths of everyone. The pedalling heroes of today are as popular as the heroes of the circus in Ancient Greece.'[16] Galetti, who became famous for the consistency of his cycling (he was known as 'the Human Stopwatch'), won the Giro three times in a row, from 1910 to 1912 (although in 1912 the race was awarded to a team rather than an individual). Once he had retired from the sport he went back to his day job as a printer, but he also continued to ride. In his late forties, in 1930 and 1931, he completed the Milan–San Remo twice in succession.

Popular heroes and myths began to emerge. Giovanni Gerbi, like so many of his contemporaries and those riders who were to come after him, started cycling as a delivery boy and continued to do so as a baker and builder. He rode in the second Tour de France in 1904 when he was just nineteen. During that race, angry spectators had attacked a group of riders during the second stage, in the middle of the night.[17] According to some versions, Gerbi lost a finger in the clashes that followed, but subsequent photos seem to show that all his fingers were still intact. Henri Desgrange described the events he witnessed as director of the Tour: 'The drama lasted a few seconds. I remember only the sight of a pile of bikes on the ground . . . I didn't even see poor Gerbi fall. There was a second as the following cars came to a halt, then I saw a horde of savages with long sticks in their hands starting to flee through the fields.' Gerbi's nickname '*il Diavolo Rosso*' (the Red Devil) was said to have been given to him by a priest because of a red cycling top he was wearing as he rode, by mistake, right into the middle of a religious procession. Stories about Gerbi's courage and rebellious nature were repeated until they became popular legend. It was said, for example, that he would train with bricks tied to his bike. In 1932, at the age of forty-seven, he rode the entire Giro (although he went over the maximum time limit, so he was not an official finisher). On arriving in Milan he found that everyone except his wife had gone home.[18] A bar and literary society exists today in Asti, his home town, dedicated to the memory of this great pioneering cyclist, and is adorned with bikes, artwork and images linked to his life.

Early racing was nasty, brutish and very, very long. It was a test of endurance as much as speed, a sport not for the faint-hearted. 1914 saw the last Giro before Italy entered the war in May 1915. The race set off at midnight from Milan and a number of top riders left the competition altogether after they encountered a thunderstorm, snow and flooding. On the third day, an Italian rider led on his own for 350 kilometres before he was caught just 30 kilometres from the finish. Later on, in the south of Italy, the race leader went missing completely, He was only found a day later, with a high fever, in a hay loft. Only eight riders completed the Giro that year, which included (sadistically) the longest stage ever – 430 kilometres (from Lucca to Rome). That year was the first in which time rather than points decided the winner of the race. Early riders were, to coin a phrase first used in France, 'slaves of the road'.

When Italy entered the First World War in May 1915, the bicycle was seen as a key – and a new – weapon in military strategy. Bicycle sections were formed within many of the older army units and bikes were used to transport men and supplies to and across the wide front. Cycling volunteers had already been called into the army in 1908 and twelve cycling battalions were employed by Italy in the conflict itself. Technology was developed to keep pace with the military use of the bike, with special reinforced frames, camouflage paint and a place to stow a rifle. As one propaganda publication claimed, this set-up offered great advantages over previous forms of transport: 'these were horses which could be carried on your shoulder, and which didn't need to eat or drink, nor did they ever run away'.[19] Bikes allowed for swift and silent movement behind the lines and improved communications; they were also easy to repair and maintain and used no petrol. In Italy's war effort, the bike was crucial, and many ex-cycling soldiers were to ride as professionals after the conflict was over. One of those who didn't make it was Carlo Oriani, who had won the 1913 Giro. He died after contracting pneumonia after swimming across the wide Piave river in the chaotic retreat from Caporetto in 1917.

Ottavio Bottecchia, who would go on to ride in the Tour de France after the war, was constantly on his bike during the conflict. Later, he recalled 'a long ride in the mountains, with a machine gun on my back, which I was to take to a lookout post that was under heavy fire. I had to ride on paths and animal tracks which were steeper than those of the Galibier or the Izoard [big mountain climbs often ridden on the Tour]. I arrived at my destination later in the evening after a risky alpine climb. The next day I found out that my efforts had not been in vain. The Austrians attacked in the night and had failed to take the post thanks to the new machine gun.' After 1918, the cycling units were to become part of the myth of the war, and the nationalist poet Gabriele D'Annunzio dedicated verses in tribute to them.

All countries need heroes. Still a young nation in 1915, Italy's heroes were rather thin on the ground. There were those from the wars of the Risorgimento – most notably Giuseppe Garibaldi – but few new heroes had emerged in the forty-five years since the unification of the country. In 1887 Lieutenant Colonel Tommaso De Cristoforis died with his men as his unit was wiped out in a place called Dogali during Italy's ill-fated colonial adventure in East Africa. For a time, 'the five hundred dead' of Dogali provided good heroic material – streets were named after them, and even the huge Piazza dei Cinquecento in front of Rome's central station – but this myth was not enough on its own. As a new global conflict began, new martyrs would be required.

Being wounded in war had always been good for the making of heroes; the idea that giving part of your body for the struggle, or fighting to the death, was vital to the creation of national myths (think of Lord Nelson, who lost an arm and an eye, and ultimately his life, for the sake of his country). In fact, the whole concept of 'the beautiful death' was a key component of national myths – often encapsulated in short books dedicated to war victims, many of which were published after the First World War.[20] Edmondo De Amicis's classic patriotic novel *Cuore* is full of characters who lost limbs for the greater good of the fatherland.[21]

Garibaldi himself had been injured during the Risorgimento, and this episode formed a key part of one of the most important songs to come out of that period: 'Garibaldi fu ferito'. Garibaldi's boot – complete with bullet hole – can still be admired in the Risorgimento museum housed inside the monumental marble monument known as the '*Altare della Patria*' in the centre of Rome. The bullet which supposedly penetrated that boot is itself to be found in a glass box in Garibaldi's house on Caprera, an island off the coast of Sardinia.

These were and are relics of a new religion – the religion of the nation.

Enrico Toti gave his life for Italy, but in this case not a limb. Born into a poor family in Rome in 1882 (the year of Garibaldi's death), his father was a railway worker. Following in the family footsteps, Toti also went to work on the railways, but in 1908 he suffered a horrific accident in which he lost a leg. Quickly, Toti found a means of overcoming his handicap – the bicycle. Removing the left pedal, he now began to cycle everywhere, earning money partly as a kind of circus freak and a participant in sideshows in Rome and elsewhere. He even decided to cycle round the world, gaining sponsorship from a number of sources.

After a series of false starts Toti apparently made it all the way to France, Belgium and Denmark, and even as far as Sudan in 1913 (or so he claimed). Other accounts have him passing through Moscow on an earlier trip from Rome and even getting as far as Lapland. For Enrico Toti, 'the bicycle was liberty'. Toti was a patriot and a nationalist, and one of the many urban myths linked to his life was that he was forced to remove an Italian armband when in Vienna, which, it is said, increased his hostility towards the Austrians. Many of these stories were recorded posthumously, as Toti's life was rein-vented after the war to fit in with his supposedly heroic martyrdom.

When Italy entered the war in 1915 Toti tried time and again to join the regular army, but his physical condition made this impos-sible. No army could recruit a one-legged man, no matter how good a cyclist he was or how zealous a patriot. Moreover, Toti was nearly thirty-four by this time – an eccentric older mascot among the raw, often teenaged conscripts who tended to dominate the infantry. Despite his handicap, however, Toti refused to give up hope. Twice it seems he made his own way to the front on his bike, offering to help behind the lines and pleading for some sort of supporting role, however minor. On one occasion he was arrested by his own side on suspicion of being a spy. Not everyone appreciated his zeal. Many Italian soldiers were less than enthusiastic about the war anyway,

and looked down on Toti as someone 'who wanted to die at all
costs'. A frustrated Toti wrote to his sister about the 'two wars' he
felt he was fighting, one against the Austrians and one with his own
army, which would not let him participate in the conflict. On 5 July
1915 he wrote: 'I was entering a trench in the Cormons area: they
found me, a General was called, and the Carabinieri sent me pack-
ing straight away.'

It was around this time that a group of volunteer cyclists achieved
national fame by riding off to the war from Rome itself. Within
weeks, Toti himself was back in the war zone, amidst the administrative chaos of mobilisation of a country fighting its first national
conflict. From this point on, his movements are difficult to trace,
and contradictory accounts turn up in his biographies, letters and
official reports. Lucio Fabi has written of an 'anti-history' around
Toti's life which emerged in parallel with the official (and often
retrospective) heroic version.

For some time, Toti helped out behind the front line, continuing to perform his 'act' in order to finance his presence there. Daily
letters to his sister provide the best evidence of his state of mind
in this period. His attempts to reach the front line were frustrated
by the army hierarchy, at least according to Toti himself, although
again Lucio Fabi claims that 'he tended to bend reality towards
his vision of the world'.[22] In early August, the army lost patience
with Toti, and he was unceremoniously packed off back to Rome.
Four months later, the official version of events recounts that Toti
was 'sent' back to the war zone as part of back-up for the army.
He certainly returned to the same area as before. Once there, Toti
became an early 'war collector', selling debris as a kind of memorial
of the conflict. After the war, in the suffocating poverty of the 1920s,
a whole generation of Italians in the mountains would eke out a
living from the dangerous accumulation of the metal from bombs
and bullets and other military debris.

Toti continued to write letters begging to be allowed to fight at
the front; he felt part of the 'class of invulnerable people' (he used

a kind of pre-fascist language). He also felt that he could be an example for others and that he was blessed – 'nothing will happen to
me'. Toti's bicycle wanderings saw him end up with the 3rd division
of the Bersaglieri cyclists, probably as a sort of mascot. Many soldiers
found Toti somewhat annoying, his nationalist zeal at odds with the
harsh, muddy and cold reality of the war, with its constant association with death and injury. One sergeant wrote about Toti that 'he
was a bizarre type, who enjoyed battle . . . he turns up when there
is more work to be done'. Toti was also 'insulted' by some soldiers
'who had been affected by subversive propaganda'.

In April 1916 Toti was injured in the trenches. After a period
in hospital, he was soon back – and close to the front line. At that
moment the 3rd Bersaglieri were ordered to attack the Austrians at
quota 85, east of Monfalcone. These were the real killing fields, and
they were also to claim Toti's life, along with the lives of a number of
other soldiers who would never find fame in death.

One way or another, Toti was near the front line when he died
on 6 August 1916, not far from Monfalcone, above Trieste. In the
official record of what happened that day Toti was described as a
'volunteer in the Bersaglieri cyclists' battalion'. The rest of the bulletin read as follows:

> despite being without his left leg, after having provided important
> support in the battles of April . . . On 6 August he threw himself
> towards the enemy trenches and continued to fight with pride,
> although he had been injured twice. After he was hit by a third
> bullet, he threw his crutch towards the enemy and, with a heroic
> cry, died while kissing the feather on his helmet [the symbol of
> the Bersaglieri], showing that stoic character which is worthy of a
> truly Italian soul.[23]

It was also said that Toti had cried 'Nun moro io' (I do not die) as he
did, in fact, die. His 'noble' gesture was often described as 'sublime'
and later versions spoke of the 'word of mouth' spreading the news

of Toti's heroism, which 'shook the dead in their graves'. But Toti's 'gesture' was also, if it ever actually happened, totally useless from a military point of view. In August Toti's story was made public, but it was to be a few months before a full propaganda effort would take shape.

It was in the autumn of 1916 that the powerful myth linked to Toti's death was born. Its creator was an illustrated newspaper called *La Domenica del Corriere*, and the colour image on its front page (published on 24 September 1916, nearly two months after Toti's death) was by the celebrated illustrator Achille Beltrame. One version of events was thus fixed visually in the popular imagination. Toti, wearing full uniform, is depicted throwing his crutch at the Austrians as he dies in the midst of a fierce battle, standing above a trench, leaning only on his rifle for support. In the illustration, Toti is surrounded by dead Austrian soldiers, with Italians behind him. The byline reads: 'The heroic end of the *mutilato* Enrico Toti. Injured for the third time, he gets up and throws his crutch against a retreating enemy' (the last part was an added detail, not even in the original dispatches).

Toti's martyrdom formed the basis of an extremely potent myth, one which was to lead to dozens of monuments, plaques and books. His published letters were studied in schools everywhere, and were particularly successful during the fascist period. It was also a myth intimately connected to the sport and practice of cycling, and many of the monuments dedicated to Toti depict either his bike or a bicycle wheel. Of course, as in most patriotic myths, the greater part of this story was pure fiction.

Toti never had a full uniform (and therefore no official feather on his helmet, although he has a feather and a kind of uniform in some photographs from the war) and it is unclear if he even died anywhere near the trenches. The 'I do not die' line is also suspicious. Exactly who had heard him cry out amid the gunfire? Some versions even claim that Toti was shot by a sniper while, worse for wear after a few drinks, he was haranguing the enemy.

Nevertheless, the image of a last dying gesture by a one-legged man was a powerful one, and it was far too valuable for the facts to be allowed to get in the way of its use by the army, the government and assorted nationalists (as well as the fascists, after the war). Toti soon received a posthumous military gold medal, although this was in fact a special medal from the king – an admission that Toti had not actually been in the army at all. Memorials and books proliferated after the end of the war.

Fascism idolised Italy's war heroes. The whole *raison d'être* of the movement was based around the glorification of war. Many future fascists had direct experience of the war and Mussolini himself made much of his own minor war injury. A number of leading nationalists (and futurists) died in the trenches. The Toti myth quickly became the most important symbol of heroism for the fascist movement after the war. Toti was perfect for fascist propaganda, with its concentration on the heroic minority who took part in the war, and the demonisation of those they considered to be pacifists, shirkers and deserters. D'Annunzio dubbed Toti 'the divine despiser of the Austrians' and Mussolini used the myth of the dead cyclist as a way of dividing fascists from those he saw as Italy's internal enemies, as symbolised by the pacifist-socialist parliamentarian and militant Francesco Misiano. In 1920, Mussolini wrote: 'The Italy of tomorrow will not be that of Misiano, but will be that of Toti.'[24] In many ways, he was to be proved right. Misiano was thrown out of parliament by the fascists in 1921 and forced into exile, while statues and tributes to Toti adorned squares and cemeteries across Italy.

After 1918, a 'war of the monuments' pitted pacifists, socialists and anarchists against pro-war nationalists and fascists. In some areas, anti-war sentiment made it impossible to commemorate the conflict, or even to fly the Italian flag. Socialists put up anti-war monuments all over Italy, and these became the objects of fascist violence. People were attacked merely for wearing a uniform.[25] In this climate of fear and civil war, Enrico Toti's funeral was a natural flashpoint, especially as the procession went straight through the subversive 'red' neighbourhood of San Lorenzo in Rome. The funeral, which was organised purely for symbolic and political reasons, took place on 24 May 1922, the seventh anniversary of Italy's entry into the war, and some years after Toti's death. Toti's first resting place had been in the Monfalcone military cemetery close to the battlefield itself, where it was adorned with a rifle and a crutch. In 1922, Toti's body was exhumed and carried across Italy (through Trieste, Bologna and Florence), becoming a rival of sorts to 'the unknown soldier', who had been buried in a special tomb in the capital in 1921. Even in death, Toti seemed to be forever on the move.

Clashes and violence on the day of Toti's second funeral left three people dead, as workers fired on the fascists escorting the coffin. Today, Toti's modest grave can still be seen near the entrance to the huge municipal cemetery in Rome. Under the fascist regime, in many monumental statues throughout Italy the small, frail figure of Enrico Toti often turned into a fascist superman: naked, muscle-bound, proudly exposing his body to Austrian bullets. Later, two massive submarines were named after Toti, in the 1920s and again in the 1960s, as well as numerous streets, schools and public buildings.

Toti also played a part in creating his own myth when he was alive, selling signed photographs of himself to finance his frequent bicycle escapades. He often told his own life story, claiming that he had covered 20,000 kilometres on his bike. Newspaper reports of his 'epic' ride were used – by Toti himself – to try to convince the military hierarchy that he should play an official role in the war. Across the world, before the war, Toti became a Fellini-like personality, on the edge of the nomadic world of travelling circus performers and street actors. He refused to accept the role of invalid, exhibiting his injury with pride, highlighting it through his single-pedal bicycle.

Propaganda surrounding the life of Toti later reinvented the young Roman as a kind of Zelig, or a Forrest Gump, who had been seen 'at the head of many patriotic demonstrations'.[26] This is an old trick. Take a well-known personality and move him – posthumously – like a pawn into various key moments of pre-war and wartime history.

Toti fitted the bill perfectly, the emotive power of his mutilated body combining well with fascist and nationalist rhetoric. So much for the myth. But what was the real story of Toti's participation in the war?

Many of the doubts around the official version of Toti's death relate to the terrain itself. How did a man with one leg even reach the area, during an attack, under fire? There are many accounts of this celebrated death, and, while some include the celebrated 'throwing of the crutch', others do not. As Lucio Fabi wrote, 'It seemed like a film, later it would become one.'[27] For some, Toti did indeed become an official soldier, but only in the brief moments before he met his end. Other versions talk of complete invention, of a banal death behind the lines and the idea – by some bright spark – of a new myth. Very soon Toti's life, but above all his death, would become a political question, and the 'control over the myth' an extremely important issue for the Italian state.

Of his famous bicycle, nothing more was seen. Toti lived on after his death as a war hero, a martyr, Italy's most important victim of the war alongside Cesare Battisti, an Italian socialist born in Trento (then part of Austria) who was executed by the Austrians for treason in that city in 1916. Fascism used Toti's name for propaganda purposes throughout the period of the regime. His story was so well known and so often related that mere mention of his surname was enough to evoke instant images of selfless heroism.

In 1932, on the tenth anniversary of the 'March on Rome' which had seen Benito Mussolini appointed as Prime Minister, the Italian fascist government declared that the area where Toti died would henceforth be known as a 'holy zone'. A new monument was erected there to the one-legged martyr. Yet when Italian and German troops fought as allies between 1940 and 1943, memories of the First World War were still fresh. After Italy pulled out of the military alliance with Hitler in September 1943, the Nazis in northern Italy destroyed this homage to Toti. It would be rebuilt again by Italian volunteers in 1948.

Today, the myth of Enrico Toti is considerably less potent, in part because of its over-use under the fascists, for whom he was 'the spirit of Italy itself'.[28] Nonetheless, interest in his life story (and especially in his cycling achievements) has remained high. A film was made in 1955 based on his life.[29] Today his tomb lies largely ignored, but those original monuments to Toti and his bicycle still stand all over Italy and are particularly prominent in those parts of the country that saw conflict in the war.

The whole Toti myth fitted badly with the anti-war sentiments so prevalent in post-1945 Italy, and radical historians of the 1960s unveiled the truth about the true horrors of the conflict. Little space remained for patriotic myths and 'beautiful deaths'. The reality of the war had been far from heroic. Most men were conscripts. Death was commonplace, horrific and often barely noted. Millions of bodies were never even identified. Survival was an end in itself.

But Toti's name at least lived on in cycling mythology. In 1948 a *gregario* named Vittorio Seghezzi was in the Italian team in France in order to help his captain Gino Bartali, who was to win the Tour in extraordinary fashion. But Seghezzi also managed to win a stage (the final sprint in Paris). Earlier, in the Lausanne–Mulhouse stage, one of his pedals broke and he was forced to ride for 82 kilometres with one leg doing all the work. Not surprisingly, this feat earned him an extraordinary nickname: 'the Enrico Toti of the Tour de France'. In the 1960s and 1970s Gianni Motta was one of the top cyclists in Italy. After a nasty leg injury severely hindered his movements, Motta became known as 'the Enrico Toti of Italian cycling'.

The bike had been to war. Now many of those soldiers who had ridden in the Great War were to become professional cyclists. One of these ex-soldiers would go on to win the Tour de France, twice, in the 1920s. And if cycling was the sport of the underprivileged, nobody was poorer than Ottavio Bottecchia, the first Italian to triumph in the Tour.

The Life and Mysterious Death of Ottavio Bottecchia, the First Italian to Win the Tour de France

'*Sono qui per gli schei*' (dialect of the Veneto – I am here for the money)

> – Ottavio Bottecchia, France, 1923

'It would be dangerous to follow Bottecchia up a mountain pass, it would be suicidal . . . his progression is so powerful and regular that we would be asphyxiated'

> – Nicolas Frantz (Tour results: second in 1924, fourth in 1925, second in 1926, winner 1927–8)

Ottavio Bottecchia's face had poverty and war written into it. Lined, gaunt and furrowed, he looked as if he had never had enough to eat – something which was more or less true until he became a successful professional cyclist in the early 1920s. Bottecchia's face in the photos we have is always etched with tiredness and stress, caked in dust, his thin, muscle-bound legs covered in mud and grime. Where the next meal was coming from had always been something of a worry for the Bottecchia family, and Ottavio took up cycling, and decided to ride in the Tour de France, purely for the cash. He had even ridden on his own (without any team support or sponsorship) in the Giro in 1923, finishing first among the so-called 'isolated' riders, and fifth overall.

He was born into an extremely poor rural family in the Veneto in 1894. As the eighth child – his name even sounds like *ottavo*, the Italian for 'eighth' – he spent less than two years at school before starting work as a cobbler and he also earned money as a builder and woodsman. It is said that he learnt to read and write through the sports pages of newspapers. Bottecchia's father emigrated, like millions of other Italians at the time, and tried to find work in Germany.

But was Bottecchia Italian at all? Although he had been born and brought up in what was nominally Italy, and had fought valiantly for 'his country' in the war, he didn't actually speak Italian, only the local dialect, and some later claimed that he was actually French. This assertion was made on numerous occasions after Bottecchia's successes in the Tour in the mid-1920s. In an attempt to kill off this rumour, after Bottecchia had become famous and his nationality had become something of great importance, *La Gazzetta* published his birth and residence certificates.

In that decade, the Tour was a sadistic enterprise. The stages were ludicrously long (one alone took twenty hours to complete), team support ranged from poor to non-existent and the 'roads' were appalling. Most stages lasted at least fourteen or fifteen hours, and sometimes longer. The mountain paths were often freezing and extremely arduous. Punctures were commonplace, and you had to fix them on your own. Riders weren't even allowed – according to the rules – to help other riders during the race, or have them help you, even in times of emergency. It was inhuman, a test of endurance and of an individual's willingness to tolerate pain, and only someone like Bottecchia, driven by poverty and hunger, could have survived it.

The torture of the Tour routes of the 1920s was, however, a vast improvement on the way in which Bottecchia had lived his life up till then. He had spent four years in the combat zone during the First World War (he was born in a tiny settlement just 10 kilometres from Vittorio Veneto, scene of the last battles of the Great War). Unlike Enrico Toti, however, Bottecchia was actually part of the elite cycling Bersagliere division, with their special folding bikes (with space for a rifle or a stretcher).

Brought up near the front line itself, his main job during the war, thanks to his local knowledge, was to ferry messages and supplies back and forth from town to town, trench to trench, by bike. In so doing not only was he therefore always 'in training' for his future career, but was also constantly in danger of being captured by the enemy. This happened on at least two occasions, and his heroic escapes earned him a silver medal for his actions in November 1917, when, in the official bureaucratic language of the state, 'calmly and bravely under violent enemy fire he returned fire efficiently and in a deadly manner with his own machine gun, inflicting serious damage on the enemy and stopping their advance. Forced on numerous occasions to retreat, he ignored the danger and carried his weapons with him so that he was able to open fire again and again.'[1] During the war Bottecchia was also subjected to a gas attack, and contracted malaria.

In 1919 Bottecchia migrated to France to work as a builder. It was there, like Alfredo Binda after him, that he began to race and train seriously as a cyclist. This emigration was also at the heart of the theory that he was not Italian at all, but French. His poverty affected his whole family and his first-born daughter died in 1921 at the age of just seven months. Bottecchia had socialist sympathies, and was a convinced anti-fascist. Back in Italy, he began to make a name for himself with some good placings in one-off races and in the Giro in the early 1920s. Journalists characterised him with references to his humble origins and sports writer Bruno Roghi wrote that he was badly dressed and smelt of goat's cheese. Despite earning good money from the sport, Bottecchia always travelled third class on trains and never made much of his extraordinary (relative) wealth after his victories in France in the 1920s, although there are rumours of family jealousy and rivalries, of lovers, of flashy cars and of needy hangers-on.

In 1923, when he was nearly twenty-nine, Bottecchia rode in his first Tour de France (although even then he was the youngest rider in his team). Only three Italians took part in that race and Bottecchia was unknown in France, and almost unheard of in Italy. His name was frequently misspelt but he soon gained a number of nicknames, among them 'the Woodsman', 'the Builder', 'Botescia' and 'Enigmatique'. Ottavio Bottecchia began the Tour as a *gregario* for the French rider Henri Pellissier, but his performances were so strong that he nearly won the Tour. The history of cycling has been written by the exploits of ex-*gregari*.

It was only when Bottecchia donned the yellow jersey in 1923 that the press were forced to take note. Italian journalists were dispatched to cover the race as Bottecchia was the first Italian to wear yellow at the Tour. For the writer Paolo Facchinetti 'it was as if a revolution had taken place'.[2] Stories began to circulate. Bottecchia, it was said, had stopped and got off his bike in order to have a wash and a drink during a mountain stage. Nonetheless, he kept winning and his determination and strength took him through the most difficult stages time and time again. In his first Tour he finished second.

He soon gained a reputation as a machine-like rider who never gave up and he was likened to a 'human train'. Armando Cougnet wrote that 'for Bottecchia, to ride is to work, each turn of the pedal is like a blow of the worker's hammer'. A famous photo of Bottecchia sums up his career, and perhaps an entire epoch of cycling. The cyclist is on his own on the Col d'Izoard in 1924, on a steep mountain track, the path in front of him littered with stones. He is so tired that his bike is skewed to one side with effort. Behind him is a large car and the clouds are below. There are no spectators to be seen.

In 1924, Bottecchia was back in the Tour, and this time he won the entire race, becoming the first Italian to do so. That year he took the yellow jersey on the first day and stayed in front until Paris, destroying the opposition in the mountains. The yellow jersey seemed his own private property. *La Gazzetta dello Sport* began to sell thousands of papers on the back of its reports from France. As a token of gratitude the newspaper launched an appeal for Bottecchia to which even Mussolini contributed (as the first person to give money, with one

lira, although the overall total raised was over 61,000 lire). More
stories emerged. It was said that Bottecchia had stopped to walk for
a while on the Izoard mountain stage (some accounts say he walked
for three kilometres uphill), and was followed by journalists on foot.
During the walk he whistled army songs as he strode on, pushing
his bike. Others commented on his propensity for silence. However,
Bottecchia wanted his victories to be remembered, and he named
his daughter Fortunata Vittoria (Lucky Victory). Such success in a
foreign land was against all the odds. After all, Bottecchia was on his
own – alone – against the French (the nation *and* its cyclists) and
even against those who in theory made up in his own 'team'. The
final blow came from the Tour organisers, who created courses which
seemed designed to destroy Bottecchia and to allow a Frenchman
to win. There were also rumours of attempts to poison Bottecchia's
food and sabotage his bike.

With the 1924 Tour win, he made enough money to open his
own bike factory; there are still Bottecchia bikes in production today.
Astonishingly, 1925 saw Bottecchia win the Tour again, this time by
more than fifty-four minutes from the second-placed rider. For Gian
Paolo Ormezzano, Bottecchia adopted entirely new tactics, taking a
big lead early on and controlling his rivals' progress in the mountains.
In all, he won nine stages on the Tour, and held the yellow jersey for
thirty-four days of racing. In Italy, however, he was unable to repro-
duce this form. Alfredo Binda, for example, was never troubled by
Bottecchia on Italian soil.

Bottecchia's death at the age of thirty-three, while cycling, has been
the subject of countless debates and conspiracy theories ever since
it occurred. On 3 June 1927 – less than a month after the death
of his brother in a car crash – Ottavio Bottecchia was found lying
near his bicycle at 9.30 on an ordinary roadside near his home
in the Friuli region. He had gone out to train that morning and
was horribly injured. He died twelve days later in hospital, leaving his wife and two children under four. Mystery still surrounds

the circumstances, his death at first being registered simply as the result of a bike crash.

More than eighty years since this tragedy, the circumstances of Bottecchia's death have still never been fully explained. Italy being Italy, the conspiracy theories have been numerous, with books published periodically about the 'Bottecchia murder'. All we know for certain is that the cyclist's body was found on the ground, after he had been out training on his own. The official inquest was brief and hardly satisfactory.

There were and remain three main theories about Bottecchia's death. One was that he had simply fallen off his bike after feeling ill, although his injuries seemed too severe for that to carry much weight. Another (which did not make the Italian press at the time) was that fascists had beaten him to death. Many people suffered a similar fate in the 1920s in Italy under fascism, and Bottecchia's opposition to the regime was well known and – for the fascists – infuriating. That they would go as far as to murder him in broad daylight is unlikely, but not impossible. The third hypothesis was also one of murder, but this time without a political motive: Bottecchia had been killed by a jealous husband, or by a crazed peasant. Years later, a local peasant confessed to the murder of Bottecchia (he said he had beaten him with a stone), after claiming that he had caught him stealing grapes. Strangely, at that time of the year there were no grapes to steal. Other more bizarre versions included anarchist or fascist plots, and the actions of an angry group of French cycle fans. Fingers were even pointed at his jealous wife. Recently, new accounts of Bottecchia's death have included an (unlikely) mafia hit, and have drawn on the confessions of a dying Sardinian emigrant as well as the recollections of a local priest.

What was interesting about these theories was not so much their convoluted nature, or the extraordinary number of books and revelations that were produced over the years, but the fact that the arguments have gone on for so long, and without any satisfactory outcome.[3] Even today, writers, journalists, cyclists and locals still argue about Bottecchia's death. This in itself tells us a lot about contemporary Italy, a country where the justice system is not seen as legitimate by many, and where disputes over the facts of the past, over history and memory, can drag on for years. The death of Ottavio Bottecchia, wrapped up as it seemed to be in the politics of fascism as well as very possibly linked to questions of money and sex, was a perfect 'case' for the Italians. It also sold newspapers, and it still sells books. As in Leonardo Sciascia's extraordinary novels set in the Sicily of the 1960s, an Italian detective story has no culprit and can never have one. There is no denouement where Hercule Poirot, or his Italian equivalent, calls everyone into the room, goes through the evidence and announces the name of the killer. In Italy, the Poirot solution simply would not work. Nobody would accept his authority, just as they don't accept that of magistrates, lawyers and historians.

So the Bottecchia case remains open, unresolved, a mystery without end, open to numerous interpretations and always liable to reappear, once again, with 'hidden revelations' from a peasant on his deathbed, or a policeman, or a family member. Perhaps it had all been a simple and familiar story; maybe Bottecchia had merely fallen off his bike, hit his head and died, as so many other cyclists did in the twentieth century (among them brothers of both Fausto Coppi and Gino Bartali). But the truth is that the mystery itself has become the story, and in this way Bottecchia's epic life and lonely death have been kept alive over the years, both in print and in the stories told by journalists, fans and the people from his home area.

The Bottecchia myth was there from the very beginning, in the literary form of the pieces sent back by a young Orio Vergani to *Il Corriere della Sera* in Milan. Vergani boasted that, while sitting in a bar in Paris, he invented the details of races he hadn't seen. As he wrote, he described Bottecchia's victory 'in the only way I could, that is with my imagination'.[4]

The fascist daily *Il Popolo d'Italia* extolled the simple virtues and generosity of the cyclist, his honesty, dignity and generosity. Here was a rider who 'had collected together quite a good sum of money but had used it all to help his brothers and sisters and his relatives' (and he had a lot of mouths to feed, including more than thirty nephews and nieces). Fascism claimed Bottecchia as one of its own after his death, as soldiers watched over his funeral and his tomb and huge crowds (as well as blackshirts) attended his laying to rest. If, as some writers claim, Bottecchia had been murdered by fascist thugs, this ceremony was in particularly bad taste. Other writers also extolled Bottecchia's virtues. For Henri Desgrange, cyclist, journalist and inspiration behind the Tour de France, Bottecchia was 'a great champion, and at the same time the living synthesis of the virtues which make up a great champion'. Bottecchia's legend also includes the desperation of a man defeated by the elements, and by terrible bad luck. In the 1926 Tour he gave up in the mountains, after five punctures during the first stage. It is said that he sat on a wall and cried. It is also said that he told journalists that he was not coming back: 'I have had enough of the Tour. This is the last time. You need to think too much.'

Bottecchia's career was shorter than most – the war took his best years – but it included two victories and one second place on the Tour (in just three years) – and these were the hardest Tours in history. In Italy, his results were modest, but the fame he gained in France made him a rich man, especially in comparison with the abject rural poverty of his youth. Yet in most of the books and stories about Bottecchia it is his death which takes precedence. His astonishing feats on the bike have been replaced with a series of competing hypotheses about his demise. And this is a pity because Bottecchia's heroic riding in 1923, 1924 and 1925 deserves to be remembered in itself, and forever in cycling history.

The legend of Bottecchia, the first Italian to win the Tour de France, something no Italian was to do again until 1938, has remained strong, particularly outside Italy. A monument has since been unveiled in the place where he was found dying, in the Friuli region in which he lived, and books and films have been dedicated to his life, as well as a special cycling route. Only Coppi has had more books published about him than Bottecchia, and many have been dedicated entirely to the conspiracy theories surrounding his death in 1927. The official version of this event, inscribed on the monument which now stands at the spot where he fell, is that of a fatality: 'A world famous cyclist/while he was out training to prepare for even harder races and more much-yearned-for victories/he was struck down by a lethal illness and fell in this part of the road/Helped by the people of Peonis he nonetheless died in the hospital in Gemona'. The evidence is still inconclusive, but locals are convinced that it was indeed a simple cycling accident. The irony was lost on nobody, at the time, or since. After surviving the entire war and the bitter hardships of the Tour, this extraordinary man perished during a banal and routine training session, close to his home.

PART II

Cycling as a Mass Sport

The 'Champion of Champions'. Costante Girardengo and Novi Ligure, Cycling's Capital

'Every time he rode on to the track [at the end of a race] the ground was wet and he was soaked by rain, snow and mud from the storms and hurricanes which came from the skies'
— *Giovanni Mosca*[1]

Before Coppi and Bartali, and before cycling became a modern sport, there was a series of champions, heroic deeds and bitter rivalries. The first great champion, the rider who paved the way for all the others in the modern era, was Costante Girardengo. Girardengo was a force in cycling just as the sport really took off, and he was the first cyclist to become truly rich from riding a bike, as well as the first to achieve mythical status in Italy after his death. Costante Girardengo, Italian cycling's earliest 'super-champion', was born close to Novi Ligure in 1893. Situated in the north-west of the country between Genoa and Milan, Novi was then a nondescript market and railway town. It was also on a series of borders, lying between the hills and rice fields of Piedmont and the coastal region of Liguria. It was here that cycling guru Biagio Cavanna also lived and worked as a cyclist before becoming a trainer and celebrated masseur. Another 'super-champion', Fausto Coppi, was also born nearby in 1919.

There is no single geographical, political, economic or bike-based justification to explain why, from the 1920s right through to the early 1960s, Novi Ligure developed into the *Caput Mundi* of cycling, producing two of the greatest cyclists in Italian history. What happened was probably down to chance, the emergence of one extraordinary champion, linked to a guru-masseur who gathered cyclists around him and created further champions. Cyclists then flocked to be part of the milieu of a town which lived and breathed the sport. Right up to the 1960s, Girardengo's house was a modest street-corner villa in Novi, but he certainly made money from cycling, as he built up a property portfolio which included a large country dwelling and a hunting lodge.

After his retirement, the Girardengo myth both created and reinvented Novi Ligure as an international capital of cycling.[2] His example was followed by other locals as a possible way out of poverty. Many of these young men were willing to do the donkey work for their team, and Novi Ligure was a kind of factory for producing *gregari* in the 1940s and 1950s. The excellent hill routes in the area, classic training circuits, as well as the proximity to Milan and the agricultural drudgery of the economy probably did the rest, helped by the mild weather of the Ligurian Riviera, where cyclists started to train in the winter, and which was also on the route of the most prestigious classic of them all – the Milan–San Remo.

There were direct links between the careers of Girardengo and Coppi beyond the places in which they grew up. Most notably, both were discovered (to some extent), trained, nurtured and massaged by Cavanna, over a period of some forty years. Girardengo even raced against Cavanna in his youth, and then with Coppi and Bartali towards the end of his career. It is said that when he worked as a delivery boy Coppi delivered goods to Girardengo himself, on his bike. Today, cycling tours of the town and its environs take in both Girardengo- and Coppi-inspired sites. Sports journalist Emilio Colombo adopted Girardengo almost as his muse, inventing the term '*campionissimo*', which would later also be applied to Fausto Coppi.

Girardengo was the fifth of nine children and he was born in a farmhouse in the Italian countryside long since eaten up by Novi

Ligure's modest urban sprawl, and which now carries an unassuming plaque dedicated to the cyclist. His father was a farmer who later opened a bar and tobacconist's. Like Coppi after him, Girardengo had become a delivery boy after leaving school. He then went on to work in a factory in Sestri Ponente, the 'red' working-class suburb of Genoa. His job as an industrial worker allowed him to avoid conscription and to continue racing during the war, although he had an embarrassing brush with the authorities, who accused him of avoiding conscription. Meanwhile Bottecchia, a peasant not working for an 'essential' wartime industry, was forced to play a full part in the conflict. Girardengo later worked in an Alfa Romeo plant in nearby Tortona. It was through that job, with its 38-kilometre daily commute, that he built up his cycling muscles. The war did not pass by Girardengo entirely, however, as he was affected by the European-wide Spanish flu epidemic and it was said that he was close to death. His diminutive stature helped him gain another, perhaps more inauspicious nickname, 'the little man of Novi' (or 'the Novi runt'). He does indeed seem small in the many photos we have of him, always dwarfed by the surrounding crowds. His other nickname was also linked to his physical appearance: '*faina*', a small weasel-like animal. On the bike he seemed even more diminutive.

As a racer he was versatile, able to triumph in the one-day classics as well as in the Giro. Among modern champions, he was also the first cyclist to create a strong team of *gregari*, dedicated to his success. Girardengo made the Milan–San Remo a private fiefdom, winning it six times in ten years, as well as being controversially disqualified in 1915 after crossing the finish line first. He certainly earned another of his nicknames, 'Mr San Remo'.

Like Coppi after him, Girardengo often won from the front, after long, solitary breaks. In 1918 he left Tano Belloni thirteen minutes behind in second place on the way to San Remo. Gian Luca Favetto takes up the story: 'a chance event, and he took his opportunity as if it was his destiny. At Rivalta Scrivia he broke in order to avoid a series of holes in the ground and two riders who were about to fall on top of him, but he was so powerful, so tough that he did not slow down. His 180km break, on his own, on dirt tracks, was a record. It was the first Milan–San Remo victory for the Novi runt.'³ On his arrival he was greeted by two 'human walls' of soldiers, fresh from the war which was still being fought to the north-east of the country.⁴ Only Fausto Coppi in 1946 would ever win with such authority in this race, and only Eddy Merckx in the 1960s and 1970s ever dominated this 'classic' in the same systematic way. Winning the Milan–San Remo (before it became a race largely for the sprinters in the 1990s) set down a marker for the season. It showed the other riders, right from the start, who was boss. A psychological blow was dealt to all challengers. For the others, from March onwards, it was catch-up time.

Girardengo's record in the Giro was not that extraordinary. He only won twice overall, in 1919 and 1923, but in both years he dominated the race. In 1919 he became the first rider to lead the Giro from start to finish, winning seven out the ten stages. His overall margin of victory was over fifty minutes. Four years later, in 1923, he won eight of the ten stages, but his winning margin in the end was a mere thirty-seven seconds. Thanks to this dominance in certain years, Girardengo was identified with the Giro and another of his nicknames, 'Gira', was a play on the word Giro. He rode in eleven Giros in an extended career, participating in the race for the last time well into his forties in 1936, when he dropped out after four stages. Some of his achievements were the stuff of legend. In 1919 he rode the extraordinarily long (665-kilometre) one-off Rome–Trento–Trieste race, winning all three stages in some twenty-five hours of racing (including the Trento stage by a staggering forty minutes). This race was politically symbolic, linking as it did Italy's capital and two newly conquered and much-prized cities from the war. But, like Bottecchia, defeats were also part of the Girardengo myth, such as the famous incident when he allegedly drew a cross in the dust after withdrawing from the 1921 Giro.

As a professional sportsman, Girardengo took his race preparation extremely seriously. He abstained from sex, it was said, and there were even claims that he wore a kind of chastity belt when racing. Girardengo claimed: 'cycling is a sport which requires personal sacrifice. You need to be careful about what you eat, your digestion, your sexual activity.'[5] But, as with Bartali, this preparation did not go too far. Girardengo, like Bartali and many other cyclists right up to the 1970s, was a heavy smoker. His trainer and masseur Cavanna took great interest in Girardengo's pre-race activities, so much so that the racer complained that Cavanna would check up on his every movement. Novi Ligure was a small place. Word got around.

He was the first Italian cyclist to achieve true national fame, and he had his own fan base. During and after his career, Girardengo became a household name. Songs were written about him, as they were about great football stars like Inter's great forward Giuseppe Meazza. It seems that his name even entered the Italian language. In Pier Paolo Pasolini's short story 'La Notte Brava', published in 1965, one of the Roman street kids uses the phrase 'a Girardengo', which apparently signified 'somebody who didn't tell the truth, who never got to the point, who tried to become your friend under false pretences'.[6] All other cyclists were compared with him, and Binda, his successor-rival, was dubbed 'the Girardengo of the Costa Azzurra'. The writer Mario Soldati professed to being 'in love' with the cyclist, and explained how a whole generation came to 'adore' Girardengo in 1919 after three and a half years of war. Costante was well known as a 'gentleman' and liked to dress elegantly. So popular was he that fans named their children after him, and some of these even became cyclists themselves, such as Girardengo Bernardini, a fine cyclist in the 1940s and 1950s who rode in a team sponsored by Girardengo himself.[7] The son of Costante's sister, Osvaldo Bailo, also became a professional cyclist in the 1930s and 1940s.

Costante Girardengo hailed from an Italy of another age, a country still linked to peasant values or those of the small town. Like Coppi, his favourite activity outside cycling was hunting. His wife was of good peasant stock, the very opposite of glamorous. He had met her when he was just twelve, as she lived on a nearby farm.

Girardengo finally stopped riding professionally in 1936, at the age of forty-three, and only then as a result of a serious accident. After that he opened a bicycle factory in Alessandria and continued to run a farm near Novi. Perhaps Girardengo was also the first cyclist to make serious money after his racing career had finished, as an astute businessman but also by cashing in on his fame. A Girardengo motorbike was produced in Alessandria in the early 1950s.

Too good to be part of a proper rivalry at his peak, he was 'the absolute King of cycling in the 1920s'.[8] Girardengo's closest competitor was Gaetano 'Tano' Belloni, who specialised in coming second. This ability *not* to win earned him the title of 'the eternal second placer', a nod to the fact that he finished behind Girardengo twenty-five times over the years. But this duality never functioned in the same way as that of Guerra and Binda, or Coppi and Bartali, because Belloni was never able consistently to beat Girardengo. This was a one-way rivalry, in which the hierarchy never shifted, and it worked more as a sympathy vote for the 'unlucky' Belloni than as a true competition for victory. A further rivalry followed with Binda, but this was one challenge Girardengo was destined to lose, as the younger man dominated Italian cycling from the late 1920s onwards. After hanging up his pedals, Girardengo, like many other champions from that time, became the trainer of the national team. In this role, he was well known as a disciplinarian. In the 1930s he would scour the bars of Paris in search of his riders to ensure that they got a relatively early night on the eve of the Tour.

Girardengo was also involved in one of the most mysterious episodes of cycling history, which has inspired a series of books, stories and myths.[9] Novi Ligure was not always the semi-prosperous town it is today, and its low life harboured a number of characters who lived on the edge of the law. They were known at the time as 'bandits'. The most famous of these men was Sante Pollastri (also known as Pollastro), bank robber and anarchist, 'the Robin Hood of Novi Ligure'. Pollastri was a childhood acquaintance of both Girardengo and Biagio Cavanna, and a passionate cycling fan. Estimates of the number of people murdered by Sante Pollastri and his gang range from seven to seventeen. After going on the run, Pollastri escaped to France and here there are tales of secret meetings with Girardengo, and claims that it was the cyclist who betrayed the bandit to the police. His life of crime was brought to an end in Paris, in 1927. Tried in France and then in Milan in 1929 (in a show trial where one of the prosecution lawyers was the leading fascist Roberto Farinacci), he spent the next thirty years or so in the terrible island prison of Santo Stefano and other high-security institutions. In official documentation against the date of release was the word 'Never'. But Pollastri was eventually released, thanks to an amnesty, in 1959. The mysterious and quixotic story of these men's lives later formed the basis of one of the best books on the history of cycling; it is a book which is a model in terms of the way it understands the sport as part of Italian history and culture, Marco Ventura's *Il Campione e il bandito*.

But what about Girardengo's relationship with fascism? Very little research has been done into this sensitive subject. In many photos from the time, Girardengo is portrayed alongside fascists, either during or outside of races. But this was not unusual. Fascists were everywhere, highly visible, throughout the 1920s and 1930s. But he clearly helped fascism make cycling part of campaigns in favour of the regime. In 1938, as national coach, he masterminded Gino Bartali's victory at the Tour de France. He was said to have been a personal friend of Mussolini's sons, Bruno and Vittorio, and took part in propaganda campaigns, as when he donated the gates of his villa to be melted down 'for the nation'. Certainly there is no evidence that Girardengo ever took part in any activity which could vaguely be described as anti-fascist. Today in Novi Ligure a huge, glossy and modern museum in the town is dedicated to the two 'super-champions' who lived and rode there. The former capital of Italian cycling now lives, to some extent, off its glorious past, and this museum acknowledges that without Costante Girardengo there would have been no Fausto Coppi.[10]

*   *   *

In 1924, Girardengo also contributed to one of the most unusual stories from the Giro, when he pulled out of the race along with a series of other top racers after a dispute over pay. Without their big stars, the race organisers needed something unique, and their decision led to a sight which would never be repeated: a woman riding in the Giro d'Italia.

That year, thirty-four-year-old Alfonsina Strada (née Morini) became the only woman to race in the Giro d'Italia. But she was not satisfied with a bit-part role. Alfonsina was determined to complete the whole gruelling race. This was no mean feat. After all, nearly two-thirds of the ninety starters failed to make it to the finish line. One stage took her nearly fifteen hours to complete, and she arrived almost three and a half hours after the stage winner that day. On that stage, she was outside the maximum time, but on the first occasion the organisers were lenient with her. Another marathon stage (from Bologna to Fiume on the Dalmatian coast) took Alfonsina twenty-one hours. This time she was excluded from the official classification, but carried on riding alongside two men who were only taking part in order to complete the race. By the end, she had ridden every centimetre of the 3,613 kilometres of the race, invariably on her own and often in the dark. Sometimes she even beat some of the other racers, all of whom were, of course, men.

Along the way she handed out photographs of herself and signed numerous autographs. Emilio Colombo defended her in *La Gazzetta dello Sport*. Even Mussolini wanted to meet her. After 1924, the story of Alfonsina Strada became one of the most well-known tales from the history of the Giro, inspiring numerous articles, cartoons, popular stories and even entire books. Strada herself lived off her fame for years afterwards, racing all over Italy and in France, especially on the track. Yet her private life was marked by tragedy. Her first husband was committed to a mental asylum and he would die there in 1942. She hailed from a desperately poor family of peasants (she had three sisters and six brothers) from the countryside near Castelfranco Emilia but she later moved to Milan in order to continue her cycling career and subsequently ran a bike shop. Alfonsina continued to ride in exhibition races right up to the 1950s and in the early days a rival had to be invented for her in order to keep the public interested.

Her participation in the Giro, in fascist Italy, had caused scandal and led to all kinds of sexist comments in the newspapers and among the general public. Her hair was cut short, she wore shorts (and the very sight of her bare legs was apparently disturbing to many) and she rode a 'man's bike', which also caused widespread shock. Journalists wrote long pieces describing her as 'muscle-bound' and cartoonists had a field day with smutty jokes about male fans waiting for her to ride by, hours after the main group had passed. Her story remains unique in the history of cycling. The male-dominated world of the Giro had been breached. Unfortunately, it was a brief experiment. When Alfonsina tried to sign up for the Giro in 1925 she was turned down. Everything was back to normal again.

4

The 1920s and 1930s. Alfredo Binda, 'the Dictator', and Learco Guerra, 'the Human Locomotive'

'Binda was extraterrestrial'
– *Luigi Macchi*[1]

Cycling has always thrived off rivalry, but Alfredo Binda never really had a proper rival. He was around for Girardengo's last years (though Costante was already in decline by the time Binda started winning) and Learco Guerra challenged him for a time. For the rest of his career he dominated the sport like a 'dictator' (one of his nicknames) and his victories were so frequent that they almost became boring. A cult of personality developed around him, almost as if he was a kind of god. He simply pulverised the opposition. But he was also lucky. During his victory in the 1925 Giro, it was said that he did not have a single puncture. In the end, Binda became too successful for his own good. Every historian of cycling knows that in 1930 the organisers of the Giro d'Italia paid him *not* to compete, as his successes had become too predictable. The no-show fee was 22,500 lire – as much as he would have been awarded had he raced and won. Not bad money for doing nothing. Perhaps this offer was not so surprising. In the three years leading up to the infamous bribe not to ride, Binda won twenty-six of forty-one stages at the Giro. Nobody, not even Merckx, or Coppi, or Bartali, has ever dominated a stage race in this way.

By the time he was being paid not to appear at all, Binda had already triumphed in the Giro five times, and had been crowned world champion on three occasions (1927, 1930 and 1932). In 1929, after easily winning the Giro yet again, the Milanese public jeered Binda because of his domination of the sport, and it was at this point that the organisers of the race started to contemplate paying Binda to put his feet up. During the 1929 Giro he won eight successive stages and this record run became known as the 'imperial' series. His total of forty-one stage wins was only surpassed by sprinter Mario Cipollini in 2004, a sad reflection on what the sport of cycling had become by then.[2] The only thing missing from Binda's record was success in the Tour de France. He only took part in one Tour, in 1930, and although he won two stages he withdrew from the race after falling an hour behind the yellow jersey.

Alfredo Binda was a cycling superstar whose fame surpassed that of Girardengo before him and all his contemporaries. For Bruno Raschi, Binda was also the first cyclist to attract a female fan base. Raschi also argues that Binda brought the sport into the modern age, forming a kind of bridge between two different epochs, that of the 'heroic' pioneers and that of cycling as a sport with mass appeal and a national following. Many experts, including Ormezzano and Brera (to name just two very distinguished journalists, both great Coppi fans), still rank Binda as the greatest Italian cyclist of all time. Binda was also a star on the international stage, travelling to the United States to take part in celebrity six-day races.[3]

As a rider many writers described Binda as 'flying' (a description later applied to Coppi) and Francesco Arcangeli wrote that his pedalling style was so easy that he seemed to be pedalling 'on nothing' or 'on air'. He was often described as elegant and 'classy'. For René Vietto he was 'the greatest of all time. His style is incomparable. He could have set off with a cup of milk on his back, and it would have still been full when he arrived. No weakness. No sense that he was tired. He was at one with his bike. Elegance, purity, an artist. He was the epitome of beauty in action.'[4] Ormezzano later described him as 'perfect'.

After a few minor wins in France and then back in Italy, Binda won his first Giro in 1925 at the first attempt. In 1927 he completely dominated the race, winning all but three of the fifteen stages and leading from start to finish. Only Girardengo had ever won a major race in this fashion. Binda was not a specialist in any particular aspect of the sport but simply the best at doing everything a cyclist needed to do, whether it be in the mountains, the time trials or the sprints. His climbing was so impressive that he became known as 'the lord of the mountains'. Perhaps only Eddy Merckx of the later riders can be compared with him. The Giro was his again in 1928, 1929 and 1933 and, of course, in 1930 he 'won' without even racing. The authorities were worried. Binda was popular – hugely so – but the sport itself was becoming dull. Cycling thrives on competition and rivalry, but Binda eliminated the competition. Learco Guerra won a massive fan base in part thanks purely to his ability to challenge Binda every so often – although he won only one Giro. As a winner, Binda was both popular and unpopular. His dominance was only really challenged when other factors intervened: falls, team tactics, politics.

Binda's team manager was the legendary Eberardo Pavesi – 'the Lawyer' – who ran the Legnano team which Binda rode for, with its green shirts.[5] But he was not an athlete in every sphere of his life. For energy he occasionally ate an enormous quantity of eggs, and he smoked – something unthinkable for a contemporary athlete but common in the inter-war years and afterwards. Binda's 'water' bottle sometimes contained what it was intended for, but often this was fortified with coffee or wine. He was also an amateur musician, which led to yet another nickname: 'the trumpeter of Cittiglio'. His total dominance is summed up by a story from the Giro di Lombardia in 1926. Binda crushed his opponents on a cold and wet day, winning by twenty-seven minutes. He had time to collect his prize and shower. As he got off the train in Varese on his way home some riders were still racing. In 1927 after yet another victory he had enough breath left to play his famous trumpet.

*   *   *

Like all cyclists of that time Binda's origins were extremely humble. As the tenth child (of fourteen) of a rural family from Cittiglio, a small town in the hills above Lake Maggiore in the north of Italy, his parents could not support him and he was forced to emigrate and live with his uncle, earning his keep as a plasterer in Nice. As with millions of other Italians, the country of his birth could not provide him with a decent living. Alfredo only took up cycling thanks to his brother, Primo, but he quickly began to set the pace as a professional. With his fame came other rewards and he shifted thousands of copies of his memoirs. His photograph was pasted up in bars and cycling clubs across Italy. Forms of 'doping' available to cyclists in the days when Binda was racing were fairly primitive. Some riders believed that huge quantities of raw eggs, downed all in one go, would help. Binda claimed to have 'taken' thirty-four eggs before and during the 1926 Giro di Lombardia. After retirement, he went on to be an extraordinary cycling manager during the golden age of Italian cycling, working with both Bartali and Coppi in the 1940s. His successful 'double career' was not unique. Many ex-cyclists (including his great rival Learco Guerra) also became team managers in the post-war period. The distinctive aspect of Binda's long career was the level of success he enjoyed in both careers, above all at the Tour, where he led Italian riders to victory in 1948, 1949, 1952 and 1960. Money flooded into Binda's life, and he was able to buy a whole street of houses in the east of Milan (where he had 130 tenants) as well as a large rural villa near his home town.

But if Binda was a modern cyclist, the sport itself had not quite caught up with him. If every cyclist had 'their' photo, the most famous one of Binda seemed to encapsulate an entire epoch. He is crouching by the road, his bike abandoned by his side, trying desperately to remove a tyre with his teeth. This photo symbolised a whole pre-modern period of cycling, and even a moment in history. Vergani wrote about 'working-class cycling, the sport of the poor, muddy roads, tyres pulled off from wooden wheels with teeth, [it was] a simple, straightforward sport'.[6] Binda was often glamorous, 'perfect', unbeatable: a superstar, but even he sometimes had to get his hands dirty in order to win.

Like so many early cyclists, Binda had great courage and endured immense pain in order to race. In the 1926 Giro he fell horribly on the first stage after his brakes failed and he was forced to throw himself to the ground. The harsh rules at the time required fallen racers to receive no outside assistance whatsoever if they wanted to continue. After forty-five minutes, Binda was able to ride on – and he recovered to win six stages and finish third overall. When asked what his secret was, he famously replied in his local dialect: 'Ghe voeren i garùn' – 'you need the legs'. In the 1920s and 1930s Italians rarely spoke the official, national language. Almost everyone spoke some form of dialect, a practice which identified local heroes with their home towns.

As with all celebrated cyclists, Binda's 'life' and career consists of a series of popular stories repeated over time. Ultimately, they all merged into one. These tales about Binda were passed down through the generations by fans, fellow cyclists, journalists and writers. Binda's is a rags to riches tale, the story of the poor emigrant who made good. But it is also a story of physical elegance and sporting style. Binda's hair was always perfectly slicked back, he was good-looking in a classical, matinee idol way and he dressed stylishly. Like many other film stars and sporting heroes, his physique and the way he carried himself mattered to his public; it was a part of his appeal, and his image was reproduced endlessly in the mass media of the time and avidly consumed by the public.[7] Binda's trousers were always perfectly pressed and he often sported a cravat. For Angelo Zomegnan he was a 'symbol of elegance' and a role model. Binda is usually described as quiet, reserved, a gentleman, and yet he drove fast cars, played the field and was an extremely snappy dresser, and many photos show him attired in a garish dressing gown. All in all, he comes across as a bit of a dandy, conscious about his appearance. He would sleep late, often until midday, an eccentricity in a place like Cittiglio, where people usually rose at or before dawn. His mother would put critics of his sleeping habits firmly in their place: 'When he is in bed, at least I know where he is.'

Women were known to swoon in front of Binda, but his career was meticulously planned and organised, and his private life took a back seat. Unusually for a sporting star of that time, Binda only married when his cycling career was over, preferring to remain single while he was still an athlete. When he eventually married a beautiful twenty-year-old at the age of fifty, his family was able to benefit from the social mobility his wealth from cycling had created, and of his two daughters one became an architect and the other a lawyer.

Binda's fame was truly national. Carlo Levi, the anti-fascist writer and painter, was consigned to exile by the fascist regime in 1935. His place of exile was a tiny village in the deep south of Italy, in remote Basilicata. In 1945 Levi published his experiences in his celebrated documentary novel, *Christ Stopped at Eboli*. The book had a profound impact on the understanding of the Southern Question, and was widely translated. Levi wrote that the book's title 'comes from an expression by the people of Gagliano [Levi's fictitious name for the actual village of Aliano] who say of themselves, "Christ stopped short of here, at Eboli" which means, in effect, that they feel they have been bypassed by Christianity, by morality, by history itself – that they have somehow been excluded from the full human experience'.[8]

But Gagliano had not been bypassed by the history of cycling, or its popularity. In his book, Levi depicts a southern worker who rides an old bicycle and dreams of emulating the epic feats of Binda and Guerra, two cyclists whose roots were firmly in the faraway north of the country. Cycling, as with other sports, had become the glue which bound together the national identity. Put in these terms, Binda's life and his sporting career appear faultless. If he did have a fault (if it can be called such) it was that he was *too* good, so much so that nobody else could get a look in. He had no fragile side, no weak points, no Achilles heel. Binda was great, but he inspired admiration, not adoration. For example, the public never loved Binda as they loved Coppi (with all his injuries and his troubled private life) or Bartali (who lost to Coppi as often as he won). Carlin (Carlo Bruguglio), the famous journalist and caricaturist, called Binda '*il grande antipatico*', which translates loosely as 'the great unsympathetic one', and captured the cold and calculating side of his nature.

Binda's lifestyle mattered to him, and his fans were interested in all its details. His image was important to his success. He presented himself as an arbiter of good taste. Rich, famous and handsome, he always took his holidays in the posh resort of Alassio in Liguria. Like Cittiglio, this town became part of 'Binda's kingdom'. Fans would turn up there looking for their hero and a special Nice–Alassio race was organised in his honour. But this superstar was also, on occasion, approachable. Binda could often be found sitting outside a town bar, immaculately dressed as ever, happy to chat with admirers and friends. He would, it was said, give out 'lessons in behaviour' from his position of fame and fortune. Binda was not just a sporting model for others, but a model for life itself. He was a *divo*, a public figure with a private life. Although Binda was wealthy and famous and drove big cars, his life was also full of the simple stories which marked him as an economic migrant. He had met his wife in the garage where he would stop to fill up his car. He had not been born into money. He had known the grinding poverty of rural Italy and the humiliation of being a migrant.

Nor was he by any means an intellectual. His daughter Lauretta wrote that her father 'was lacking in culture, but was able to fill this gap with great intelligence. His education was based upon the observation of the world around him. He used to say that he learnt how to behave "in society" by watching the behaviour of those who he took to be able and valid people.' He claimed to have read only one book in his life – Alessandro Manzoni's classic novel *The Betrothed* – but he read all the papers, every day, from first to last page. Moreover, his origins were sometimes betrayed by the way he spoke, and his Italian was a mixture of Cittiglese dialect and French.

The places linked to Binda's life and his cycling career changed as a result of these connections. Like Girardengo and Coppi with Novi Ligure, Binda put Alassio on the map: it became a cycling town. Cittiglio, meanwhile, also became part of the history of the sport. The Giro passed through the town, and Binda's big villa was the centre of operations for his team and regular training sessions, which would usually take in the famous Ghisallo climb – up to and past the church dedicated to cyclists.

Binda always claimed to be uninterested in politics, but he was a 'good fascist'. In fact, politics *was* an important part of Binda's life – and is largely ignored by the hagiographies which have appeared in print. His relative activism under fascism is almost always played down in accounts of his life and career, and is excised completely from the account on the website of the museum in Cittiglio, where his interest in 'politics' is shifted forward to the 1950s. After the war, Binda justified his 'fascism':

> It is easy to understand my political beliefs. I go to church and I have liberal tendencies but I was a fascist, when everyone was. I was political secretary [of the Fascist Party] for five years, at Cittiglio. Nobody has ever criticised me for this. After all the fascists gave me a hard time during the war as I didn't want to join the party. I am not a communist. When someone owns property, they can't be a communist. Everybody joins the party which defends their own interests, without exception. I have always defended my own interests, and that which I have earned through hard work. An industrialist earns money through the labour of his workers, and he should take care of them. But I pedalled with my own sweat and I can't accept my money being given to others.

This statement is a mix of myth-making (the self-made man) and self-justification (not *everyone* was a fascist, after all). Other cyclists clearly kept their distance from fascism, most notably Bottecchia before him and Bartali afterwards. Binda not only embraced the regime, but also represented the fascists in local politics and thus benefited from the largesse of the dictatorship. But unlike many pre-war fascists in other walks of life, Binda stayed on his political path after the war, being elected as independent councillor in Cittiglio in the 1950s and 1960s. His sporting success seemed to give him the perfect alibi for his activities under the fascists. He even seems to speak 'like a fascist' in documentaries. Often, Binda painted himself – and is depicted – as a minor rebel. Fascism's relative lack of interest in cycling allowed him to escape the worst of the demands of propaganda imposed on footballers, racing drivers and boxers.

With the war over, Binda refused to rest on his laurels and simply enjoy his huge fortune. He became national team manager – at a time when the Tour de France was still a competition for national teams – and his fame as manager almost eclipsed that of his time as a rider. For in the golden age of cycling, Binda found himself in charge of the greatest set of riders ever to represent Italy: Bartali, Coppi and Magni – to mention just the leaders. Perhaps only a man with his experience, charisma and character could have made such a success of that job, at that time.

Binda finally retired from the world of cycling in the early 1960s. Thereafter he lived a comfortable life, dividing his time between Cittiglio, Milan and the Ligurian coast. He died quietly in 1986, having found time to drop in and check on his own obituary, personally, at the *Gazzetta dello Sport* offices. The Binda museum was opened in Cittiglio in the same year and in 1995 was moved to Vararo, near the Cuvignone climb which Binda would cycle up almost every day during his long career. It is thus intended to be a museum which can be reached by bike. Binda's strong links with his home town have continued to develop since his death and he is also remembered in his 'summer residence', Alassio, on a special wall which bears names associated with the international jet set (including Ernest Hemingway) who once frequented this seaside town.

Many of Italy's most respected cycling writers have rated Binda as the greatest Italian cyclist of all time. The debate continues, as does his fame: in 2002 an Italian stamp was issued bearing the former champion's image.

During his career, the search for a convincing rival for Binda was unceasing. The first candidate was Ottavio Bottecchia. Their backgrounds were similar: both came from peasant stock, from big families, and both were forced to emigrate. Each man learned his trade as a cyclist outside Italy. But there the similarities end, so much so that Ormezzano has even described them as opposites. While Bottecchia remained essentially a peasant, even in victory, Binda transformed himself into a gentleman, albeit a *nouveau riche* gentleman. As cyclists the two men could not have been more different. Bottecchia led from the front. His tactics were simple – keep riding, wear out the opposition, take control (and the lead) and keep it. He was never a sprinter of note, nor successful in one-day races. Binda on the other hand was a tactician: cold, calculating, technical and cynical. The Bottecchia–Binda rivalry did not work for one crucial reason. Bottecchia was famous for his exploits in France, and never put up much of a show in Italy. Binda, conversely, never showed much interest in the Tour, and became a sporting superstar thanks to his constant success on his home turf, and in particular in the north (although he was hugely popular in Rome and well known in the south). In the 1920s, Girardengo challenged Binda for a time, but he had lost much of his potency once Binda began to win consistently. Binda was Girardengo's heir, the new '*campionissimo*'.

In the end, only Learco Guerra came anywhere near to fitting the bill as a credible rival for Alfredo Binda. Guerra was born in 1902 in San Nicolò Po, a village close to Mantua in the Po Valley. His father had a penchant for names associated with literature and Greek mythology and one of his brothers had been called Ivanhoe.

Learco is a Greek name which translates as 'judge of the village'. Like Ganna before him, Learco became a builder by trade, and, like so many other future cyclists, he learnt how to ride as part of his job or on the journey to work. The region was a hotbed of socialism, particularly among rural day labourers, and strong unions and cooperative movements were established throughout the Po Valley as workers and peasants organised themselves against landowners and employers. In December 1919 Mantua erupted and riots and demonstrations paralysed the town. The origins of this movement lay with events in Rome. As the new parliament was being sworn in, a number of socialist deputies left the chamber in protest at the presence of the king. They were then attacked outside in the street by nationalists. Unions called a general strike.

In Mantua these protests quickly took on a revolutionary fervour. Demonstrators ransacked local barracks and weapons were seized. The crowd was fired upon by the *carabinieri*. In the end, six civilians (including two trade unionists) and a soldier died. Mass arrests followed and 173 of those taken into custody were eventually convicted.[9] Learco Guerra was influenced by these events. In the local elections of 1920 the socialists won a crushing victory in the Mantua area (taking control of fifty-nine of the sixty-eight councils) and Guerra was said to have participated actively in the campaign. Soon, however, the fascist squads arrived. Violence descended on the socialist movement, with beatings and the destruction of cooperatives and socialist buildings.

Called up to do his military service, Guerra was enrolled into the cycling division for eighteen months. On his return he went back to the building trade with his father, with whom he would often ride in tandem. In 1926 he began to take part in local amateur races and for years he rode as an *isolato*, without any real back-up, before he was finally taken on by the Maino team. At the age of twenty-seven his career had begun. His first Giro was in 1929, and he rode as a *gregario* for his team captain, finishing in twenty-fourth position. Guerra's career finally took off in 1930. Soon, his great strengths

in time-trial racing and the ability to keep going started to come
to the fore. At that Giro he took two stages and finished ninth. He
then finished second in the Tour, winning another two stages and
wearing the yellow jersey. He would be runner-up in the Tour again
in 1933. He also won the Italian national championships that year,
and was described in *La Gazzetta dello Sport* as riding 'as fast as a
motorbike'.[10]

A different *Gazzetta* journalist gave him a nickname which
stuck – 'the Human Locomotive'. From an unknown amateur,
Guerra was now one of the most popular riders in Italy. At times
he seemed unstoppable. In 1931 he was the first rider to wear
the pink jersey, which had just been introduced at the Giro. (The
colour pink was an obvious reference to *La Gazzetta dello Sport*;
the newspaper responsible for organising and creating of the Giro
was famously printed on pink paper.) In the same year he took part
in one of the most extraordinary races ever organised, an interminable time trial to decide who was to be world champion. This
time, nobody could stay with Guerra, not even Binda. He became
a national hero, and his popularity was exploited by the fascists.[11]
In the 1933 Giro the Guerra–Binda rivalry reached its peak. On
the sixth stage Guerra had a terrible fall after his bike touched
Binda's close to the finish line, putting the man from Mantua out
of the race and into hospital. Binda went on to win, but Guerra's
fans were furious.[12] He got his own back in 1934, his greatest year
and the only time he managed to win the Giro ahead of Binda
(who retired after six stages). In that race Guerra won a Binda-
esque ten stages overall. As with all great rivalries, Italian fans were
divided into *Guerriani* and *Bindiani*, and accusations over tactics
and favouritism flew back and forth: 'there was no end to the arguments in the newspapers and bars of Italy'.[13] Learco Guerra was
represented as a kind of superman, strong as an ox, unstoppable
with his thick cycling goggles and swept-back hair. He was rough
and ready, unlike Binda, with a smile so wide that it was described
as looking like a 'money-box'.

For a time, Guerra was seen as, at last, the man who could actually 'challenge the hegemony' of the 'unbeatable' champion, Alfredo Binda. Girardengo's fans now seemed to transfer their affections to Guerra, the 'anti-Binda'. Gian Paolo Ormezzano has argued that the Binda–Guerra rivalry reflected territorial and cultural divisions in Italy. While both riders were clearly from the north of Italy, Guerra's riding style (and perhaps his underdog status) seemed to gain him a fan base above all in the south, and he was especially popular in Naples. Others described him as 'the people's cyclist'. Less has been made of a possible political rivalry, despite Binda's adherence to fascism and Guerra's earlier socialist sympathies. Yet things became much more complicated during Mussolini's twenty years in power. It has been claimed that Guerra was held up by the regime as the ultimate 'fascist' rider, and as a result gained many fascist fans, while Binda attracted a more oppositionist fan base. As Stefano Pivato has argued, 'Binda was the hero of sporting anti-fascists, Guerra was a champion who incarnated the ideals of Mussolinian Italy.'[14] His name also helped: *guerra* means war, and this was a regime permanently on a war footing. Despite their personal opinions or pasts, or what they actually did in Italy outside the sport (there is no evidence of Guerra taking part in explicitly pro-fascist political activity) their different cycling styles and the way they were represented by the regime seemed to create two contrasting and politicised fan bases.[15]

Bruno Roghi has made more lyrical and poetic (and rhetorical) distinctions between the two cyclists: 'those interested in aesthetics love Apollo, the crowds adore Dionysius. Binda is lyrical, Guerra is dramatic. His eyes aflame, his muscles in tumult, his pedalling furious, his bike pock-marked by his crude power, his cheeks are puffed out. Learco Guerra is riding by.' Guerra took a long time to retire, and continued to ride occasional races, even during the war, as well as appearing on the track on numerous occasions for appearance money.

Binda continued to challenge Guerra even when the two had stopped riding against each other. In 1948 Binda took over as national team manager from Guerra, with extraordinary results in the Tour. Guerra, meanwhile, carved out a career as a successful team manager and bike manufacturer in the 1950s, in particular through his work with the Swiss rider Hugo Koblet (the first foreigner to win the Giro in 1950, wearing a 'Guerra' shirt) and the spectacular climber from Luxembourg, Charly Gaul (winner of the Giro in 1956 and 1959). Guerra's team also won with Italian rider Carlo Clerici in 1954. But Guerra was diagnosed with Parkinson's disease in the early 1960s and his condition quickly worsened. When he died in 1963, Binda attended his funeral in Mantua and Bruno Raschi produced a poetic piece for *La Gazzetta dello Sport*: 'after thirty years,' he wrote, 'Binda is alone'.[16]

Italy began to dominate world cycling in the late 1920s. The world championships, alongside the Tour, were the only occasion in the cycling calendar where riders would ride specifically as Italians, representing their country and themselves at the same time. In 1927, the inaugural world cycling championships were held in Germany. It was a triumph for Italy, as their riders finished first, second, third and fourth in the one-day road race, the most prestigious part of the whole event. But in 1928 there was an embarrassing incident during the same competition. Both Binda and Girardengo pulled out close to the end of the race and the regime, furious at the riders' apparent lack of application, insisted that heavy bans be imposed upon them.[17] Suitably chastised, Binda went on to be crowned world champion again in 1930 and 1932. By the early 1930s, Binda's fame was worldwide. Special books were published to celebrate these successes, which were exploited by the fascists making the most of the prestige and the boost to national identity which they hoped would reflect well on them. Binda's record in the world championships was exemplary: he only finished outside the top six once in seven such races. No wonder the fascists were so enamoured of him. And when Binda didn't win, some other Italian invariably stepped up to the mark in his place.

In 1931 the cycling authorities decided, in their wisdom, to turn the world championship road race into a mammoth time trial, in which each rider would cycle against the clock. The city chosen to host the first such race was Copenhagen, where the track was 'as flat as a billiard table'.[18] The remarkable feature of this event was its length. One hundred and seventy-two kilometres for a time trial was a record, and something not seen since, a form of torture given that the riders would have to cycle on their own, against the wind, without company, for the entire distance. As he rode, Binda became desperate for water and had to stop and knock on someone's door to ask for a drink. Riders weren't even permitted to drink while they cycled. It was said that Binda's eyes were so inflamed at the finish line that he couldn't open them. Many other riders were exhausted, and withdrew altogether. But this was the perfect scenario for Learco Guerra, who was well known for his ability to keep going at speed for long periods of time. The first racers set off at 7 a.m. on 26 August; Guerra was the twelfth rider to depart.

Nobody could live with Learco over such a distance, and he won by more than five minutes from the second-placed rider after five hours of pedalling, with Binda some nine minutes behind. Guerra's feat that day was quite extraordinary, the stuff of legend and never to be repeated (not least because nobody would ever again dare to set such a distance in a time trial). After that victory *La Gazzetta dello Sport* called Guerra 'the complete champion, an irresistible fighter'. The railway workers who transported Learco back to Italy covered the train with graffiti: 'Long live Guerra world champion'. It later turned out that Guerra had removed his gears in order to make his bike lighter. He had ridden all 172 kilometres of the time trial with a fixed gear.[19]

The 1932 world championships were held in Rome and, after his triumph the previous year, Learco was the favourite to win. The president of the Italian cycling association called for team discipline behind Guerra's bid: 'That is an order,' he told the team before the race. Binda later claimed that he had agreed to help Guerra, his great rival, until the last lap (of a total of three). It was 1 September and the sun was beating down on the course. On that final lap a Spanish rider made a break and Binda stayed with him. He was then joined by another Italian, Remo Bertoni. With 10 kilometres left to go Il Duce, Benito Mussolini himself, turned up in a car and followed the riders for a short time before leaving. Binda broke and made a triumphal finish, arriving alone at the line, where he was carried forward by a huge crowd. Bertoni was 4.52 minutes further back.

Despite Mussolini's lukewarm interest in the race, the Italians had won again, this time in their own capital. For the first time, radio commentary of the race was broadcast to the listening public at home and in bars all over Italy. Binda had his third world championship in six years and he could once again claim to be the best cyclist in the world. Two years later, Italy would win football's World Cup in Rome, and they would retain the trophy in France in 1938. Italy was leading the world in the most popular mass sports of all, football and cycling, and the regime was well aware of the importance of winning over the hearts and minds of the millions of sports fans.

Fascism promoted cycling despite, and not thanks to, Il Duce. Mussolini was only ever photographed on a bike two or three times in his life, despite being presented by the regime as 'Italy's first sportsman', and he never attended a Giro d'Italia. Put simply, he was not particularly interested in cycling. Other sports and pastimes were much more important to Il Duce – above all football and motorsport. Fascism nonetheless intervened and invested heavily in cycling, as it did in every sector of public and private life in Italy, organising special races and exploiting the victories of Italians for its own ends. Some cyclists were also openly fascist. Pietro Chesi, for example, was a blackshirt and a rider good enough to win the Milan–San Remo in 1927.[20] Binda's and Guerra's victories were used to the full, and it was important to the regime that the Italians triumphed in the world championships. But sport could also be a double-edged sword, providing alternatives to fascism and creating opportunities for dissent.

So popular did cycling's heroes become that they could also be seen or held up as anti-fascist, or at the very least non-fascist. Their success sometimes gave them the power to resist.[21] The most famous example of this was Gino Bartali, the great Tuscan rider of the 1930s and 1940s. Bartali was a fervent Catholic and dedicated his victories to the Pope, rather than to Mussolini. The Catholics, for their part, saw in Bartali an opportunity to create a non-fascist Catholic hero, and they proceeded to do precisely that. This battle was played out in full during and after the 1938 Tour de France. Bartali won that race after the fascists had 'persuaded' him not to ride in the Giro, which he had won in 1936 (a race the regime used to push their campaign for self-sufficiency, calling it the Giro of Autarchy) and 1937. But although Bartali's victory was presented as a victory for Mussolini and the dictatorship, things were not as straightforward as they seemed.

The fascists tried time and again to force or cajole Bartali into crude propaganda for their own ends, but he invariably refused them, even under pressure. They had pushed him into taking part in the 1938 Tour, hoping to boost further Italian sporting prowess and success following the World Cup win in France, and the fascist and sporting press made great play of Bartali's victory, but the man himself declined to wear a black shirt or to make political capital out of his triumph. It is said that Mussolini did not even meet Bartali on his return to Italy after the Tour was over. Bartali was awarded a medal for sporting valour, but it was only a silver medal. Many thought that victory in the Tour deserved a higher honour.[22] At the same time, the connection between Bartali and the Catholic Church, which had been fostered and reinforced as an alternative to the 'new fascist man', was given a great boost. Unlike football, cycling did not lend itself quite so clearly to straightforward political manipulation. Even when national teams competed, as they did in the Tour, it was the individual riders who attracted interest from the fans. Italians supported Bartali in the Tour largely because he was Bartali, not because he was Italian. The legend of Bartali did not therefore disappear with the collapse of the regime in 1943, but was represented with great power after the war had ended.

PART III

The Golden Age

War and Post-war. Cycling, Resistance and Rebirth

'The bicycle was like the air that I breathed . . .'
– Giovanni Pesce, partisan leader

'Many women were on their knees, with their children by their side . . . the wide road was packed with people who were crying I-T-A-L-Y, I-T-A-L-Y, I-T-A-L-Y . . . Sport, at that moment was a flame which lit up the nation'
– Bruno Roghi describing cyclists
entering the city of Trieste in 1946 [1]

With the onset of the Second World War, the bicycle was dumped by the Italian army. More advanced technology now became an integral part of the 'total war' which engulfed Italy, with the use of tanks, armoured vehicles, jeeps and motorcycles paramount. Cities were systematically bombed while the entire country became a battlefield, the Allies fighting the Germans with Italians on both sides of the conflict. Yet, although no longer a military requirement, the bicycle remained a crucial means of transport for civilians during the war years. Petrol shortages and damage to road and rail networks meant that many Italians relied almost entirely on their bikes to get around. After September 1943, the anti-fascist resistance recruited militants in the mountains, the countryside and the cities of northern and central Italy. Lacking resources, guns and back-up, the partisans and those supporting them often fell back on the humble bicycle for communication. Messages, weapons and even bombs were carried by bike, often by women and at great personal risk. To combat this, the Germans and the Italian fascists set up checkpoints and made frequent searches of bikes. At one stage in the war the Germans banned the bicycle altogether, only to revoke this decision when it became clear that none of the country's factories could operate without their workers, most of whom travelled to work by bike. With the increasing strength of the resistance, the Germans began to see 'every cyclist . . . as a rebel ready to shoot'.[2] The bike began to be viewed as dangerous, as subversive, as a vehicle of democracy.

During the resistance, secret documents were hidden in bike frames and crucial messages delivered all over Italy by brave cyclists who supported the anti-fascist struggle. For example, forged identity papers were transported back and forth across central Italy by Gino Bartali, winner of the Giro and the Tour in the late 1930s. In the cities the bicycle was both a crucial and a silent means of attack and escape. Giovanni Pesce, partisan leader in Milan, went so far as to say that 'without the bicycle the partisans of the GAP brigades in the cities could not have survived'.[3] Special permission was needed to use a bike in wartime, but it was difficult, if not impossible, to check on the use of millions of cycles.

Many cyclists were also partisans, including such key figures as Luciano Pezzi, Alfredo Martini and Toni Bevilacqua. The 1909 Giro winner Luigi Ganna donated a number of the bikes he manufactured to the resistance. In some cities bicycle shops were used to exchange information and as meeting places. Like everyone else, cyclists found themselves caught up in the horrors of war. Many were held as prisoners of war or deported to camps in Germany. Some did not survive, but those who did were prepared to suffer all kinds of hardships on their bikes after the war was over. Nothing in the future could be as bad as the pain they had endured, so the young men who took up cycling again after the war seemed almost to enjoy their suffering. At least they were being paid for it.

After 1945, those who had been cyclists before the war quickly returned to the sport. Six years had passed and all were eager to make up for lost time. The fans were equally impatient to see their heroes in action – and to find out if they were still alive. The stage was therefore set for the start of Italy's golden age of cycling, and in a country marked by temporary graveyards and rubble, provisional bridges and unexploded bombs and Allied checkpoints. Against this backdrop, great cyclists like Fausto Coppi, Gino Bartali and Fiorenzo Magni were to take part in racing which would capture the imagination of an entire nation, in an epoch that would be defined by sporting achievement. Now the cycling could begin again. In 1946 the Giro itself was resumed. It had a mission, as indicated by the name given to it by its organisers: *il Giro della Rinascita* – the Giro of Rebirth.

In 1946 Italy was emerging from a war which had affected every single one of its citizens, rich and poor, young and old, men and women, communists and fascists. After the Italians pulled out of the alliance with Nazi Germany in September 1943, a vicious civil war then tore the country further apart. In April 1945 Mussolini was captured and shot as he tried to escape to Switzerland, disguised as a German soldier. His body was then strung up by the feet from a lamppost for all to see in Milan's Piazzale Loreto. Nor did 1945 mark the end of the suffering. Bloodletting and revenge after the war was officially over led to at least 15,000 deaths. Homelessness was rife and many people lived in shacks or even caves. Life was hard, and many Italians were reduced to living from hand to mouth. Criminal behaviour reached an all-time high, particularly in 1946. The prisons were overflowing and riots spread like wildfire up and down the country. Meanwhile, those who had been deported for refusing to fight for Mussolini and Hitler, or for being political activists, or because they were Jews, struggled to make it back to Italy. Many thousands had already died in the camps during the war. This was a country on its knees, where civilians had been as much a part of the struggle for victory as ordinary soldiers and generals.[4]

It was in this context, in a landscape marked on every street corner, in every field, on every beach by the signs of the war – bullet holes, bombed-out housing blocks, orphans and widows and widowers, babies born as a result of prostitution or rape, plaques, crosses and monuments to mark the martyrs on one side or the other – that cycling, the most popular sport of all, began to recapture the imagination of its fans and fire the passions of sporting rivalry.

The cyclist Renzo Zanazzi had been conscripted into the Italian army and after the armistice between Italy and the Allied armed forces was officially announced on 8 September 1943 his division was confined to barracks in Milan. Zanazzi took the opportunity to escape, change his uniform for civilian clothing and hide out at home. He was therefore officially a deserter and at that point he joined the resistance in the city, becoming involved in various improvised attacks on German troops. On many occasions he was on the verge of capture (he used his speed on a bike to get away) but he was able to remain in the city and resume his career as a cyclist at the end of the war. In June 1946 he duly took up his place in the Giro of Rebirth. He would be riding in the Legnano team, with the great Gino Bartali as his captain.

The Communist Party daily *L'Unità* was clear about the significance of this Giro d'Italia, the first since 1940 and following hot on the heels of the highly symbolic Milan–San Remo of March 1946: 'this Giro makes the idea of the unity of our nation concrete . . . in just one week the convoy has passed through cities and villages, like the beads on a rosary, and when the Giro passes, these landscapes are revitalised . . . the dusty and multi-coloured convoy brings a new and original tone to what was already there'.[5]

Italy's national cycling race began a year before the Tour resumed once again in France, despite massive bombing and damage to the infrastructure, with bridges down and roads heavily potholed. It posed all sorts of problems, not the least of which was where the race should take place. Extensive damage to the already weakened

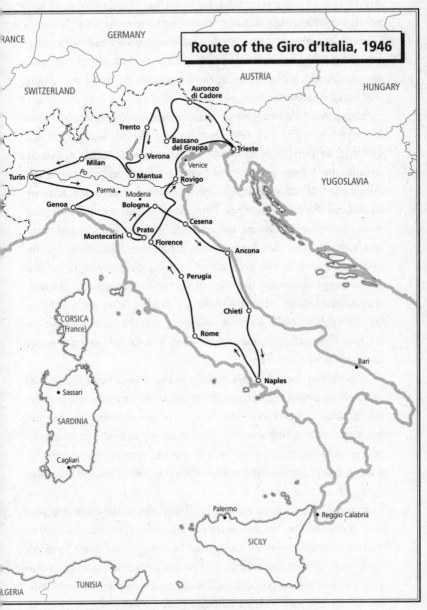

Route of the Giro d'Italia, 1946

GERMANY

SWITZERLAND

AUSTRIA

HUNGARY

FRANCE

Auronzo
di Cadore

Trento

Bassano
del Grappa

Verona

Trieste

Milan

Mantua

Rovigo

Venice

YUGOSLAVIA

Turin

Po

Parma

Modena

Genoa

Bologna

Prato

Cesena

Montecatini

Florence

Ancona

Perugia

Chieti

CORSICA
(France)

Rome

Bari

Sassari

Naples

SARDINIA

Cagliari

Palermo

Reggio Calabria

SICILY

TUNISIA

ALGERIA

15 June–7 July 1946. The race began and ended in Milan.

southern road and rail network restricted the Giro largely to an area north of Naples, but the race passed close to some of the cities worst affected by the war, from Naples itself, which had suffered carpet-bombing, occupation, near famine and the breakdown of civil society, to Cassino, where an entire town had been flattened by fighting and aerial bombardment.

Stages were also designed so as to make common connection between events in the First and Second World Wars, with the crossing of the Piave, Bassano del Grappa and highly symbolic finishes in Trento and, it was hoped, Trieste, which was under Allied control and was disputed territory. Such was the uncertainty in Italy at the time, over key issues such as the constitution, and who was actually running the country, that the Giro began without a definitive route having been established, and negotiations continued even as the cyclists were setting out on the race. This was a tough Giro, and the state of the roads was appalling, much worse than before the war. Of the 3,350 kilometres to be covered by the cyclists, only 2,500 were on asphalt. On many stages, as *L'Unità* reported, the dust meant that 'you could only recognise the cyclists by their hats'.[6]

The idea of the Giro as a rebirth of the nation soon reached all sides of the political spectrum, from the far right to the communist left. *L'Unità* dubbed the Giro the 'race of the people' and 'a sporting event which transcends itself, becoming something which we might call a social fact if we did not want to resort to hyperbole . . . a social fact in terms of the interest shown by the people who are also protagonists of the race'.[7]

Every single cyclist in the race had been affected by the war in one way or another. Some had been partisans, others fascists. There were cyclists in the Giro who, months earlier, might well have fired on each other during the civil war. Now they were riding in the same peloton. But not everyone was allowed to take part. Fiorenzo Magni, one of the strongest of the challenging pack after Coppi and Bartali, had fought with the fascists and was excluded from the 1946 Giro for that very reason. He was to be readmitted in time for the 1947 Giro.[8]

Certain riders openly professed their communist beliefs. Vito Ortelli, who led the Giro for six stages, was a member of the Communist Party, as was Mario Spinazzi. Alfredo Martini had taken part in the anti-fascist armed resistance.[9] Others, most notably Gino Bartali, supported the Church and the Christian Democrat Party. All had seen death and suffering and had experienced Allied bombing or German gunfire. At one point, the riders even met the Pope. Pius XII wrote to *La Gazzetta dello Sport* exalting the Giro and promising an audience with the cyclists if they should pass through Rome. It was not an easy race for those taking part. Spinazzi described how the cyclists had to change their own tyres, just like the 'isolated' riders from the pioneering days of the sport. This was also a race of inexperienced riders, further evidence of its being one of 'rebirth' and renewal: of the seventy-nine riders who started, just under half were making their debut in a Giro.

Every rider in that Giro had a wartime story to tell. Fausto Coppi, the winner of the 1940 Giro (and thus still the defending champion, despite the fact that nearly six years had passed since the last one) had been a British POW in North Africa, and had cycled home through war-torn Italy from Naples, risking his life on at least one occasion. His brother Serse had fought with the fascists (he claimed to have done so against his will) and according to some accounts he had even been put on trial by partisans. Coppi's great rival, Gino Bartali, meanwhile, remained in Italy during the war, and had numerous close shaves himself.

Two of Coppi's most faithful *gregari* of the future – neither of whom rode in the 1946 Giro, both turning professional in 1948 – saw action in the war. Ettore Milano had joined the partisans after having been conscripted to fight on the Russian front after Hitler's invasion of the Soviet Union in 1941. Andrea 'Sandrino' Carrea was less fortunate than Zanazzi during the war. He had been deported and interned in Germany, and ended up in Buchenwald, of which he recalled 'hunger, thirst, cold'. Of the three thousand who left the camp on a 'march of death', only eight hundred reached their destination. It took Carrea months finally to make it home and when he did so he was reduced to a skeleton, weighing just 40 kilos.

The experiences of the post-war cycling generation – all of whom were young men of fighting age during the conflict – represented those of all Italy during the period. Now they were taking part in sporting events, but the political rivalries of the past were certainly not forgotten, and neither was the context in which these races were taking place.

During the Giro of Rebirth, which took place between 15 June and 7 July 1946, dramatic events in Rome and elsewhere ran concurrent with the race itself. On 13 June, two days before the start of the race, the king, Umberto II, left Italy and would not set foot on Italian soil for more than fifty years. He had lost a referendum on the monarchy held on 2 June. Italy was now officially a republic. On 25 June, the Constituent Assembly, the first national body in Italy's history to be elected by full, universal suffrage, sat for the first time.

Politics and cycling vied with each other for the public's attention. L'Unità noted that the famous sports journalist Giovanni Mosca had failed to be elected for the Monarchist Party, and that 'today he had hoped to be in Rome in another guise from that of a journalist'. On 28 June, Italy elected its first president of the new republic. Cycling, moreover, was presented as a democratic and egalitarian sport, in the words of Daniele Marchesini 'in perfect harmony with the times'.[10]

Some sixty journalists followed the Giro, eventually outnumbering the riders as they dropped out. And, in an age without television, it was the journalists who brought the race alive for their readers, transmitting the idea of rebirth through their words. They constantly drew comparisons between Italy and the Giro d'Italia, and stressed how the effects of the war were being overcome through cycling. Orio Vergani, for one, alluded to the conflict, and to the memory of the war, in many of his reports from the race. 'In front of us,' he wrote, 'there was peace. On the sides of the roads, there was war.'[11]

L'Unità pursued the theme, writing about the 'war damage . . . and the roads where the workers are reconstructing buildings . . . the miracle of the ongoing reconstruction, which will create structures which are as good as before, and better than before, because these areas have seen blood spilt by Heroes of the Liberation.'

It was impossible for cyclists and journalists to ignore evidence of past destruction and the widespread feeling of a new life beginning. In Ancona, which had been heavily bombed, there was no running water, but in Milan, although Bianchi's bicycle factories had also suffered bomb damage, their team still took part in the race. Crosses stood everywhere and Gianni Brera wrote of a land 'of hunger, of raped cities and villages'. With the rebirth of democracy, politics took centre stage, not least among the Giro riders. One of the 1946 teams was close to the Communist Party, and wore a shirt bearing the Italian flag. Yet, beyond such pressing issues brought about by the war, its memory and the sense of reconstruction taking place, the Giro was also able to make history all on its own: *sporting* history – although it was always much more than that.

In 1946 Italy became transfixed by the one great rivalry that would define a generation, divide families and friends and produce more newsprint than all other topics put together, a rivalry which was sporting and personal, political and regional all at the same time. This was the year that cemented the Coppi–Bartali duel, a rivalry that would only end with Bartali's retirement in the late 1950s and Coppi's death in 1960. The era of Coppi and Bartali stands head and shoulders above those of other notable modern sporting rivalries. Later generations perhaps saw similar comparisons – we might think of Anguetil and Poulidor (cycling), Ali and Frazier (boxing), Borg versus McEnroe (tennis), Prost against Senna (motor racing) or Ovett and Coe (athletics) – but in none of these cases did the rivalry run as deep, or perhaps have such universal ramifications, cutting across and influencing politics, society and culture, as this one did. Coppi and Bartali's rivalry forced fans and even impartial observers to choose sides, and remained powerfully symbolic for years after both riders retired from the sport, and even after their deaths. It is no exaggeration to say that this was the greatest individual sporting rivalry the world has ever seen.

It is normal to argue that Bartali and Coppi 'divided Italy', and in many ways this is true. But it is also true that Italians were united in their interest in, and passion about, the Bartali–Coppi duel *per se*. Cycling fandom and discussions about cycling implied that Italians were actually talking about – just talking, *not* killing each other over – the same subject. In this sense, the rivalry itself was a sign of renewed unity, of renewed national identity. As Leo Turrini has written, 'Bartali and Coppi were Italy. The best part of Italy. An Italy which was beginning, again, from nothing, from a defeat. An Italy which was beginning again on its bikes.'[12] At the end of the Giro d'Italia, less than a minute separated the two great rivals at the finish line, Bartali winning by forty-seven seconds. All the others simply made up the pack, with the third-placed rider some fifteen minutes behind.

In a purely sporting sense (beyond Coppi and Bartali that is), this was a low-level Giro, both in terms of the numbers of riders and their quality – thanks to the war most had not had an acceptable level of training for such a race. But the race itself was dwarfed by its symbolic, political and economic importance. It was a race born of necessity, of needs which went far beyond those of cycling itself.

Great power was thus attributed to cycling, even the ability to heal the wounds of the war itself, to 'mend in twenty days that which had been destroyed by five years of war'.[13] *La Gazzetta* wrote:

the Italians want to embrace one another, and if misunderstand-ings and obstacles aim to hold back the completion of this innate desire, the Mother Land, our common land, our common sense of mourning should help us overcome these misunderstandings and break through these obstacles. The Giro d'Italia has been reborn to serve a higher duty which transcends itself. Its prob-lems are part of its success. Neapolitans and Turinese, Lombards and Laziali, Veneti and Emiliani . . . All Italians [all] part of a single civilisation and with one heart and they all see the Giro as a mirror in which they can recognise themselves.[14]

Although such language would not have been out of place under the fascist regime, which the *Gazzetta* had faithfully served as a propaganda mouthpiece for twenty years, there was nonetheless something new, something democratic, about these sentiments. Italy was no longer a fascist state, but a nation of people not designed merely to serve the interests of Mussolini and his supporters. Nonetheless, the power of the Giro to solidify, but also to divide, had still to be demonstrated. The greatest test of this power came early on in the 1946 Giro, with the planned arrival in Trieste and the extraordinary events which surrounded a day of cycling, violence and intense debate.

Trieste had been contested territory for decades. In the First World War, between 1915 and 1918, 571,000 Italians had lost their lives so that Italy could 'regain' a relatively small amount of land – which included Trieste, the jewel in the crown, the city which had served as the main port for the Austro-Hungarian Empire, and where Slovenians, Italians, Austrians and writers, entrepreneurs and intellectuals created a melting pot which included a large Jewish community with its own huge synagogue. After 1918, Trieste was under Italian rule, and fascism was at its most aggressive and violent in this part of the country.

In the 1920s and 1930s, fascism 'Italianised' Trieste, repressing the Slovenian population, banning non-Italian languages and forcing 'Slavs' to Italianise their surnames. During the Second World War, the city became the site of bloody conflict, a nexus of civil and class war, ethnic hatred and political extremism. The Nazis set up the only death camp on Italian soil in Trieste, in a former rice mill known as the Risiera di San Sabba. In the Risiera, close to the city's football stadium, Slovenian and Italian anti-fascists were tortured and killed, with some being gassed, and their bodies were burnt in special ovens. Many Jews passed through the Risiera on their way to Auschwitz.

In May 1945 it was payback time as Tito's partisans liberated the city from the Nazis, set the clocks back to Yugoslav time and fired on Italian nationalist demonstrators. Many Italians and non-communists were arrested and deported, and thousands were killed, often without even the perfunctory tradition of a summary trial. After the war this entire border area came under Allied control. Soviet, French, American and British troops divided up the area into zones, as in Berlin and Vienna, in part as a buffer (for the latter three nations) against the communist East.

In 1946, this explosive mix became an international issue of great importance. Negotiations were taking place in Paris in an attempt to broker a compromise and the Cold War was about to begin in earnest. Allied soldiers, local communists, Slovenes, Italian nationalists and neo-fascists all jockeyed for position in the city. Many were terrified of a communist takeover, while others, after twenty years of prejudice and dictatorship, steadfastly refused to accept government from Rome. Tensions in the city were thus close to breaking point. In Europe, perhaps only in Berlin was the beginning of the Cold War felt or fought out so keenly as in Trieste.

The timing of the proposed arrival of the Giro in Trieste was therefore either disastrous or perfect, depending on your point of view. With discussions in Paris continuing, reports of the furious debates dominated the newspapers. The talk was of an 'ethnic' dividing line between Italy and Yugoslavia, and the big powers were all deeply preoccupied with the question of where East was to be divided from West. An iron curtain was being drawn, and its precise position would be crucial to the future of millions of people. The division of the area into zones was expected to be carried out on 3 July 1946, during the Giro itself.

Thus it was at this key point in the history of Trieste that a national cycle race decided to try and finish a stage in the city.[15] From the outset it was clear that this Giro was deeply entwined with political issues and international disputes. On 14 June, in an official statement the President of the Council of Ministers declared that the Allies would not allow a stage to take place in Trieste, and that the Rovigo part of the Giro would now finish at Vittorio Veneto, the scene, in November 1918, of Italy's final victory of the First World War. That such a statement about a sporting event was made by the Italian cabinet showed how important this stage had become. The sport of cycling now had diplomatic connotations, and neither side was about to back down.

The Rovigo–Trieste stage had originally been planned for 30 June, and had been talked up in the media – in particular through the feverish nationalist rhetoric of *La Gazzetta dello Sport*. It wasn't just the stage finale in Trieste which mattered so much, but the fact that a strong team had been put together whose name, Wilier Triestina, and sponsorship had strong links with the city.

The very name of this team had patriotic connotations. Italians often use the letter W as an abbreviation for the word *viva* – 'long live' – so it is common for cycling and other sports fans to hold up banners reading '*W l'Italia*' or '*W il Giro*'. They would also demonstrate their support for cyclists with slogans such as '*W Coppi*' or '*W Bartali*'. The patriotic expression '*W l'Italia, liberata e redenta*' (Long live Italy, liberated and redeemed[16]) gave birth to the name Wilier. Moreover, for some of the cyclists on the team, this was also a personal issue.

Local man Giordano Cottur (described by Facchinetti as 'pure Triestino'[17]) was the Wilier Triestina team captain, a very strong rider and probably one of the best Italian cyclists never to win the Giro. He came third overall three times in the race (on two occasions behind Coppi and Bartali), seventh and eighth on one occasion each – and this despite losing his best years to the war. Bald of head and thin of features, he seemed to have suffering etched into his very body. His victory in the first stage of the race in 1946, which gave him the pink jersey, brought the Trieste question to the heart of the

Giro, and the way in which the race was imagined and represented (largely at the time, as we have seen, through the press and to a lesser extent radio). For *L'Unità* Cottur 'was in a hurry to get to Trieste'. The eyes of Italy were on the race, and the debate over the as yet unconfirmed Trieste stage raged on in the newspapers.

Cottur was born in 1914 in Trieste (not a part of Italy at the time) and on the day after his first birthday Italy declared war on the Austro-Hungarian Empire. Anti-Italian riots broke out in the city, leading to the destruction of a statue of Giuseppe Verdi, and deportations of Italians. Cottur's father had been a champion cyclist and had his own make of bike, which Giordano rode as soon as he could, training on the steep hills above the city. He fought in the conflict and in later years tended to celebrate his birthday a day late, so that it coincided with the anniversaries of Italy's declaration of war.

Not surprisingly, the 1946 Giro was hot news in Trieste itself, especially after Cottur's victory on the first day. Special editions of the city's newspaper, *Il Piccolo*, were published to coincide with the race. Cottur's early triumph was presented as a response to the exclusion of Trieste from the Giro itinerary. This is how *Il Corriere della Sera* reported the first day:

> Yesterday we learned that the Trieste stage has been removed from the Giro. The convoy will not be allowed to cross the Venezia–Giulia zone in order to carry its fervent salute to this most Italian of cities. Today we saw a response to this ruling. Cottur, a cyclist from Trieste riding for a team sponsored by a Trieste company, on a Trieste-made bike, won the first stage of the Giro d'Italia. When he rode in to the Turin velodrome, alone, the crowd recognised him, and the applause for the winner – through a kind of tacit agreement – became an ovation for Trieste. The celebration of this sportsman developed into a passionate display of patriotism.[18]

La Gazzetta dello Sport drew links between Cottur and the 'Trieste question' from the very beginning. Bruno Roghi, *La Gazzetta*'s most important cycling journalist at the time, described Cottur's first victory in the 1946 Giro (and his subsequent donning of the pink jersey) in language similar to that employed under the fascists:

> There, in the distance, a reddish spot in the dusty road, is an athlete who has broken away from the group. His pace is imposing, his progress is forceful. His pallid and sharp face appears like the bow of an aerodynamic bomb when combined with his bike. An athlete from Trieste, the Trieste we all feel part of, flew towards the finish line of the first stage of the Giro d'Italia. You know what his shirt looks like: it is red, fire-like. It is the shirt of the Wilier Triestina team, marked with a halberd symbol [a weapon consisting of a long shaft with an axe blade and a pick, topped by a spearhead: used in fifteenth- and sixteenth-century warfare, it is the symbol of the city]. The blood of our hearts has stained the shirt which covers the arms and the torso of a Triestine athlete.

The dramatic events during the stage which had been designed to end in Trieste were to cement it in sporting history, the history of that city *and* the history of Italy. As with Gino Bartali's victory in the Tour of July 1948, the 1946 Trieste stage has acquired mythical status in terms of its political and social impact. Paolo Facchinetti goes as far as to say that it was 'only thanks to Cottur' that the Giro reached Trieste, and in this way 'an ethnic civil war was prevented'.[19] The facts themselves, however, seem to suggest otherwise. Violence was *provoked* by the Giro, and it was along both ethnic and political lines.

In the absence of historical research into the events themselves what now emerges is a popular story that has been handed down through time, usually in the words of (cycling) journalists. This story is also supported by other reports in the newspapers of the time. Based largely on the most detailed account in Facchinetti's volume, this is the story as it has usually been told.

Originally the Allies in control of Trieste had refused to give permission for the race to end in the city. This was not a ban applied just to cycling. The Allies would not allow the local football team, Triestina, to play at home at that time for fear of violence, but the decision to ban the stage caused great controversy within Trieste – and in the rest of the country – and the Italian government applied political pressure in order to allow the Trieste finish to go ahead. Fevered negotiations continued even after the Giro was underway and on 22 June the Allied Military Command reversed its ruling and said that it would permit the Rovigo–Trieste stage to reach its original destination. At the last moment, the Giro organisers had won their battle to reach a town which lay within contested territory. Or had they?

The 228-kilometre stage set off from Rovigo at 6.25 on the morning of 30 June with just forty-six riders of the original seventy-nine in the group, including Bartali and Coppi. Such was the uncertainty in that region that the Trieste finish had only finally been fixed that morning and, as the city was outside Italian jurisdiction, all the riders were issued with special passes which would allow them to get through checkpoints. On the way, the cyclists crossed the Piave, symbol of Italy's defence of its country against the armies of the Austro-Hungarian Empire in 1917–18, during the First World War.

Things went quite smoothly until the group reached Pieris, just inside the so-called Zone A, about 40 kilometres from Trieste. There the cyclists encountered makeshift barricades which forced them to stop. Then they were pelted with stones from the surrounding fields. One cyclist – Egidio Marangoni – was quite seriously hurt, and some thought he had actually been killed. Many riders threw themselves into ditches to avoid trouble, including Coppi and Bartali (although other versions have Bartali hiding in a car and Coppi behind a fish basket). Shots were then fired, probably it seems by those guarding the route of the Giro. Other accounts mention barbed wire, petrol barrels and other obstacles. Some claimed that the cyclists themselves were fired upon. At that point, most of the racers refused to continue.

L'Unità gave its own side of the story. A car following the race and flying the Italian flag entered the disputed territory of Zone A. After this 'a group of irresponsible people reacted with stone-throwing directed against the cyclists who ran away'. Thus, according to *L'Unità*, the attack on the Giro had been largely spontaneous, a 'reaction'.[20] Most other versions, however, accept that the attack on the Giro was planned, that it was an ambush. News of these events soon reached Trieste, and wild rumours spread, including one which claimed that some of the riders had been murdered. This situation was then exploited further by local nationalists (dubbed 'fascists' by *L'Unità*), who went on the rampage, attacking Slovenes and 'Slavs'. In the riots that ensued 'a number of stationery shops, bookshops and restaurants owned by Slovenes were burnt down'. A Slovenian newspaper was targeted and there were attacks on its offices, in scenes reminiscent of the anti-Slovenian riots and violence of the early 1920s. Two general strikes were called, symbolising the deep divisions in the city. One was in protest at these incidents in Trieste, and the other was linked to the ambush of the Giro.

Who was behind the dramatic attempt to stop the Giro reaching Trieste? Facchinetti attributes the attack on the Giro to 'slavs', 'pro-slavs' (*sic*) and 'communists' (pro-Titoans) – *slavcommunists* – who tend to be amalgamated into a kind of amorphous group of 'anti-Italians' (although some were clearly Italian). The evidence for this claim is extremely fuzzy. No arrests were made and no trial was held. The assailants, whoever they were, made their escape through the fields lining the Giro's route.

By then, however, the mystery assailants had achieved their purpose. The stage seemed to have come to a halt, and would not end in Trieste after all. Furious discussions ensued among the riders and the race organisers about what to do next. Most of the cyclists, understandably reluctant to carry on towards the city, wanted to abandon the stage. Who could tell what else was awaiting them on the road into Trieste? But one small group, led by Cottur, was determined to continue. After two hours of toing and froing, a compromise was reached. In terms of the race (and the leadership board), the Giro was deemed to have finished at Pieris, but those who wanted to carry on into Trieste would be helped to do so, although any further racing would be purely symbolic (apart from the victory in the stage and the prize money, which was still on offer). The Giro organisers later wrote that the 'honour' of the race was at stake.

A rather motley (and brave) group of seventeen riders, now less than half of the total left in the Giro at that point, decided to 'race on' (including the whole Trieste team plus assorted other cyclists) while Bartali, Coppi and most of the top journalists went straight to Udine, where the next stage was due to begin. What happened next is unique in the history of professional cycling. A US Army truck picked up the seventeen intrepid riders and their bikes and drove them, with an armed military guard, to the seafront of Barcola on the edge of Trieste. There they were dropped off. With just seven flat kilometres remaining to the finish line, and most of the riders somewhere else altogether, the 'race' began again.

It was no great surprise that Cottur broke away to win, and was engulfed by the crowds who had gathered in the local cycle stadium. There a banner greeted the cyclists – *Sporting Trieste welcomes the 'girini'*. Amidst the confusion Cottur's bike was stolen, although it was later returned. Cottur was greeted as a conquering hero, a symbol of Trieste's Italianness, but the arrival of the Giro was also symbolic of the fact that the war had finally ended, and that normal life was beginning to return, even in this troubled region. The fact that a local rider had won, in a local team (with the word *Triestina* on their shirts), and despite a violent attack from 'slav-communists', added to the momentousness of the occasion. Symbolically, the cheering crowds who welcomed Cottur were also welcoming Italy itself back into their city, the Italy of the old days, before the bloody divisions of the conflict with its occupations, arrests and hardships. Cottur later remembered that moment as a 'marvellous day', adding that he saw many people in tears: 'The Giro was associated with Italy and Trieste wanted to be Italian.'[21]

The events of 1946 were described in glorious nationalist rhet-oric by Bruno Roghi in *La Gazzetta*, who saw the Giro in simplistic terms as a unifying, nationalist force. The finishing of the stage in Trieste had been a moral obligation, a demonstration of nationalist pride. For Roghi 'the Giro d'Italia has done its duty. It has gone, once again, to seek out the Italians. It has gone out to say to the Italians that they should be united and love each other . . . the Giro had to go to Trieste, precisely in these sad and painful times, in order to help out this sister of ours who is in danger and to bring her the solidarity of all her Italian brothers. The Giro went to Trieste.'[22]

Not surprisingly, the so-called 'pro-slav' or 'communist' press was more sceptical about the ability of the Giro d'Italia to change the world. At that time the print press was the main source of ideas, opinions and news. Non-communist anti-fascists also exploited the attack on the Giro for propaganda purposes: 'the savage and planned attack carried out by Tito's followers against the cyclists on the Giro as they crossed the Zone A border is an eloquent sign of how much liberty and democracy would be enjoyed by Italians if this area was to fall under the control of the Yugoslav regime'.[23]

But far from easing the violence – as in Roghi's vision of a unify-ing force, or in Facchinetti's claim 'it is clear that the arrival of those 17 cyclists in the city helped to avoid an ethno-political conflict between Italians and Slavs'[24] – the arrival of the Giro also sparked scenes reminiscent of a civil war. In Trieste, rioting continued for at least two days. Two people were killed amidst attacks on 'slav' and 'communist' buildings and 'communist' violence directed at the police and Allies.

Giorgio Fattori wrote at the time that 30 June marked a turning point in history: 'From today, Venezia Giulia has become synonymous with a pink shirt, a pink shirt of the Giro and of its Italianness',[25] and in the years after 1946 the Trieste stage became legendary. In purely sporting terms, Cottur's victory was meaningless. It changed nothing in the overall balance of the Giro (official time-keeping having ceased at Pieris), but those seventeen cyclists who rode into Trieste were part of an event which went way beyond anything to do with a bike race. They were riding into history.

A sporting event had seemingly transformed Italy. A stage of a cycle race had become 'an historic event which is part of the memory of the people of the border lands'.[26] Such powers were also attributed to other moments from sporting and national history after the war, among them Coppi's epic solo victory in the Milan–San Remo of the same year. In this period of rebirth and reconstruction, it was as if sporting moments took on special significance. But the vicious ethnic and political violence in Trieste in the wake of the events of 30 June 1946 do not fit with this comfortable and unifying narrative – and have thus been quietly removed from most versions of the story.

In the record books, too, the whole story is glossed over – and often slightly falsified. The 139-kilometre stage 'finished' at Pieris, but was 'won' by Cottur (after 'six hours', in Trieste), with two other riders from his team behind him (and, of course, rumours of a fix were rife at the time and continue to this day). In other records, the stage is simply 'cancelled', removing Cottur's final ride that day from sporting history. The most complete records describe the arrival in Trieste as 'symbolic' with the stage ending in Pieris and every rider having the same time.[27]

The great Italian journalist Dino Buzzati once asked himself this question, in print. 'Is this strange thing called the Giro d'Italia of any use?' Then he answered his own question for his readers. 'Of course it is. It is a stronghold of romanticism besieged by the squalid forces of progress.' In 1949, in one of his famous series of pieces about the Giro, Buzzati described the Giro's passage through Trieste (on the way to Udine) as a moment of national unity:

Brought to life by the sprint, the cyclists entered the city, and at that point the atmosphere of the Giro suddenly changed. All at

once, there was no longer any difference between one racer and
another . . . Bartali was on the same level as Carollo, Coppi equal
to Malabrocca, Leoni to Brasola. We were suddenly met by fantastic crowds, appearing out of nowhere, swarming on roof terraces,
a jubilant population raining flowers from the sky, and flags, flags
again and again. There was no longer any difference between the
great champions and the boorish commoners, nor between the
racers and members of the caravan; the same applied to Ronconi
and the motorcycle messenger, Cottur and us, the reporters – we
were truly equal. Because we were all Italians.

Sport was to play a key role in the post-war history of Trieste, too,
and the authorities on both sides of the Iron Curtain were well aware
of the importance of football and other sports in terms of national
propaganda within and outside the city. Triestina football club was
subsidised directly by the state in the 1940s and early 1950s, and the
team was given special dispensation to remain in Serie A despite being
relegated in 1946. Under the astute management of Nereo Rocco,
Triestina finished second behind the unbeatable *Grande Torino* team
in 1947. The Yugoslav government responded with its own Trieste-
based team – Amatori – which played in the Yugoslav league.

Once the 'Trieste question' was resolved in 1954 (with Trieste
itself remaining in the Italian orbit, and the mass exodus of some
250,000 or so ethnic Italians from the Yugoslav-controlled Istria
region into Italy), Triestina became far less important politically,
the money dried up and the club slipped out of Serie A, never to
return. As the city ceased to be a literal battleground between East
and West, although it remained on the front line of the Cold War,
the possibilities for propaganda linked to sport diminished. That
day in 1946 was a moment when sport, politics and history came
together, and when sport itself became part of history.

When Giordano Cottur died at the age of ninety-one in 2006 the
press was fulsome in its praise of him. Right up to the end of his

life he had continued to ride his bike around the city and work in his cycle shop. Cottur and Wilier Triestina bicycles are still being produced and the modest shop in the city centre still bears his name.

The winner of the 1946 Giro may have been Gino Bartali, but for many the moral victory went to Cottur. After the final stage, in Milan, Bartali and Cottur were given garlands and both wrapped themselves – literally – in the Italian flag, as the Trieste rider completed a kind of lap of honour with the overall victor. Mussolini had never been a great fan of cycling, and fascism never exploited cycling in the same way as it had tried to do with football or boxing. But the new republican state was to be a different animal, where this massively popular sport was to be deeply involved in politics on a daily basis, as well as with everyday questions of religious identity, morality and social change.

The Guru. Biagio Cavanna and the Lost World of Italian Cycling

'Cavanna was Homer. Blind and at the centre of a fascinating and cruel Iliad'

— Claudio Gregori[1]

'My whole life with Fausto Coppi was accompanied by his voice, his breathing, the sounds of the wheels turning, the smell of sweat and the sharpness of his spiky bones, which were both fragile and formidable at the same time, which I felt pulsing in my blind man's hands . . . massaging his legs was like playing a guitar'

— Biagio Cavanna[2]

In the sport of cycling, even those who take a direct part in racing (the cyclists) often never really knew what was happening overall, how far they were ahead, or behind, what was round the next corner up the mountain, or what was coming up towards them from below. Even with today's earpieces, radio contact and satellite TV, they still rely on information from others. In the past word of mouth, hearsay, rumour, snippets of news and rapidly chalked up times were all they had to go on. This information was notoriously unreliable, and often deliberately so. Managers would sometimes give false times to their team or their rivals in order to create confusion or for psychological reasons.

Biagio Cavanna was blind for much of his life, yet he was a constant presence at races all over Italy, and was always at Fausto

Coppi's side. It was said that he knew instinctively when Coppi was in the lead. He also felt and massaged every muscle of his riders' bodies. He could tell, he claimed, just from his touch if they were ready (or not), and predict their future in the sport if they were just starting out. It is often said that he also knew if they had trained properly. Cavanna was a symbol of how cycling was understood in its heroic age, through smell, touch, words and noise.

Cycling fans rarely saw their heroes before and during the golden age, but they could feel their presence, they read and heard about them and they understood when they were about to pass by. 'Coppi's coming,' 'Bartali is nearly here,' 'Where is Magni?' These were constant cries on the road in the post-war period. For one celebrated French cycling journalist, the words 'Coppi is coming' characterised an entire historical epoch.[3] The same was true of fans in bars listening to the radio, or reading *La Gazzetta dello Sport*, anxious for news of their idols (and those they wanted to lose). Cycling was a sport which was both sensed and narrated. It smelt of 'urine and sweat'.[4] Cavanna, in such a world, was a powerful figure. For a long period, Novi Ligure was an international centre of cycling, from the time of Girardengo right through to the end of Coppi's career. And the nerve centre of this cycling capital was Biagio Cavanna's house, with its live-in stable of cyclists.

Giuseppe 'Biagio' Cavanna was born in Novi Ligure in June 1893, and he cycled in his youth, winning a number of races. In 1937, in his mid-forties, he lost his sight as a result of dust getting into his eyes. He then wove his magic with a whole generation of cyclists, from the two 'champions of champions' (Girardengo and Coppi) to a whole generation of *gregari*, ready and willing to do their master's bidding (in training) and follow their captain's orders (on the road). Part of this 'magic' was due to the 'substances' Cavanna would supposedly prepare for 'his' riders, and stories abound of the content of these substances, and their effects. He was never a simple masseur, and his presence alongside Coppi acquired mythical proportions for fans, cyclists, journalists and writers. Gianni Brera wrote that Cavanna 'knew everything about cycling'.[5]

The training regime in his Novi stable was harsh. Every morning, Cavanna's cyclists would leave in a group and ride for 200 kilometres or so, whatever the weather. 'For Cavanna the main principle was this: ride, each and every day. He would knock on our doors at 4, 4.30 a.m.'[6] After coffee and bread and with another bread ration for later, the riders would be packed off. On their return, Cavanna would check their muscles, to see if they had really ridden all that way. Part of the ride would be against time, and part in a group, over local hills and foothills. Cavanna was a big man, both tall and large, with huge hands, and in his later years he always carried a stick. His daughter married one of Coppi's most faithful *gregari*, Ettore Milano, in 1950.

Cavanna lived among cyclists for fifty years, in Via Castello in the centre of Novi Ligure. His life was cycling, twenty-four hours a day, seven days a week. He set up a unique kind of cycling school, where young men would live the life of professional riders, and train with the champions who lived in the town. Each evening, the riders would all eat around one large table and the subject of conversation was always the same: cycling. This was a time of great poverty, both for Novi Ligure and for Italy in general. Often, aspiring young cyclists would pay Cavanna in kind with food, his favourite thing of all. As he used to say, 'People eat in order to live, I live in order to eat.'

Although Cavanna could not see, he had his spies and those who used their eyes for him. In this way he kept a tight control over his young riders. One remembered, 'we all went to bed early. Everyone knew us in Novi. There was no point going to bed late, as he would have found out about it. And in any case Cavanna would turn up himself, with his stick, to check on us.' Cavanna could often be very frightening; he flew into rages and he scared the young cyclists under his control. Riders were born and made. As he said, 'there are those who are born to climb easily, those who are ready to sprint, those who can pedal with the regularity of a Swiss clock, and those destined to be *gregari*. It is big mistake to try and be that which you cannot be.'[7]

By the end of the 1940s, Cavanna had moulded a group of riders who dedicated their lives and their professional activity entirely to Coppi, and to Cavanna himself. They lived, trained and rode together. Coppi's success was also down to this almost military preparation, to the bonds he forged with Novi, Cavanna and the group of *gregari* prepared there. No cyclist before or since has had such a loyal and disciplined group of *gregari*. Coppi was not an individual; he was part of a group, almost a sect, under the control of the guru Biagio Cavanna. Cyclists would make pilgrimages to see Cavanna, to have their muscles felt by his famous hands, to hear his judgement on their chances of making it in the world of professional cycling.

With the deaths of Cavanna and Coppi that world came to an end. Cavanna died on 21 December 1961, heartbroken, it was said, at the passing of Coppi in January the previous year. Their double demise symbolised the end of two eras at the same time – that of Novi Ligure as the capital of cycling, and that of the heroic, popular age of the sport in general. Novi Ligure now lives off the memory of that time. If no longer the world capital of cycling, it has reinvented itself as the storehouse for the memory and nostalgia of the sport.

Fausto Coppi and the 'Coppi Myth'. The Fragility of Greatness

'The perfect myth'
     – *Gianni Mura on Coppi*[1]

'He was flying. It was beautiful. He was flying'
     – *Giovannino Chiesa*[2]

Mary McCarthy wrote of Venice, 'Nothing can be said here (including this statement) that has not been said before.'[3] The same might be said of Fausto Coppi. His short life was under the microscope even when he was alive, and has been worked over in minute detail since his premature death in 1960.[4] What remains more or less untouched by study, or even reflection, however, is the Coppi myth. Why did he generate so much love, and hatred, while he was alive? And how has the Coppi myth endured since 1960?

Let us try and provide some answers. Coppi's fame can be put down to an extraordinary talent, but it was also linked to his well-known frailty. He was a mass of contradictions, a man of the people and a superstar, a peasant's son with expensive tastes. He was a winner, but his bones were liable to shatter with every fall. Coppi gave his fans much satisfaction, but he also disappointed them with his selfishness, his tendency (as with his petulant withdrawal from the 1948 Giro, at the height of his fame) to behave like a spoilt child, and his occasional tactical lapses. He also elicited strong feelings of jealousy (he was 'too rich', and he wouldn't retire), pity (when he was injured, in his late thirties) and hatred (mainly from Bartali's fans). And Fausto Coppi died prematurely, mysteriously and tragically, cementing the Coppi myth for ever, while he was still a professional cyclist. 'The whole world,' it was said, 'cried for him.'⁵ During his life, every inch of Coppi's body was considered, analysed, photographed and debated. Competitors and allies also fell into the same obsessive trap. They looked to his body for physical signs of form, since he never seemed to tire. Thus arose the story of the vein in his leg, whose prominence, or otherwise, was said to indicate if he was on top of his game. Rival cyclists would stare at Coppi's leg, hoping to see the vein bulging, indicating that he was not on form. For many, Coppi was a god, superhuman, someone far too important, too powerful, to inhabit such a frail, breakable body. He was remembered after his death in religious terms,⁶ his sporting feats so impossible that they had to be explained by other means. With his barrel chest and extraordinarily long legs, Coppi was often described as a freak. It was as if he had been born to ride a bike, so ungainly was he off the saddle, so elegant on it.

Other theories about Coppi's success are more prosaic. There are claims that he was doped. Stories about his use of drugs, something about which he was quite open, and which often raised a smile in the 1950s, have been doing the rounds for years. Some claim that Coppi was 'running on dope' throughout his career, that he was *bombato*, amphematines and other stimulants being known as *la bomba*, 'the bomb'. There have always been those willing to mutter darkly about Coppi's early death, and whisper in your ear that 'something strange happened there'. As with so many other mysteries, all sorts of stories surround Coppi's tragic end, including versions which claim that he was poisoned as part of a complicated vendetta.

When discussing Coppi, we need to be aware of the dangers of reading the history of his mythical status backwards, as in hindsight: 'the risk, when talking about Coppi is that everything is legendary and it is easy, when discussing Coppi after his death, to say that he was predestined to become a legend'.[7] Each anniversary since that tragic event seems to strengthen the myth. It has become almost 'an obsession . . . no athlete is missed like him'.[8] And since his death, the Coppi fable has gathered pace. Numerous monuments are dedicated to him in Italy and France – and are frequently being added to – and in 2000 his birthplace became a museum. A television film based around Coppi's life attracted huge audiences in 1999, close to the eightieth anniversary of his death. In the award-winning feature-length cartoon film *Belleville Rendez-vous* (2003) one of the cyclists is clearly based on Fausto Coppi. At least three books have been written about Coppi in French. In 2010 the Coppi myth was stronger than ever.

If Coppi was a superman, he was also susceptible to very human frailties. The 'weakness' most associated with Coppi during his lifetime had nothing to do with his cycling at all, but with his relationships with women. Many never forgave him for leaving his wife Bruna (whom he had married in 1945, just after his return from the war) and their small daughter, Marina, for a married woman, Giulia Occhini, who had her own children. Occhini was dubbed 'the White Lady' by the press after turning up at Coppi's side at a race wearing a white coat. The nickname stuck. Even worse, Coppi openly procreated outside wedlock, producing an 'illegitimate' son whose very physical presence created a scandal. Coppi was thus an adulterer, and in a society where adultery was openly practised but rarely discussed and certainly not flaunted. It was also illegal, although the legal authorities seldom cracked down unless inspired to by personal prejudice, the strength of ideas linked to morality, or where political pressures forced them to step in. Coppi's adultery exposed this hypocrisy for what it really was. This whole story, for many, was far too close for comfort.[9]

The Coppi case could not be ignored. Everyone knew about the affair, and the cuckolded husband could not be bought off, or silenced. So a show trial was held, and Coppi was forced to submit to a humiliating series of punitive measures – from his son being born abroad, to his inability to give that same son his surname, to his new partner being denied access to her children from her marriage. But it was not the adultery alone which so enraged public opinion. Coppi, the peasant's son, the delivery boy, the man who spoke in local dialect, had got above his station. He employed servants who wore white gloves, he lived in luxury and ate oysters, and he was openly having sex with a married woman who came from a class above him. Moreover, it was a commonly held belief at the time that sex was an impediment to sporting success. Girardengo had even worn a chastity belt. Coppi's affair with 'the White Lady', it was said, was also undermining his sacred gift as a cyclist. The irony was that the Coppi–Occhini adultery trial dealt a fatal blow to the legal framework upon which it was based. By revealing it to be absurdly punitive and out of touch with modern society, the state was forced to abolish these laws altogether (although not until 1968–9, after two separate decisions by the constitutional court ruled that they were unconstitutional and discriminatory). Fausto Coppi and Giulia Occhini's legal martyrdom changed Italy, but this did not make things easier for them, only for those who came after them.

Coppi's entire life was a spectacle, a show, a piece of theatre. He was always metaphorically on stage, riding between packed rows of crazed fans up and down mountains, applauded and booed, loved and hated, touched and spat at, cried over, shouted at, patched up, whispered about. He was both pantomime hero and villain. He fell frequently, but got up again and again. Most of his life was a heroic success story, but some of it was pure farce and it all ended in unlikely tragedy. He lived a celebrity's life after 1945, under total scrutiny, and he died from a disease which everybody in Italy thought was a thing from the past.

Fausto Coppi had no private life. His every turn of the pedals was scrutinised and discussed, his every statement mulled over and dissected. There are photographs of a near-naked Coppi in the changing room, in the bath, even in bed, and, of course, thousands of photographs of Coppi on his bike. There is even a film of him screaming in pain after yet another fall. His mere presence was exciting. Millions of fans lived for the moment when he would race by, in a blur. *'Arriva Coppi'* – 'Coppi is coming' – was a cry frequently heard on the roads and in the mountains of Italy after the war. But Coppi was also merchandise: his body was sold as public property and he drove himself to the limit for his fans, for his sponsors and his family. People paid just to see him, in thousands of ride-bys that were little more than guest appearances, happy for the chance to see the celebrity at first hand. Velodromes would be filled with spectators willing to glimpse him cycle past. His presence alone would double the gate. Coppi was and still is instantly recognisable; his face has been reproduced hundreds of times; the mere sight of his angular features is enough to inspire comment, in Italy as elsewhere.

Over time, the darker aspects of the Coppi story began to fade. The vicious debates over his affair with 'the White Lady' developed into a comforting tale of an Italy once 'conservative' but now modernised. Everyone became a Coppi fan in the end, even the *Bartaliani*. His early death gave the Coppi myth an unshakeable advantage over his rival Gino Bartali, who grew old before a new generation of fans, and became something of a figure of fun. Many things he may have been, but Coppi was never a figure of fun and his death elevated him to mythical status. He did not live long enough to be regarded as ordinary. Ironically, as Gianni Mura has written, his 'absurd death guaranteed him immortality'.[10]

Coppi stopped dividing Italians after he died. Moreover, the *Coppiani* wrote the history of Italian cycling, with Coppi at its heart. Gianni Brera was easily the most important of these writers, dedicating hundreds of articles to Coppi as well as a kind of non-fiction novel.[11] Gian Paolo Ormezzano is another noteworthy *Coppiano*, and his history of cycling puts his hero centre stage. Both Orio Vergani, the prince of Italy's cycling journalists, and his son Guido were potent contributors to the literary creation of

Coppi as 'the Heron'.[12] The Coppi myth gained strength over time but was progressively stripped of its problematic features. It became a reassuring soap opera, a rags-to-riches story, a human tragedy spiced with (a touch of) sex, an oddity from an increasingly distant past. Unusually for Italy, this was a story about the past that united Italians in a nostalgic, rosy glow. This rare power kept the myth alive and kicking far beyond that of other cyclists and other events.

And the Coppi story continued through the surviving members of his family, who tried – and failed – to avoid publicity, before eventually accepting their role as purveyors of the myth. His daughter Marina, with her striking resemblance to her father, began to appear more and more frequently as a representative of the Coppi family, and there was a rapprochement with Faustino, Fausto's son with 'the White Lady'. 'The White Lady' herself lived out the rest her life in Novi Ligure, before a car accident in 1991 left her in a coma. She died in January 1993. She had always argued that she had her own identity, and had a right to her own name, and she fought hard for her civil and marital rights.

Coppi's first wife Bruna had lived more quietly in the same small town until her own death in 1979. Many of the Coppi family are part of the local, but still powerful, Coppi industry. In Castellania there is a small museum, the cyclist's gravestone (alongside that of his brother) and a small farm producing Coppi family wine. In the town itself, down the hill, stands the super-champions' museum, dedicated to Coppi and Girardengo. Races are often held nearby, or pass through Castellania, and there are a number of well-worn cycle tracks in the area which attract thousands of amateurs each year. Riders who rode with Coppi, above all his faithful *gregari*, Carrea and Milano, stayed on in Novi Ligure, and in turn continued to feed the Coppi myth, turning up at celebrations and telling their stories again and again. Their loyalty remained rock-solid long after their team captain and friend was dead. They are still at their captain's side.

After Coppi's death, Novi Ligure became a place of endless fascination and intrigue for Coppi fans and gossip-mongers, with its two widows, its two fatherless children and the ongoing disputes over Coppi's legacy, his memory and his friends and colleagues. Jean-Paul Ollivier's book about Coppi begins with a description of the *omertà* and bitterness which still pervaded that town in the 1970s.[13] In 1978, eighteen years after Coppi's death, Ettore Milano was still not on speaking terms with Coppi's first wife or his daughter. Locally, the acrimony of the very public separation and affair lasted for decades.

Yet the greatest, most authentic carriers of the Coppi myth are not his family, or the journalists, or even the writers inspired by him. They are the former fans who worshipped Fausto and the cyclists who rode with him, and who passed his story down. It is still common, right across Italy, to chance upon iconic photographs of Coppi in bars, especially the classic 'bottle' photo taken with Bartali during the 1952 Tour. It has often been blown up and invariably takes pride of place at eye level beside another equally iconic presence, the coffee machine. Former fans still tell stories about Coppi. In a country where football now dominates all sporting conversation, closely followed by motorsport, cycling has survived in the national imagination but invariably through images or associations from the distant past, rather than through cyclists of the present or more recent past. The Coppi myth invaded every part of Italy, just as the Giro itself took on a mission to visit every corner of the country.

All the best and most famous writers and journalists in Italy – and in many other countries, above all in France – wrote about Fausto Coppi. He proved to be an irresistible subject. It was as if writing about Coppi was the acid test. To name just a few, the list contains journalists and writers of the quality of Dino Buzzati, Curzio Malaparte, Giorgio Bocca, Enzo Biagi, Indro Montanelli and Gianni Celati. Some built their entire careers around writing about Coppi. The relationship was often a symbiotic one: they created the myth, but the myth also created them, and the same could be said of radio broadcasters. Given this wealth of material, it is clear that there is almost nothing new to be said or written about Fausto Coppi, the

man or the cyclist. So a different tactic is required. We can write
about what has already been written about Coppi, and about the
relationship of these writers and journalists with Coppi and his
myth. We can analyse the myth, and try and place it in a historical and social context. Why were so many well-to-do intellectuals
fascinated by the son of a poor peasant? What was it about Coppi
and the sport of cycling which drew in writers and fans so totally, so
completely, so obsessively?

There are other reasons why writing about Coppi is so difficult.
The story of his life seems set in stone, consisting of a series of oft-
repeated stories which have been passed down by word of mouth or
in print. Very little about Coppi's life was secret, or remains still to
be discovered. There is no smoking gun.

But there *are* new things to be said about 'Fausto Coppi the
cyclist' and 'Fausto Coppi the man'. The myth is a fascinating one.
The attention itself is worthy of attention. Descriptions of Coppi
deserve more analysis. To say something new, we need to break up
these stories and analyse how they have changed and developed over
time. As with all popular and frequently repeated tales, the Fausto
Coppi story is replete with omission, invention and exaggeration.
It is also a myth overlaid with questions linked to national, political, religious, sporting and social identities. This was a true *national*
myth, in a country singularly lacking in such things.[14] The Coppi
story is not just a story about Coppi, but a story about Italy and
Italians. It is impossible to understand the Italy of the 1940s and
1950s without serious reference to Coppi, and to cycling. But above
all, we cannot comprehend how that Italy is understood today without talking about Coppi's contemporary meaning.

But what has already been said about Coppi can also be organised
in a different way, around themes and reflections, flashes of his
life, his routines and races. We can start with the earliest descriptions we have – that of a young Fausto Coppi, perhaps at the age
of thirteen. He is in Novi Ligure, on a bike. But this is no thin,

sleek racing bike. It is a fat, heavy, black delivery bike, with a big frame at the front for carrying groceries and meat. Even on the flat, riding a vehicle of that kind is hard graft. Coppi is working, delivering goods for a local store. He is given a note. It contains the name and address of his next delivery. The name is a famous one: Girardengo! The great cycling champion from Novi. Coppi rides up to his hero's villa and makes the delivery. Girardengo himself, dressed as ever in his most elegant clothes, answers the door. He doesn't notice the gaunt figure riding off into the distance. Eight years later, that boy will win the Giro d'Italia. The delivery boy story, even if apocryphal, is a key element of the Coppi myth. It tells of the master and the apprentice, it roots Coppi's story in the milieu of Novi Ligure and it underlines the intimate connection between Fausto Coppi and 'his' land, his locale, the topography of his home town and its surroundings. Today these places still form the central, fixed elements of the Coppi myth.

The details of Fausto Coppi's life and career are familiar. He was born in September 1919 to a poor family in the tiny Piedmontese-Ligurian hill town of Castellania. His father was a subsistence peasant, making just enough to survive and keep his family alive from small plots of poor, backbreaking land. Coppi was undernourished as a child, as were millions of Italians in the 1920s and 1930s, and some have diagnosed his gait as the result of rickets, and his notoriously fragile bones as a consequence of poor diet. Castellania made Fausto Coppi. He 'was part of its people and had all the signs of that place'.[15]

Not content with tilling the soil, Fausto found himself a job as a delivery boy in the relatively thriving Novi Ligure, a railway town down the hill from Castellania towards the sea. This movement away from the land was enough to have him branded as 'bourgeois' by some commentators – as 'not poor enough' to make it as a cyclist. Such an attitude reveals much about the social levels enjoyed by many Italians – in the 'rich' north of Italy – only seventy to eighty years ago.

Coppi's job required much cycling, carrying food and goods to the

citizens of Novi Ligure. It was here that he first began to fall in love
with the bike, as training and work merged into one. Despite its apparent fragility, Fausto's body seemed designed for cycling. Many have
commented on his physical gaucheness when walking or standing, and
of the transformation into elegance, the way he became 'a heron' once
on a bike. His legs were extremely long and his chest stuck out as if
he somehow had an extra lung attached to it, an organ which could
contain seven litres of air. This combination of physical attributes was
perfect for a cyclist. Many fellow cyclists identified this near-physical
deformity as Coppi's 'secret' (but there were a number of other theories
as well). Fausto also had a very low heartbeat, essential for a professional cyclist. His body, its very form, was part of his mythical status.

Chance had it that Novi Ligure was the most important centre
for cycling in Italy. If he had grown up elsewhere, or emigrated,
like so many of his compatriots, perhaps he would never have
become 'Fausto Coppi', and would have remained a delivery boy
or become a bricklayer. When Coppi was young, Novi Ligure lived
and breathed cycling. It gave birth to champions, and to those who
would ride by their side. It was the ideal place for a budding young
cyclist to grow up in. Novi Ligure provided Coppi with the perfect
geographical, political, cultural and sporting context in which to
succeed and brought him together with the most accomplished and
experienced trainer-masseur in Italy, and perhaps in the world at
that time: Biagio Cavanna.

The meeting between Cavanna and Coppi was to change both
men's lives, and the history of the sport.[16] Cavanna identified Coppi's
potential early on, and groomed the cyclists who were to ride with
him for the whole of his career. Cavanna imposed a punishing training regime on his riders, and built a formidable *esprit de corps* among
them. Thanks to Cavanna, Coppi began to race locally – and the
results were spectacular.

Coppi became a professional cyclist in 1938 and he made his Giro
d'Italia debut in 1940. Despite losing nearly six years to the war, he
won the Giro d'Italia five times and the Tour de France twice.[17] On

two occasions he won both races in the same year. He was also world champion in 1953 and won numerous other classics. Coppi was the complete rider, a climber of power and grace and an extraordinary time-triallist. No career has ever contained so many moments of spectacular riding as his. His accomplishments wrote and rewrote the history of the sport.

Coppi's myth really begins to take shape in 1940. It is the familiar story of the apprentice beating the master, and marks as well the beginning of *the* rivalry. Bartali, his team captain, was off form that year, and Coppi, the young, inexperienced *gregario*, took his chance. In terrible weather, on the road from Florence to Modena, which takes in the long, winding climb to the Abetone pass, Coppi attacked and broke away. It was to be the first of the nearly sixty lone attacks which made his name – and turned him into the most famous sportsman of his age and probably the most spectacular cyclist in history.[18] He almost never lost once he had broken away from the pack. Nobody could live with him.

Orio Vergani later recounted what he had seen that day. 'Under rain mixed with hail, I saw Coppi come into the world. I saw something new: eagle, swallow, heron? I can't say, something which, under the beating rain and the drumming hail, and looking as if he wasn't tired, was flying, literally flying up the hard slopes of the mountain, amidst a silent crowd who had no idea who he was, or what to call him.'[19]

Coppi never lost the pink jersey and Bartali finished way down the field (he was injured after running into a dog early in the race). On 9 June Coppi rode into Milan with a lead of two minutes and forty seconds over the second-placed rider (Enrico Mollo) and a massive forty-six minutes ahead of Bartali.[20] He had won the Giro at the first attempt, at the age of twenty. The upstart had beaten his captain, and in doing so overturned the rigid hierarchy of the team. Bartali was furious and would remain so for the rest of his life. It was to be the first of many disputes in their careers, and thereafter their lives were to be inextricably linked.

If Coppi's life had been a novel, it would have been rejected as being too unrealistic, too fanciful. On 10 June, the day after Coppi's victory, Mussolini stood on a balcony before a huge crowd in the Piazza Venezia in Rome (with live radio broadcasts to almost every other major piazza in every major Italian city) and made a short, fiery speech. Italy had declared war on France and Great Britain, and Coppi was a soldier, albeit one who had been given special permission to ride in the Giro. Bruno Roghi depicted these events in belligerent terms. The Giro 'was won by a soldier on leave and sporting Italy felt the power of a new and forceful combativity'.[21] Two days later, Coppi was in an army barracks. The Giro would not run again until 1946. For a time, Coppi's fame kept him out of the fighting, and he continued to race, but it is said that after a while an unsympathetic colonel refused to offer him such protection any longer.

Before he set off for the war itself Coppi was able to establish another part of the myth, this time in the deserted Vigorelli velodrome in Milan on 7 November 1942. A motley crowd filed in free to watch Coppi add 31 metres to the world one-hour record. Cavanna was at the trackside. Coppi's record, which stood until 1956, was not ratified by the authorities until 1947, and there have always been mutterings about it being a fix. Italy, after all, was at war at the time, and the fascist government would have been happy for any kind of propaganda victory. Coppi never tried to break the record again. He later admitted to taking amphetamines in order to keep going that day in Milan.[22]

Fausto Coppi's participation in the war was very brief. He fought in North Africa but with little apparent enthusiasm, and most of his war was spent in a British POW camp where, it is said, he caught malaria. Months in a prisoner-of-war camp were not exactly the best preparation for a professional athlete, but Coppi's experience was no different from that of many other Italians during the war. Most were reluctant soldiers, millions were taken prisoner and many tried desperately to return to their homes, amidst the ruins of the conflict and the violence of the subsequent civil war. For a time, survival was all that mattered. Few of the soldiers were heroes, nor did they desire to be. Coppi had been captured on 13 April 1943 and finally returned to Italy in February 1945, with the war still in progress. He got back on his bicycle as soon as he could, aware that he had lost some of potentially his best years. Even then, he had to beg for help. A local paper put out an appeal to its readers to donate a 'cycle for Coppi'.

After a few races in the south, and in Rome (he was later to learn that his parents had unwisely invested his savings in useless war bonds), Coppi set off for home on his bike. His apocalyptic journey north from Caserta to Castellania must have looked (and probably felt) a bit like a Giro d'Italia – like one of his famous solitary breaks – but this time he really was alone, without prizes, timekeepers, opponents or crowds. The popular writer Gian Franco Venè later used Coppi's ride to tell the story of Italy, and of the Italians.[23] It was an odyssey, an epic but anonymous ride towards a new life, and a new career. It was also dangerous, and it is said that Coppi risked death on more than one occasion. He finally made it back to Castellania and returned to training immediately. It was time to make up for lost time. Cycling's golden age was about to dawn, and Fausto Coppi was soon to become a superstar.

Coppi's life offers the perfect metaphor for the Italian experience between the 1930s and the 1950s. His war was similar to that of many others – and at the same time exceptional. His experiences were those of millions – but he was also unique. This made Coppi and his story glamorous, out of reach, star-studded – but also approachable, understandable, within the grasp of ordinary people.

There have been cyclists who have won more races than Fausto Coppi. But with Coppi it was not just the winning which created the sense of history, of myth. It was the way he won. Coppi's victories were spectacular, dramatic, unrepeatable. They lived on in the memory and bore endless retelling. They were the stuff of which dreams were made.

It is rare for a cycle race to symbolise a key moment in a country's history; rarer still for one moment, in one particular race, to encapsulate a significant sense of change for an entire nation. In Italy, this happened twice in two years between 1946 and 1948, once on home soil and once in France.[24] The first incident took place outside a tunnel, just before the Turchino Pass 500 metres above the Ligurian coast, and it involved the most popular, talked-about, successful and unlucky rider of the 1940s and 1950s, Fausto Coppi.

The 1946 Milan–San Remo, commencing on 19 March, was the first post-war classic and the first big race in Italy since 1940. Coppi made his mark with one of the most extraordinary rides of all time. As the group edged out of a shattered Milan – with rubble everywhere, La Scala still closed and thousands living in hovels or on the streets – the crowds began to gather. Within a month, Mussolini's body would be stolen from an unmarked grave in Milan's municipal cemetery, a pathetic attempt by fascists to keep the myth of the dictator's memory alive. The return of the Milan–San Remo meant that Italy was slowly getting back to normal again.

Coppi made his first break extremely early in the race: just outside Milan itself, at Binasco, where he attacked along with a small group of other riders. One fellow cyclist later said that 'we saw him go at Binasco, and then I next bumped into him at dinner'. The Turchino tunnel had just been reopened. When Coppi emerged alone from that tunnel into the light, with ninety miles still to go, his feat began to take on mythical proportions. That moment was relayed by journalists who were describing what they had seen, or what they imagined they had seen. Pierre Chany of *L'Équipe* wrote these celebrated words, which made a direct link between cycling history and the history of Italy itself.[25]

The tunnel was of modest dimensions, just 50 metres long, but on 19 March 1946 it assumed exceptional proportions in the eyes of the world. That day it was six years in length and lost in the gloom of the war . . . A rumbling was heard from the depths of those six years and suddenly there appeared in the light of day an olive-greenish car stirring up a cloud of dust. '*Arriva Coppi*' the messenger announced, a revelation only the initiated had foreseen.

Coppi rode more than half of the race alone. He didn't simply beat the other riders, he pulverised them. They were rendered invisible. The second-placed cyclist, Lucien Teisseire, was fourteen minutes behind. Bartali, his great rival, was another ten minutes behind that. In modern cycling terms, twenty-four minutes represented an abyss. At that moment, Coppi and Italy became one. They were fused together. A myth of endurance, of a superman in peasant's clothing, had come into being, and for many it wiped out, if only briefly, bad memories of the war. As Ormezzano wrote, 'the idea of "one man, alone" was born that day . . . it was him, Fausto Coppi, the best lone cyclist of all time'.[26] Coppi's solo arrival led to the famous announcement on the radio that 'music will be transmitted' while the commentators waited for the second-placed rider to turn up. In his popular history book, *Vola Colomba*, Gian Franco Venè dedicated twenty-two pages alone to the Milan–San Remo race.[27] Coppi himself was, as usual, very modest in victory. His post-race words were brief – 'I am pleased to have won. Hello, Mum' – and soon became a classic in their own right. Much later, in the late 1960s, a popular TV quiz series would be presented by former professional road racer Vittorio Adorni. The programme was entitled *Ciao Mamma*.

The Milan–San Remo classic had always been the benchmark for all the other riders and for the season as a whole, and continued to be so after 1946. Girardengo made the race his own, and Coppi and Bartali fought for supremacy on the route both (but especially Coppi) knew so well, so close as it was to Fausto's home town and his regular training circuit. Only Binda never really took it seriously,

although he did win it three times. As it was the first race of the
season, the winner was sending out a strong signal. In winning by
fourteen minutes in 1946, Coppi confirmed that victory in 1940
had been no fluke, and the message went out clearly to Gino Bartali
and to the whole of Italy and beyond. But the race was not a turning point in any real terms. It had no genuine social, economic or
political impact on Italy. Apart from that of Coppi himself, it didn't
actually change anyone's life, but it took on enormous symbolic
importance. It provided a moment for exaltation, of joy, the birth of
a myth, a memory to be repeated and passed down through generations. Normal life had returned and with it the great sporting heroes
who would both inspire and divide millions of fans: in cycling,
Coppi and Bartali, and in that other symbol of Italy's rebirth, the
Grande Torino football team of the 1940s.[28]

June the tenth 1949 marked the ninth anniversary of Italy's entry
into the Second World War, and the year that Fausto Coppi won
his first Giro d'Italia. In 1949, one particular stage was a brutal one,
but it was not the distance from Cuneo to Pinerolo which mattered,
rather the five mountains to be climbed on the way. Coppi broke
early and attacked with no other cyclists in sight but amidst huge
crowds and with a convoy of cars and scooters surrounding him. His
ride over the mountains in the 1949 Giro is the most legendary lone
break in Italian cycling history. He rode unaccompanied for nearly
200 kilometres. The times of the Giro alone tell the story. Gino
Bartali trailed in second, nearly twelve minutes later. The race leader,
Adolfo Leoni, lost twenty minutes. The year 1949 was a particularly
poignant one for sports fans. In May, just a month before the Giro, a
plane had crashed into the side of the Basilica of Superga near Turin,
killing all of its passengers and crew. That plane was carrying the
Grande Torino football team, which had won four championships in
a row after the war (and was on its way to a fifth). That tragedy was
still fresh in people's minds as they followed Coppi's progress across
the mountains of Italy and France.

As Coppi progressed, his ride became a key part of the myth of the man and it was then that the radio commentator Mario Ferretti pronounced the words which, ever since, have been associated with Coppi's career, and indeed with Ferretti's own: '*Un uomo solo è al comando; la sua maglia è bianco-celeste; il suo nome è Fausto Coppi.*' The entire stage took over nine hours to complete. Coppi 'flew like a heron' and eventually won the Giro with a massive twenty-three-minute advantage over Bartali.

Dino Buzzati wrote one of his most celebrated pieces about that stage in which he compared Coppi and Bartali to Hercules and Achilles.[29] Over the years that moment has been immortalised in plays, exhibitions, concerts, films and photographs, monuments and plaques, street signs, museums, archives and even in an entire book.[30] In 2009, as the Giro d'Italia returned to the Cuneo–Pinerolo stage to celebrate and consecrate Coppi's memory, a plaque was placed at the precise point at which he had begun his break. The ceremony was held in the presence of Coppi's two children, Marina and Faustino, and Claudio Ferretti, the son of Mario Ferretti, whose name was also (and forever) linked to that day of racing.

The Stelvio Pass, in the north-eastern corner of Italy, peaks at 2,758 metres above sea level. It is the highest road pass in Italy and the third highest in Europe. On 1 June 1953, the Giro riders attempted that mammoth climb, which rose for some 25 kilometres through forty-eight bends, many of them hairpins, for the first time. Huge banks of snow were piled up on the side of the road. And, in addition, this ride was filmed.[31] Coppi arrived two minutes and eighteen seconds ahead of the rest, and went on to win the Giro for the fifth time. In the film he seems, as so many others have written, to be flying, riding without effort, floating across the landscape, up and up, further and further away from the following pack, among the pack Bartali himself. All we can hear is his breathing, and at each hairpin Coppi looks down at his ant-like rivals, and then up at the crowds gathered on each corner, at the climb still to come.[32]

It is as if he could have ridden forever, right up into the sky, forever gaining precious seconds on those behind him. At the top there is now a memorial plaque which reads simply *A Fausto Coppi dagli sportivi della Valtellina*. Every summer, cyclists of all shapes and sizes attempt this climb and in recent years the road has been closed to traffic once a year to allow up to five hundred riders to try and reach the top en masse.

One photograph in particular is always associated with the Stelvio Pass stage, and it is one of the most frequently reproduced of all those of Coppi on his bike. It shows the words *Viva Fausto* carved into the snowbank, visible as Coppi rides past, his outline etched against the whiteness. Coppi seems to be taking in the message; it is almost as if he is being confronted here by his own myth, with the unreserved love and dedication of his fans, with the totality of his life as a public figure, as someone who, no matter what he does, can never disappoint. The photograph also encapsulates the link between Coppi and his fans, their intense desire to see him, to encourage him, to participate in his victories. Years later, the man who carved the words met Faustino Coppi and told him how he had snapped a broom in half and used the stick 'like a big pencil', and had then begged a photographer to take a shot as Coppi went by.[33]

Tragedy and fragility were, and remain to this day, central to the Coppi myth. The absurd death of Fausto's brother Serse, his partner in life and on the track, and a kind of alter ego, was something from which he never recovered. Fausto's cousin Pietro Coppi remembered, 'Fausto was never the same' after 1951.[34] Many agree with him.[35] It is said that Coppi did not eat for three days after his brother's accident, and that he wanted to give up cycling altogether. The Tour de France was due to start just four days after the tragedy and Coppi's heart was not in that race. He finished tenth overall.

On Coppi's death the brothers were reunited, and they now lie side by side in Castellania, just as they were during many races, when Serse would often protect Fausto. While Fausto was taciturn and shy, Serse was a *bon vivant* and a ladies' man who drank and smoked, and liked to dance and sing. It is said that he was extremely well endowed; also that the brothers were often mistaken for each other, but this was never the case when they were racing. As with identical twins, they would sometimes complete each other's sentences. In the loss of a sibling, as in so many other aspects of their lives, Coppi and Gino Bartali were also united, for Bartali's brother Giulio (also a cyclist) had died after his bike hit a car in Florence in 1936.[36]

Dino Buzzati dedicated a beautiful piece to Serse in 1949: 'Who among us is not familiar with this unique counterpoint to the great champion, a "doppelgänger", a younger "twin" brother who shares the same face, same blood, the same last name, but is in a way pitiable because he does not share his brother's athletic abilities – of whom he is almost an ironic imitation.'[37] Less than two years after Buzzati's article, Serse was dead, at the age of twenty-six, after an apparently trivial fall during the Giro del Piemonte in Turin in June 1951. Renzo Zanazzi remembers seeing Serse looking 'a bit shaky' after the race. Nobody expected him to die so suddenly of a brain haemorrhage, after feeling unwell in his hotel room.

According to Orio Vergani, Serse death's robbed cycling of 'a happier yet uglier Fausto'.[38] Serse was by no means a bad cyclist, and had even won the Paris–Roubaix Classic in 1949, albeit in extremely controversial and unlikely circumstances. The first rider to the finish line that day had taken a short cut, by mistake, and Serse had won what he assumed to be the consolation sprint for the minor placings. It was said that Fausto had put pressure on the authorities to award Serse a joint victory, which they duly did. Even when Serse won, he was always in his brother's shadow.

Unlike Fausto, Serse was totally lacking in cycling style. He was held up to constant ridicule. It was said that he was the only professional cyclist in the world who did not know how to ride a bike. He was compared in the saddle (at various times) to an accordion, a duck and a giraffe. Again, in this he was the opposite of his brother, of whom it was often said that he was born to sit in the saddle.[39]

Dino Buzzati, once again, got right to the heart of the relationship between the two brothers. I make no apologies for quoting again from his extraordinary (and eerily prophetic) 1949 portrait of Serse:

> Here's the fascinating hypothesis – that Serse is Fausto's lucky charm, his guardian spirit, a sort of living talisman, a little like the magic lamp without which Aladdin would have remained a beggar. Who knows – perhaps the secret of his champion brother lies within Serse? If Serse were to give up cycling, perhaps the magic would disappear, and Fausto would suddenly find himself without strength, like a limp rag. Partners, then – they are so close that neither is capable of living without the other.

Coppi inspired devotion among his millions of fans, but even more so among his close circle of *gregari*.[40] This group was more than a family; it was a kind of sect, in which everyone worked in the interests of one man, 365 days a year. Unlike many of today's teams, Coppi's squad was stable, and the entire group became famous, including his brother Serse. They were a gang, a clan, a solid group of men dedicated completely and utterly to the success of one man. Coppi's *gregari* trained with him and often lived with him. They fetched and carried his water and his food, they reined in breaks and they took him (some of the way) up mountains. They were not supposed to win, ever. It was not their job, and they followed their task to the letter. The most famous of Coppi's *gregari* was a double act, the good-looking former partisan Ettore Milano, with his slicked-back hair, and the less handsome Andrea Carrea, who climbed mountains for Fausto.

One oft-told story perfectly sums up the total dedication of Coppi's *gregari* to their leader. In the 1952 Tour Carrea ended up in a leading group on the Alpe d'Huez and, purely by chance, took the yellow jersey. Unlike almost every other rider in the history of cycling who has won a stage or led a race, Carrea's reaction was one of despair. He had upstaged his captain, stolen the limelight. His yellow jersey was a terrible error. Even when Coppi congratulated him, he was not satisfied. He felt out of place; the roles had been reversed (but just for one day). Carrea even felt the need to humiliate himself for the cameras, having his photo taken in the yellow jersey while he polished his boss's shoes. The next day, his torment was over. He freed himself of the yellow jersey, and Coppi went on to win the Tour overall. Normal service had been resumed.[41]

Coppi's *gregari* were not in it just for the love of their captain, however. Every *gregario* wanted to ride for Coppi. They earned good money, better than most cyclists and certainly more than the other *gregari*. Every time their captain triumphed, they shared in the winnings. Fausto's fame rubbed off on them a little (there was plenty to go round) and they shared in the triumphs of those years. After Coppi's death, his *gregari* became a key part of the memory of the golden age of cycling, contributing with their memories to books about Coppi (the best ones, by Marco Pastonesi, are collections of stories told largely by *gregari*) and turning up at events, commemorations and anniversaries. Both Milano and Carrea lived out their lives in Novi Ligure in modest fashion, the last survivors of a formidable team which had shaken the cycling world to the core – Coppi's angels.

Coppi continued riding throughout the 1950s, well into his late thirties. This was not a popular decision and many journalists and fans began to resent the older Coppi, regarding him as a mediocre rider. They couldn't deal with the stark evidence of his decline, his age, his normality. Memories were still fresh of his 1946 Milan–San Remo break, of the Stelvio, of his victories at the Tour. But Coppi's decision to keep on cycling was ruining those memories. It was an insult to his myth, to his past. He was, as Bruno Raschi wrote, 'trying to outlive himself'. And he was also seen as greedy, as exploiting his legion of fans (their hopes, their dreams, their willingness to pay to see him, as in a freak show, when he was just another cyclist, pedalling along in the group, never in contention for victory) without being able to reward them with the victories as in the old days. It was difficult for the fans to accept Coppi as a 'normal' rider, as part of the peloton, as someone way back off the pace. Too strong, too vivid, were the memories of those solitary breaks, those sprints to the line, the total domination of a race. Many blamed Coppi's failure to retire on Giulia Occhini, who was, it was said, used to a rich lifestyle and needed to be kept in the luxury to which she was accustomed.

For his critics, although they would never have written this explicitly, Coppi 'died at the right time'. It was easy to write about Coppi the myth, much easier than it was to analyse a Coppi who seemed determined to destroy that myth. Coppi's death offered a poetic way out of this impasse – the perfect tragedy – and was to inspire volumes of rhetoric for years to come.

Other writers treated Late Coppi with more kindness. The poetry encapsulated by the ageing Coppi was apparent, as he rode in the group, with occasional flashes of his former greatness, and with a team still dedicated to him. He was still the Coppi of old in many ways, still beautifully elegant in the saddle. During the 1955 Giro, the writer Marcello Venturi saw Coppi as a kindly father in dignified sporting decline. Many fans would still turn out just to glimpse him ride past. When the Giro passed through Novi there was 'a single cry: Coppi!'.[42] But such moments were no longer for Coppi's direct benefit, and in that same Giro he famously broke away with Fiorenzo Magni to destroy the chances of a young pretender, Gastone Nencini, and hand Magni an unexpected overall victory. It was said in that stage in 1955 that a glance between the two old rivals had been enough. They worked together perfectly from that moment on. It was to be one of the last times that Coppi would have an influence on the outcome of an important race.

Fausto Coppi was a thin, rather ugly and unassuming man, with a pointed nose. He had been a shy and reserved boy, with a fragile physique and a distended chest. Only later in his life did he discover that his formidable chest gave him extra lung power which no rivals could compete with. Gianni Brera identified strongly with Fausto Coppi – they were both from the north of Italy and the same generation. He wrote that Coppi looked like you and me but 'he was clearly not a normal man [with a] tiny body, which appeared to mirror the bitterness of centuries of working-class poverty, and yet was able to climb mountains'.[43]

Coppi looked nothing like an athlete – until he sat on a bike. Gino Bartali compared him to a 'bald cat'. Others have said that he was like '*uno scorfano*' – a scorpionfish, to which ugly people are often compared in Italy. But all this changed when Coppi climbed on to the saddle. 'Off the bike, he seems a scorpionfish. On the bike, he is simply divine.'[44] Coppi's fragility fascinated writers and fans. For Roger Bastide he was like a figure from a church stained-glass window, a religious icon, a martyr.[45] Coppi's body was misshapen, and its warped nature helped to make him into a great cyclist. He only became human, real, he only made sense when he started to pedal. For Malaparte he was 'a man alone, a sad man . . . his life is made up only of movement. Blood flows through Gino's veins, but petrol runs through those of Fausto.'[46]

Coppi's body, its form, its shape, its every angle and bone, was the subject of constant analysis and speculation. On his bike, he was elegant, light, a heron, 'almost aristocratic', as 'light as a seagull'.[47] But then, of course, came the time (every day) when he had to get off, and then he became a normal (and malformed) person once again. 'His shoulders are those of someone with rickets, his face seems that of a worker with tuberculosis, he had long arms, his veins stick out, his chest protrudes like a bird's breast. He is a fragile and vulnerable figure.'[48] Perhaps this was why Coppi was so reluctant to retire. Once he was in the saddle he was a different person. Once he stopped riding, some claimed, he would die.

Coppi's fragility was intensely physical. His bones were always breaking, he fell badly, he often ended up in hospital. A list of his injuries down the years reads like a wartime bulletin:

1939: a fall at Castellania. Damage to his ankle

1942: collarbone at the Vigorelli track in Milan

1950: broken pelvis in the Giro d'Italia

1951: collarbone in the Milan–Turin

1952: shoulder blade on the track in Perpignan

1954: head and knees hurt while training after being hit by a
       spare car wheel

1956: displaced vertebra in Giro d'Italia, damaged again (despite
       special corset) during world championships that year

1957: thigh in training in Sardinia

1959: head injuries after being hit by a tractor while training.

This physical fragility was connected by many to Coppi's psycho-logical make-up. He was criticised for a tendency to pull out of races, and some claimed that he allowed Bruna to wear the trousers in their marriage, and was manipulated by Giulia Occhini during their affair. Moreover, this frailty also extended to Coppi's decision to carry on racing right through his thirties. Final proof of the deli-cate nature of 'the heron' came with his death from a disease most people assumed had been eradicated.

As if all his victories and falls were not enough to give Coppi legen-dary status, there was also his scandalous private life. Scandalous, that is, by the standards of the time. Coppi had always been the object of the attentions of female fans, and of the press. In the 1950s he left his wife to move in with Giulia Occhini, whom French hacks had dubbed '*la dame en blanche*' thanks to her white coat, a phrase which was quickly translated into 'the White Dame' or 'the White Lady'. Occhini had been spotted in a white coat at a number of races and it became impossible for the couple to keep their affair secret. Enrico Locatelli, Occhini's husband, was a big Coppi fan, and he had introduced her to the cyclist in a hotel in 1948, when he had encouraged his wife to ask him for his autograph. The affair began, it seems, on Capri in 1953.

Adultery, along with the 'crimes' of 'the abandonment of the matrimonial bed' and 'being a concubine', was illegal at the time in Italy, as was divorce, and 'the White Lady's' wealthy husband pressed the police to arrest her. They did so on 9 September 1954. Normally, such drastic measures were not taken in these cases and a compromise was reached, but Locatelli insisted that the letter of the law was to be laid down. The affair was so public that the authorities felt obliged to act. Occhini spent three days in prison and was later forced (again by law) to live with her aunt in Ancona, relatively far away from Coppi. For a time, the cyclist had his passport confiscated, which prevented him from racing abroad. At the subsequent trial in March 1955, where the accused also included the maid who had supposedly helped the pair to meet, both were convicted, receiving conditional sentences of two and three months respectively. Coppi was subjected to a degrading interrogation by the judge, which was reported verbatim in the papers. Meanwhile, the now pregnant Giulia was refused permission to see her two children from her marriage to Dr Locatelli. It was to take five years of legal argument before she would be allowed even to meet them again.

Coppi left his wife Bruna, although he remained close to Marina, and journalists, while condemning the 'immorality' of the most famous cyclist in Italy and the 'dame' (an epithet she hated, seeing it as a way of making her seem haughtier than she was), nonetheless used the scandalous liaison to fill reams of newsprint and to shift tons of editions of newspapers and popular magazines.

The Coppi scandal had parallels with that involving another immensely popular sporting figure of the same period, Valentino Mazzola, the Torino midfielder, whose affair with a young Sicilian caused outrage in the late 1940s. The harassment of Coppi's family, as with Mazzola, continued after his death. Despite his mother giving birth to him in Argentina (in 1955) to escape Italian legislation, Faustino, Coppi's son with Occhini, was officially 'recognised' by Occhini's husband, Dr Locatelli. This absurd loophole was not closed until the 1970s. Only in 1978 was Faustino permitted to use the surname Coppi. The 'White Lady' scandal only increased Fausto's already immense fame. Cycling's most spectacular superstar had now become an actor in a complicated love triangle, part of a soap opera, front-page news even when he wasn't racing on his bike. The public, while pretending to be shocked, lapped it up. Nothing about Fausto Coppi was allowed to be private – his body, his sex life, his every decision open to scrutiny – and today, more than fifty years after his death, little has changed.

On 2 January 1960, with most Italians still on holiday following Christmas, news began to filter through of Fausto Coppi's illness. He was 'in a very serious condition' according to *L'Unità*. But it was already too late. That same day the tragic news was announced on the radio in these words: 'Fausto Coppi's big heart stopped beating fifteen minutes ago . . . his name echoes on the highest mountains.' Crowds gathered outside the hospital on the news of his death. His funeral was scheduled for 4 January 1960, at 10 a.m., but the enormous number of people attending forced the family to move it back to the afternoon of the same day. On 8 January 1960, an official communiqué from the health ministry announced to the world that Fausto Coppi had died of malaria, a statement that did nothing to prevent subsequent years of controversy over what was considered to be an entirely avoidable loss. There have even been accusations of murder. After a cycling/hunting trip to Africa in late 1959, Coppi contracted a rare form of the disease, which went undiagnosed, and he died in agony at the age of forty.

Fausto Coppi was duly buried in Castellania on 4 January 1960. In the film and photographs we have of that day, we can see Coppi once again climbing a hill, with all its hairpin bends. But this time he is not on a bike; he lies in a coffin, inside a hearse, and his destination is the place in which he was born, the tiny village from which cycling had allowed him to escape, but which he had never really left behind. An immense crowd lines the winding road up to the

village, as the funeral cortège passes. Many of the mourners are
themselves on bikes, or are pushing them up the hill. The faces of
those in the fields are those of rural Italy, a pre-industrial country, a
nation which had first-hand experience of poverty, of manual work,
of the countryside and of its hardships, of early death. This was an
Italy which saw in Coppi a man who was both a modern-day hero
and one of them: fragile, magnificent, self-made, but still a man of
peasant stock. His mother emerged from that world and never left
it. For years after, she wore black, having lost both sons to cycling-
related accidents. Photographs show her laying wood on the fire.
She had lost her teeth and it was almost as if she had been plucked
from a neorealist film. After Coppi's death, no sporting hero would
ever come close to him, his death only confirming the power of his
myth. Brera himself also largely gave up writing about cycling after
1960. As Mario Fossati wrote, 'that funeral removed a great part of
cycling's history, perhaps all of it'.[49] After Coppi, what was the point
of writing about cycling at all?

Coppi's death in 1960 shocked Italy. Thousands of mourners filed
past his body in Novi Ligure and around 50,000 hiked through the
muddy fields up to Castellania. The press in Italy, France, Switzerland
and Spain dedicated special pages and editions to stories from
Coppi's life, and tributes poured in from riders, writers, ordinary
fans and politicians. *La Gazzetta dello Sport* wrote that 'his name
echoes from the highest mountain tops' and that 'the whole world
said goodbye' to the *Campionissimo*.

Today Castellania is home to a variety of monuments, messages
and signs which both encapsulate and continue the Coppi myth.
One monument lists Coppi's victories and achievements, while
another dedication, in French, confirms his international standing.
Close by, there is a citation by Orio Vergani which highlights the
way Coppi's status was created by journalists and writers. The popular and mass nature of his fame is marked by the multitude of small
offerings left by fans over the years, and the simplicity of the site
itself.

Italy, meanwhile, was on the way to becoming something else altogether: industrial, then post-industrial, rich and individualistic, a centre of fashion and design. With time, fewer and fewer Italians would be prepared to work manually for a living as Coppi himself had done. Fewer and fewer would be ready to make the sacrifices which had turned Coppi into a champion – the early nights, the total dedication to his sport, the millions of kilometres, the pain of the broken bones, the frozen hands, the aching muscles, the tight chest, the hunger and the thirst, the mud and the shit. At Coppi's funeral, the crowd behaved as if he wasn't dead at all, lining the roads as they had done during his races. *Arriva Coppi! Arriva Coppi!* But this time it was a different crowd, their faces etched with the pain of shock and mourning, and there were none of the ecstatic smiles or the gesticulations of the race crowds. If Coppi lived on, it was only in the imagination. After 1960, Coppi became a saint and a martyr.

Every year in Castellania a group of largely old men pay tribute at the graves of Serse and Fausto Coppi, before moving on to the nearest bar to share stories about the old days. Fausto never had the chance to grow old.[50] He was to have ridden in the 1960 Giro d'Italia, twenty years after his first, thrilling victory in that race, and his team was to have been managed by his great rival, Gino Bartali. It was not to be. From 1960, Bartali was a man alone.

The Bartali Myth. July 1948, Palmiro Togliatti and the Tour de France

'In Italy the only subjects of conversation are cycling and Bartali: in homes, in bars, in restaurants, in churchyards, even in the offices of the political parties'
— *Emilio De Martino, 1948*[1]

'Rumours do not survive unless they make sense to people'
— *Paul Thompson*[2]

A 'Bartali myth' has existed in Italy for sixty years. It claims that a cyclist – Gino Bartali – saved Italy from revolution and civil war in July 1948 by winning a series of stages at the Tour de France. The Bartali myth provides us with a powerful set of indicators concerning Italian national and political identity, and the stereotypes which have marked that identity. It also gives us a rare example – for Italy – of a version of the past which (now) unites rather than divides. The Bartali myth is one of the exceptions which proves the rule. A unifying narrative around which people can agree, something which brings a smile to their faces, a myth which also feeds other myths, above all that of the 'good Italian' as well as the so-called *arte di arrangiarsi* (the 'ability to muddle through' often applied to southern Italians).

It is not my intention here to prove the Bartali myth 'wrong'. In its stronger version, the story about Gino Bartali's role in history clearly presents a largely (but not necessarily entirely) false interpretation of the events of July 1948. What is interesting is both the history *of* the myth, and its interpretation *as* and *within* history. This way of understanding the Bartali myth tells us a lot about both the events of July 1948 – but much more about Italy since then – and the way in which Italians have understood their own past and created or reinforced their own identities.

Gino Bartali was one of the greatest cyclists in the history of the sport.[3] Born into poverty in the rural Florentine suburb of Ponte a Ema, he became a professional cyclist in 1935 at the age of twenty-one, against the wishes of his father. After his brother Giulio died in a cycling accident, Bartali was tempted to give up the sport altogether, but was enticed back by a series of victories. In 1936 he won his first Giro d'Italia and he repeated that victory the following year. In 1938 he rode in the Tour de France for the first time, after the fascist regime had expressly ordered him *not* to enter the Giro in order to prepare for the French race. Bartali duly won the Tour, becoming only the second Italian to do so, and he thus became a sporting celebrity. Yet his relationship with fascism was strained. Bartali's father had been a socialist, and the socialist factory owner Gaetano Pilati, who employed him, was killed by the fascists in 1925.[4]

Bartali never joined the Fascist Party, despite pressure to do so, and was reluctant to contribute to fascist propaganda (although he perhaps unwittingly did, through his victories, and the timing of them). A devout Catholic who wore sandals when he wasn't racing, he became known as Bartali the Pius (*Bartali il Pio*). During the Second World War, Bartali remained detached from fascism. Moreover, it later emerged that he had saved the lives of hundreds of Jews by riding across war-torn Italy with false papers hidden in his bicycle – at great personal risk. The documents were destined for the town of Assisi, the centre of an underground organisation which hid Jews in convents in Tuscany and helped them escape persecution. The whole story only emerged just before Bartali's death, as the cyclist was reluctant to talk about what had happened, even with his own family.[5]

An extraordinary climber who was immensely strong in the saddle, Bartali never lived the life of an athlete. He drank, smoked, enjoyed coffee and preferred talking to sleeping. With his crushed 'boxer's' nose (the result of a cycling accident) and his tireless and generous style, Bartali built up an immense following from the 1930s onwards, and not just in Italy. Only Fausto Coppi would be able to compete with 'the man of iron' (another of Bartali's nicknames) in terms of his immense power and the longevity of his career.

Gino Bartali had been held up as a role model well before 1948. As the most successful Italian cyclist of the mid-to-late 1930s, he was perfect material for exploitation by the Catholic Church: a winner, extremely famous and deeply pious. Thus, the Church exploited and created the myth of Bartali as a Catholic idol and as a *non-fascist* hero.[6] At the same time fascism tried hard to ride piggyback on Bartali's success as 'the man of iron' and 'the conqueror of France', and publicised his victories for its own ends. Bartali's myth was always fought over.

The battle over Bartali raged throughout the 1930s, and then into the 1940s and 1950s, albeit in the latter stages without the fascist element. The Bartali myth was part of history, and had its own social explanations, but it also survived in a form which had some autonomy from both history and society, in different epochs, and right through the war years.[7]

After a long break thanks to the war, Gino Bartali returned to professional cycling in 1946 (although he had ridden thousands of kilometres during the war). He was by then over thirty years old, and the pressure from the younger and faster Coppi was immense. The 1946 Giro was an epic battle between the two men. Bartali held on to win the overall race by forty-seven seconds from Coppi. By the time Bartali rode in the 1948 Tour, however, he had been written off by many commentators and fans.

Bartali's myth continued to play an important part in post-war Italy. Every Italian took sides – they were either *Bartaliani* or *Coppiani*. The divisions were bitter – and political. Coppi was, at the very least, an anti-anti-communist; he didn't hate those on the left. This was enough to make him the idol of many of those who stood on the 'red' side during the Cold War. When he was persecuted for his private life by the Italian state, the left sprung to his defence. 'Coppi . . . [was] widely believed to be a Communist. In fact he was not, but ideology was so pervasive in Italy that Bartali's rival *had* to be a Communist.'[8]

Bartali, on the other hand was, for many, clearly on the other side of the Cold War divide. As well as being extremely pious, he was a member of Azione Cattolica (translated as Catholic Action, the Catholic social and movement formed in 1924) and a personal friend of Alcide De Gasperi, Prime Minister of Italy and Christian Democrat leader. Indro Montanelli famously merged the two men, calling Bartali 'De Gasperi on a bike' or the 'De Gasperi of cycling'.

In September 1947 the Pope made an important speech from the balcony of St Peter's, 'To the men of Catholic Action'. It was a call to arms. A huge crowd packed the wide square below him. 'The time of reflection and of projects has passed. Are you ready? In the religious and moral camps, the opposing fronts are becoming more and more clearly defined. It is time to put ourselves to the test.' In this 'hour of action', the moment to act decisively against the Communist threat, the Pope employed a cycling metaphor. 'This difficult competition, which St Paul spoke about, has begun. It is a time for intense effort.' He then did something extremely unusual. He named an individual, a sportsman, a cycling star. 'The winner can be decided in an instant. Look at Gino Bartali, member of Catholic Action. Often he has earned the right to wear the much-sought-after "jersey". You should also participate in a championship of ideas, so you can conquer a much more noble form of victory (1 Cor., 9, 24).'[9] This was a rare and highly significant moment. It showed how important cycling had become in everyday and political life, and how central Bartali himself was to the popularity of the sport.

So if supporting Coppi against Bartali was in some sense a left-wing act, this was often because of Bartali's undeniable links with the Catholic Church. In 1948 the Pope received the riders of the Giro d'Italia in Rome. During the bitter election campaign which ended on 18 April that year, Bartali's name was used to mobilise support for the Christian Democratic Party (the *Democrazia Cristiana*, or DC) and against the left-wing popular front, which included the Communist Party. Both Bartali and Coppi were offered places in DC lists, which they turned down. De Gasperi's party won a crushing victory in the general election, and Bartali sent his friend a telegram of congratulations.[10] There was now no doubt in anybody's mind as to which side of the widening gulf in Italian society Gino Bartali stood on.

These political divisions were never as clear-cut as they seemed at the time. Many left-wing fans supported Bartali, especially in his native ('red') region of Tuscany, but also elsewhere. Communist Party leader Palmiro Togliatti was a Bartali fan, for example, and this would play a part in the Bartali myth. With time, moreover, the divisions between *Bartaliani* and *Coppiani* began to fade and diminish.[11]

Bartali was not the favourite to win the 1948 Tour de France. He was nearly thirty-four and had just been beaten by 'the third man', Fiorenzo Magni, at the 1948 Giro. In general, the pendulum seemed to be swinging towards the younger Fausto Coppi. But Coppi had decided not to take part in the Tour that year, and Bartali was captain of one of the two Italian squads sent to the race, which, unlike the Giro, was organised with national teams. The Tour began on 30 June 1948, and the route was to cover nearly 5,000 kilometres of the French countryside, with much of it taking riders through the Alps and the Pyrenees.

The early stages of the 1948 Tour were ones of mixed fortune for

Bartali. He won three (including two in a row) and wore the yellow jersey for a day. One victory was particularly important for later narratives of the Tour, and became an integral part of the myth. On 7 July the Tour was due to finish in Lourdes for the first time, and Bartali won the stage. This victory was followed by a mass held for all the cyclists at the sacred place of pilgrimage. The journalist Emilio De Martino wrote, 'Our Madonna of Lourdes has become Our Lady of the *Giro di Francia*'.[12] There are various other stories linked to the Lourdes stage – of a private visit to the holy grotto by Bartali, as well as a special medal which was supposedly given to the riders, and which Bartali allegedly put on his handlebars. Many elements of the subsequent myth were added retrospectively following the outcome of the race so as to fit more comfortably with the myth as it developed. Bartali was destined to win; he was blessed; he was 'carried by angels'; his victory would often be described as 'a miracle'. In sporting terms, it was.

Despite his stage victories, Bartali seemed to be off the pace. He had lost ground to the French rider and home favourite, Louison Bobet (who was only twenty-two) at various points in the race and by 13 July he had slipped well behind the home favourite. He languished way back in seventh place. Nobody gave Bartali any chance of winning the Tour, and it is said that a number of journalists took advantage of the proximity to the Italian border during the day off in Cannes to leave the race altogether. According to some, this behaviour infuriated Bartali, and played a part in his eventual comeback and victory.

July the fourteenth 1948 was a rest day at the Tour and the riders were in Cannes to prepare for the next stage – the first real mountain stage of the race. That day, the leader of the Italian Communist Party, Palmiro Togliatti, was shot three times (once in the head and twice in the chest) as he was leaving the parliament building in Rome. His would-be assassin was a young right-wing Sicilian student called Antonio Pallante. It was 11.30 in the morning. Nothing could have inflamed anti-fascist passions quite as much as this event. It brought back very bad memories, notably of the murder of socialist deputy Giacomo Matteotti by fascists in Rome in 1924. Togliatti was adored by the communist base, and was the all-powerful leader of a mass party which could boast over two million members. His nickname was 'il migliore', the best, and a powerful cult of personality had been constructed around him by the party. His shooting was both a sign of a return to the past, and a signal for many militants that the revolution (put off for so long, not least by Togliatti himself) could finally begin.

News of the shooting spread fast, as Togliatti was rushed to hospital. Strikes and demonstrations broke out all over the country, and a general strike was called officially for the next day by the CGIL – the trade union federation closest to the Communist Party – at 6 p.m. By the time the Interior Minister Mario Scelba rose to make a statement to parliament the following day, at least fifteen people had died in clashes and hundreds had been injured. The violence and protests were both spontaneous and organised. The revolution had not been planned for July 1948, but many had been waiting for this moment for a long time.

The 1948 strikes and movements in the wake of the shooting of Palmiro Togliatti on the steps of parliament represent one of the great silences of Italian historiography.[13] At no other point in the history of the republic did a political movement emerge on to the streets on such a scale, with such organisation and with such revolutionary intent. In some areas, the moment was certainly of an insurrectionary nature. Guns reappeared from their hiding places, well oiled and ready for use. Shootouts took place between the police, the army and armed demonstrators all over Italy. In Rome, militants openly called on their leaders to 'give us the go-ahead'. They were ready to act.

Factories were occupied in most of the northern cities, including that of Fiat, in Turin, where the president, Vittorio Valletta, was taken hostage in his office by armed workers. Police and *carabinieri* were attacked and disarmed in numerous places. Barracks were besieged, prefects' offices occupied, tramlines soldered together and MSI (the neo-fascist party), PSDI (anti-communist social democrats), Liberal Party and DC offices ransacked and sometimes burnt down. Although the clashes were not of the same nature in the south, there were street battles in Naples and Taranto. In other towns prisons were besieged in order to release imprisoned partisans or demonstrators. Piombino, in Tuscany, was taken over by a kind of soviet, with road blocks being erected. In some cities there were negotiations between the authorities and the demonstrators, and a curfew was declared in Genoa. Barricades went up almost everywhere. Former partisans turned up on the streets in numerous cities brandishing guns. Occasionally, *carabinieri* and policemen fraternised with demonstrators.

The miners of Abbadia San Salvatore, on Monte Amiata in Tuscany, who had a long tradition of militancy, tried to cut off telephone links between the north and the south of the country. As the army arrived, many residents took to the hills to escape capture. Two policemen had earlier been killed. More than three hundred people were later tried for their supposed part in the events in that Tuscan hill town after 14 July.

In Rome there were attempts to occupy the Palazzo Chigi, the Prime Minister's residence. It looked and felt like a revolution, but also like a continuation of the civil war. In Pisa a young neo-fascist rode a horse into the middle of a left-wing demonstration, firing a pistol. He was pulled from his mount and shot dead. In Milan, during a demonstration in the Piazza Duomo, the secretary of the local communist federation, Giuseppe Alberganti, told the crowd: 'On 18 April we counted the votes numerically. Now we will weigh things up: politically.'[14] In the north and centre of the country, peasants and sharecroppers demanded concessions from employers or landowners. In the end nearly seven thousand people were charged or arrested across Italy, with nearly 1,800 in

Tuscany alone. Many were communists, including the Mayor of Genoa.[15]

After three days, however, the 'movement' quickly died down. In some places this was due to repression by the forces of law and order. In others – after some prevarication – strikes were called off by the Communist Party and its union representatives. In the end, after 16 July, the workers drifted back to their factories and order was restored. The after-effects of the strikes were extremely far-reaching, creating a double split in the union federation which still exists today, more than sixty years on. Togliatti, for his part, made a full recovery and continued to lead the Communist Party right up to his death in 1964.

At the very moment Togliatti was shot, Bartali was more than twenty-one minutes behind the leader in the Tour, Louison Bobet. The next day, 15 July, might have been made for the Tuscan. It was cold, wet and foggy, as Emilio De Martino put it, a day of 'mud, gravel, water',[16] a day designed for a 'man of iron'. Bartali rode the 274 kilometres of the thirteenth stage in over ten hours, including a number of terrifying mountain climbs and descents. Amid the snow and fog of the Izoard, Bobet fell back dramatically and Bartali, the 'new human locomotive' (as *L'Unità* called him) took over. He broke the resistance of French cyclist Jean Robic on a descent, and it was said that he was already in his hotel when Bobet finished the stage. Bartali had gained over nineteen minutes on the leader in one day's racing, and was only just over a minute behind the race leader. It was the stuff of which many legends would be made. The victory in the mountains was both epic and heroic. Meanwhile, Italy seemed on the verge of civil war, with strikes and demonstrations spreading across the country.

The following day, Bartali finally broke Bobet's resistance and took the yellow jersey on the way to yet another victory. He went on to win a third stage in a row on 17 July, and arrived in Paris on 25 July as the overall winner, more than twenty-six minutes ahead of his nearest rival. By then, many of Bartali's *gregari* had left the Tour for one reason or another. In all, Bartali won seven stages. There were, De Martino commented, 'no more adjectives available' to describe what had happened.[17] It was quite simply the greatest three days of cycling in the history of the sport. In more than twenty-eight hours of riding over three mountain stages, Bartali had demolished the opposition.

But was there any connection between these two apparently separate and unconnected events, the shooting in Rome and Bartali's victory in the Tour? Let us begin to unravel the Bartali myth, starting with the famous 'phone call'. As news of the Togliatti shooting reached Cannes, where the Tour 'caravan' was preparing for the next day's race, some of the Italian journalists, as we have established, left immediately to return to Italy. It is also claimed that many would soon return to France, galvanised by Bartali's success. However, other accounts have it that many journalists had already abandoned the Tour, given Bartali's position in the race classification. There are a number of different versions concerning *when* and *where* the racers – Bartali among them – heard about the attempt on Togliatti's life.

Team manager Alfredo Binda claimed in his autobiography, published posthumously in 1998, that 'at the Tour we didn't know what had happened that day [in Italy]'.[18] However, most other versions (and, above all, the account at the heart of the myth itself) have the news reaching Cannes on the 14th itself. This breaking of the news is usually followed by a key component of the myth – a 'phone call' between DC leader and Prime Minister Alcide De Gasperi and Gino Bartali.

According to the now accepted version of events, De Gasperi phoned Bartali in Cannes on the evening of the 14th and made an explicit request that Bartali win the race 'for Italy'.[19] Amidst a crisis which touched every corner of Italy, with armed revolutionaries on the streets of Rome and the country almost cut in half (phones were down, the lines cut) by the events in Abbadia San Salvatore, the

President of the Council of Ministers found time to make a phone call to a cyclist in a hotel in France? De Gasperi was a notoriously cautious man, not given to extravagant gestures. It is perhaps not surprising that a few people claim that such a phone call never took place at all. Bartali himself only began to acknowledge many years later that 'the call had taken place'.[20]

For a long time, then, Bartali was not one of the propagators of his own myth. In his autobiography, published in 1979, and based on a series of meetings and interviews with the writer Pino Ricci, the link with Togliatti is kept to a bare minimum and no mention is made of the De Gasperi 'phone call'. Bartali himself plays down the importance of the myth. 'I never gave much weight to the idea that I had "saved the fatherland", on the day of the victory on the Briançon, with the attempt on Togliatti's life which had paralysed the nation.'[21]

The phone call began to take shape in the 1970s and 1980s – it was mentioned explicitly by Bartali on camera in an Istituto Luce documentary made in 2004 – and then appeared in many new publications as a complete dialogue (although almost always with small differences in the 'conversation'). The phone call was also recalled by other cyclists, among them Bartali's support rider Giovanni Corrieri. However, Binda's version of events ('we didn't know about Togliatti until the evening of the 15th') excludes the call completely. It seems that the call became concrete sometime in the post-war period, as the myth itself was reinforced in the public consciousness as a widely believed account of what had actually happened.

There are various versions of the phone call between De Gasperi and Bartali, on the evening of 14 July. Some claim that leading DC politician Giulio Andreotti also spoke to Bartali. The most repeated version includes the following dialogue: De Gasperi: 'Do you think you can still win the Tour? You know, it would be important, and not just for you.' Bartali, modest as ever, tells the Prime Minister of Italy that he will try his best to win the stage – but that the race will be difficult.

In the huge celebratory volume *La Leggenda di Bartali* (1992), written by Romano Beghelli and Marcello Lazzerini, there is an extremely detailed account of the call and the conversation that supposedly took place. This is the version which later turns up (with changes) in all the subsequent books and articles on Bartali and 1948 – complete with the De Gasperi call (and extended dialogue), the supposed 'lessening of tensions' in Italy and the celebrations of Italian fans at home and abroad. Here the Bartali myth is fully in place.

A further detail in the Beghelli/Lazzerini book which is not present in many other accounts is the 'explanation' offered to Bartali of the possible political and social importance of his victory. This is attributed to both Binda and Bartolo Paschetta, a Catholic activist, journalist and friend/fan of Bartali who had turned up to support him during the Tour. According to the Beghelli/Lazzerini volume, this was the interpretation given to Bartali for the reason behind the phone call: 'Gino, you know that you are a popular hero. Your victory could help lessen the tensions in Italy. We need some strong emotions, something encouraging, in such a sad and dramatic moment. That is why the President of the Council called you.'[22]

Here the myth is simply being laid out – in hindsight – for the benefit of contemporary readers. Once again, it reinforces the idea of Bartali as a naïve hero, happy to help but outside political power games. As I have tried to show, however, there is good historical evidence which casts doubt over whether this phone call ever took place. It seems that it gained in veracity over time, and was embellished with more and more detail. If Bartali had not won three stages in a row, and the Tour overall, the phone call myth would not have been required. In the end, perhaps Bartali gave in – and accepted the inevitability of his own myth.

Beyond the phone call – be it fact or fiction – there are many other mythical elements to the events during the rest day in Cannes. According to another version, Bartali gathered his team together on the beach and told them that it was unlikely the Italian riders would finish the Tour if Togliatti did not survive. It was this conviction, it is said, which led Bartali to make an all-out attack in the mountains on 15 July. Moreover, the phone call signifies that De Gasperi himself understood the possible importance of Bartali's progress in the Tour. That is, he thought a sporting event could influence Italian history. Meanwhile, as the Tour continued, the Bartali myth began to take full form.

The first element of the myth is the supposed effect the victory had on the movement back in Italy. This effect is described in various ways, but most of them talk of 'distraction' and of a 'calming influence' introduced by the news of Bartali's success. This 'calming influence' apparently had its first impact in parliament, where the announcement of Bartali's success in the chamber allegedly took place in the middle of a tense debate about the events taking place in the country. This was supposedly the work of a deputy called Matteo Tonengo from Chivasso, who brought the news to his fellow parliamentarians 'in an agitated state'.[23] In some accounts this announcement was met with applause, in most it helped to calm down parliamentarians (for a time), although some, including Giulio Andreotti, claim that its effects have since been exaggerated.[24]

Secondly, we have the parts of the myth linked to Togliatti himself. Once again, here the stories do not always tally, but many people claim that the communist leader asked about Bartali's progress on coming around after a successful operation to remove bullets from his head and chest. With the passing of time, this request for news about Bartali has been turned into Togliatti's *first words* on sitting up in bed, a moment which coincided with a clear sense in Italy that 'the revolution' was doomed to fail. According to another part of the myth, Togliatti had actually been discussing cycling when he was shot.

Thirdly, there is the Bartali effect on the streets. Did Bartali's series of victories have any influence on strikers and demonstrators – or those who might have been tempted to strike or demonstrate – across the border in Italy? As Stefano Pivato and others have pointed out, there is no evidence that they did.[25] On the ground, there is little sign of any 'calming influence' caused by the events of 14–16 July 1948, which in many cases (and particularly in Tuscany, where Bartali had many fans) took on a more extreme form as time passed. Pivato found no proof of a 'Bartali effect' either in prefect and police reports or in the accounts of local militants and trade union leaders. This does not mean that there was no 'Bartali effect' at all – in fact, it is entirely plausible that people were interested both in 'the movement' and in Bartali's victory, as one Alfa Romeo worker later claimed.

Yet it is not clear what any evidence of such an effect would look like. Many of the accounts of the Bartali myth are *circular* – they simply repeat the 'facts' of the myth with reference to previous versions, with perhaps the addition of a couple of changes or 'errors'.[26] Two parallel (but separate) events, a cycle race and a revolutionary upsurge, have become posthumously linked, and this connection has become more and more difficult to avoid over time.

Bartali's mythical salvation of Italy has developed into a commonplace through journalism, the writings of popular historians, word of mouth and the later versions – repeated time and time again – put forward by Bartali himself. On his return, Bartali, along with the other Italian riders in the Tour, was received by the Pope, to whom he presented his yellow jersey, De Gasperi and the President of Italy, all of whom thanked him for his victory and, it is said, for the part he played in deciding the fate of Italy in July 1948. Bartali was awarded a number of medals and honours by the Italian state after the Tour, and was welcomed back 'as a national hero'.

There is no doubt that the Bartali myth was first propagated by the Catholic press. As Pivato has shown, the Church was able to reinforce and build on the pre-existing 'Bartali myth' in July 1948, and to do so with some force. It was in the Catholic press that the idea was first expressed that Bartali had not only performed a miracle, by winning the Tour at the age of thirty-four, ten years after his last victory in that race, but at the same time had 'saved Italy' (and he had done so 'willingly', knowing that winning at least the Izoard stage would be important for the outcome of events back in Italy).[27] This story was given added force by Bartali's victory in Lourdes and his visit to Bernadette's grotto, where he left his winner's bouquet. Bartali's race had been 'under the protection of the Madonna'[28] and De Gasperi sent a telegram to Bartali in which he said that he had helped overcome 'divisions and aversions'.

Catholic writers claimed to have seen people abandoning political meetings in order to follow the Tour. The revolution had been, in short, 'toned down thanks to turns of the pedal'.[29] All of these pieces appeared in the immediate aftermath of the Tour.[30] But sports writers also picked up on the religious connotations of Bartali's victory. The very participation of Bartali in such a race smacked, according to Emilio De Martino, of 'something mystical, nostalgic, romantic'.[31]

The Bartali myth was not the first time that sport had been attributed immense powers in influencing domestic politics and history. It played a key part in the consensus strategy adopted by the fascists under Mussolini, especially in the 1930s with the World Cup victories of 1934 and 1938, and this prevailed after the Second World War. In 1946, as we have seen, it is said that the efforts of a few riders to reach Trieste during the Giro had 'saved the city from civil war'.[32]

It would be difficult to argue that Bartali himself promoted his own myth in the period after 1948. In his first written piece on the 1948 Tour, contemporary events back in Italy were ignored completely. Bartali justified his victory in cycling terms alone, through his desire to prove his critics wrong, to show that he was not 'too old' to win another important race. In 1963, in his first published autobiography, he did not even mention Togliatti by name (but only 'a well-known politician who had been shot in Rome').[33] Sixteen years later, a new autobiography was published, which was again extremely coy about the link between the movement of 14 July and the Tour de France.[34] Only in 1992 did *La Leggenda di Bartali* begin to redress the balance.

The myth changed with time. The idea that the 'defeat' of the civil war was due in part to Bartali's triumphant progress at the Tour moved from being mainly a 'Catholic story' (with clear political overtones) into a national myth, accepted and repeated in a variety of media. The seeds of this shift, however, were there right from the start. The nationalist content of the 'revenge victory' against the French, in France, made the Bartali myth extremely exportable and flexible. Emilio De Martino's articles were embued with nationalist and mystical rhetoric (with language which had changed little from the 1930s). National pride had been restored – as the hyper-patriotic *Settimana Incom* newsreel film, *Grazie Gino* (1948), confirmed.

The myth was thus able to successfully change and remould itself to suit a different Italy, and later still an Italy where cycling today has lost much of its popular appeal; where it is a sport which is viewed through rose-tinted spectacles, free from the divisions it once created. Romano Beghelli and Marcello Lazzerini's *La Leggenda di Bartali* of 1992 is a prime example of this transformation. For Beghelli and Lazzerini, 'with that amazing success Gino defeated civil war'.[35] The Tour was 'the only happy moment about which Italy could – finally – agree'.[36] For others, similarly, Bartali's victory had a 'sedative power', it was an 'emotional anaesthetic' which helped to 'free the hearts and minds of Italians from the spectre of a fratricidal conflict which had come back to haunt the nation for forty-eight hours or so'.[37] For Indro Montanelli 'Bartali's victory calmed everyone down, it lessened the tension, it captured attention. But the revolution would not have broken out in any case because Togliatti, as we know, didn't want it to do so.'[38]

Some historians also call the myth a 'popular' one, 'a mythological idea which took hold in people's minds'.[39] Lack of evidence did not prevent the myth becoming hegemonic; it was part of people's dreams, of their imaginations. As in the title of the most popular book about Bartali, he was a man who 'saved Italy by pedalling'.[40] The myth also made a great story, one that could survive endless retelling. In some ways Bartali's victory felt unreal even as it was happening. Emilio De Martino described the race as 'a fairy tale'.[41]

Even if most commentators hesitate about backing the idea that Bartali had 'saved Italy from civil war', they do at least go along with the idea that his victory 'helped to lessen the tension in the country'.[42] Bartali had become a kind of lightning conductor for the social and political tension of the time.[43] It was, as another writer put it, 'the summer of the attempt on Togliatti's life, with Italy on the verge of a civil war, and then the nostalgia came with the years which followed, made happier by Gino's yellow jersey'.[44] 'Gino did not save Italy, but if some good news (Togliatti is alive) was added to some more good news (Bartali has won easily) then the effect on Italy could only have been a positive one.'[45] There is wishful thinking here – fiction based on hindsight.

Myths are key to the ways in which national identities are constructed and transmitted through time.[46] Moreover, as John Dickie has argued, 'nations . . . cannot exist without being imagined . . . the imaginary dimensions of nationality explain the power nations exercise over the way we think and act'.[47] The Bartali myth is part of a 'conceptual map of the world', a 'story' given added power by the presence of 'others' (the French – their cyclists, their fans, their race). We are dealing here with a powerful 'social fiction' which took root through the endless retelling of a story: a myth which became part of the nation's history of itself.

If the Bartali myth helped create a sense of national identity, it also worked in many other ways. It served the needs of the communist hierarchy, as it played down the importance of the 1948 'insurrection', and the strong signs of rebellion against the party line which were seen all over Italy, especially in working-class cities like Milan, Genoa and Turin. Furthermore, the story helped to reinforce the idea of Togliatti as a man of the people, as somebody perfectly normal and yet holding an extremely responsible position. He was a cycling fan, a proper Italian. The cult of personality around Togliatti was created by such attributes. For the communists, moreover, the Bartali myth allowed them to 'forget' the embarrassing evidence of preparations for an 'hour X' among some militants – a planned revolution – after their defeat in the elections in April.

Those who participated in the July events were also interested in perpetuating the silence about those days, and they thus also left the Bartali myth uncontested. For those who had thought that they were taking part in a revolution, the defeat was a bitter one – and with it came the realisation not just that the class-war elements of the resistance were destined to disappear, but also that the Communist Party itself was uninterested in those elements of the struggle.[48] The result was silence, anger – and repression – along with a sense of powerlessness. There was no desire therefore to carry forward an alternative version of the past. Thus, the Bartali myth was left in place also by those who could have proved that it was false, the active participants in 'the July days'. A pact of silence about 'the July days' was created, and the Bartali myth became a part of that pact.

For other reasons, the Bartali myth story has survived and appeared to gain strength over time. Clearly for the Church and the DC this was a 'good story' – it underlined the cohesive power of religious institutions in Italy and the crucial role of De Gasperi in 'keeping peace', but it also gave continuity to the long-standing Bartali myth which the Church had helped to create in the 1930s.

And there is more. The Bartali myth fits perfectly with that of the 'good Italian', the idea – both powerful and widespread – that Italians (in the Second World War in particular, but also in terms of the Italian empire) had 'behaved well' as occupiers and imperialists.[49] Accepting the Bartali myth empties the events of July 1948 of any serious meaning. As with many interpretations of the fascist 'March on Rome' in 1922 as a 'recital' and not a revolution or a coup, the Bartali myth transforms the revolutionary events of July into theatre – a farce, something even less important than a cycle race. It is also a unifying myth. Italians were united around a common national

symbol – an Italian winning a sporting competition in a foreign land
– and this took precedence over the internecine struggles – the civil
war – inside Italy itself. Bartali's myth was reassuring.

Finally, the myth fitted well with the idea that, deep down, Italians
were part of one nation, and that the ideological or class differences
which divided them were only skin-deep. What really mattered was
a common sense of being Italian. It was this message that emerged
from the popular series of Don Camillo books and films, set in
rural 'red' Emilia, where the clashes between a communist mayor
and the local priest are always resolved through a kind of collaboration for the common good. It is no surprise therefore to learn that
Giovannino Guareschi, the author of the Don Camillo books, was
one of the first and most quoted proponents of the Bartali myth.

For the cyclists themselves, the myth was also a handy way to
underline (or exaggerate) the power of their sport, as well as a good
story to be repeated – with embellishments or deletions as required.
Bartali himself began to embrace the myth towards the end of his
life, and it was disseminated by others in the cycling milieu, riders,
journalists and writers. With time, the myth-story took on a set
format, trotted out whenever *that* Tour or the Togliatti shooting and
its aftermath were mentioned.

Bartali's myth provides historians with a fascinating insight into
the workings of memory, popular history and the ways in which
sport, politics and history frequently coincide. A sort of umbilical
cord now links the two stories (the revolution, the Tour). They have
become one narrative with a clear causal connection between Gino
Bartali's victory and the failure of the 1948 'movement'. This story
also links the worlds of Catholicism and communism – through
two of its most representative figures – creating a tale around which
national identity can be recognised and understood. The myth was
at first – and in part – a political and religious construct, but it
quickly took on a life of its own, and its particular features allowed
it to permeate fully public consciousness as well as every possible
vehicle of cultural transmission of the past – apart from the bulk of

official historiography, which has in any case largely ignored both Bartali and the 1948 strikes. It might be possible to separate these two narratives in order to place them in their context, but we will never be able to dismantle the Bartali myth. That is now part of history.

The Supporting Cast: The Gregari of the Golden Age and the Black Shirt

No history of cycling's golden age can be complete without reference to the lives and careers of that epoch's *gregari*, the support riders – or to the anecdotes about them. Giovannino Corrieri was a professional cyclist who for six years – from 1948 to 1954 – rode almost exclusively as a *gregario* for Gino Bartali. In 1955, after Bartali had retired, Corrieri spoke to the writer Marcello Venturi after he had won a stage. 'I have always been a *gregario*, a donkey, a horse with a cart to pull . . . my job was not to win . . . but to help someone else win . . . the kilometres I rode were not for me, they were kilometres for Bartali.' Corrieri would only fetch water for 'the dry mouth of the captain', not for himself. Sometimes he carried up to five bottles of water at a time. Often, he would prepare the victory for Bartali, and then 'the captain would move ahead and forget me, and at the finish line the applause was all for him'. Corrieri had some regrets about his role as a *gregario*: 'If I had been more selfish, who knows how many times I would have won?'[1]

All the great riders of the golden age had their own faithful *gregari* – the *fedelissimi* (the super-faithful). For Coppi, the most important *gregari* were Andrea Carrea and Ettore Milano while, for Bartali, Corrieri played this role. Ettore Milano was described as Coppi's 'lieutenant', above all after the death of Fausto's brother Serse in 1951. Milano remembered the strong bond between the team and their captain: 'we lived with Fausto, we slept in the same place, we ate together, we drank together, we spoke together'. These men were totally dedicated to their captain: 'we gave everything, even our souls, and it was still not enough' (Carrea). This was an era in which cyclists were 'covered in sweat, dirty, straightforward, generous'.[2] For Milano being a *gregario* 'was our job. A real job . . . we sweated. But it was never painful . . . I have no regrets,' while Carrea has said, 'I always rode with Fausto and for Fausto.' Coppi inspired love and affection. He lived and trained together with his *gregari* every day, many of whom lived in the same house in the same town. A cyclist at that time spent more time with his team than with his family.

Once in a while – albeit very rarely – a *gregario* could have his day of glory. He might be allowed to win a stage, or even to hold the yellow or pink jersey (if only for a day). Milano won one stage in his whole career, in the 1953 Giro. This constant sacrifice inspired frustration (as with Corrieri and Bartali) and sometimes even hatred. Many *gregari* were convinced that, given the chance, they also might be able to win something (at least once in a while). But they were destined to stay well out of the limelight. Only the very best escaped from *gregario* status to become champions themselves.

In 2008 I travelled from Milan to Novi Ligure to meet Andrea Carrea. He spoke almost entirely in a local dialect which was difficult, if not impossible, for me to follow, and I relied on friends to 'translate' for me. Carrea's house in the countryside just outside Novi was full of pictures of Coppi and mementos from his cycling days. We then went to a special event at the super-champions' museum, where the crowd included a host of former cyclists from the golden age, including Renzo Zanazzi and Ettore Milano. It was like a roll-call of 'Coppi's angels'.

The most faithful *gregari* were rarely 'seen' by the press or spectators. They were silent, modest, always in the background. They seldom appeared at the key stages of the race. They broke away only to stop breakaways, and never broke alone. Their real home was in the group – *il gruppo* – the peloton, around their captain, almost as bodyguards. *La Gazzetta dello Sport* journalist Marco Pastonesi has written a number of beautiful books dedicated to these characters, including a series of interviews with those who rode with Fausto.[3]

The most popular *gregari* were those linked to the golden age. In the 1950s, in a break with tradition, some *gregari* became so famous that the popular actor and comedian Ugo Tognazzi dedicated one of his TV personalities to them – Gregorio il gregario.[4] At that time, some were almost as well known as the champions themselves. In the 1940s and 1950s, with the Tour organised around national teams, this created a big problem for a nation which boasted both Coppi and Bartali, neither of whom was willing to be a *gregario* for the other. A compromise was reached. Both riders would be captains, with their own set of *gregari* which they themselves would choose. Such a complicated situation gave rise to frequent polemics and debates in the press, and among the riders themselves.

There are few sports where coming last consistently can make you famous, and reasonably rich. In the world of Italian cycling, coming last briefly turned a journeyman cyclist called Luigi Malabrocca into a household name in the 1940s.[5] Malabrocca is an extremely unusual name – today there are only three people in the whole of Italy with that surname – and radio commentators' penchant for referring to him by this slightly weird surname was one of the reasons behind his rise to prominence. It was also almost perfect for a cyclist who was trying to be bad. *Mala* sounds like a shortened version of *malato* (sick), and *brocca* is similar to *brocco*, a word used to describe somebody who is useless at something, like a poor football player. Thus *Malabrocca*: you couldn't have made it up. His name briefly became an expression, a noun, an insult used in everyday speech to mean 'bad', '*un Malabrocca*'.

In the post-war euphoria of the Giro, people suddenly became interested in the role of last-placed cyclist, and cash prizes began to be awarded to the worst rider in the overall classification, who also wore a black vest. This choice of colour had political connotations. Fascism had imposed the black shirt on many people (although not

on Gino Bartali), and its militants had worn that colour with pride.
By making the last-placed rider wear black, the organisers were
(wittingly or otherwise) underlining the fact that a black shirt was
now taboo, and that fascism was over. Vincenzo Torriani, the race's
boss for years, had anti-fascist sympathies and he probably had a
role in the choice of colour. It was also a brilliant marketing move.
Crowds would wait around for the last rider to arrive, and not leave
straight after the stars had finished, and further forms of rivalry were
created beyond those involving Coppi and Bartali.

The use of the black shirt was surely ironic. For twenty years,
those wearing black shirts – the fascist uniform – had bullied people,
beaten them up and 'commanded respect' (through violence). This
was no longer true. The black shirt was now out of fashion, the
colour reserved for those designated the worst of all, behind everyone, the least powerful.

Malabrocca was quite a good rider, and would go on to become
Italian cyclo-cross champion, but he quickly saw the financial possibilities of coming last, and became a specialist in that art. This was
nothing short of surreal in sporting terms. Being the worst of all
earned Malabrocca far more money than the person slightly better
than him, on paper (the penultimate rider, who nobody really cared
about, and who didn't wear the black shirt). Given the money
involved, coming last was by no means easy. There was an intense
struggle to be very bad, and riders became experts in coming last.
There was no room for error here. You got nothing for second from
last place. 'Arriving late,' as Dino Buzzati wrote, 'is their job.'

Aldo Bini, a cyclist good enough to wear the pink jersey at the
Giro in the 1930s and who beat Bartali to win a Giro del Piemonte,
was the overall winner/loser of the black shirt in 1949 (although it is
said that he rode most of that race with a broken hand). Malabrocca
had competition for last place, and he also had to remain within
the maximum time allowed for the riders each day in order to avoid
disqualification. He recruited his cousin, a policeman, to keep
him informed as to the maximum finishing time available (which

changed) and to help him through the chaos at the end of each stage, when most of the crowd had gone home and traffic was back on the roads. Soon, Malabrocca had his own fans, who displayed slogans such as 'Long live last place' and 'The victory of the proletariat will also be yours'. After asking who the leader was, the next question on people's lips was 'Who has the black vest?'

With a lot of time on his hands (after all, he was in no hurry) Malabrocca would often stop for a drink or even a meal, accepting invitations from fans en route. Other riders became jealous of the money he was making and tried to get him to divide some of his 'losings' with them. In 1946, he duly arrived some four hours after Giro winner Gino Bartali (overall) and the myth of the black vest was born. He repeated his losing feat in 1947, coming in nearly six hours behind race winner Fausto Coppi, but in 1949 he found himself up against a fellow maestro of defeat, Luigi Carollo.

The duel with Carollo was an epic one, after his new rival discovered that he simply couldn't keep up with the group, and began to compete with Malabrocca for the kudos, and the money, of coming last (and staying there). Carollo wore two huge watches so as to be able to keep an eye on the maximum time, and each rider would hide so that the other would be fooled into thinking they were ahead (or behind, depending on your point of view). On one stage, it is said that Carollo was forced to ride a child's bike borrowed after his own broke down.

Meanwhile, the race organisers were losing patience. The timekeepers, in particular, were tired of waiting for hours for the black vest competitors to arrive, and threatened to go on strike. In the end, Carollo took away Malabrocca's black vest, arriving a massive nine hours and fifty-seven minutes behind race winner Coppi. After that marathon battle, the public slowly lost interest in the fate of the black vest. The names of Malabrocca and Carollo, however, remained part of the memory of the rebirth of cycling after the war, and of an epoch when poverty was rampant, and where coming last could earn you enough to feed your family. The country had been reborn in

1946 as a democracy, with a constitution whose First Article claimed that 'Italy was a nation built on work' – and cycling fitted perfectly with the ideology of a meritocratic, egalitarian society where work mattered and was accorded value.

It was a lonely business, wearing the black vest. Malabrocca himself recounts how he rode the whole famous Cuneo–Pinerolo stage, like Coppi, entirely alone, but in last place, without cheering crowds or the support of the 'convoy'. The black shirt riders did not have the luxury of riding in the peloton; they had no slipstream to work with, no friends, no team. If they fell, there was nobody to help them. If they had a puncture, they had to fix it themselves. In the 1949 Giro, Malabrocca hid from Carollo in a tank of water, only to be discovered by a local peasant, an episode which inspired this surreal dialogue: 'What are you doing?' 'Riding the giro.' 'In my tank?' His popularity was such that letters addressed to *Malabrocca, Italia* reached him at home, and he was asked to appear in a popular cycling comedy film with top Italian comedy star Totò.

But Malabrocca had other cycling stories to tell. In 1946 he had been among the seventeen riders taken to the edge of Trieste in a US Army truck in order to 'complete' the stage of the Giro. Over his long career, Malabrocca was not a consistent loser. He was an above average rider who won some fifteen races. With the advantages, the prize money and fame afforded by the black shirt 'victory', last place became a much-prized possession for a time, and some very skilled riders competed for this prize. In 1951 the black shirt was abolished, after protests from other riders who saw their achievements being superseded and ridiculed, in the press and by the public, by the clownish antics of the competitors for that prize. In 2008, rather desperately, the tradition was renewed, this time with a 'black number' which carried no prize money. But nobody could really be bothered about this tradition any more, however, and the reform failed to inspire even a fraction of the interest it had created in the 1940s.

Dino Buzzati wrote one of his most famous pieces from the 1949 Giro about the black shirts. 'Malabrocca,' he wrote, seemed like a 'name from a fairy tale . . . if he didn't exist, we would have had to invent him.' For Buzzati, 'the last rider becomes, in a sense, the standard-bearer for all the other destitute and needy on this earth'. In the time-trial stages, the black jersey rider would always be the first to start. Buzzati was intrigued by this reversal of interest. 'What a strange feeling it must be for him to be first: ahead of him, two traffic policemen on motorcycles are clearing the road; behind, a team car is following just for him, plates with his name mounted on the grille and the back; and people applauding at the edges of fields.'

Looking back, the black shirt led to feelings of nostalgia, for the days when cycling was more ordinary and a genuinely proletarian sport. In 2006 *L'Unità* wrote this eulogy when Malabrocca died at the age of eighty-six: 'Once the black shirt was discarded, a myth was also done away with. Those who come last have lost the dignity conferred upon them by memory . . . on Sundays groups of so-called "amateurs" fill themselves with pills and climb the Stelvio because they want to be a super-champion, and not the black shirt. Goodbye, Malabrocca, hero with a normal, human face.'[6]

Innumerable stories and jokes were told about the black shirts. In one, an autograph hunter asked Malabrocca to get him Fausto Coppi's signature. Malabrocca replied that he would be happy to oblige, but that he never got to meet Coppi. His job was to stay as far away from Coppi as possible – all the time. Recently, a lovely book dedicated to the story of the black shirt, filled with tales of the tricks, stratagems and intrigue around the battle for last place, was reissued.[7] Malabrocca was even adopted as a symbol of the virtues of taking one's time by the Slow Food movement, and in Milan in 2009 a play was put on based on Malabrocca's life and career.[8] The myth of the black jersey lives on today as part of the history of the golden age of cycling.

The Golden Age on the Track. The Surplace, or the Excitement of Nothingness

Italian cycling's golden age was also a golden age for the velodromes which had been built in every city and in many smaller towns in the north and centre of the country. Track racing was spectacular and dangerous. Bikes had no gears and no brakes, falls were common and specialists became skilled at using the steeply sloping tracks to their advantage. Gimmicks were introduced to make riding even faster, such as specially adapted motorbikes, including special versions known as stayers, which created slipstream and allowed riders to reach speeds which would be impossible on the roads outside. It was also, at times, mesmerising to watch, as riders went round and round the track in a blur. There was little specifically Italian about this, apart from the immense popularity of all forms of the sport, and the fact that, in the golden age of cycling, Italians were also better at track racing than almost everyone else.

How did track cycling work? The most popular kind of race was the *inseguimento* (chase), in which two riders would challenge each other over short distances. The key to victory here was always to start to sprint *behind* the other rider, thus exploiting his slipstream and the element of surprise. Over time, this led to the extraordinary practice of the 'surplace', where cyclists would remain motionless on their bikes waiting for their rival to crack, and then take off. Riders were not allowed either to put their feet on the ground or go backwards more than 20 centimetres during the surplace. It was a strange kind of spectacle. For minutes on end, and sometimes for much, much longer, absolutely nothing would happen. Then there would be a blur of movement, and it was all over.

During the surplace, parts of the track would become covered in perspiration, making it treacherous for the race itself, once it finally began. At first, the crowd would often heckle the riders ('Hurry up, I've got a train to catch' was a classic) but then silence would descend on the stadium. The spectacle was surreal, but fascinating, a test of endurance and nerve, a physical game of chess which then exploded in a blaze of wheels, light and energy. The foreplay, for many, was much more exciting than the climax.

Giovanni Borghi was born in the working-class neighbourhood of Isola in Milan in 1910. His father ran an electrical goods shop which was destroyed by Allied bombing in 1943. At that point, the family moved to a house in the countryside, near Varese, to the north of Milan. After the war, the Borghis began to invest in consumer durables and white goods, opening a series of factories which, by the time of Italy's 'economic miracle' in the late 1950s, employed nearly 10,000 workers. These products were given the name of Ignis, and Giovanni Borghi, or Mister Ignis as he was known, was a throwback to the paternalistic bosses of the past, always turning up at his factories to talk to the workers and take personal charge of production. The journalist Camilla Cederna compared him to a sultan. He is credited with inventing the fridge-freezer, and when Italians purchased their first fridges in the 1950s and 1960s they often chose an Ignis. Mister Ignis also understood the value of sponsorship, and was one of the first big businessmen in Italy to use sport to promote his products. His basketball team was immensely successful, but his real love was cycling. In the Giro, his star was the Spanish sprinter Miguel Poblet, who won twenty-three stages over the years as well as many classic races.

On the track, Borghi sponsored Antonio Maspes, the greatest Italian specialist track rider of all time. Track racing was perfectly adapted to the sponsor's needs, especially when transmitted live on TV. The surplace meant that the camera would be fixed on a motionless cyclist for a long time, and it was said that Maspes would stop in front of an Ignis banner, thus giving twice the value in advertising terms. In 1955 Maspes 'went into surplace' for thirty-two minutes before winning the world championships. Not surprisingly, he became known as the 'king of the surplace'. Remaining rigidly still, upright and unsupported on a bike did not come naturally or easily; it required rigorous training, massive leg and arm strength and intense concentration, and Maspes would spend hours at the Vigorelli velodrome, Italy's most famous indoor racing track, on his own, holding the surplace position while the janitor of the stadium read him the daily papers from the stands. Maspes became so famous, and so closely identified with Ignis, that he even appeared in the *caroselli*, the celebrated short TV advertisements which were popular at the time on Italian state television. These little films, for which the law stated that the product could only be mentioned at the end, attracted huge audiences in the 1950s and 1960s and it was said that Italian children would only be sent to bed 'after *carosello*'.

Born on the edge of Milan, where he lived all his life, Maspes would often speak in the local dialect. His house was a stone's throw from the Vigorelli velodrome, where big road races would often begin and end. His track racing tactic was simple: take off as late as possible. Maspes became the jewel in the crown of the Ignis empire, winning seven world sprint championships in the 1950s and 1960s (in 1955, 1956, 1959, 1960–62 and 1964) and numerous other trophies and titles. By the end of his career he had won the national sprint championships an astonishing fourteen times. He could cover 200 metres from a standing start in eleven seconds. As with Coppi and Bartali, the track had its own great sporting rivalry, this time between Maspes and his main challenger Sante Gaiardoni, who played the part of the 'eternal second-placed rider' (and only won one world title to Maspes's seven). When Maspes died in 2000 at the age of sixty-eight he earned a resting place of honour among

Milan's elite in the Famedio, the principal entrance of the city's beautiful Cimitero Monumentale. Maspes was a big man, with a large face and enormous leg muscles. According to Maspes himself, none other than Biagio Cavanna told him his legs were like those of Girardengo. Two of his world titles were won at the Vigorelli, and the track is now named after him. Sadly, however, the Velodromo Maspes Vigorelli is now closed to cycling altogether.

Maspes didn't hold the world record for a surplace, however. On 27 July 1968, with students in revolt all around the world, Italian TV transmitted the Italian track championships. The pursuit final was between a rider from the suburbs of Milan, Giovanni (Vanni) Pettenella, and Sergio Bianchetto from Padua, and the race would be going out live from the track in Varese, under a baking sun. Pettenella had been good enough to win gold in the same event in the 1964 Tokyo Olympics. As the transmission began – with commentary from the celebrated sports journalist Nando Martellini (who would later commentate on some of the most famous football matches of all time, including Italy's celebrated 4–3 victory over West Germany in the 1970 World Cup semi-finals) – not much was happening. In fact, nothing at all was taking place. The riders were in a kind of never-ending surplace. They had ground to a halt after an incredibly slow first lap. Martellini interviewed a few people, as the crowd and the TV audience waited for something to happen on the track. This was only the first race; the winner would have to win two to become world champion.

In theory, the race was supposed to last three laps, but neither rider seemed about to crack. Slowly realisation dawned that something historic – albeit extremely boring and yet endlessly fascinating at the same time – was taking place. Gradually crowds began to turn up at the stadium after seeing the 'race' on TV. They had stopped work in order to observe . . . nothing. Martellini stopped the transmission, saying that he would come back on air 'in a few minutes'. He was being optimistic. The surplace record at that time was held by Maspes, and stood at an hour. As time went on, the crowd began to chant: 'or-a, or-a' (hour, hour). It seemed that they were calling for *more* surplace, for the record to be broken (although they could just as well have been asking for it to end, as *ora* also means now). When Martellini came back on air, the 'race' was in almost exactly the same position as when he had left it. On the track, the cyclists were in deep concentration, sweating profusely, their muscles straining. A new record came closer and closer. Suddenly it was broken. More than an hour had passed.

Then, after sixty-three minutes, the tragic epilogue. Bianchetto moved slowly forward. Had he decided to sprint at last? No. After swaying from side to side he simply collapsed, rolling down the track past Pettenella and having to be revived with smelling salts. Pettenella pedalled through to the finish line. He had won without even racing – and (perhaps fortunately) the second race was cancelled. The two riders were like ancient Roman gladiators. Survival was what mattered. In order to avoid such events being repeated, limits were soon put on the surplace (the current regulation sets a maximum of three minutes) and this bizarre practice came to an end.

Six-day racing was huge business throughout the world in the nineteenth and twentieth centuries. The rich and famous, as well as more 'popular' fans, would turn up to see cyclists ride for hours and even days on end, round and round cycle tracks. Sponsors paid for trackside advertising and various forms of entertainment. The big stars would usually 'race' in such cases alongside a track specialist – who would do their dirty work for them, allowing them to sleep (often on small beds inside the stadium). For a time six-day cycling events were also big in the USA, attracting Italian stars such as Alfredo Binda, who travelled by steamer to the States, training on special exercise bikes during the voyage. The races themselves were denounced as cruel and inhuman: in some ways they were similar to the marathon dancing competitions which became popular in America during the Depression (as depicted, for example, in Sydney Pollack's 1969 film

They Shoot Horses, Don't They?). Six-day races really did last six whole days (and nights), but they were often not real races and were closer to show business than sport. Riders would take drugs to keep them going. The show had to go on. For six days and six nights. Later, the more absurd aspects of this exploitation were toned down.

In Italy, the king of six-day racing during the golden age was Ferdinando Terruzzi, a cyclist from the working-class neighbourhood of Sesto San Giovanni, just outside Milan, an area known for a long time as 'Italy's Stalingrad'. Born in 1924, Terruzzi was a professional cyclist for sixteen years (1949–65) and during that period he won twenty-five six-day races. He did the donkey work for the big stars, riding with Coppi and Anquetil in what Pastonesi calls 'a sport which no longer exists'.[1] Six-day cycling saw riders reach spectacular speeds thanks to the use of special motorbikes and cars.

Terruzzi's nickname was '*il Gatto Magico*' (the magic cat), and it often seemed that on the track he had turned into a kind of animal. He 'sprinted like a leopard, and ate like an ostrich'.[2] Meanwhile, off the track, the six-day events were grand affairs, where champagne flowed and pop stars attended. Camilla Cederna wrote that Giovanni Borghi had 'transformed the Palace of Sport into an immense nightclub'.[3] The middle of the track would be filled with dinner tables and waiters would serve food and drink while the riders whizzed around and around. Terruzzi kept his head so far down on the bike in order to maximise speed that he often injured his nose on the wheel itself. So graceful was he that Coppi claimed he could 'ride on the edge of a bath tub'.[4]

The six-day race in Milan in 1961 took place at the height of the country's 'economic miracle', in what was the capital of the boom itself. Fourteen thousand fans packed into the Vigorelli and the police were forced to hold others back on the streets. Inside, an orchestra had been assembled and the popular singer Mina performed. So many members of the audience were smoking that it was difficult to breathe properly. Track racing continued to be extremely dangerous, and the fans demanded speed and circus-like tricks, such as standing straight up on the pedals or crouching down behind the seat in full flow, at 60 kilometres an hour. Terruzzi finally retired at the age of forty-one, much to the dismay of his many female admirers.[5] Six-day racing died out along with track racing itself. Attempts to revive the tradition in the 1990s were sad affairs. Cyclists had lost the ability to ride on the track at all (right up until the 1980s, most professionals were adept at track racing) and Italy's great tradition in track racing ended abruptly. Velodromes were demolished or left to crumble. As the maverick cultural commentator and journalist Luciano Bianciardi had predicted in 1971, Maspes was the last of his kind.[6]

The Rivalry to End All Rivalries: Coppi and Bartali

'The Coppi–Bartali duel created great enthusiasm in the crowds, those massed waves of sports fans we came across in Piedmont and Liguria. The duel has taken on tones like those in Ariosto's epic poetry, it is a fair and fascinating contest between modern cycling champions'

– L'Unità, *18.6.1946*

'By the end of the 1940s an entire generation of European sports fans would find it impossible to mention one without the other'

– *William Fotheringham* [1]

The Tour de France, 6 July 1952. The two most famous cyclists in the world are climbing yet another mountain: the Galibier. As on so many other occasions in the past, they are together: Coppi in front, Bartali just behind him. A bottle is passed between the two. Later, Coppi will break and win the stage. He will then go on to win the Tour. At that instant a photographer with a wonderful name – Wafrido Chiarini – captures a shot which unites the two men in a single/double movement. It is the perfect photograph, like Capa's dying soldier in Spain or his image of an American soldier being shown the way by a diminutive Sicilian peasant during the Second World War.

* * *

On 10 July 1952, the 'bottle' photo first appeared in *Lo Sport Illustrato*. In the caption to the photograph the question which has dogged that particular image ever since was first raised: who is passing the bottle to whom? In the original publication the answer was Bartali – but it could just as easily have been Coppi. The photograph itself does not provide the answer and, after all, the riders were riding together, on the same Italian team. The image has since become one of the most famous Italian photographs of all time, and not simply in terms of sport. Daniele Marchesini devoted an entire chapter of his pioneering book *Coppi e Bartali* to this image.[2] And it is also a photogaph which has inspired endless debate. Everybody has an opinion, but nobody, it seems, has yet come up with the definitive answer.

The latest attempt to draw a line under this seemingly endless controversy came in a special book published in 2010 to mark the fiftieth anniversary of Coppi's death. Here the name of the photographer changes (again): he is now Carlo Martini, who worked for *La Gazzetta dello Sport* in the fifties. According to cycling expert Pier Bergonzi, the mystery of the 'bottle' photo 'is for cycling like the way the enigma of Mona Lisa's smile relates to the history of art'.[3] Vito Liverani, now in his eighties, a Milanese photographer and friend of Martini's, said that he had never revealed 'the truth' before, but that 'the time had come' to do so. Liverani confirmed what had been stated in 1952–3 when the photo first started to do the rounds: Bartali was passing the bottle to Coppi.[4] But despite the caption to the photograph, Bergonzi was not convinced: 'It is better if . . . each of us continues to interpret the photo as they wish.'[5] Liverani's 'truth' was not enough to end more than fifty years of controversy.

There they are, then, the two great rivals, reproduced in thousands of bars, in dozens of books and numerous advertisements, frozen in time in competition as well as in alliance; and the debate itself is also caught in a time warp – it can never be closed, it is destined eternally to divide Italians, but also to unite them in that division and in memory. Over time, the story behind the photograph has mellowed, becoming one of those 'stories around which cycling fans link together in a communality of spirit. This is something which does not happen with any other sport.'[6] The 'bottle' photograph has also become a way of forgetting and simplifying the rivalries of the past. Divided memories and versions have become united through nostalgia. The 'conflict between them has ended up by becoming one, expressed by a single word: Bartalicoppi'.[7] As William Fotheringham has written, 'the photograph shows Italy united . . . Italians cooperating in spite of their apparent difference'.[8]

The Bartali–Coppi rivalry was one shot through with contradictions and ambiguities, just like the famous photograph. It was also a dynamic rivalry, forever going through change. For one thing, despite their rivalry, the two became friends of a kind, and at times they even helped each other out. Both riders also made a great deal of money from their rivalry. They understood how much they needed each other; their success was symbiotic. Moreover, each man was well aware of the strengths of his rival. Each respected the other, so much so that sometimes they ignored the fact that they had to race at all. When that happened, someone else, a 'third man' perhaps, might even win. It was later suggested that the rivalry was bound by fair play – Bartali himself said 'we fought a bitter war, but it was a sporting war'[9] – but this was certainly not true all the time. Only hindsight allowed their intense rivalry to be reinvented as an example of Italian sportsmanship, in a sporting world where fair play was the exception not the norm.[10]

Although the beginning of the duel is often set at 1940, it was in 1946 that it really began in earnest. Fans took sides, dividing Italy into *Coppiani* and *Bartaliani*. Nobody remained neutral. In oral history interviews carried out in the 1980s and 1990s, many people recalled vividly which side they had been on.[11]

But how did they make their choice? How did people become *Coppiani* or *Bartaliani*? Part of the answer was down to geography.

Bartali attracted fans from the centre of the country (in particular in his stronghold, Tuscany), while Coppi was all-powerful in the north. The south was probably more *Bartaliani*, but evidence is inconclusive either way. Another influence was religion: '*Bartali il Pio*' was openly and deeply Catholic, Coppi only meekly religious. Bartali also carried forward his own set of loyal fans from the 1930s, while Coppi's fan base was younger, more modern, more urban, more post-war, perhaps more democratic, less fascist. Many fans made a personal choice, based on emotions, or their own family, or a race they had seen, on chance. Politics certainly played its part. For Giorgio Bocca, the choice was instinctive: it was 'love [for Coppi] at first sight, like being struck by lightning'.[12] Bocca's Piedmontese roots probably also played a part in his own decision as to who to follow. For many Bartali represented the values of Christian Democracy, and, as the Cold War set in, political divisions within Italy became more pronounced. Bartali's obvious willingness to allow his name to be used for ideological reasons was another factor.

As cycling's millions of fans were divided into two groups, so the rivalry began to dominate the sport itself. The two most important teams (the bicycle manufacturers Bianchi and Legnano) were captained by Coppi and Bartali respectively. Colours became associated with the rivalry. Newspaper sales soared as they concentrated on the endless battles on and off the track, as well as the gossip. For Marchesini, more space was dedicated to the rivalry than to 'Mussolini under the fascist regime'.[13] This is some claim. All other riders (and sports) were consigned to a minor, supporting role, which was rather harsh on many of them, and in particular on 'the third man', Fiorenzo Magni, whose career was probably damaged by the power of the great rivalry, but who was also sometimes able to profit from the one great flaw in both Coppi and Bartali: a weakness where the other man was concerned.

What exactly was the relationship between Coppi and Bartali? Fellow cyclists and journalists have spoken of occasional hatred, and there were certainly periods when they were not on speaking terms or referred to the other as 'that bloke over there'. But there was also great respect, and the rapport changed over time. Cycling is an intimate sport, a sport of male bonding. On thousands of occasions Coppi and Bartali shared the same hotel, the same private space, the same stretch of road, the same restaurant table. Again and again, they climbed mountains together, took part in exhibition races, stood on podiums, passed each other water or food. They saw each other more than they saw their own wives, children and mothers. In the Tour de France they were part of the same national team, as they were at the world championships. The greatest cycling competitions in the world, the Tour and the Giro, were reduced, for a time, to a two-horse race. The Tour became 'a kind of private competition between the two greatest living riders'.[14]

Neither man was in control of his own myth or fame. Over time a *double* myth has emerged, the story of *two* riders and *two* men: a new surname that runs into one word: *CoppieBartali* (CoppiandBartali). It is now impossible to tell Fausto Coppi's tale without reference to Gino Bartali, and vice versa. Leo Turrini's excellent biography of Bartali tries to tell his story without mentioning Fausto Coppi, for a large slice of the book at least. It is a heroic effort, but in the end he is forced to give in to the inevitable. Today, in death, even more than in life, the two men are together. Giorgio Bocca wrote that after Coppi's death Bartali was 'perhaps the most hurt of all'.[15] In the second half of the 1950s, the divisive nature of the rivalry became less pronounced. With time 'Even the *Bartaliani* became *Coppiani*, partly through obligation, partly through conviction, partly through nostalgia'.[16]

The unenviable task of managing the egos and talents of Italy's great cyclists within one team, at the Tour, fell to a cycling legend: Alfredo Binda. Would 'the Dictator' be able to harness the greatest rivalry in the history of the sport for the good of Italy? At the very least, Binda had been handed a poisoned chalice. Things came to a head in 1949, when both riders were due to take part. Before and throughout those post-war Tours, plots, myths, counter-plots and conspiracy theories were hatched and splashed across the press. The greatest sporting rivals of the century were not only being asked to ride 'together', but to help the other win. The result was explosive, hilarious, fascinating *and* victorious, and Binda was the architect of this national, sporting and personal triumph. He had only ridden in one Tour during his racing career, winning two stages before retiring in 1930, but as a manager he was to guide the fractious Italian team to four overall victories in thirteen years.[17]

In 1948, with Coppi absent, Binda masterminded Bartali's extraordinary victory. His elegant figure, seen standing in the team car, became almost as celebrated an image as that of the cyclists themselves, and he dealt effortlessly with the press and their incessant questions about inter-team rivalry. As with Italians and football, the role of the manager, in strategy and tactics, was seen as being as important as that of the sportsmen themselves. Bars and front rooms all over Italy were dominated by discussion of Binda's handling of his two superstars, and the tactics for each stage. In France, Binda was admired and hated in equal measure.

The year 1949 – with both Bartali and Coppi in the team – was Binda's *annus mirabilis* as a manager. Before the Tour began Coppi insisted that the team ride for him, and that Bartali be excluded. Binda could not accept such a diktat (Bartali had after all won the Tour in 1948), and so he brokered a fragile deal which was agreed by both men in the seaside town of Chiavari early in 1949. The agreement was simple but at the same time ambiguous, as the press release stated: 'the two riders have agreed to take part in the Tour with common intentions and in solidarity with each other, and to help the other with the single objective of promoting the best result overall for the one or the other'. Of course, this was not the end of the rivalry between the two men at that particular Tour, but just the beginning, and Binda would have to manage the race. It would be a very delicate operation. Binda even spoke on behalf of Coppi and Bartali when their relationship deteriorated so much that they

refused to communicate directly with each other. Acres of newsprint were expended on covering the negotiations between Coppi
and Bartali concerning their role in that race, even before the Tour
began. Who would be team captain? Who would win the Tour?
Who was really in charge?

There would be no team captain, and both Bartali and Coppi
would have five *gregari* each, in the same team (of twelve riders).
This meant that a *second* Italian team took part, with Magni as
captain (known as the Italian cadets, with six riders overall). Binda's
deal, in theory, allowed events on the road to dictate the hierarchy
within the race – it had a built-in flexibility. The most in-form rider
would naturally emerge from this trio. For a time, Magni was in
the lead, but when Coppi took control in the Alps, Bartali (and
his *gregari*) backed his rival and the Italian team triumphed. The
two then worked together all the way to Paris. Tactical agreement
let Bartali win a stage on the way home as compensation. Binda
was thus able to keep the two men on board. In 1952, a similar
compromise (this time with three captains) saw Coppi win again,
with Bartali effectively a part of the support team – but as a *gregario
di lusso*, a five-star *gregario*. Binda is usually credited with convincing
Coppi to carry on that year after a nasty fall left him thirty minutes
down on the leaders. Binda used his regret at never completing a
Tour himself to convince Coppi not to withdraw. Bartali and Coppi
had great respect for Binda, and his experience as a rider.

As Coppi rode into the history books (including this one) during
his epic solitary breaks through the mountains, Binda was always
at his side, handing him little notes telling him his distance from
his rivals. It is said that Coppi never entirely trusted Binda, and
would keep the slips of paper in his pocket to check against the
official distances later. Some have called the 1949 Tour *il Tour degli
imbrogli* (the Tour of trickery).[18] It is testimony to his charisma and
intelligence that Binda managed to carve out a role between these
two great cyclists, becoming a kind of judge, diplomat and part
of a triumvirate which seemed to represent various aspects of the

Italian 'character'. 'Bartali, Coppi and Binda were often depicted in newspaper articles as ambassadors or ministers who have the task of holding up the good name of Italy abroad.'[19] Bartali called Binda an 'ambassador' while *Il Corriere della Sera* dubbed him 'the Prime Minister', but he was also known as '*il generalissimo*' – 'the five-star general'.[20] Some claimed that it was impossible to argue with Binda, and he remained close to both Bartali and Coppi in private as well as in public.

In this way, Binda became part of a great sporting and national story, long after he had stopped cycling professionally. In France, where he had lived for some time, his mastery of the language helped him keep part of the press and public on his side. Descriptions of *the* rivalry often assign Binda a key role as the architect of Italy's overall victory. Binda's orders were seen as crucial to Coppi's decisive break in July 1949. As the *Corriere* headline put it, 'Bartali had a puncture and fell, Coppi waited for him. Binda cried out "go, go" and Fausto took the yellow jersey'.[21]

One of the features of the ways in which the rivalry has always been interpreted is the idea that Bartali and Coppi somehow encapsulate different features of the Italian national character. Thus, taken together, CoppiandBartali seemed to represent 'Italy'. Many journalists and writers have tried to produce a synthesis of this division. Curzio Malaparte, for example, wrote an extraordinary essay, first published in French in 1949, entitled 'Les deux visages de l'Italie: Coppi et Bartali' (The two faces of Italy: Coppi and Bartali).[22] For Malaparte, 'international sport may never see their like again, in the same moment, two champions who encapsulated two essential aspects of the modern world'.[23] He saw in Coppi and Bartali 'two different representations of the world, two different ways of understanding the universe and the meaning of life'.[24] Their rivalry was faultless, unrepeatable, sublime: it touched on deep philosophical and existential themes (materialism, the very existence of God) and reflected changes in society and history: Bartali was the *past*, Coppi the *future*. But it also mirrored regional differences. Bartali grew up close to Malaparte's home town and the writer would dedicate an entire book to the 'Tuscan character' whose title can be translated as 'Damned Tuscans'.[25] The cover of the French edition summed up Malaparte's argument perfectly. Two Italys face each other, and superimposed on these Italys are two enormous faces: those of Coppi and Bartali.

Malaparte is by no means the only writer or historian to have attempted an analysis of Coppi and Bartali. Complex insights into the division between the two men, and its symbolic nature, were almost *de rigueur* in the 1940s, 1950s and 1960s, and continue to appear to this day. Everyone had their own take on which parts of Italy, and Italians, the two men symbolised.

Much later, Giorgio Bocca wrote that Coppi was 'reflective, shy and modest, but not lacking in elegance, well-mannered but, at times, cold and vengeful'. Bartali, on the other hand, was 'fearless, rude, superTuscan but also a good person'.[26] For Rino Negri, beneath it all Bartali and Coppi were both very much Italians.[27] Yet, they were clearly not the same kind of Italian. Together, they epitomised different sides of what were seen as national characteristics, but these characteristics were so fragmentary as to be contradictory. Their unity lay in their disunity, and they changed over time.[28]

During their careers, Bartali's and Coppi's dualism was fault-less, unique. It was almost as if it had been constructed artificially by an artist working with a businessman, a sports promoter and a historian. The two were divided in everything, at least superficially. Theirs was 'an opposition about everything', a 'complete split'.[29] As Gianni Mura wrote in 2009, they epitomised 'old age and youth (even if there was only five years difference between them), red and white (but Coppi voted for the Christian Democrats like Bartali, and they both signed a pro-DC manifesto in 1948), the chatterbox and the quiet one, the man of iron and the man of crystal (Coppi broke thirteen bones in his career), the man faithful until death to his wife Adriana and the adulterer who left his wife Bruna and his daughter Marina for Giulia Occhino, a doctor's wife, who was known as the White Lady'.[30]

Although they were fierce rivals, Bartali and Coppi, and their fans, needed each other. The rivalry was very good for business. Sponsorship, advertising, newspaper sales and other revenues increased hugely if both men were taking part in a race. The two riders were thus forced upon each other, continually asked about 'the other one', each pushed into an obsessive relationship with his eternal antagonist. Both had careers which went beyond the rivalry (especially Bartali, already a superstar when Coppi came on the scene), but it was a challenge which brought the best out of them.

The two riders complemented each other, and they allowed easy conclusions about the 'two Italys' they supposedly represented to be drawn. 'Two different personalities, two different "races", two different nervous systems, two different ways of understanding life, struggle, pride.'[31] Much of this was forced, over-literary, even untrue, but it also reflected a near total divide among fans which needed explanation. Amidst the rush to analyse and dissect, one simple fact was often forgotten. If they had not been such extraordinary cyclists, nobody would have written a word about them.

If Coppi was a symbol of Italian modernity (in sport itself, and in terms of Italian society), Bartali was its antithesis. In the words of one cycling writer, 'the opposition to the Coppi model was resistance to modernity itself'.[32] For many, Coppi was a vital symbol of Italy's reconstruction and its economic miracle, of 'a poor people who were looking for redemption and who were riding towards reconstruction'.[33] He 'personified . . . a desire for rebirth, for renewal'.[34]

This modernity could also be seen in the attitudes of both men towards their sport. Coppi paid attention to what he ate (he employed a dietitian in the 1950s), his medical 'help', his clothing, his training regime, his adoption of new cycling materials. His body itself was, for Ormezzano, 'the first real scientific laboratory in cycling' and he is often described as 'the first modern cyclist'.[35] Coppi brought cycling into a new age.

Bartali, on the other hand, was not scientific at all. He came from an era when cyclists simply got on their bikes and rode. He never cultivated the same blind loyalty among his *gregari* as Coppi. His training regime was haphazard (like his tactics) and he never had Cavanna and his team to rely upon, nor the milieu of Novi Ligure. While Coppi's team was spot-on and extraordinarily loyal, Bartali's *gregari* were more like a group of individuals, apart perhaps from Corrieri, whose intense loyalty was nonetheless always tinged with anger and regret.

Coppi's modernness meant that he had no God to rely on in times of difficulty. He believed in God, but didn't believe that God could help him win. As Curzio Malaparte wrote, while Bartali was 'protected by the saints', Coppi didn't 'have anyone to look after him from above . . . he is alone, alone on his bike. Bartali prays while he pedals, Coppi, the rationalist, the Cartesian, is sceptical and full of doubt and only believes in that engine which has been entrusted to him – his own body.' Coppi joked that God 'has more important things to do than think about our bikes'. Bartali, on the other hand, was 'seen' being pushed up hills by angels, and went on his knees to thank the Madonna after winning a stage in Lourdes. To cite Malaparte's beautiful analysis once again, Coppi 'knew that perhaps Bartali will go to heaven before him. But what does he care? Fausto Coppi wants to be first in this world.'[36]

In sporting and human terms, this rivalry reached its peak (or its low point, again, depending on your view) at the 1948 world championships in Walkenberg in the Netherlands. On that infamous occasion, both riders (especially Coppi) were so obsessed with their enemy *not* winning that they cancelled each other out. In a normal race, this might have been acceptable, but on that particular day they were both supposed to be representing Italy. Unlike with the Tour of 1949, no binding agreement had been reached between the two before the race (and *that* agreement was in part the product of the events of 1948). As a result, they rode against each other and not for the team. They lost all interest in any other aspects of the overall result. Once both were sure that the other would *not* win, they withdrew together. Boos rang out as the two cyclists got off their bikes and disappeared. It was said that they even followed each other into the dressing room.[37]

Both men were banned for two months after what became known as the 'shameful episode of Walkenberg'. Although the ban was quickly overturned, the stain on their reputations remained. The duel had become so all-encompassing that nothing else mattered, nobody else existed in their minds. There was no race, there were no other riders, there wasn't even an Italian nation; there was only Coppi against Bartali. As Orio Vergani put it, 'the problem for one rider was to stop the other one winning, and vice versa'.[38] And this was also a result of their near total domination of the sport, on a world stage, in the late 1940s. In the post-war period, as Ormezzano wrote, beyond those two riders 'there was nothing else to Italian cycling'.[39]

While the intense competition between Coppi and Bartali divided Italy, the French were not far behind. Italians seemed split more or less evenly between the two cyclists, but the French clearly preferred Coppi, with his 'thin look and melancholic face' (Manlio Cancogni). He was described as 'the most French' of the Italian riders. The French appreciated Coppi's modesty and spectacular racing brain.[40] Bartali appeared to antagonise them. People perhaps remembered his 1938 victory, the year Italy won the World Cup in France. Fascist Italy (although not Bartali himself) made much of that double victory in France. *La Gazzetta dello Sport*, for example, wrote this in 1938: 'A command came from the Italy of Il Duce: Victory. Bartali, champion of the Legnano team, has obeyed.' Bartali was at the centre of some furious arguments on the Tour in the 1940s, and these also involved Coppi at times. In 1950 the whole Italian team withdrew from the Tour (with Italian cyclist Magni in the lead) after scuffles in the Pyrenees. Many French fans found the domination of Italian cyclists in that period hard to stomach. Memories were still fresh of the 1940 military invasion, especially in the border regions through which the Tour and the Giro would often pass. Coppi's popularity in France has been seen by many as a force which brought together the two countries after the war.[41]

The dualism between the two cyclists carried on well after Coppi and Bartali stopped riding against each other. In 1960, just as they were about to embark on an unlikely joint venture, with Bartali as manager and the younger man as rider in the Giro, Coppi died, leaving his compatriot as the eternal orphan of one of the great sporting relationships of the century. From that moment, Bartali was destined to talk about (and for) a man who could no longer speak for himself. In death, as in life, Coppi found it extremely difficult to shake off Bartali, and the feeling was reciprocated. Although his most famous successes had seen him riding alone, with time Coppi almost always came to be associated with his great rival. The older Bartali was like someone who had lost an identical twin or even a limb, a sad figure, a man forever in the shadow of his former rival.

Gino Bartali retired as a professional cyclist in 1954 and lived off his fame until his death in 2000. He tried his hand at bicycle manufacturing and even invested in Bartali motorbikes. As a living legend, he was frequently to be seen at the Giro and other races and had his own cycling team for a time, which he ran without any great success. Unsurprisingly, his marriage was rock-solid to the last, and he would pray daily in the private chapel he built in his Florence home. Numerous books and articles were dedicated to his career and to the 'Bartali myth', including some of the first academic studies about cycling. Some saw Bartali as a figure of fun in old age, and he let himself be exploited by tacky television chat shows.

In Bartali's home town of Ponte a Ema there is now a glittering museum and a big fountain built around the theme of cycling. A bar in the town bears the name '*L'Intramontabile*' (the timeless, the eternal one) after the local hero (also the name of the 2006 TV film). The museum offers the usual collection of bicycles, shirts, photographs and books, but it also contains some notable Bartali memorabilia, such as his famous sandals.[42] Right next to the new museum there is a remarkable example of the political divisions which marked Italy after 1945, and of which Bartali himself was a part, and which were also present in the cyclist's birthplace. There, on the walls of the Casa del Popolo, are two highly political (and unusual) plaques. One, from 1972, contains an anti-fascist sentiment linked to a desire for 'social justice'. The other refers to the execution of Julius and Ethel Rosenberg, accused of spying for the Soviet Union in the USA and executed in 1953. The Cold War was still etched on the walls in Bartali's home town, right into the twenty-first century.

In November 2009 a very strange demonstration took place in Florence. The demonstrators included cycling fans and cyclists with their bikes. They were protesting about the closure of the Bartali museum as a result of a dispute over funding and its management. This also led to the cancellation of the special race held (in theory, annually) in Gino Bartali's memory. There seemed to be a real risk that this huge new museum would actually be forced to close its doors for good. Some of Bartali's family, it seems, wanted to transfer some of the material in the museum to the Ghisallo national cycling site. The Ponte a Ema museum reopened in March 2010, but the issues at the heart of the dispute over Bartali's memory had not been resolved. Gino Bartali's myth lives on, but his legacy is not an easy one to manage.

'The Third Man': Fiorenzo Magni, His Secrets and His Triumphs

'People say that I was unlucky to ride with Coppi and Bartali . . . it isn't true. I was very lucky. Those two devils taught me how to lose properly'

– *Fiorenzo Magni*[1]

'He who votes for the Christian Democrats votes for Coppi and Bartali; he who votes for the MSI votes for Magni'

– *banner in Rome, 1952*

Like Orson Welles in the 1949 film of the same name, Fiorenzo Magni was 'the third man', a nickname pertinent in a number of ways. It was an obvious reference to Magni's difficult but important role in relation to CoppiandBartali. He was nearly always mentioned after CoppiandBartali, almost permanently in their shadow. But when the other two didn't win, he often did, and his relationship to *the* rivalry was both problematic and complicated. Magni managed to carve out a space for himself despite the power of those two great riders. His tactical awareness and particular strengths – his opportunism, his strong team of *gregari*, his power over long stages, his downhill racing – allowed him to take advantage of any slips made by Coppi or Bartali. Never a great climber, Magni often managed to stay in contention through sheer bloody-mindedness. He never gave up. Moreover, Magni was also 'the third man' because of his uncomfortable past (as with Welles in the film), his role in the war and his awkward position after 1945. Unlike the Welles character, Harry Lime, however, Magni was distinctly unglamorous. His private life was of no interest to the press, he went bald prematurely, he avoided publicity. Magni did not sell newspapers. To date only one book has been written about him, and even that is short and not very good.[2] Histories of cycling usually assign Magni a minor, walk-on part.

Fiorenzo Magni was undoubtedly the most important 'other' Italian cyclist in the 1940s and 1950s. In any other country, and at any other time, he would have been a superstar in his own right. But in an era dominated by CoppiandBartali, he was relegated to a supporting role, perfectly encapsulated by his nickname. His cycling successes (he won three Giri d'Italia and many other races) were not reflected in his fan base. Finally, the reference to 'the third man' underlined his ability to hide in races and the many ways in which he was so different from his two main rivals. A film was made about Magni in 1951, a year when he won a series of victories. Its title? *Fiorenzo, il terzo uomo*.

Magni was immensely strong, and his courage was legendary. While Coppi was fragile and his bones often shattered, Magni was even more of a 'man of iron' than Bartali. He was a 'lion', able to win again and again the toughest, most bone-shaking classic in world cycling, the Tour of Flanders, which takes place largely over slippery and bumpy paved paths, with short, brutal climbs known as 'walls'. So successful was Magni in that race that legendary cycling journalist Mario Fossati wrote 'when you hear the name Tour of Flanders you immediately think of Fiorenzo Magni'.

Like Coppi and Bartali, 'the third man' had become a strong cyclist through work, and like his future rivals his early life was marked by family tragedy. He was born in the small Tuscan town of Vaiano, near Prato, in 1920 and when he was seventeen his father, with whom he had also cycled, was killed in an accident. He was already well known in cycling circles by the time Italy entered the war in June 1940 and in 1942 he won the Giro del Piemonte. But at that moment other events, which had nothing to do with sport, took over Fiorenzo Magni's life. To all intents and purposes, Magni's cycling career was put on hold until 1947, well after the conflict was over. In order to tell Fiorenzo Magni's story we now need to leave cycling altogether and immerse ourselves in the bloody and violent civil war which marked Italian history from 1943 to 1945.

After entering the war in 1940, fascist Italy had suffered a series of humiliating military defeats in Greece and North Africa. The Italian people turned against the war and the ruling class was looking for a way out. Desperate times required desperate measures. July 1943 was the last straw, with the invasion of Sicily by Allied troops and the carpet-bombing of Rome. On 25 July the Fascist Grand Council voted to remove Mussolini from power, and the king had him arrested. Secret negotiations were opened with the Allies, and an armistice was signed with the Americans and the British on 3 September 1943 and announced to the world, by radio, five days later.

Officially, the war against the Allies was over, but the reality was that Italy had two governments. In the south the king set up his own new state, while in the north Mussolini, sprung from prison by the Nazis in October, was made head of a puppet government under German control. Hitler's troops flooded into Italy. The Allies fought their way up from Sicily. Italy was divided politically and militarily. Every Italian faced some stark choices, among them the struggle simply to survive. In parts of the country young men and women joined the fledgling anti-fascist resistance movement. Others responded to the call from Mussolini and Hitler. Italians thus stood on both sides of the divide.

As a promising twenty-three-year-old cyclist, Magni became involved early on in the civil war that raged throughout central and northern Italy from 1943 to 1945. He fought for a time on the 'wrong side', the losing side, with the Italian fascists and the Nazis, although he later played down the 'fascist' nature of the choice he had made in 1943, presenting it as a kind of duty: 'when you were twenty, when they called you up, you either went up to the mountains [joining the anti-fascist partisans] or you obeyed. There was no other choice.' In recent years, in Italy, those 'young men' (like Magni) who ended up on the 'wrong side' during the war have been the subject of furious political, historical and cultural debate.[3] Some argue that those men were inspired by a sense of patriotism, while others assert there could be no justification for opting to fight under Mussolini and Hitler. Many, like Magni himself, have claimed that they were only following orders, as young men conscripted into the fascist army and threatened with prison or even summary execution if they deserted. Magni's own story as a young man was also part of a wider history which still divides Italy today. The choices he made in the mid-1940s would haunt him for life and mark his cycling career. As in so many other areas, the dividing line between politics, history and sport was a fine one indeed. Above all, Magni would always be associated with the first bloody battle of the civil war, which took place close to Vaiano, an event which has become known as the 'massacre' or the 'battle of Valibona'.

Stuart Hood, a captain in the British Army being held as a POW by Italians near Parma, was released along with thousands of other prisoners on or just after 8 September 1943. He then joined one of the first partisan groups which formed all over the country, as former POWs and anti-fascists armed themselves and took to the hills. The charismatic leader of Hood's tiny band of brothers was an older man with military experience, 'a sergeant-major in the Italian army called Lanciotto Ballerini who, at the time of the armistice, loaded a machine gun, various rifles, ammunition and hand grenades on a truck and drove up into the hills'. In January 1944, Ballerini's inexperienced partisans, all eighteen of them, were on the move across Tuscany. They took refuge, Hood remembered, 'in the hills at a group of peasant houses where we slept in the barn for two or three

days'. It was an isolated place, known as Valibona, just seven kilometres from Fiorenzo Magni's home town of Vaiano. Hood noticed,
with some trepidation, that nobody had been put on watch that
night, an oversight that led to tragedy.

> We were surprised and surrounded by a force of 50 or more
> Fascist militia. After a gunfight that lasted a couple of hours, we
> broke out. The machine-gunner was dead. The barn was on fire.
> Ballerini was killed. One of the Russians was captured and shot on
> the spot. I escaped with one of the Yugoslavs. The Italians, several
> of whom were wounded, were taken off to prison in Florence . . .
> The action I had been involved in was, I discovered, the first
> armed clash between the Fascist militia and partisans in Tuscany.[4]

Some fifty or so fascists and *carabinieri* had come just before dawn,
from two directions. A Russian partisan, Andrey Vladimiro, heard a
noise as he got up to urinate. He raised the alarm but it was too late.
After a lengthy shoot-out Ballerini, thirty-three, was hit in the face
by a bullet. Vladimiro was executed after being captured. Another
partisan died in the fire that broke out in the barn. Other prisoners
were horribly beaten while a number of fascists were also killed.[5]
When the battle was over, the remaining partisans disbanded and
some of the survivors were able to continue their resistance activities. Stuart Hood joined other partisan groups and took the battle
name of 'Carlino'. He later wrote a memoir from that time called
Pebbles from My Skull, in which he described Ballerini as 'a fighter,
a Communist . . . fearless himself but with no knack of leading
men'.[6] Ballerini's funeral in Campi Bisenzio, his home town, drew
big crowds, despite efforts by local fascists to prevent it taking place.
Photographs of the dead partisan were distributed in great numbers,
so much so that the fascists arrested the photographer responsible
for printing them.

The 'massacre of Valibona' was no ordinary wartime skirmish,
but as the first armed clash between fascists and partisans in that

part of the country it was a notable event which informed post-war radical politics, especially in the area around Valibona, in Prato and in Campi Bisenzio. It started to build the myth, and gave the movement its first martyrs, and the stories of heroism inspired other partisans. In addition, the story also encouraged hatred and created a desire for revenge.

Many locals were convinced that Fiorenzo Magni had been among the fifty-strong fascist militia (part of the *Guardia Nazionale Repubblicana*) which took part in the attack. A number of eyewitnesses claimed to have seen Magni at Valibona on the day of the massacre and some even assigned him a leading role in the killings. In one version, that of Ballerini's widow, Magni was accused not only of killing the partisan leader himself, but of boasting about it afterwards.[7] 'Magni from Prato, the cyclist,' she was quoted as saying, 'was proud of having killed him.'[8] Little, however, is certain about Magni's direct participation in this battle, or his role in the rest of the war. Magni himself denied taking part in the round-up and killings, although he admitted to being part of a fascist militia and, it is said, retained his right-wing views after the war.

In December 1945 a judicial enquiry was opened into the 'Valibona massacre' and Magni's name appeared on a long list of so-called collaborators under investigation. It was said that the group of which he was a part had used 'particularly harsh' forms of torture, and had a big meal to celebrate the killings of January 1944. Moreover, according to official documents unearthed by the historian Mauro Canali, Magni had connections to the notorious 'Carità Gang', a group of fascists well known for their violence who operated alongside the Nazis in Tuscany and the Veneto during the war. Some accounts claim that the *Banda Carità* took part in the massacre of Valibona itself.

The *Banda Carità* took its name from its leader, Mario Carità, who participated in fascist violence in Florence in the early 1920s and remained part of the movement throughout his life. A trial was held of many other members of the gang in Padua after the war, where tales emerged of sadistic torture meted out by the group in Tuscany and Padua. In his book *Le spie del regime* (*The Spies of the Regime*), Mauro Canali cites US documents which seem to show that, according to the Allies, Magni 'became the leader of a terroristic group which hunted down partisans' in Tuscany in 1943 and 1944, before the liberation of Florence. Other documents claimed that, after moving to Milan, Magni continued to take part in 'anti-partisan activities' and had links to the *Banda Carità*.[9]

Here the wartime stories of the two Tuscans Magni and Bartali converge. It is often said that Gino Bartali was arrested by the *Banda Carità* during the war, as he rode back and forth across central Italy with secret documents hidden in his bicycle frame, that the gang threatened to kill him but in the end let him go. The line between life and death was a thin one at that time, as similar stories relating to the activities during the war of both Fausto and Serse Coppi confirm.

At the end of 1946, twenty-four former fascists, Magni among them, were sent for trial. The accusations against them were extremely serious: if found guilty, they faced long prison sentences and possibly even the death penalty. In January 1947 the trial opened in Florence. For the magistrates in Florence, Magni was officially on the run, a fugitive from justice, and a warrant was issued for his arrest. The mother of Lanciotto Ballerini was there for the prosecution, as was his widow. Emotions were, not unnaturally, running high. The prosecution asked the court to send Magni to jail for thirty years. But if Magni was not present at the trial, his lawyer, Gino Martini, was. And he was a very good lawyer.

Martini called a number of witnesses in defence of his client. Three famous Tuscan cyclists were first on the long list – Gino Bartali, Aldo Bini and Alfredo Martini. All three knew Magni well and all had ridden with him before the war. But only Alfredo Martini would testify at the trial. One of Gino Martini's aims was to show that

Magni had taken part in the resistance after moving north following the battle of Valibona. Thus, Alfredo Martini was described in an official document as an 'ex-partisan'. According to Magni's lawyer, Martini would be able to confirm that Magni had been 'forced' to enrol in the fascist army and he had also been of 'great help' to the anti-fascist cause. In addition, other witnesses would be called to testify that Magni had intervened in favour of prisoners whom 'he knew had anti-fascist sympathies' and had helped out local anti-fascists. The picture painted by Magni's lawyer was that his client had played an active role in the resistance, despite having been part of a fascist militia. Various members of the Magni family confirmed that they were anti-fascists and that Fiorenzo was aware of this and had taken no action. Magni's lawyer also argued that there was no evidence against his client, and nothing to show that he had actually participated at Valibona.

Regardless of the claims of Magni's lawyer, Alfredo Martini's testimony at the trial was very short and carefully worded. According to the trial records, he simply stated the following: 'Magni is a cyclist who seemed to me to be a very good person up until 25 July 1943.' But Martini made no comment on the case before the court: 'no specific facts were mentioned in favour or against Magni'. It was a straightforward character reference, and it is difficult to see how it could have had much influence on the case itself, especially as it reserved judgement on Magni's activities during the civil war itself, something which was not surprising given Martini's left-wing sympathies.

There was a further twist to the Valibona mystery. Documents unearthed in 2010 and presented by the defence at the original trial revealed a completely unexpected version of the story. According to two official letters, written in 1945 in defence of Magni, the cyclist had helped out the anti-fascist resistance during his time in Monza. This evidence, which contradicts that in the US archives cited by Canali, claimed that Magni was involved in transporting anti-fascist newspapers and in such a way provided 'precious' help

The Age of Pioneers. The cyclists take a rest during a race in Sicily, 1908.

The 12th Bersaglieri (rifle) cycling division 'conquers' Monte Nero, a mountain now in Slovenia. June 1915.

The third Milan–San Remo race, 1909. Pierino Albini is at the head of the group. Behind him, wearing a cap, is the French cyclist Emile Georget, who would finish second overall, an hour behind the winner, Luigi Ganna.

Ottavio Bottecchia, 1926.

Enrico Toti, one-
legged war hero and
cyclist, photographed
in 1916, the year of his
death.

Cyclists are forced to negotiate a level crossing on the route during the Giro di Lombardia.

Learco Guerra during the second stage of the Giro d'Italia, 1933.

Poster for the Velodromo Vigorelli, 1935.

Alfredo Binda tries to remove a tyre with his teeth, 1920s-30s.

Gino Bartali (centre, with an outline of France and a cross on his jersey), 1930s.

From left to right, Fabio Battesini, Costante Girardengo, Learco Guerra, Alfredo Binda.

Alfredo Binda at his desk during the fascist era. On the left is a bronze of Benito Mussolini.

Monte Cassino in ruins after the fighting of the Second World War, 1949. The Giro d'Italia route went past Cassino that year. In the background there is a cycling shop.

The race moves slowly through the rubble of the war during the Giro of Rebirth, 1946.

Giordano Cottur is carried aloft by huge crowds during the 1946 Giro. Trieste flags are very much in evidence.

Renzo Zanazzi (on the right) goes the wrong way at the end of the final stage of the Giro of Rebirth in Milan, despite the best efforts of a policeman. The other cyclist is Oreste Conte, who would win the stage.

The fourth stage of the 1952 Giro d'Italia – the Giro passes through rural Tuscany

Gino Bartali praying in Siena, 18 September 1948. After winning the Tour de France, Bartali offered his yellow jersey (framed, in the middle of the photo) to St Theresa, the patron saint of children, in the Church of Santa Petronilla.

Gino Bartali eating with fans massed outside during the Tour de France, 1940s.

Gino Bartali in the Giro di Lombardia, 26 October 1952.

Graffiti by cycling fans along a Giro route, 1940s.

Fausto Coppi celebrates winning the world championships for the only time in his career in Lugano, Switzerland, 30 August 1953. To his left is his mistress 'the White Lady' Giulia Occhini.

'Viva Coppi.' The fourth stage of the Giro d'Italia, 1952.

'Coppi you are Italy.' The fourteenth stage of the Giro d'Italia, Turin–Brescia, 1954.

The celebrated Merano–Monte Bondone stage, the twenty-first of the Giro d'Italia, 1956. Charly Gaul is carried off, exhausted, after finishing the stage in the snow. He would go on to win that year's Giro.

The sixteenth stage, between Bologna and Madonna di San Luca, of the Giro d'Italia in 1956. Fiorenzo Magni rides on, biting down on a piece of inner tube because of the pain from a broken collarbone. He would finish second in the Giro, behind Gaul.

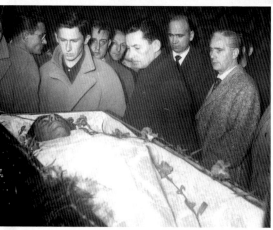

Distraught fans and relatives file past Fausto Coppi's coffin.

Fausto Coppi's funeral at Castellania, near Novi Ligure, 4 January 1960. Fans line the road up to the village where Coppi was born and where his family lived.

Death notices for Fausto Coppi. Tortona, northern Italy, 2 January 1960.

Felice Gimondi at home in the town of Sedrina near Bergamo with his family, after winning the Tour de France at the age of twenty-two in 1965. Gimondi is standing in the doorway, hands on hips. To his right is his mother, Angela.

Giro d'Italia, near Rome. 1950s.

The Coppa Bernocchi race, Lugano, Switzerland, 12 October 1952.

A six-day race at the Velodromo Vigorelli, early 1960s. Note the advertising on the track and the row of scooters beside it.

A crash at the Velodromo Vigorelli during the six-day race, 7 August 1961.

TV programme *Processo alla tappa*, late 1960s. The presenter, Sergio Zavoli (centre), is flanked by leading journalists Gianni Brera (to his right) and Bruno Raschi.

Vincenzo Torriani, patron of the Giro, in his usual position, standing up in the organiser's car, 1966. At his side is the popular TV presenter Mike Bongiorno.

Eddy Merckx during the thirteenth stage of the Giro d'Italia between Cortina d'Ampezzo and Vittorio Veneto, 1968 (which he went on to win). He is wearing his world championship jersey after winning that race in 1967.

Eddy Merckx at a doping test at the end of the second stage of the 1968 Giro d'Italia. Saint Vincent, France.

Eddy Merckx in his hotel room after being thrown out of the Giro for a controversial positive doping test at Albisola. 2 June 1969.

The Goodwood rifle-shot. Giuseppe Saronni wins the world championships in Goodwood, England, in 1982, after a stunning sprint finish.

Marco Pantani leaves his hotel room in Madonna di Campiglio, Trentino, after being suspended from the Giro while in the lead with two stages to go. 5 June 1999.

Doctors Francesco Conconi and Michele Ferrari flank Francesco Moser during his preparations for another attempt on the world hour record, 1986.

The interior of the Madonna del Ghisallo church near Lake Como, northern Italy.

and had given 'notable' service to the 'liberation cause'.[10] Another letter backed up this version of events. These documents seemed to show that Magni had taken part in activities which helped resistance organisations in the north and in Tuscany (despite being part of the armed fascist group the GNR). These points were backed up by witnesses (many of whom were related to Magni). If these documents were a reflection of what had really happened in the war, Fiorenzo Magni (like Gino Bartali, his great rival) had indeed taken part in the resistance. Were these documents invented? They were official letters, on headed paper. They certainly seemed, and still seem, genuine. If they were genuine, much of the 'political history' of Fiorenzo Magni needs to be rewritten. Up to now, none of the accounts of the case have even mentioned this aspect of the trial, or of Magni's past.

On 24 February 1947 the court reached its verdict. Despite a series of witness statements and the report made at the time by the fascists themselves (dismissed as propaganda), the court was unable to decide if Magni had 'participated in the action at Valibona'. As a result, the judges declared that his 'crimes' fell under the amnesty of June 1946. In terms of the charge of 'military collaborationism' the judges argued that the fascists involved had acted for 'political reasons . . . in a period when all social and moral values had been subverted'.[11] They had also been 'following orders'. Thus, although Magni and others had 'collaborated' with the Nazis and the fascist army, this charge fell under the amnesty for fascist prisoners passed thanks to Communist Justice Minister Palmiro Togliatti in June 1946. Some of the accused were found guilty of 'harsh forms of torture', but many of these charges were overturned on appeal.[12] There was no mention of the 'resistance' version of Magni's past. If the judges had been influenced by the arguments of Magni's lawyer, they decided not to mention this evidence in their final judgement.

Magni had been officially banned from cycling after the war, which meant he could not ride in the 1946 Giro, and there is confusion about the reasons behind that ban, which was imposed by the

UVI (the Italian cycling association). Some versions have it that this ban was directly related to Magni's activities in the war, and his trial, others that he had been caught riding under a false name (which may also have been part of an attempt to cover up his past). But although the court's word was final, the trial's outcome by no means convinced everyone. Some later claimed that Magni had got off scot-free because of his fame as a cyclist. The stench of fascism, of having taken part in a massacre, stuck to Magni for years. Ever since Valibona, any number of contrasting accounts, rumours and smears have done the rounds about Magni's role in the war, and in particular the events of January 1944.

Within cycling circles, however, Magni's life story is often related nowadays as a reassuring tale of national unity, above all through his lifelong friendship with communist sympathiser, former partisan and cyclist Alfredo Martini. Grateful for his testament during his trial, Magni later said, 'my best friend was Martini the Communist who came to the court and said under oath: "I know Fiorenzo well. Those charges are all absolute rubbish" [not quite the same phraseology as that in the official trial documents]. I realised that day that men are more important than their ideas.' Whatever the truth about Magni's wartime activities, the legacy of his war record lived on after the conflict and the fact that he was cleared in the trial in 1946–7 made little difference to his political reputation. Many saw him as a fascist who had participated in an infamous massacre. Above all, as a direct result of his activities after 1943, Magni remained a hate figure for many in his home-town area, and when the Giro passed through the area in 1947 it is said that some locals tried to attack him.[13]

Whatever the truth about the 'massacre of Valibona', it is known that Magni decided to move north in 1944, and this was probably a wise decision. Many thousands of fascists were killed in the violence which followed the official end of the war in 1945, a period of blood-letting which became known as *la resa dei conti*, 'the settling of accounts'. Magni has spent most of the rest of his life living in the prosperous city of Monza, near Milan, where he later opened a lucrative car showroom, which, as I write, is still going and still bears his name.

Magni's political reputation stuck with him after the war. There is direct evidence of criticism of him in the post-war period, and of chants of 'fascist' being directed against him (after his 1948 victory, in Milan, for example). He never confessed to his past, although he did try to explain it away. It is fair to assume that Magni was hated by many of those on the left,[14] and it is also true that much of the language used to describe him might have had fascist overtones – he was a 'lion', a 'man of iron', a 'formidable' hero; he rode 'as if he were in battle', he 'roared'. For one analyst, Magni 'represented' the right, although the cyclist himself never played a direct part in politics after 1945.[15]

Much of Magni's career was destined to be interpreted in a political sense, a sign of the way sport and politics were always inextricably linked in Italy, as well as of the Italian interest in conspiracy theories. In 1951 he finished second in the world championships, held in Varese. It was said that fellow team member Toni Bevilacqua, who had taken part in the resistance (and who finished third overall) refused to help him win because he was 'a fascist'. For Magni this story was a 'lie', but it is interesting that so many people shared this belief at the time. An incredible one and half million spectators were estimated to have watched the race.

Journalists on the left were hostile to Magni for some time, especially immediately after the war. Memories were long, and bitter, and the civil war lived on in people's minds for many years. Magni was not particularly famous in cycling terms in 1947, but he would soon become so, and his fame brought back uncomfortable and recent memories from his wartime past which would haunt him for some time.

There is no doubt that some of this bitterness remains even today. When a photograph of Magni was used to promote the Giro d'Italia in March 2009 in the official local government publication of Campi Bisenzio angry protests were issued by a local left-wing association. This statement appeared on the internet:

> After 8 September 1943 Fiorenzo Magni supported the Italian Social Republic [Mussolini's puppet government] and on 3 January 1944 he took part in the Battle of Valibona, during which many comrades were killed including Lanciotto Ballerini. Tried and cleared (thanks to an amnesty) he has never denied his adherence to the fascist side of the war. (*Il Cantiere Sociale Camilo Cienfuegos*)

Such local debates had an immediate effect. When the Giro stage began from Campi Bisenzio in May the same official local government publication had changed the photograph on its cover from one of Magni to the far less controversial and more classic image of Coppi and Bartali. Magni was still *persona non grata* in the area where he had been born, even in the twenty-first century.[16] Unlike in other home towns of great cyclists (Ponte a Ema for Bartali, Castellania for Coppi, Cittiglio for Binda, Cesenatico for Pantani) Vaiano has no Magni museum, nor any reference to Magni on its website. Such an omission can only be politically motivated.

Very few winners of the Giro d'Italia have been booed as they crossed the finish line. Alfredo Binda was sometimes heckled in the 1920s because he was too good. His victories had become too predictable. But by 1948 things were different. Italy was divided between Christian Democrats and communists, and between *Coppiani* and *Bartaliani*. When 'the third man' won that Giro, his victory was unacceptable to many. This was not just because of his 'dark' past, but also thanks to the manner of his triumph.

The Giro of 1948 was given an astonishing build-up in the press. Everyone expected yet another Coppi–Bartali battle, but it never materialised. The race was dominated by less famous riders: Cottur,

Ortelli, Bevilacqua and Magni. After falling nine minutes behind near the start, Magni took part in a breakaway on the Bari–Naples stage, and climbed to only a minute or so back from the leader. He took the pink jersey just before a series of brutal mountain stages.

With the race nearing its end, Coppi finally made his move, winning two stages in a row and coming right back into contention. But just as journalists and fans were gearing themselves up for another Coppi triumph, the race became mired in controversy. After the tough Pordoi mountain stage Coppi could not understand how Magni had managed to stay in touch, as he was known for his weakness on big climbs. Word spread that Magni had been 'helped' uphill, and some claimed that he had been pulled by a car. Coppi and his team demanded that action be taken against Magni: they wanted him thrown out of the race altogether.

As the stage came to end, amid claim and counter-claim, the race jury considered the evidence before them. There were no photographs or TV pictures to go on, only the testimonies of riders, fans and officials. The first verdict of the Giro jury was clear. Magni had indeed been 'helped' – pushed – up the mountainside. The jury's judgement went even further. The pushing had 'evidently been planned'. Organised cheating had taken place. But the punishment for this cheating seemed rather mild: Magni was docked a mere two minutes, which still left him wearing the pink jersey. William Fotheringham has no doubts about the pushing, writing that 'his supporters had pushed him up the toughest mountain passes. They had been brought in by the coachload and specially positioned for maximum effect.'[17]

Coppi then took the radical and controversial decision to withdraw from the entire race in protest, along with his team. Efforts continued late into the night to persuade him to change his mind, but he would not budge. It was not until his team failed to show up for the next day's stage that journalists and Coppi's legions of fans finally realised what had happened. Fausto Coppi, the most famous and popular cyclist in Italy, the winner of the Giro in

1947, had pulled out of the race in protest, despite being just behind the leader.

Fans, journalists and others were furious and they took out their frustration on Fiorenzo Magni. Alongside '*Viva Coppi*' and '*Viva Bartali*' now appeared '*Abbasso Magni*' (down with Magni, usually written with an upside-down W). Coppi's withdrawal left the world of cycling in shock. Not only were his many fans enraged, even neutrals felt that justice had not been done. Magni was not only seen as a cheat, but as someone who had conspired to defraud legions of Coppi enthusiasts.[18] The fans took their revenge on Magni on his way to Milan. He was booed mercilessly throughout the final stages, as he tried to cling on to his slender eleven-second lead.

The final sprint in the Vigorelli velodrome in Milan saw the 'ferocious' crowd reduce Magni to tears, and the police had to escort him away. He had responded to the crowd by winning the sprint, the stage and the overall race. Guido Giardini, the only Italian journalist who would witness Magni's victory in the Tour of Flanders the following year, wrote, 'this dreadful episode will remain in the memory for a long time'. *L'Unità* was harsher than the crowd itself, claiming that the Giro had ended when Coppi pulled out, and its reporter, Attilio Camoriano (a former partisan himself), was blunt: 'we are not interested in today's race'.[19] Thus Magni, the winner of the Giro, had to endure boos, whistles and hostile banners, such as this one: 'Long live Coppi cycling champion, down with Magni the pushing champion'.[20]

Magni's triumph had been transformed into a kind of 'trial', with the crowd delivering a guilty verdict. Most fans wanted Coppi, and wouldn't accept that someone else had won, nor the manner in which the race had panned out. *L'Unità* wrote of 'boos for Magni, an angry shouting crowd' and of 'fruit being thrown'. For Magni, this was a bitter pill to swallow, but it made him a stronger man and probably a better cyclist. He would get his revenge on the *Coppiani* in future years, and he was even to become an ally of his great rival during a final, dramatic Giro victory in 1955.

Part of the hostility directed at Magni was clearly political, and certainly linked to the battle of Valibona. As the 1948 Tour came to an end Alfonso Gatto, a communist poet and cycling enthusiast, wrote a highly critical piece in *L'Unità* in which he made a link between the accusations of cheating levelled against Magni and his fascist past. Gatto called those who had supposedly 'pushed' Magni 'collaborationists', an obvious reference to the 1947 trial.[21]

The fact that the Giro had been won by a former fascist was something of an embarrassment, but it was also in its way a sign of a return to normality after the war. Ex-fascists were in every walk of life – working as judges, architects, policemen and administrators as well as in the world of sport. Italy did not banish them from society altogether, and so the legacy of the civil war continued to haunt Italy for years after 1945. The irony was that Magni's participation in the Giro was partly a result of the amnesty of 1946, which had been passed thanks to the Justice Minister at the time, Palmiro Togliatti, the undisputed leader of the Communist Party. When Gatto attacked the 'spirit of conciliation' which had, he claimed, helped Magni win the race he was, if indirectly, criticising the actions of Togliatti himself.[22]

The only consolation for Magni was a telegram from the Mayor of Prato, a communist called Menichetti. The telegram was a simple one: 'In the name of our citizens we congratulate you on your fine sporting victory which is a reward for all your efforts and brings honour to our city. Menichetti sindaco, Prato.' Symbolically, this gesture was an important one. It was also a sign of the divisions of that time, and since, that a message as straightforward as this could carry so much weight. Later Magni said, 'I was very pleased by the solidarity I received from the Communist Mayor of Prato.' Magni's story was both a reflection of the divisions of the war but also of the way the country came together after it.[23] Time is a great healer, and Magni's cycling exploits soon won over many of the doubters. By 1951 even *L'Unità* had changed its tune, describing Magni's second victory as 'a result of his courage, tenacity and strong will'. By then he was something of a national hero, having beaten the Belgian Rik Van Steenbergen and the Swiss Ferdinand Kübler to overall victory following the first foreign triumph in the Giro a year earlier.

While hundreds of books and millions of words have been dedicated to the Coppi myth, the competing (and complementary) Magni myth has received very little attention. Certain black marks have dogged Magni's career. His 1948 victory was never really accepted at the time, and still bears the taint of cheating. Moreover, it is often claimed that Magni would organise his *gregari* to pull him along for many kilometres at the beginning of stages, to save energy. This practice was not officially banned, but it was not something which, for example, Coppi or Bartali were seen doing very often. 'In the early part of each race . . . Magni would be pulled along, literally, by some of his *gregari*, holding on to their trousers so he did not have to pedal and could save precious energy for the end of the stage.'[24] Then there was Magni's relationship with his team of *gregari*, which is also often seen in political terms. According to one recent book, Magni was 'a despotic and needy champion, almost a dictator of the teams which he captained'.[25] Perhaps this alleged attitude to his *gregari* also smacked of fascism. He later said that he knew where all the water fountains were, but *he* never stopped at them. That was something he left to his *gregari*. But the Magni myth also contains some positive elements, some of which have come to the forefront in recent years. These date back to his extraordinary victories on the slippery pavement paths of Belgium, in the late 1940s and early 1950s.

Despite his three Giro victories, the Magni myth is most strongly associated with one race in Belgium and a Giro he lost in 1956. It is a myth linked to a sense of courage, strength and the will to continue against all odds. In some ways, it is one which also connects with Magni's fascist past, with its dreams of Italian victory abroad.

In April 1949 Fiorenzo Magni took a train to Ghent in Belgium, accompanied only by his bike, one humble *gregario* (Tino Ausenda) and a *Gazzetta* journalist (Guido Giardini), whom he had informed of his intentions by phone. Ausenda was one of Magni's most faithful *gregari*, described by Rino Negri as 'a worker of the pedal, serious and extremely tenacious . . . he would give his all for Magni'. He was also, it was said, a communist sympathiser.

Magni had decided to ride the brutal one-day classic known as the Tour of Flanders. It was only his second visit to Belgium and in the corresponding race in 1948 he had been forced to withdraw, after slipping and damaging his bike. He had no team and no technical back-up. If his bike was damaged, he was out. Now, he was going to try again. The three men stayed in a small hotel near the station before the race. The odds were against Magni: he was in a hostile land, despite (or perhaps because of) the large number of Italian emigrants who lived and worked there. Of the 220 riders who started the race, 185 were from Belgium. After his failure in 1948, Magni had prepared his equipment with great care. It is said that he had wooden rims on his bike (to absorb the bumps and cobbles), as well as foam around the handlebars (for the same reason).

The Tour of Flanders that year provides one of the great stories from the golden age of cycling. The risks were enormous, but in those days you could indeed win on your own, with just a bike and a few spare tyres wrapped around your body. But you needed great bravery, luck and massive determination to succeed. Everything else was superfluous. One of Coppi's most faithful *gregari* once said of his captain, 'if he had had Magni's grit, he would have won twice as often as he did'.[26] Magni's victory in the 1949 Tour of Flanders is also a story of his stubbornness, and his desire to gain the respect of his fans (and of Italian emigrants abroad) against all the odds. He lost Ausenda quite early on when he withdrew after a puncture. Giardini waited in vain for ten minutes for Ausenda, and then ordered his car to drive on up to Magni at the front. From that point, Fiorenzo was on his own.

Magni spent most of the race, with its 268 kilometres of cold, bumpy, wet and slippery terrain, in the lead. Giardini, despite being in no way a religious man, resorted to prayer in the hope that Magni's bike would hold out on the tough terrain. The race was won at the sprint, after nearly seven and a half hours of riding. In the early part of the race, Magni had gained a big lead, and spectators at the side of the road helped him with tea and beer. He loved cold weather and he is said to have described rain and low temperatures as 'money in the bank'. Magni also thrived in the heat. Tactically, his strategy was simple: break, and hold on as long as possible. Keep going. Magni's race was reminiscent of Bottecchia in the 1920s. One man, alone, abroad, with the odds stacked against him. Just thinking about it brings to mind mud and sweat, muscles screaming with pain, jarring bones. This was sport at its least glamorous, but its most glorious. Giardini phoned in his piece from Belgium. His prayers had been answered. He had had his 'heart in his mouth' for the whole race.[27] Many saw the triumph in Belgium as a magnificent reply to the whistles and boos of the 1948 Giro. For Emilio De Martino, Magni had been 'alone against two hundred others, alone against the terrible cobbles, the wind, the doubting public, alone against the wickedness of man'. In 1948, in Milan, 'the people had attacked Fiorenzo Magni in a ferocious manner', something De Martino described as 'the saddest and bitterest moment of our sporting life'. The Flanders triumph was also 'revenge' for that treatment.[28]

A year later, Magni was back on the cobbles. This time he had a team of sorts. Ausenda was there again, but Magni also had support of the quality of the former partisans Bevilacqua and Martini. It was as cold as the previous year. Colder. Some parts of the course even had snowdrifts. Once again, Magni attacked near one of the steepest 'walls'. A number of riders gave up along the way, too frozen to continue. When Magni reached the famous wall of Grammont, with its 18 per cent incline, he was alone, more than five minutes ahead of the field. If the 1949 victory had failed to hit the headlines, by 1950 Magni had become a hero, especially for the Italian emigrants in Belgium, many of whom worked in appalling conditions in the country's coal mines.[29] The 1950 race saw Magni take eight and a quarter hours to cross the finish line, two minutes and fifteen seconds ahead of the great Belgian rider Briek Schotte. Later, Schotte was quoted as saying that 'Fiorenzo was like a non-stopping express train. Once he had set off he only stopped at the finish line.'

In 1951 Magni won in the manner of Coppi, with the next rider over five minutes back (the biggest winning margin since 1922 in the race). The packed crowds recognised Magni immediately, shouting out 'it's him, again, it's him' as he rode past. Four rides, three victories. Other riders in those races spoke in awe-struck terms of his speed and strength. One said that you needed a motorbike to catch him. In 1951 Magni stepped off his bike at the finish line, exhausted, and vowed never to ride the course again. He was as good as his word. His name would always be associated with that race and those three consecutive victories. He had become, forever, 'the Lion of Flanders'.

The Magni myth was and still is a combination of ideas associated with his courage, his obedience to the higher needs of the nation and the dramatic nature of his riding style. Magni was known for the spectacular and dangerous way he rode downhill, where he often tried to catch up after losing ground on the climbs themselves. This is how Mario Fossati described such moments: 'we would be on the Iseran, or the Stelvio, or the Galibier. He [Magni] emerged from the icy clouds, from the water and the rain, or in the cold air of the Alps and the Pyrenees, on the rough and dangerous asphalt. Then Fiorenzo would undo his foot straps and disappear into the abyss.'[30] Magni was also a formidable road racer on the flat, and he broke the world record for 50 kilometres in 1942 (after failing in an attempt on the world one-hour record) and that for 100 kilometres soon afterwards.[31] But he also had a good tactical brain, and always rode with a strong team of *gregari* by his side.

Magni's myth is also connected to his willingness to sacrifice personal ambition 'for his country' and he was popular because he was seen as unlucky. In 1948 Magni was excluded from the Italian world championship team, despite having won the Giro d'Italia. The power and popularity of Coppi and Bartali led to this omission, and the controversy over Magni's 'pushed' Giro victory probably played a part too. Despite this disappointment, it is said that Magni spent his time handing out food and water to those who were selected, in particular his friend Vito Ortelli, who finished third. In the end, as we have seen, the team selection proved disastrous, as Coppi and Bartali showed little interest in the higher ambitions of the nation. After both retired well before the end, Magni later said that he would have 'ridden on until my pedals gave way'.

Again, in 1950, Magni paid a high price because of both the individual power of Bartali and Coppi and the need to play a supporting role for the good of his country. Leading the Tour by over two minutes, Magni never had a chance actually to ride with the yellow jersey on his back (although he had worn it on other occasions and would wear it again in the future). After a number of Italian riders had been physically threatened (and even attacked) on more than one stage by hostile French fans, Bartali insisted that the whole Italian team withdraw, and he refused to change his mind.[32] The team stayed up late into the night arguing with their captain. Gianni Brera, who was present, recalled that night in his celebrated (and hostile) open letter to Bartali, written long after the event and published for the first time in 1974.

> You spoke in ridiculous French. You were smoking my Gauloises with a tenacity which smacked of masochism. Magni was wearing a yellow hat on his head and wore an evil frown. He would happily have beaten you up there and then, along with everyone else.[33]

Magni was captured in a famous photograph folding up an unworn yellow jersey into his suitcase. He had 'obeyed' once again.

For a long time, Magni was very angry about the way he had been 'forced' to fall into line. Bartali claimed that Magni was 'dead tired' and would never have won. Over time, however, Magni's views mellowed. Years later, he refused to blame Bartali for what had happened. He accepted his 'bad luck' philosophically. It could also be argued that Magni indirectly paid the price for his support of Mussolini during the war, whose invasion of France exacerbated French–Italian tensions in post-war Tours.

Few of Fiorenzo Magni's victories were easy, especially in the Giro d'Italia. He won the Giro three times (1948, 1951 and 1955) in just nine attempts, an extraordinary achievement in the age of Coppi and Bartali, and he remains the oldest rider to win the Giro (at thirty-five in 1955).[34] Yet all of his three victories were tight, in doubt until the last stages of the race. If we add up the winning margins of Magni's three Giri triumphs, we reach a grand total of 130 seconds. No wonder he was quoted as saying that 'time is sacred'. In 1955 it looked as if he was heading for another glorious defeat. A fresh-faced young pretender from Tuscany, Gastone Nencini, was taking the world of Italian cycling by storm. Magni was 1.29 minutes down going into the penultimate stage from Trento to San Pellegrino.

Nobody gave Magni a chance, but the conditions were in his favour. It was a tough stage, but there were no big mountains (Nencini was a better climber than Magni) and it was cold and wet, his favourite conditions. For once Magni was lucky, as Nencini suffered a series of punctures, and Magni also received precious help from his old enemy, Fausto Coppi. 'We understood each other without saying a word,' Magni would later say, 'we didn't have to agree anything beforehand with a notary. We used to exchange favours without the need to get the chequebook out.' The two veterans broke with 160 kilometres still to ride, with Nencini desperately trying to catch them. Crowds massed on the roadside to catch one last glimpse of their heroes almost as if they knew they were in their prime. Magni let Coppi win the stage. Nencini, in tears, lost over five minutes in one day. The Giro was Magni's, by thirteen seconds.

The cementing of the Magni myth came in 1956 with one of the most celebrated photographs from the golden age of Italian cycling. The race in which the photograph was taken has acquired its own mythical status for, at the age of thirty-six, it was Magni's last Giro. Magni simply refused to let anything stop him finishing the race, and he came home second. He wouldn't give in in the face of the snow and cold on the legendary Monte Bondone stage, nor after a series of injuries left him with broken bones that meant that he was unable to grip the handlebars properly, and had problems braking. Magni himself takes up the story of his physical problems on that Giro:

> In the 1956 Giro I fell on the descent from Volterra and I broke my collarbone. The doctor said to me, 'You can't ride'. But I put some rubber sponge on the handlebars and I rode the time trial. I used up four pairs of shoes by trying to brake. Then I rode over the Apennines. But on the uphill time trial at San Luca the pain was too much, so Faliero Masi cut a tyre for me and tied it to the handlebars and I held it in my teeth. The next day, in the Modena–Rapallo stage, I fell again and I broke my upper arm. I fainted with pain. I was already on a stretcher. But I got up and the group waited for me. And I finished the Bondone stage in the snow.

This is the famous image we have from that Giro. Magni had broken his collarbone with ten stages to go, but he carried on regardless, his only palliative a piece of inner tube attached to the handlebars, gripped in his teeth. In this condition, he finished the Giro and in particular the apocalyptic Bondone stage in the snow where nearly half the riders withdrew. Fans held up banners praising Magni's courage, 'Viva Magni. The beast still does not fall even when injured', 'Bravo Magni. You are symbolised by your pride, you fight with audacity. Young people follow his example'. His grimace became his trademark, but it was an expression which also marked the end of the 'heroic' epoch of cycling history.[35] Coppi carried on racing right through the 1950s, but he was a shadow of his former self. The age of Bartali, Coppi and Magni was over. Magni kept a blow-up of the photograph by his desk in his car showroom in Monza, where he continued to work well beyond retirement.[36]

Fiorenzo Magni remained very much within the world of cycling after he retired. He outlived both Coppi and Bartali and he became a leading figure in the running of one of the most beautiful cycling museums in the world, the imposing glass structure perched on top of the Ghisallo climb, with its stunning views over Lake Como. Both the peak and the museum are visited by thousands of cyclists and enthusiasts every year. Magni was sprightly into his nineties, giving numerous interviews to the press and writers. He became a kind of living memory of the golden age of cycling. He would wake every morning at 5.30, and drink two and a half glasses of warm mineral water – something he swore was essential to good health.

Thus an autonomous Magni myth was created, and is told through the stories and images discussed in this chapter. During the 2001 Giro, Magni was afforded the ultimate honour for any Italian cyclist, as a stage was planned to pass right by his house in Monticello Brianza. Nonetheless, the real power of cycling's golden age lay in the figures of Coppi and Bartali, evidence of which can be seen through the books and films dedicated to that period of sporting history.

The 1956 Giro saw the end of the golden age of Italian cycling. After that, the sport began to live largely in the past despite continuing in the present. At the time, and since then, the power of CoppiandBartali obscured almost everything else. On the fiftieth anniversary of Coppi's death in 2010, dozens of books on Coppi were published or reissued. Everyone else, no matter how good they had been, was relegated to the sidelines. No other comparable myth emerged to challenge that of CoppiandBartali, and other riders (both those who rode with Fausto and Gino, and those since) were inevitably seen as bit-part players, 'orphans', or simply compared (usually unfavourably) to those great stars. A number of budding cyclists in the sixties, seventies and eighties appeared to freeze after being named 'the new Coppi' (hardly anybody was compared to Bartali). Neither journalists not cyclists ever again reached the heights of the immediate post-war era. Coppi and Bartali had created unprecedented interest in the sport, and their departure left a gap which nobody was able to fill.

After Coppi's death, only Eddy Merckx was able to challenge his power on the bike (but in many other ways his life was much less interesting off the bike) and Marco Pantani later created levels of fan hysteria which could be compared to the golden age. The Moser–Saronni rivalry filled endless pages of newsprint, but bore no comparison to the CoppiandBartali age in terms of the races themselves or the drama they had produced. The shadow of the 1940s and 1950s hung over Italian cycling for the rest of the century, and beyond. Nobody was able truly to emerge into the limelight. Apart from Merckx, those who followed were pale imitations, mere parodies, bad copies. Yet their stories are certainly worth telling and analysing, and even looking back the golden age would not have been the same without them. The present, as always, affected the way the past was understood.

The 1956 Giro and the End of the Golden Age. Bicycle Thieves and Motorways

'His face was no longer that of a man'
— *Gianni Cerri, describing*
Charly Gaul on his arrival on
Monte Bondone in 1956

Monte Bondone towers over Trento, a sleepy, beautiful little city in the north-east of Italy which was the scene of bitter conflict in the nineteenth and twentieth centuries. For years, Italian nationalists argued that the Risorgimento – the unification of Italy – could not be completed without the addition of Trento and Trieste. Italians in Trento campaigned for annexation and Garibaldi marched an army through Trentino in the 1860s in an attempt to repeat his heroic feats in Sicily. In 1915, Italy ended up going to war with Austria-Hungary over these so-called 'unredeemed' lands. It took more than four years of trench warfare and hundreds of thousands of lives for Italy to gain small amounts of ground, including Trento and Trieste. Trento was ideal cycling territory, the starting point for a series of challenging mountain stages.

On 8 June 1956, a Giro d'Italia stage was set to finish on Monte Bondone. The popular twenty-three-year-old Luxembourg cyclist Charly Gaul – the 'angel of the mountains'[1] – began the day way down the field in twenty-fourth place, nearly seventeen minutes behind the race leader, Pasquale Fornara. Gaul was a specialist climber, and he rode with particular skill in the cold, but he had lost a lot of time in previous stages and most experts thought the Giro was finished. *La Gazzetta dello Sport* wrote on the same day, 'the decisive part of the race is over'. That day, however, the Bondone area was hit by a freak snowstorm and cold snap. The weather was so bad that meteorologists have since carried out detailed studies on the reasons for the sudden drop in temperature.

It was four degrees below zero, and Gaul won the stage on his own on the last climb (which rose from 192 metres to 1,300 above sea level in 16 kilometres and thirty hairpin bends), in short sleeves, without even a hat towards the end, after a series of terrifying descents on the earlier parts of the stage where he used his feet as much as his frozen brakes. Only one of the twelve motorbikes on the Giro was able to accompany him up the mountain. Fornara pulled out at the start of the Bondone climb, while Gaul finished nearly eight minutes ahead of the second-placed rider, specialist sprinter Alessandro Fantini, who ended up wearing a leather jacket. It was obvious that Fantini had not climbed the last mountain under his own steam.[2] In their desperation, the race organisers actually encouraged this assistance for Fantini and others, as the whole Giro was at risk. Too many cyclists were dropping out. Alpine troops also helped out on the climb. There are many stories of riders hitching lifts in cars that day and remounting just before the end. But Gaul did the whole thing on his bike, and still finished first.

It is said that after the race was finished (Gaul took over nine hours to cover the course that day) he couldn't open his mouth and his shirt was frozen to his chest. He fainted after getting off his bike, and then sat in hot water for half an hour. When he emerged he had no idea where he was, or what had happened. 'That day surpassed anything seen before in terms of pain, suffering and difficulty,' wrote the former Tour organiser Jacques Goddet. Years later, Gaul said that a banana offered by a spectator had been his 'salvation'. To make matters worse, Gaul's entire team of cyclists withdrew that day from the Giro: he was on his own, without *gregari*. His manager Learco Guerra kept Gaul going when he told him that he was 'dying of cold'; Guerra replied that he could 'go ahead and die, but with the pink vest on'. It is also said that Guerra organised a hot bath and new kit for Gaul *along* the route, in a roadside hotel.

The first twenty-three riders in the race before that terrible stage were either forced to retire or rode in over ten minutes behind the Luxembourg cyclist. Some drank grappa or tea in an attempt to keep going, while others sheltered in farmhouses and bars. Many fell victim to the ice, mud, sleet and rain. In all, forty-four riders pulled out on the same day (newspapers referred to the finishers as 'survivors', as if they had taken part in a battle), more than half those who had started the stage. Fausto Coppi, who was following riders from his Carpano team in a car (Coppi had pulled out earlier in the race) advised them to 'stop, have a hot bath' and then carry on. Spanish rider Federico Bahamontes, 'the Eagle of Toledo', was found in a ditch by a peasant, who later phoned Trento to say, 'I have a cyclist here with me, he doesn't speak Italian, what should I do with him?'[3]

Journalists reporting on the race were well aware of the importance of what they had just witnessed. Giuseppe Ambrosini, 'typing with frozen fingers', wrote of a 'real drama'. Emilio De Martino predicted correctly that 'this day will become part of history'. Guido Giardini claimed that 'this stage of the Giro will . . . soon become legendary' and compared the day to the 1910 Milan–San Remo. For Jacques Goddet in *L'Equipe*, 'we found ourselves in the mountain stages of a prehistoric age'.[4]

There were so many heroes that day. Riders Monti and Moser 'carried on while pleading for hot water to be thrown at them'. A cyclist called Fabbri finally collapsed into a soldier's arms, crying, 'I don't want to die.' The last-placed rider took over eleven hours to reach the finish line. Fiorenzo Magni had fallen and broken his collarbone a few days earlier, but still made it to the end of this stage in third place. He was nearly thirty-six years old.[5] Two last riders turned up over an hour and a quarter behind Gaul, in the snow. He became, that year, only the third non-Italian to win the Giro. The

'apocalyptic' Bondone stage had been his triumph, and had revolutionised the whole race.

In 2006, the Giro returned to Monte Bondone as a tribute to Gaul's
feat, fifty years after that freak snowstorm. The race passed the two
permanent monuments dedicated to Gaul on its way up the same
route. But Gaul had died in December 2005, and thus missed
his own anniversary. He described the Bondone stage as 'having
marked my life, it was a source of joy and regret'. The Luxembourg
cyclist's whole career, in retrospect, became centred on that one
extraordinary day in the snow. His life had never been easy and
his tough character won him few friends in the peloton. He was a
heavy drinker and he married three times, and on retiring he lived
for a time like a hermit, in an isolated farmhouse without electri-
city. Later he became friends with another fragile climber, Marco
Pantani. He came first in two Giri d'Italia and one Tour, but he
could have won so much more.

As we have seen, Coppi, Bartali, Magni and their *gregari* represented
cycling's short but glorious golden age. This period was unique. It
was before television, and took place in a country where grinding
rural poverty was the norm, not the exception, and where the bicycle
was the main form of transport for peasants and workers alike. By
the mid-1960s, cycling had been affected by a three-pronged shift in
lifestyle, which in the long run was to prove devastating both for the
sport and its mass appeal.

First, the motor car replaced the bicycle. Not everyone had a
car, but everybody wanted one. The bike became old-fashioned, a
symbol of poverty, of backwardness, of pre-modernity. Bike firms
closed down, cycle shelters (an essential part of many factories in
the early 1960s) were replaced with car and scooter parks.[6] Italy's
cities were rebuilt around the motor car, and bikes and cycling were
largely excluded from this process.

During Italy's 'great transformation' in the late 1950s and early

1960s, as the country became industrialised and modernised, Italians thus lost touch with the bicycle. Previously, work, everyday life and leisure had been intimately associated with cycling. Italians pedalled to work and did their shopping by bike. In their days off, they went on picnics, visited their girlfriends or went to the bar by bicycle. In the First World War, many Italians fought in bike-based divisions, on cycles created specially for military action. Rural Italy was formed of social and geographical landscapes where long-distance travel was common, and where the bicycle revolutionised working time. The sport of cycling not only produced stars who had cycled every day, just to get around and to earn money, but it also created a strong bond between everyday activities and the sport itself. Fausto Coppi would often ride to Milan to see his tailor, or his manager, or to take part in races.

By the 1960s the bond with the bicycle was broken. Rural Italy had more or less disappeared, along with the peasantry itself. Italy had urbanised, and although many still used cycles for a time to get to work, working *on* a bike became less and less common. Distances changed, and were covered by other means – most notably on two-wheeled vehicles which looked like cycles, but usually required no pedalling – mopeds, the Vespa, the Lambretta. Italian peasants also purchased millions of tiny, slow, motorised three-wheel vehicles, known as 'bees' (*api*) because of the noise they made. The bike disappeared from the landscape, as the landscape itself was transformed. Inevitably, this affected the way the sport itself was followed, and understood. Italy's urbanisation was closely linked to its motorisation. Motorways linked north and south. Cars took up space, on pavements and in backyards. This was all space denied to bikes, which were literally squeezed out of the picture. And the organisation of races became a problem in itself, hindered by heavy traffic. Cars had always proved a danger to bikes. Now they became a menace. Cycling in the big cities became unpleasant and dangerous, a way of breathing in fumes and risking one's life at the same time. And this was true not just for commuters or amateurs. Even the top stars were not safe.

Not surprisingly, most people preferred to get around on a Vespa or in a Fiat 500, which were now, unlike the bike, also status symbols. Italy's economic miracle thus marginalised the bike, and cycling, at any number of levels. Bikes were left to rust, children stopped learning to ride at a young age, boys dreamt of playing football for AC Milan, Inter or Juventus, not riding in the Tour de France. These changes were not obvious at the time, as cycling enjoyed huge popularity throughout the 1970s, but in retrospect the decline was clear. Small changes signalled this transformation – the photos on popular plastic children's beach marble games changed from those of cyclists to footballers; track cycling began to lose its allure. Cycling's huge fan base, from the Bartali and Coppi era, guaranteed a mass following for years to come, but that fan base was not maintained in subsequent decades.

Italians began to use their free time in different ways, too. By the late 1950s, television was replacing other forms of leisure activities with a vengeance and for a time it revitalised cycling. Riders became TV stars, either because of their inability to construct a sentence, or even speak Italian, or sometimes because of their (much rarer) eloquence. This was above all thanks to one highly successful and innovative programme, *Il processo alla tappa* (The Stage on Trial), invented and hosted by a brilliant TV journalist named Sergio Zavoli, a man with a deep knowledge of cycling. Zavoli's language was modern, his style even more so. His short programme combined immediacy (a report on something which had just happened, the stage of a big race, usually the Giro itself, but also the Tour, interviews with cyclists during the race itself) and instant analysis.

The programme would begin soon after the stage had finished, every evening, during the Giro. In the studio, leading intellectuals rubbed shoulders with journalists and sweaty riders just off their bikes. The result was electric, controversial, often hilarious and addictive. *Il processo alla tappa* gained huge audiences, and achieved cult status over time. It ran from 1962 to 1969 in its original format, covering every Giro over that period. It was said that when the programme was at its height 'it led factories to stop work, teachers to interrupt their classes . . . prize-winning writers to talk rubbish'.[7]

But in the long run, television undermined the popularity and singularity of cycling. For one thing, physical activity became less important with the rise of television as a leisure activity at home. The classic Sunday bicycle outing was now replaced by an evening in front of the TV, often in a bar or in the room of the wealthiest person in the neighbourhood, the first proud possessor of a television. Soon every family would have their own gleaming set.[8] TV also changed the way cycling was watched, removing much of the mystique of the sport. With increasingly sophisticated camerawork and changes to technology over time (helicopters, satellites, fixed cameras), fans could follow races from the comfort of their own living rooms. There was no longer any need to wait for hours, in the rain or under a baking sun, for a possible glimpse of their heroes as they whizzed past in a blur. The whole race could now be watched close up, the cyclists' faces, their falls, their breaks, their crises, the moment they dropped out, or won – all this was now public property, devoid of mystique.[9]

Cyclists became TV stars, and in this way they were no longer stars who seemed to come from the real world. Journalism was also transformed. The literary invention of Orio Vergani and others was replaced by a more televisual style, and the commentators themselves became stars (above all Adriano De Zan). Cycling journalists began to write more frequently about the past. Bars would fill up in the afternoons for the last part of stage races, which would be watched, like motorsports, by men sitting in smoky back rooms, staring at TVs attached to the wall. In the end television killed off the fairy-tale qualities associated with cycling. Coppi's fame was built largely in an age before television. His heroic exploits were passed on by word of mouth, listened to on the radio; or they were seen in the flesh, not transmitted by TV. The cyclists who came after Coppi became inseparable from their TV images.

Television thus took many fans off the streets, and created a new set of celebrities who had nothing to do with the sport. It also helped to create a levelling out which made cycling into a sport like any other one. Given the choice, motorbikes and fast cars were much more attractive to people, and far more in keeping with the consumer demands of everyday Italian life. The Gran Premio and *la partita* replaced the Giro stage as the main sporting passion for Italians. Cycling was relegated to the back pages. It was no longer, after the 1970s, *the* national sport.

Italy's great economic transformation in the late 1950s and early 1960s was also reflected in a whole series of cultural phenomena – art, literature, journalism and, of course, cinema. After the Second World War, Italy was still a country where the most important means of transport, after walking, was the bicycle. In 1948, Vittorio De Sica and Cesare Zavattini created one of the most celebrated films in cinema history. It was called *Bicycle Thieves*, and tells a simple story of an unemployed man, in Rome, who wanders around the city looking for his stolen bike, which is crucial to his job as a poster hanger. De Sica's film was an international success, and it depicted a city full of bicycles, where the bike was simultaneously a status symbol, a means of employment and a prized possession. In one scene, hundreds of football fans leave their bikes outside the stadium before watching the match. When the troubled star of the film tries to find his own bike, he is confronted by a veritable forest of bikes.[10]

Yet this forest would soon disappear from the streets of Rome. The swift demise of the bicycle can be seen in the shape of a Hollywood film set in the same city. In 1953 the international success of *Roman Holiday*, starring Gregory Peck and Audrey Hepburn, exported an iconic and fashionable new mode of transport which had two wheels but required no pedalling. The Vespa (and the Lambretta) began to replace bikes in the late 1940s (just after *Bicycle Thieves* was made) and were nippy enough to allow people to pop around the back-streets of Italy's cities. Millions of Vespas and Lambrettas were sold in Italy, revolutionising the lives of Italians of all ages.

The unmistakable buzz of the scooter filled the days and nights, and families used the Vespa or Lambretta for day trips to the countryside, as two people could fit on the large seats. This motorisation or 'micromobility' affected above all the lives of young people and made private vehicles available to the working class for the first time. Networks of friends widened, as did the ability to cross town without the need to rely on largely inefficient public transport systems, especially on the periphery and late at night, outside the commuting rhythms of the working day. The Vespa and the Lambretta were modern status symbols (and not just in Italy). Bikes were for the old, and the poor. Boomtime Italy ran on petrol, not pedal power.

By the early 1960s, therefore, Italy was unrecognisable. Production lines in Turin and Milan were spewing out cars, and those same workers were buying them. In 1958, 370,000 cars were produced in Italy. By 1963 this figure had risen to 1.1 million. Cars on the roads in Italy rose from 1.4 to 5.4 million over the same period.[11] Traffic became a feature of the landscape for the first time, and a massive and significant national engineering project created the Motorway of the Sun, the Autostrada del Sole, which links northern and southern Italy, Milan and Naples (and opened in October 1964). Bicycles were not allowed on motorways.

Once again, cinema provided Italians with a wonderful representation of the way their country was being transformed. In 1962, at the peak of the economic miracle, Dino Risi released *Il Sorpasso* (*The Overtaking*). The main star of the film was Vittorio Gassman, but even he was outshone by the other star of *Il Sorpasso*, a beautiful, sleek, all-white Lancia Aurelia B24. Where *Bicycle Thieves* showed a poor Italy, struggling to rise again from the horrors of the war, *Il Sorpasso* revealed an arrogant, thrusting Italy, a country which was becoming motorised and where speed was seen as a sign of wealth and power. In the end, the message of the film was bittersweet – the boom had its downside after all. Nonetheless, despite the cautionary message of the film, the image which it portrayed was of an Italy where the bicycle was no longer part of society, nor a prized possession. The films were less than twenty years apart, but they might have been from different centuries.

PART IV

After the Golden Age

14

Gastone Nencini: The Forgotten Lion

'It wasn't a man who won, but his character'
— comment after the 1960 Tour de France[1]

In the late 1950s, Gastone Nencini developed briefly into the most victorious and popular Italian cyclist of the post-golden-age era. He was born in 1930 in Bilancino, close to Barberino di Mugello, a small town in a desperately poor part of rural Tuscany just 25 kilometres north of Florence but a world away from that city culturally, economically and socially. Poverty was grinding, children struggled through school, illiteracy levels were high and whole villages depopulated. The Autostrada del Sole snaked through the hills in a series of tunnels and bridges, but nobody passing in their cars really noticed Barberino di Mugello, either then or now.

It was in a small village close to the Mugello area that a radical priest, Don Lorenzo Milani, set up a special school for poor children in the late 1950s. His work there would later galvanise an entire generation, and in particular the movements which erupted in Italy around 1968. Don Lorenzo's account of his experiences in the book which was published as *Letter to a Schoolteacher*[2] made his school a model for anti-authoritarian education. If the vast movement which radicalised the schools and universities of Italy in the 1960s had a manifesto, this was it. The state school system had failed the children who attended Don Lorenzo's school. They had learnt little, and had often been terrorised by a system which put them at the mercy of authoritarian teachers. Gastone Nencini could easily have been one of those children, but his escape route from poverty was simple: *pedalare, pedalare.*

Nencini came from this world, but he wanted more. He saw cycling as a way of 'emancipating himself from his origins' (Severino Saccardi) and he was used to hard, backbreaking work. His father was a horse trader and Nencini worked in a sand quarry in order to buy himself his first bike, against the wishes of his family, who regarded it as a waste of money. His nephew and biographer Riccardo later wrote that 'it was the Mugello which made Gastone taciturn, and the war which had just ended did the rest'.[3] Nencini quickly broke away from his home town and joined a cycling squad in Florence, the SS Oltrarno. Like so many of his compatriots, Nencini had emigrated to one of the cities of Tuscany from the countryside, as Italy was transformed by the economic miracle. From there he was signed up first as a *gregario* for Pasquale Fornara before becoming a star in his own right in the mid-1950s.

Gastone's rural Tuscan origins were often linked to the way he cycled, to his grit and courage and his never-say-die attitude. 'The Florentine people loved him because he was like that: generous and unpredictable. His reserve and his harsh Mugellian peasant's face which only occasionally opened out into a broad smile.'[4] More negatively, Nencini was often accused of a lack of tactical awareness and of not possessing the discipline of a real athlete: 'he would give his all from the start to the finish. He was always on the attack. Sometimes his energy ran out before the end . . . he smoked twenty cigarettes a day and he did not live a very healthy life.' His national team manager, Alfredo Binda, had a different view. For Binda, Nencini was 'tenacious, courageous . . . a fighter . . . he won with his strength, but in the battle he used his head as well as his legs'.[5]

Often, fans and journalists made connections between Nencini's very appearance, his upbringing and the way he cycled. He was described by Bruno Raschi as 'a magnificent beast always ready to attack without reserve'.[6] One of Nencini's nicknames was '*faccia di fatica*' (tired face), almost as if effort was carved into his features. Raschi further wrote that 'he had the signs of struggle marked out on his face'.[7] Nencini rarely smiled, and it was said that he only cried once in his life (in 1955).[8]

Many regarded Nencini as the natural heir of Gino Bartali, including Bartali himself, who saw him as a kind of prodigal son. Both riders had a lack of respect for contemporary sporting mores – they were drinkers and smokers – and a rural Tuscan background in common, as well as a reputation for courage. They also shared a reputation for climbing power. Neither was ever willing to give up. Bartali was 'the man of iron', Nencini 'the Lion of Mugello'.

But the two cyclists were very different in other ways. Together they seemed to encapsulate various (and contrasting) stereotypes of what was known as the 'Tuscan character'. While Bartali was a chatterbox and a constant moaner, Nencini was reserved and introverted. Anna Maria Ortese famously wrote that Nencini was '[both] kind and grumpy . . . This cyclist has a world to win and doesn't like riding with those who have already been successful. He is a bit sad . . . [and] hostile.' According to legendary cycling TV commentator Adriano De Zan, 'Gastone was a Tuscan who rarely spoke and measured his words. When he did speak, his words cut to the bone, like a hero in a western.'[9]

Although he won both a Tour and a Giro, Gastone Nencini is best remembered, like so many other riders, for the races he lost. In particular, his 'great defeat' in the 1955 Giro is often told as one of the most extraordinary moments in the entire history of that race. With two stages to go, the Giro seemed over, and most journalists, having already decided that there was nothing more to write about, left the race altogether. Nencini had won, or so it appeared. Yet a combination of the weather, bad luck (a series of punctures) and Nencini's naïve approach to the race saw him snatch defeat from the jaws of victory. Moreover, this defeat was created by an unlikely and spectacular alliance between two ageing heroes, Fausto Coppi and Fiorenzo Magni. As the two former rivals broke above Trento on the penultimate stage, Nencini tried desperately to catch up but his vain pursuit ended in more punctures and tears. Meanwhile, hundreds of thousands of fans poured on to the Giro route to witness the swansong of their idols. *Viva Nencini* quickly turned into *Viva Coppi, Viva Magni*. Three writers in particular were covering the Giro that year – Anna Maria Ortese, Vasco Pratolini and Marcello Venturini – and each took pains to recount this dramatic change of fortune in a celebrated series of articles, all of which later became books.

The most common story told about Nencini is thus one of a bitter and unexpected debacle. In 1955 Ortese, essentially a novelist who was covering the Giro for the glossy magazine *L'Europeo*, published a series of articles which immortalised the Tuscan rider's fall from grace. 'Gastone Nencini,' she wrote, '[has been] brought down by the mediocre nature of daily life, he is no longer wearing the pink jersey, no longer a champion, he is no longer the revelation of this 38th Giro. He is nothing.' She waxed lyrical about 'Nencini's innocence, his breathless face which tried hard to contain his surprise, his joy, which had been acclaimed by everyone only 12 hours earlier, that face is now beaten, hard, unhappy, covered with sun and tears . . . as he tried to avoid the crowds along the roads of Bergamo, Como, Milan'.[10]

While he is remembered for his defeats, most of Nencini's victories have been overshadowed, in the telling, by other events. His 1957 triumph at the Giro, by just eighteen seconds from the great French rider Louison Bobet, is usually surrounded by farcical stories of conspiracies and insults. These anecdotes are often grouped together under the collective name of 'the costly piss'. The story of 'the costly piss' is an elaborate one. Nencini's main rivals in the '57 Giro were Bobet and Charly Gaul, who had won in 1956. On a key mountain stage, one version of the story has it that Bobet decided he would do something that was both a little risky and a touch arrogant

– he would urinate while standing up. Then, as now, professional cyclists usually pee on the move, without dismounting. Bobet's whole team stopped with him while he did his business. Nencini decided to do the same and Gaul also elected to stop and pee, thinking that it was safe to do so. As he was urinating, Bobet and Nencini rode past and Gaul allegedly 'made an indecent gesture with his organ of vitality'. Offended, the Italian and the Frenchman sped off, leaving Gaul trailing in their wake.

Thanks to that break, the Luxembourg rider was out of the race, but his dislike of Bobet was such that he decided to help Nencini to win, pulling him up a crucial mountain stage. The French dubbed Charly Gaul 'Monsieur Pi-Pi'. 'The costly piss' thus damaged both Bobet and Gaul, and helped Nencini to win overall, by seconds. After losing so narrowly in 1955, Nencini had won by the skin of his teeth just two years later. There are many different versions of 'the costly piss' story, however, and this is just one of them. Most of them are usually given more space than reports of Nencini's overall victory, Nencini being seen as a kind of bit-part player in a much more interesting story involving others. His victories are mere sideshows. This was also true of the 1960 Tour, Nencini's triumph.

The 'Lion of Mugello's' greatest victory was in the 1960 Tour, when he became the first Italian to win since Coppi in 1952. Nencini triumphed overall without coming first in any single stage, and thanks in part to an extraordinary Italian team (Ercole Baldini, Nino Defilippis, Arnaldo Pambianco, Imerio Massignan, who was the King of the Mountains, and Graziano Battistini, who was second overall) which was expertly orchestrated by the wily old master tactician Alfredo Binda (managing his last national team before retirement). But Nencini's only Tour victory was overshadowed by other events, and its memory is inextricably linked with tragedy.

It was 10 July 1960, a week from the end of the Tour, on the fourteenth stage of the race. Nencini was leading by just over a minute and half from the popular French rider Roger Rivière, who had broken the world one-hour record in Milan in 1957. An Italian journalist wrote of Rivière, 'he was good looking, well turned-out. Sweat didn't stick to him, it ran off him like water on grease paper.' Rivière was the golden boy of French cycling at the time, but he was often reckless. In a desperate attempt to keep up with Nencini on a fast downhill Col de Perjuret section of Mont Aigoual in the Massif Central, on a tight and slippery track, Rivière (the closest rival to the Tuscan for overall victory) misjudged the curve. He then hit a small wall, and flew through the air down a steep ravine.

Rivière had disappeared. Nobody knew where he was for a time. Then his body was spotted. He was lying in the vegetation below, motionless, but with his eyes wide open. His head was buried in leaves. A crowd of people carried him up the hill, 'like a Renaissance Christ taken down from the cross'.[11] Then a helicopter flew Rivière to hospital, but he had broken two bones in his back and was never able to walk properly again, let alone ride a bike.

Nencini's comment at the end of the stage was laconic – 'That's life.' After the victory ceremony in France, Nencini announced that he wanted his winner's bouquet to be given to Rivière in hospital. Meanwhile, Rivière's young, blonde wife kept vigil by his hospital bed, in tears. Later, Rivière admitted to using a drug called Palfium, a powerful painkiller. Some claim he had taken a dose so powerful that it meant he couldn't feel his brake levers.[12] He would die sixteen years later at the age of forty, from throat cancer, a broken man. Accounts of the 1960 Tour concentrate on this dramatic story, to the detriment of Nencini's overall victory. As Raschi wrote on Nencini's death in 1980, 'it was as if every time he experienced the joy of victory this had to be balanced out with someone else's pain'.[13] The other event which dominated cycling in 1960 was the death of Fausto Coppi. Even in triumph, Nencini could not escape the shadow of the golden age.[14] Years later, a monument was erected to Rivière at the point where he fell, and where his career ended.

Nencini's Tour victory was also eclipsed by political events in Italy itself. In July 1960 the decision by the Christian Democratic Party to form a government with the support of a small neo-fascist party caused riots and protests across the country. The state responded with excessive force, shooting dead five demonstrators in Reggio Emilia. As protests spread, the government resigned on the same day as Nencini won the Tour. Yet this was not 1948, and Nencini was not Bartali. Historians or journalists have seldom drawn connections between the events back in Italy and Nencini's victory in France. No Nencini myth was born to rival that of Gino Bartali, from 1948. Cycling appeared to be losing its power to perpetuate such myths.

By 1960, cycling was losing its hold on Italian popular imagination as well. While Bartali's victory had stopped people in their tracks (at least in the mythical versions of that event), Nencini's yellow jersey in Paris took second place to more serious political and social events occurring on the streets of Italy itself. It had little historical significance, even in retrospect. Perhaps only at a local level was a Bartali effect seen. On his return to Florence, Nencini was greeted by huge crowds as his open-topped car drove through the city, followed by innumerable bicycles and scooters. Journalist Franco Quercioli later wrote that 'the Florentines repeated what they had done when Bartali won on the Briançon in July 1948, the day after Togliatti was shot: they passed from the smoke of tear gas to jumping around for joy for their hero'.[15]

Another oft-told story linked to Nencini's 1960 Tour victory has little to do with cycling itself. With just two stages to go, the race was due to pass close to the summer residence of Charles de Gaulle (much of the Tour had been planned in De Gaulle's honour, and the first stage started in his birthplace, in Lille). So that the French president could personally greet some of the leading riders, the whole race ground to a halt. De Gaulle shook Nencini's hand (who stayed on his bike, and mumbled a modest '*merci*'), telling him that he had 'fought hard every day like a good soldier'. Journalists reported that Nencini was close to tears.[16]

The 1960 victory represented the peak of Nencini's career. In 1961 he ended up in hospital after a nasty fall and, although he

returned to the sport, he was never the same again. He took part
in three more Giri and rode in one more Tour, but only actually
finished one of these races. To all intents and purposes, Gastone
Nencini's career ended in Paris in 1960. His star had burnt brightly,
but not for very long.

There have always been rumours linking Nencini to the use of drugs,
a practice widespread in cycling at the time. In 1960 Nencini was
reportedly seen by the official Tour doctor, Pierre Dumas, 'lying in
his bed with a drip infusing primitive hormones into both arms, and
smoking a cigarette'.[17] Another writer claims that 'he [Nencini] even
handed out stimulants to the peloton to get them to chase a breakaway'.[18] In 1962, on the Tour, Nencini was involved in the notorious
'bad fish' affair when twelve riders became ill on the same stage of
the race and were all forced to withdraw. Nencini was one of those
who pulled out, and all twelve peddled the same line – that they had
eaten some 'bad fish' the night before. Many refused to accept this
explanation, including the Tour doctor (Dumas again), who claimed
that drugs were the cause. It is said that none of the hotels where the
riders were staying had served fish for supper.[19] Dumas made a statement which highlighted 'the dangers of certain types of preparation'.
The speed at which Nencini rode also caused rumours to fly. His
victory in the 1957 Giro was achieved at an average speed of 37.488
kilometres per hour, a record which stood until 1983.

For an Italian Tour winner, Gastone Nencini failed to leave any kind
of legacy to stand comparison with that of his fellow cyclists from
the golden age. The Giro paid ritual tribute to him, and during the
2007 event a stage began at Barberino di Mugello, but his posthumous fame remains largely regional, or only celebrated by real
aficionados. In some ways, this is difficult to explain. Nencini's story
had all the right ingredients for the creation of a national myth. His
victories were heroic, he won both at home and abroad, and against
foreign rivals, and he died relatively young. He also tended to lose in

dramatic circumstances. His career was short but extremely success-ful. He completed just seven Giri (winning once, finishing second once and third once) and he also rode in five Tours, winning in 1960 (and finishing fifth and sixth). It was often said that he should have won more, and that two Giri were 'stolen' from him (in 1955 and 1960). He very nearly won both the Giro and Tour in the same year, coming in just seconds behind Jacques Anquetil in the 1960 Giro.

But there was also something about Nencini's career which mili-tated against the creation of a powerful and lasting myth. He only won a single one-day classic (the Tre Valli Varesine in 1956) and his strength was in the long races, where his uphill and downhill racing kept him in the running over long periods. He did not win stages Coppi-style, and his tactical awareness was, as we have seen, unspectacular. He won his only Giro without winning a single stage, and the same was true of his Tour victory. Moreover, being an intro-vert he never captured the imagination of the public on a vast scale, beyond Tuscany. His victories bore no comparison with those of Bartali, Coppi and Magni. His timing was also wrong. The weight of the golden age was too great, and nobody could compete – at the time, or in retrospect. Coppi's ghost continued to haunt Italian cycling throughout the 1960s.

In addition, no rivalry involving Nencini existed to match those of the past or even those which were to come later. Only four books have been written about him, two by his nephew Riccardo, a leading contemporary left-wing politician in Tuscany. Nencini's premature death in 1980 was largely ignored by the world of cycling, and by Italy in general. By then, cycling was no longer the sport it had been, and this also had an impact on the importance of the history and memory of the past.[20]

Felice Gimondi and Eddy Merckx: The Postman and 'the Cannibal'

'A champion destined to ride behind another great rider'
— *Paolo Colombo on Gimondi* [1]

'If Coppi was the greatest cyclist of all time, Merckx was the best'
— *Gian Paolo Ormezzano*

It was Felice Gimondi's mother who first inspired his interest in cycling. She was the local postwoman and carried out her job on a bike, and a young Gimondi would watch her riding around the town, dreaming of the day when he would have his own bicycle. In the meantime he secretly 'borrowed' hers. 'I would wait until she got off and then start riding it myself, at first in secret and then with her permission, which she gave reluctantly.' This was the Italy of post-war reconstruction, where money was scarce. Gimondi had been born in 1942 in Sedrina, a small town in the hills above Bergamo. Soon, his mother was taking little Felice to work with her. When there was a particularly steep hill, she would send her son on to deliver the post: 'You go on ahead, you are quicker, she would tell me.'

Like Coppi, Bartali and so many others, then, Gimondi came to cycling through the world of work. But his passion for the sport of cycling was thanks to his father, Mosè, a lorry driver (he delivered gravel), who would drive miles to see races all over the region, taking

Felice with him. This was and still is cycling country, with its famous Ghisallo climb and classic races such as the Giro di Lombardia. Felice begged his father for a bike, but the family budget didn't stretch to such a luxury. It was only when a supplier preferred to pay in kind rather than cash that things changed. The payment came in the form of a bicycle, and Gimondi could now join the local cycle club. He was an immediate success, winning again and again. In 1964 he finished first in the amateur Tour de France, and a year later he rode into Paris with the yellow jersey on his back. He had turned professional, obviously as a *gregario*, with the Salvarani team (sponsored by a company that made kitchens) that very year.

Summer 1965. The Tour. The national teams were no longer part of the race (they had been done away with in 1962, although they returned in 1967 and 1968). Now all teams had a sponsor, although the national character of each was strong, to say the least. Jacques Anquetil was not riding the race, which seemed the most open for years. One of the favourites for overall victory was an intelligent rider from Parma, Vittorio Adorni, who had just won the Giro d'Italia. Adorni's team of *gregari* was impressive, including Gimondi, who was a young, virtually unknown, fresh-faced rider from a small town in the hills above Bergamo. Gimondi had finished third behind Adorni in the Giro that spring, almost thirteen minutes back. It was to be his first ride in *La Grand Boucle*. The instructions from Gimondi's team managers were clear: 'Ride a few stages, just to help your comrades.'[2] But cycling is an unpredictable sport, and its history is full of stories of dramatic role changes and overturned hierarchies, of *gregari* who became champions, almost overnight. Gimondi's chance came when Adorni had a terrible day in the Pyrenees during the ninth stage, and pulled out altogether, complaining of intense stomach pains.

To the surprise of everyone, including Gimondi himself, he now had the yellow jersey on his back, and he fought tenaciously to defend it. Without Adorni, Felice the *gregario* suddenly had a team of *gregari* to support him. On the climb up the terrifying Mont

Ventoux, where British rider Tom Simpson would die two years later, Gimondi was chased by other riders, in particular the Italian Gianni Motta and French rider Raymond Poulidor, but he held on. A victory in a later time trial secured a first place in Paris. At the age of just twenty-two, Gimondi had won the Tour at his first attempt, something only four other riders have done in the history of the race. No Italian rider would win the French classic again until Marco Pantani in 1998.

A glittering career beckoned for Gimondi. He was a modern rider, an all-rounder, good at everything and tactically astute. He was also good-looking and had a pragmatic approach to racing dictated by his background. Mario Fossati described him in this way: 'Gimondi had the muscular shape of a noble athlete, he was like a middle-distance runner.'[3] His body was thin and muscle-bound, his hair slicked back or perfectly combed. Over the next three years he would collect a full set of the great Tours – with a victory in the Giro and the Spanish Vuelta. Gimondi was looking like a combination of Coppi and Bartali, without rivals. But then his life changed thanks to the emergence of one of the greatest riders of the century: a Belgian called Eddy Merckx. The rest of Gimondi's career would be in the shadow of Merkcx.

In the late 1960s and early 1970s, Gimondi captured the imagination of a new generation of cycling fans and enthusiasts, attracted by his losing (and occasionally victorious) battles with Eddy Merckx. Whatever the outcome, the two men were fated to be considered together. From 1968 to 1972, Gimondi failed to beat Merckx, in any race. He did win the 1969 Giro, but only after Merckx was disqualified while in the lead. Gimondi's fate as second best seemed sealed in the 1968 Giro, when Merckx broke in the mountains (on the Tre Cime di Lavaredo) and won an epic stage – in the wind, the snow and the intense cold – with apparent ease. Gimondi lost over six minutes to him that day. It was around then that fans began to appreciate that someone almost supernatural had come into the world of cycling, an 'extraterrestrial' rider. 'The Cannibal' was born. For the next five years, the others would feed only off his scraps.

Like Magni in the 1940s, Gimondi was often seen as unlucky. Above all, it was said that he was unfortunate to have come up against Merckx, who was described as 'an unbeatable pedalling accountant'. Gimondi also resembled Magni in another way – in his tactical aware-ness. During the frequent battles to finish second, behind Merckx, Gimondi was always ready to forge deals and alliances.

There was something poetic about the 'gracious'[4] way in which Gimondi accepted his fate. He had found himself up against some-one whom he later described as 'almost unbeatable', but he always carried himself with dignity and skill. The crumbs Merckx left for the others were largely picked up by Gimondi. The image of the battle for second place, the constant chasing of Merckx's shadow, that of the perpetual loser (with its long and glorious history, from the 'eternal second' Belloni in the 1920s onwards) inspired songs and poems and a whole new generation of fans. Merckx needed Gimondi, and Gimondi's myth also required Merckx. Moreover, it was easy to play around with Gimondi's name: Felice. *Happy*. In the song 'Sono Felice' (I am *happy*, I am *Felice*) by Italian group Elio e le Storie Tese, the melancholy role played by Gimondi is captured to perfection: *Sometimes he* [Merckx] *rides off, he doesn't even wait for me, he leaves me with Bitossi, it drives me crazy*. Similar ideas are to be found in another popular song about Gimondi, written by Italian rock singer Enrico Ruggieri: *I am even more alone than before, and the Cannibal is already at the mountain top, and I have to press on in order to catch him*.

On many occasions, therefore, in an age dominated by TV cover-age, 'Gimondi was in trouble, he fell back, he was forced to watch that devil climb up and away.'[5] Every so often, however, the world was turned upside down: Gimondi would beat Merckx. Famously, this happened in the sprint at the end of the 1973 world cham-pionships in Barcelona. Merckx and Gimondi were among the last, breakaway group, but it was Gimondi who won ahead of his great rival. For Bruno Raschi, Gimondi's victory in that race was an example of the beautiful irrationality of sport, the way that outcomes sometimes defied all sense of logic. Raschi looked back to the early part of Gimondi's career, when he was 'king of the road and he was usurped by a young rider called Merckx. Another rider would have given up, but Gimondi carried on, stuck to his [Merckx's] wheel and waited for his opportunity.'[6]

Thus, after 1967, Gimondi's golden career came up against the unstoppable force of Eddy Merckx. The former postman from Sedrina was forced to be Merckx's foil. For a very long time in cycling terms he was a rival who never won, a bit-part player on a stage where Merckx would strut his stuff. Commentators joked about the Belgian's dominance: 'The arrival of the stage of the Giro d'Italia will be transmitted at 15.30 for Merckx and 16.00 for Gimondi.'[7] Yet Gimondi hung in there, and by outlasting Merckx he was able to win again towards the end of his long career with his great rival no longer the force he had once been. These victories were all the more sweet and memorable precisely because of the innumerable defeats Gimondi was forced to endure when Merckx was at his peak.

The rivalry with Merckx never had a personal edge. Gimondi took defeat with endless good grace and a healthy dose of realism. As he put it,

'many people think that there was a great sense of rivalry between Eddy and me, but this was true only in a sporting sense given the races we took part in. My real rival in personal terms was Gianni Motta more than Merckx. Perhaps because he, like me, is from the Province of Bergamo, and perhaps because we didn't talk to each other much either during races or afterwards. Eddy and I, on the other hand, used to talk all the time. We were friends, and we still are today.'

Gimondi's last Giro victory in 1976 was marked by tragedy. On the first day of the race, in Sicily, a little-known Spanish rider, Juan

Manuel Santisteban, hit his head on a guard rail and died almost immediately. The photos of his bleeding corpse still shock. In a beautiful piece, Gianni Brera wrote, 'in the eyes of the riders you can see pity and dismay'.[8] With Merckx in decline (he kept changing his bike in frustration), Gimondi won his last Giro without winning a single stage, at the age of thirty-five. It was his swansong, and it was also beautifully narrated by Brera, one of his greatest fans, who was reporting from the Giro for the last time. The journalist compared Gimondi to the dignified Sioux chief, calling him *Nuvola Rossa* (Red Cloud) or, in a play on his own words, *Nuvola Rosa* (Pink Cloud), once Gimondi started wearing the pink jersey.

During this final, victorious Giro ride, in 1976, Gimondi had a terrible fall on a late stage, while he was race leader. He was unconscious for two minutes and an ambulance was called. Brera reported that when he regained consciousness, the doctors asked him who he was 'in order to check on his state of shock: Gimondi regained his voice and shaking his fists cried out "eh, I'm Merckx"'.[9] Instead of taking advantage of Gimondi's misfortune, the group waited for him to recover and cycle back towards them.

This noble sporting gesture showed how popular Gimondi was among his fellow cyclists, and it prompted Bruno Raschi to write in *La Gazzetta dello Sport* about how 'moved' he had been by the 'courage' and 'honesty' shown by the group: 'A hundred men, none of them wolves,' he concluded, 'without this gesture, with its sense of chivalry . . . Gimondi would have irredeemably lost a Giro which he still has not yet won.'[10] Brera also exalted the gallant side of cycling after Gimondi's fall: '*Nuvola-Rosa* Gimondi gained the respect he deserved as a serious worker, a squeaky clean champion who shows no fear.' After the stage was over, Gimondi regained his composure and he 'was able to recall why and how he had fallen. When he was asked who he was he replied: "Gimondi Felice di Mosè."'[11]

Brera was, as we have seen, a great admirer of Gimondi – the two shared what Brera saw as 'Lombard roots'. In his last, great reportage on a long cycle race, in 1976, Brera waxed lyrical about the cycling of the past in a series of articles which, even when they referred to the present and to the race he was actually watching, seemed to look backwards rather than to the here and now. As Marchesini has written, from that period onwards cycling 'lived on as a story about the past, and not through its strength in the present'.[12] Another famous *Gazzetta* journalist, Luigi Gianoli (who was known as 'the poet'), was also a passionate Gimondi fan. Gianoli compared Felice's sense of fair play and aplomb to the ethos of the English public school (or at least his idea of what that ethos was).[13]

After retiring as a professional rider, Gimondi remained an important figure in the world of cycling. He continued to work for a living, setting up two insurance companies, and he had a share in a company making bicycle wheels. It was said that the money he earned from cycling was enough to buy him a castle near Bergamo. Mario Fossati described him in retirement as 'an elegant gentleman, with a few streaks of grey hair, and a very respectable financial position'.[14]

No rider has ever dominated the sport of cycling quite like Eddy Merckx. In the late 1960s and early 1970s, he won everything on offer, and in every possible country. He rode throughout the year, and triumphed in all areas of the sport – in the mountains, in sprints, during time trials, in one-day classics and in the great stage races. In Italy, Merckx quickly became a hero – in 1968 – and built up a big fan base. His rivals never really challenged him until his decline began in the mid-1970s. The only black mark on his career was his controversial disqualification, for doping, from the 1969 Giro, one of the most contentious moments in the history of the sport. Merckx was particularly fond of the Milan–San Remo, which he won seven times. For the first time in the history of the Giro, in the late 1960s and early 1970s, a foreigner was the undisputed king of the race for a sustained period. Foreigners had won the Giro on occasion in the 1950s and 1960s, but nobody, not even the great Jacques Anquetil, had come close to the series of victories achieved by Merckx. And it was not just the winning, it was the manner of his victories.

Merckx was not known as 'the Cannibal' for nothing. He destroyed his opponents, ignoring the favours and tactics which were an integral part of the sport before and after his reign. Merckx wanted to win everything, all the time, and he was so good that he often did just that. Such was his influence that cycling historians have often written about 'the Merckx era', or 'merckxism' (as a kind of philosophy). No individual cyclist, with the possible exception of Binda, ever had such a domineering relationship with the sport, and Merckx was world-famous, while Binda's reputation was largely restricted to Italy. Gian Paolo Ormezzano divided the history of cycling into before and after Merckx. He was also no stylist. Matt Rendell has compared him to 'King Kong . . . with uncontainable brute strength'.[15]

After winning his first Milan–San Remo in 1966, at the age of twenty, Merckx took his first Giro in 1968. He then went on to win the Giro again in 1970, 1972, 1973 and 1974. He also won five Tours between 1969 and 1974. For six years, Merckx was all but unbeatable. In 1971 he took part in 120 races, and won fifty-four of them. He wore the Giro's pink jersey seventy-six times.[16] It was around this time that a fan held up a celebrated banner at the Tour reading: 'Eddy, have pity on the others'. For nine years of his career Merckx rode with Italian-based teams. Faema (Fabbrica Apparecchiature Elettromeccaniche e Affini) was an espresso coffee-machine and boiler manufacturer, based in Milan and founded in 1945. Merckx joined the well-established Faema team in 1968, after winning two Milan–San Remos and the world championship. Faema wanted Merckx to concentrate on racing in Italy, and winning the Giro, and they took on a series of Belgian *gregari* to help their captain. In 1970 he switched to Molteni (a salami manufacturer with its main factory in Arcore, near Milan) and in 1977 he rode briefly for Fiat. Looking back years later, Merckx reflected on the influence of Italian cycling on his career: 'it was a relief to ride in Italy. It wasn't by chance that all the big riders of the era wanted to ride there. There was a structure, organisation, medical supervision.'

It is difficult, however, to write about Merckx the man. Nobody could really get to the bottom of his character, and he is often described as a puzzle, an enigma. He was 'a mystery',[17] even to his fellow cyclists, 'the biggest stranger in the peloton' (Johan de Muynck). Journalists ran out of words to describe his victories: 'all kinds of adjectives have been used for Eddy Merckx. We no longer know what to say about him.'[18] Countless pages were dedicated to comparisons with past cyclists. Just how good was Merckx?[19] Better than Coppi? Better than Bartali? Better than Binda? Others remarked on his 'normal' appearance. Luciano Bianciardi wrote that his face was like that of a man 'who checks your tyres at a petrol station'. Pier Paolo Pasolini dedicated a whole article to 'Merckx's face'.[20] Others compared him to a machine. He was boring and yet unbeatable, boring because he was unbeatable. There was something non-human about him, and the way he rode. Another of his nicknames in Italy was 'il mostro', 'the monster'. 'He rode, when the force was with him – too often – from the front, always in front of everyone.'[21] His victories had little of the drama or poetry of the Coppi era, and nothing of the sheer physical pain of Bottecchia. They inspired admiration and awe, but not adoration. Eddy Merckx was a cyclist of the TV age, who moulded his every gesture to a new form of media. 'With the sneer of the cannibal, a voracious frown on his face, Eddy Merckx crossed the finish line. As a form of celebration [after one of his numerous Milan–San Remo victories], he would raise the finger of one hand and then both to show the cameras how many times he had won overall.'[22] He had a loyal fan base, but he was also 'unloved', and many French cycling enthusiasts detested him for his utter domination of 'their' race.[23] During one Tour he was physically attacked by an angry French supporter.

Merckx was a modern sportsman in an age where technological and medical progress was rapidly transforming cycling. Nino Nutrizio used the example of Merckx to try and understand the way the sport was changing. 'Once upon time,' he wrote, '[cycling] was a struggle against suffering. Now it is marked by elasticity and changes of pace. It used to be about resisting pain.' Social and cultural changes were also explicitly linked to the Merckx era. It is often said that Merckx was the first cycling champion not to come from the working class or the peasantry. He was frequently described as 'bourgeois' and his childhood as 'spoilt'. This analysis probably says more about the grinding poverty which had produced the cyclists of the past than about Merckx's own background. His father owned a shop and, although he had a comfortable, middle-class upbringing, he was certainly not bourgeois in any modern sense. But Merckx had not come to the bicycle through work, and he had never experienced hunger or war, unlike the entire generation of cyclists before him (and many of those who cycled with him). In this sense, Merckx was different. He was the first post-war champion, and it showed. His sponsors were part and parcel of the consumerism of the boom years – with its coffee machines, its packaged supermarket food (Molteni) and its cars (Fiat). Pasolini argued in his article on Merckx that 'these are the last years of this peasant-based and proletarian sport'.[24] Looking back, it is difficult to disagree.

In 1976 Gianni Brera painted a touching portrait of a great cyclist at the end of his career, when he was no longer 'the Cannibal'. This previously 'unbeatable' cyclist was now eminently beatable, tired and – at last – almost human. The same fate was destined to befall all great riders, as it had with Bartali in 1949 or Coppi in the 1950s. The sight of an ex-champion still soldiering on, without the power he had shown in the past, provided perfect material for melancholic poetry (but also for rhetoric). As Merckx struggled towards the finish line, and Gimondi won, Brera wrote, 'Merckx comes out of this Giro, where he has been badly beaten, as an even greater figure than before.'[25]

'Meteors'. Heirs of the Golden Age

A series of promising cyclists in the 1950s and 1960s were burdened with the label of being 'the new Coppi' or (more rarely) the 'new Bartali'. None of them lived up to that billing. For some, their star burnt bright for a time, but most faded fast. Italy has a word for this kind of rider: '*meteore*'. Some of these 'new Coppis' actually rode with the great man: Ercole Baldini helped Coppi to one of his last victories, in the Trofeo Baracchi in 1957 (where two riders rode against the clock in competition with other pairs, taking it in turns to set the pace). It was said that Coppi had later confessed that it had been 'hell' trying to stay in touch with Baldini during that race. Baldini was very fast, so much so that he held the world one-hour record for a time in 1958 (his year of glory), and his nickname was 'the train of Forlì' (his home town). He also won a Giro d'Italia and the world championship that year and was widely praised as an elegant stylist. He was only twenty-five at the time, and seemed to have the world at his feet. But weight problems and health issues hampered his career. If his rise had been spectacular, his burnout was equally as rapid. In the end, he was just another 'meteor'. There were to be others like him throughout the 1960s.

One of the most charismatic cyclists of that decade was Vittorio Adorni. A regular on Sergio Zavoli's *Il processo alla tappa*, Adorni was tall, articulate, good-looking and opinionated, perfect for the new

television age. Zavoli called him 'the symbol of modern cycling'.[1]
Born near Parma in 1937, Adorni is best remembered for his Giro
win in 1965 (by more than eleven minutes, a huge margin, which
led to the customary comparisons with Coppi) and above all for
his world championship victory in Italy, on the Imola circuit, in
September 1968.

In that race he broke with a small group after just four laps and
rode the last 90 kilometres on his own, finishing a record ten minutes
ahead of the field. The race was centred around the city's motor-
racing track, with the addition of various steep hills around the city.
Contestants were required to ride eighteen laps – at 15.4 kilometres per lap a total of 277.3 kilometres. Nobody thought Adorni
could keep going for so long. (Many had previously dismissed him
as 'finished', especially when he took the radical step of agreeing to
present the TV quiz show *Ciao Mamma*.) But they were to be proved
wrong. It was a race which reminded many of Learco Guerra, 'the
Human Locomotive'. After seven and a half hours Adorni crossed
the finish line, arms raised. It had been an epic victory, watched by
enormous crowds both at the trackside (some 300,000 spectators)
and on television across Italy. Two laps from the end, Adorni had
a puncture and replaced his bike with a spare one. He was lucky
to get a spare bike at all, as the Italian team car had nearly run out
of petrol. But by then Adorni was destined to win: 'he would have
won with any vehicle, even on a woman's bike'. He was thirty-one
years old. Even today, Adorni is still referred to by fans as 'world
champion'. It was a real team effort that year. Five Italians finished
in the first six.

The world championships always prompted much discussion
in Italy over various alliances, and the Imola race saw long debate
about the friendship between Merckx and Adorni, both of whom
rode for Faema at the time but were on different national teams.
Would Adorni help Merckx? In the end, that question was turned
round, and it was said that Merckx, who finished eighth, had eased
up to allow his teammate to win (something Merckx denies). The

victory was particularly sweet for Bruno Raschi, who was also from the Parma area. Raschi finished his piece with an ode to his city and Adorni: 'We would like to be there with him, in the crowd, in the celebrations in Parma, a dear city which this evening will evoke those illustrious spirits of its past which this aristocratic cyclist is so fond of.'[2]

For much of the rest of his career Adorni was extremely adept at helping others to win, and he supported Merckx on numerous occasions. Despite his 1965 victory in the Giro, he was not really a rider suited to the big stage and he only completed one Tour. He specialised in rare but extravagant victories. Like many other cyclists around this time, Adorni also had problems with doping. He tested positive and was banned for a month during the Tour of Sardinia in 1968, and there were rumours during that year's Giro that he had avoided a test.

Those were the years in which cyclists became TV personalities in their own right, either in the studio or during the race itself (where, for a time, they could be interviewed as they raced, until this prac- tice was banned). Adorni was one of the most successful of these figures, and Pasolini wrote, 'I am convinced that Adorni will have a longer career as a TV presenter than as a cyclist.'[3] He was wrong. Adorni would be remembered as an elegant and spectacular rider, and above all for that 1968 victory at Imola.

It was one of the strangest sights of all in the history of cycling, but fans became used to it in the 1960s and 1970s. A professional rider would suddenly stop, get off his bike mid-race and stand still. Waiting. All the others would ride past. Was he mad or just eccentric? Did he want to lose? What exactly was he waiting for? The answer was a bizarre one, and was summed up in one of that cyclist's nick- names, '*cuore matto*', crazy heart – which was also the name of a famous Italian pop song of the 1960s sung by an Italian Elvis Presley impersonator known as Little Tony. Franco Bitossi was the cyclist in question, and he quite literally had a 'crazy heart'. In the 1960s

Bitossi had been diagnosed with heart-rate problems. His doctor (who also became well known as a result) advised him to stop altogether when his heart was beating too strongly. Not surprisingly, this often happened during professional cycling races – when occasionally his heart rate reached 220 beats a minute. What was extraordinary was that, despite this obvious handicap (top cyclists are often known for their extremely slow heartbeat rates), Bitossi had a long and successful career, in a world in which he was competing with heavyweights such as Merckx and Gimondi. It was often said, however, that Bitossi's heart problems were 'largely psychological'. Today they might be described as panic attacks, a diagnosis which would explain some of Bitossi's absurd losses. But Bitossi was also known as *falena* – moth – because of the smooth, light way he would win races, and because he sometimes seemed to be floating. A Tuscan, like Bartali and Nencini (who is said to have discovered him), Bitossi's father was a tractor driver. Like so many other cyclists from his generation, his background lay in a rural Italy which was fast disappearing.

August 1972. The world championships in Gap, south-eastern France. Franco Bitossi had all but won. The race was over. He was on his own, with just a few metres to go and the following group far behind. They seemed to have given up the chase. Bitossi got out of the saddle to sprint, then something incredible happened. He suddenly appeared to be cycling underwater; his speed dropped appreciably, he veered wildly to his left, and looked back more than once. Suddenly, those behind (including Merckx) were gaining on him. Just before the finish line, one of them passed him. An incredulous Marino Basso raised his hands in the air as he realised he had won, his eyes wide open in total surprise.[4] It was one of the most spectacular turnarounds in the history of sport.

Although Bitossi was a fine rider and climber, and particularly strong in one-day classics, he was destined to be remembered above all for his heart problems, and for this one, spectacular, defeat. Bruno Raschi later wrote that he had 'been afraid to win'.[5] He admitted that it had been his psychological frailty, and not anything physical, which had paralysed him as the finish line came into view. The end of the race, seen by millions on television, became known as the 'infinite sprint'. Adriano De Zan couldn't believe his eyes. 'Go, Franco!' he said desperately as Bitossi was suddenly and unexpectedly overtaken by the pack. Later, some critics drew a distinction between a 'loser', a word which was inappropriate for Bitossi given his many, many victories (he won over 140 races), and a 'non-winner', which captured more accurately his ability not to come first in the big races. He rode on until he was thirty-eight, and retained a huge fan base. On retirement, he lived quietly in Empoli, near Pisa, cultivating his allotment and becoming an extremely good *bocce* player.

Like the famous Mazzola footballing family, Gianni Motta was born close to the banks of the Adda river in rural Lombardy. His parents were farmers and Gianni worked the land himself from an early age. Like so many others before him, going right back to Luigi Ganna, he took to cycling through work, riding to and from a cake factory in Milan (the famous Motta company, of which he was no relation) every working day from the age of fourteen. That commute became a kind of daily race, or series of races, with other young men. Through success in these spontaneous competitions, Motta came into contact with the Milan-based Faema cycling team. He then turned professional in 1964 with the Molteni squad and in his first Tour in 1965 he finished third, behind Gimondi. In 1966 he won the Giro and seemed destined for a brilliant career. The last stage finished in Trieste that year, on the twentieth anniversary of the 'return' of that city to Italy after the Second World War and the dramatic Giro stage of 1946. This time there were no attacks from members of the public to deal with and all the cyclists who wanted to made it to the finish line. Motta's triumphant entry into the city was hailed by vast patriotic crowds. A star was born. He celebrated the victory in style, with a firework display and a dinner for two hundred in his home town of Groppello d'Adda.

But 1966 was to be Motta's last important victory in a major stage-based classic. With Merckx and Gimondi to contend with, he concentrated on one-day races. Moreover, for most of his career he was affected by pain in his leg after a terrible accident in May 1965, during the Tour of Switzerland, when he was hit by a press car which ran over his left leg. Sometimes his leg would go completely numb, and on other occasions he remembered 'crying with pain' during races. This injury was to dog him for the rest of his life and he retired early, at just thirty-one. In 1970 he had contemplated retiring even earlier as a result, although in the end an operation kept his career going until 1974. The idea that he was effectively riding with one leg gained him another nickname, 'the Enrico Toti of Italian cycling'. His other nickname was associated with the colour of his hair and the village where he hailed from: 'the blond man of Groppello'.

As with Gastone Nencini, many journalists saw the way that Motta rode as being driven by the extreme poverty of his youth, by a desire quickly to create a new life for himself. Mario Fossati wrote that his face was 'like that of a cat who had been caught in a trap'.[6] He seemed desperate to win and anxious for success but some say that he failed to live up to his early promise. All too quickly, Motta also gained a reputation as a cyclist lacking in discipline. Like so many cyclists after the golden age, he could not meet the enormous expectations heaped upon him by fans and journalists. He was also frequently involved in allegations of doping, and in both the 1968 and 1971 Giros he tested positive. Yet Motta was very talented and on his day could beat anyone. He was, as Adriano De Zan wrote, one of the few riders regularly to worry Eddy Merckx. But Motta's great rivalry was with Felice Gimondi. Where Gimondi was a gentleman, Motta was rude, and often expressed himself coarsely in his local dialect. In 1970, as a publicity stunt, the two riders were even recruited to the same team, but the results were poor and the experiment was quickly abandoned. After retiring, Motta set up a successful bicycle company and continued to ride thousands of kilometres a year across Italy in charity races.

Italy and Italian Cycling in the 1970s and 1980s. Crisis and the Triumph of the Collective Will

'The Giro as a place of memory for Italians today survives above
all through harking back to old emotions and ancient passions'
— *Stefano Pivato*[1]

Most commentators have argued that the political and social events
of the 1960s and 1970s had little effect on the sport of cycling in
Italy, and cycling itself had little political impact in the same period.
It is undoubtedly true that few cyclists took a strong political line,
and even fewer seemed to have any interest in the social, political and cultural movements of that time. However, the student and
worker uprisings of those years often had an influence on the sport of
cycling, and the language of the time influenced the way the sport was
understood and reported. In 1967, for example, an anti-Vietnam
demonstration in Milan led to the cancellation of the prologue to
the Giro, after clashes between students and police. Throughout the
1960s and 1970s various protesters saw the Giro as a chance to gain
support for their cause, by holding protests or blocking the road. The
TV age gave a live sport like cycling enormous visibility.

Moreover, professional cyclists began to demand more rights
partly in response to the movements which emerged from 1968.
Associations of cyclists used the language of the unions, with their
talk of 'exploitation'. But they also dismissed comparisons with
1968's students, when journalists compared certain cyclists to drug

addicts and hippies, a description they rejected. As with football, many radical students continued to follow cycling. Their memories of the upheavals of 1968 were entwined with images of Merckx and Gimondi. As in so many other walks of life, the 1968 movements both affected and were affected by sport, and cycling did not take place in some sort of bubble, detached from society as a whole and the upheavals in Italy at the time.

Fundamental changes were taking place in Italian society in the 1970s. Consumerism took hold, feeding into and from new forms of the mass media and advertising. Silvio Berlusconi was becoming a household name, first as a building entrepreneur and then as the man behind the meteoric rise of the commercial television sector in Italy, with its constant diet of game shows, scantily-clad girls, football, dubbed cartoons and American and Brazilian soap operas. At the same time, the two great ideologies which had dominated Italy began to crumble: namely, Catholicism and communism. Church attendance plummeted, and after a long struggle divorce (in 1974) and abortion (in 1981) were legalised. The Italian Communist Party, which had once had more than two million members, quickly unravelled in the 1980s. By the 1990s, the party had abandoned its name and rejected much of its own past, and split into a number of warring factions and parties.

As the twentieth century came to a close, the very idea of Italy began to crumble. Aggressive radical federalist movements in the north and the south called for the abandonment of the centralised nation-state. This state of flux clearly affected the way sport was understood. Writers struggled to embrace the great narratives of the past, where the nation and the Giro d'Italia had seemed almost inter-changeable. In a world where the global and the local appeared to be taking over from the nation-state – for journalists, cyclists and ordi-nary fans – it no longer made sense to understand a sporting event as an integral part of a country's identity. The Giro d'Italia was still a unique sporting moment in the annual calendar, but perhaps that was all it had now become. The universal meanings which seemed so clear and obvious to the writers of the golden age were no longer apparent. The Giro was now a story principally about cycling and cyclists, not about a nation or its culture.

By the 1970s, then, cycling had changed dramatically from the golden age of Coppi, Bartali and Magni. Cyclists were fitter, the equipment was better, the roads had been vastly improved, teams were organised in a businesslike way, doping was more effective (and becoming truly scientific) and there was far more money around. Racing was, as a result, much faster and much more predictable. One of the results of these changes – which were also reflections of transformations in Italy itself – was that cycling became more boring. There were fewer breakaways, fewer heroic solo rides, fewer falls. Luciano Bianciardi noted this trend in 1971, when he called the Giro 'the *Ghiro* d'Italia' (a pun linked to an animal – the *ghiro*, the dormouse – known for its propensity to sleep). Bianciardi placed the blame squarely on the fact that Italy was now a much richer country. 'Those who created cycling as a sport,' he wrote, 'went to work on their bikes from dawn until dusk . . . the kids who work for the baker today travel by scooter. They no longer want to pedal.' 'Cycling,' he argued 'is dying . . . because poverty is coming to an end, and with the end of poverty we are seeing the end of all the sports of the poor.'[2]

Technology mattered as well. Equipment failure became less significant, the weather counted for much less and new types of rider emerged – all-rounders or pure sprinters, specialists who no longer needed to ride the Stelvio on their own for hours in order to win or become rich. Time trials were more and more central to overall victory. The days of *un uomo solo è al comando* were gone, more or less for ever (although there was a brief revival with climbers Claudio Chiappucci and Marco Pantani in the 1990s). Increasingly, the peleton/*gruppo* became hegemonic over the efforts of individuals, as all the riders became faster, and team organisation much more scientific. Improvements to the sport and its participants thus destroyed much of its fascination. An intrinsically individual sport became imprisoned by the power of the collective.

But despite these transformations the decades after the death of Fausto Coppi and the retirement of Bartali and Magni saw cycling maintain and at times increase its popularity. As we have seen, Italy produced two cyclists capable of winning the Tour – Gastone Nencini in 1960 and Felice Gimondi in 1965 – but neither was able to repeat that triumph in later years. The end of national teams damaged Italy's chances. In the one-off annual world championships, where national teams still rode, Italy did extremely well.[3] But Italians in commercial teams made little impact on the Tour in the 1970s and 1980s. It was the Giro that remained the focus, the heart of Italian cycling. TV money came into the sport, increasing advertising revenue and making many cyclists, and teams, rich (and much wealthier than most of their predecessors).

The legacy of the golden age, however, remained strong. History was increasingly significant. Rivalries were usually compared to those of Coppi and Bartali, and individual cyclists were always seen in the light of their predecessors. Yet nobody really measured up to those former heroes, and although many had big fan followings, the days of Coppi, Bartali and Magni were gone: forever. In the absence of that kind of heroic cycling, the Giro became a place of memory, living increasingly off its past as it tried in vain to recapture something which could not be repeated. Cycling – and the Giro – entered what has been called 'the age of memory, of nostalgia, of regret'.[4]

The greatest Italian cyclists of the post-Merckx era in the 1970s and 1980s were Francesco Moser and Giuseppe Saronni. The two men disliked each other intensely, and opposing fans shared that animosity. Once again, Italians were forced to choose sides. Moser was also an integral part of the most extraordinary cycling family in the history of the sport. Brothers had often ridden together as professionals – think Alfredo and Albino Binda, Serse and Fausto Coppi – yet nothing came close to the Moser dynasty. Born in 1951,

Francesco Moser was one of eleven children (some claim there were twelve), and three of his brothers became professional cyclists. The Mosers hailed from the tiny village of Palù di Giovo in the mountainous region of Trentino (Val di Cembra), 500 kilometres above sea level. Francesco was thus steeped in the world of cycling from a young age, and remembered going with his father, on a tractor, to see the Giro ride past: 'it was a big party, we would eat bread with salami, and sometimes they even gave a glass of red wine to the children with the excuse that wine builds up your blood'.[5]

Aldo, born in 1934, was the first Moser to make a living from the sport. Known as 'Vecio', the 'old one', he was good enough to wear the pink jersey in the 1958 Giro – for one day – and amazingly he repeated this feat some thirteen years later in 1971. His career spanned nineteen years and he played a part in the epic snow-affected stage during the 1956 Giro. A religious man, Aldo had his own fan-priest/guru, who would follow him to all his races, and was also known as the 'cyclist-baker' because of his former profession, which involved long periods cycling up and down the mountains of Trentino delivering bread to various villages.[6]

Later, another of Francesco's older brothers, Enzo (born in 1940), became a fine rider in his own right, and was also able to wear the pink jersey – this time for two days – during the 1964 Giro. Thus three brothers from the same family were to lead the Giro at various times over a period spanning more than three decades, from 1958 to 1984. In July 2008 Enzo died in extraordinary circumstances (extraordinary for a cyclist, not for a farmer) when the tractor he was driving overturned and crushed him. Yet another brother, Diego (born in 1947), also rode as a professional. There is still a Moser bike shop in Trento, and more cyclists are now emerging from the next generation of Mosers, including Francesco's son Ignazio, and two of Diego's sons, Moreno and Leonardo.[7] In 1973 all four brothers were part of the same team (with Enzo as one of the managers). In Trentino and elsewhere the name Moser has been associated with cycling for more than fifty years.

Francesco (born in 1951) was at his best in one-day races, and he holds the record among Italian cyclists for the greatest number of victories (273 in all). His nickname was 'the Sheriff' thanks to his statuesque position in the saddle and his authority during races. Despite numerous attempts Francesco won just one Giro (in highly controversial circumstances in 1984) but he did triumph in the world championship. After retiring he became a successful local politician and continues to play a part in promoting the family's wine business.

Born in the northern industrial town of Novara in 1957, Giuseppe Saronni also came from a cycling family: his grandfather rode as a *gregario* for a cyclist called Libero Ferrario in the 1920s. Saronni tasted success very early on, so much so that his first nickname was 'the Boy' (in dialect *il balin*). Unlike Moser, who had to wait until the very end of his career to win the Giro, Saronni won his first in 1979 at the age of just twenty-one. He also triumphed in a dramatic world championship race (in Britain) in 1982 and won a second Giro in 1983. But his career went into rapid decline after that victory, something which inspired constant mutterings about doping. He retired in 1990.

In the end, then, Francesco Moser and Giuseppe Saronni won just three Giri between them, and no Tours. Neither man was particularly strong in stage races, and both were much more suited to one-day classics and stage wins. But, as Saronni later said, 'of course times had changed, but the interest which it provoked meant that our rivalry was the last to come close to that of Coppi and Bartali'.

Moser and Saronni gave birth to a highly durable rivalry. Neither rider, however, wrote his way into the history books. Saronni was a master of the sprint finish, and thus won many races, but was not a heroic individual rider in the Coppi or Bartali mould. Moser was a time-trial specialist (and he made a number of successful attempts at the one-hour record with a fantastically designed

modernist bike in the 1980s) with a fine record in one-day classics, in particular the Paris–Roubaix, which he won three times in
a row (1978–1980). Both were strong personalities and although
neither was able really to dominate in the big national races, their
rivalry was extremely important to Italian cycling in the 1970s and
1980s, when both riders provided a new generation of cycling fans
with much to argue about and admire. Nonetheless, there was also
a strong sense in which Moser and Saronni were parodying the
rivalries of the past. Their dualism was played out as much in the
media as on the track.

The bitter rivalry between Moser and Saronni in the 1970s and
1980s was very different from that of Bartali and Coppi, and its
form reflected changes to society and in the sport itself. Neither
rider was strong in the mountains, and neither was interested in
riding the Tour de France. Theirs was an Italian rivalry, for national
consumption only, and something which never really excited those
outside Italy. In fact, the 1970s was a time when the Italians lost
interest in the Tour, and the Giro isolated itself from the outside
world. This was also a rivalry exacerbated by the press, who fed off
it and sold papers via it, and it was clearly personal. Although both
riders claimed they didn't actually hate each other, they played up
their animosity for the media. Neither man was averse to disparag-
ing – frequently – the achievements of the other .

Saronni was often described as a 'wheel-hogger' by his rival's fans
– someone who didn't do his fair share of work but would then win
with a brief, killer sprint. Meanwhile, Saronni still casts doubt on
Moser's victories, dropping dark hints about doping and scientific
assistance. 'Moser was my main competitor until 1983. After 1984
he became something else, the only one of us to have access to new
training techniques. After that, Moser only challenged himself.' For
Saronni, the success enjoyed by Moser in the mid-1980s was thanks
to 'scientific changes' to the sport which, he claimed, were for the
worse, not for the better. The two riders would often simply wind
each other up. When Moser won the Paris–Roubaix classic, Saronni

was quoted as describing that particular race as 'a cycle-cross competition which should be abolished'.

In the end, the Moser–Saronni rivalry became rather like a pantomime act, and never reached the sporting heights of Coppi versus Bartali, or Binda versus Guerra or Girardengo. Nor did it move beyond the realms of sport. It never touched or cut across political or social divisions. This was a verbal duel which reflected the postmodern spectacle the sport had become. Moser's one-hour record was the culmination of this trend, a show made for TV. This rivalry was, however, long-lasting (it still rumbles on today, years after both men's retirement), and saw moments of great drama and unexpected turnarounds. In 1979 Saronni beat Moser by two minutes to win the Giro and in 1983 the thirty-two-year-old Trentino rider seemed finished. Saronni won again, and Moser abandoned the race five stages from the end, nearly ten minutes behind. But then came Moser's unexpected renaissance, an almost miraculous hour record, and victory the following year in both the Giro and the Milan–San Remo. Saronni's moment of glory came in 1982, the year Italy also won the World Cup in Spain.

The world championships are a national team race with a national manager but with an individual winner. Thanks to this dynamic, world championships have been the cause of endless arguments over the years. Cyclists who are bitter rivals throughout the season have to work together, for one day only, for the good of their country, but in the end an individual winner takes all the glory, and the team's work is largely forgotten. Often there have been accusations of rivals working against each other, rather than for a common, patriotic cause. This was the case with Coppi and Bartali, as we have seen, but the same could be said as far as Moser and Saronni were concerned, with frequent allegations that each man was working against his rival.

Italy's most successful world championship manager was Alfredo Martini, friend of Fiorenzo Magni, who ran the national team from

1975 to 1997 (a period when Italian riders won six times). Each race saw a team leader nominated by the manager. This captain would be the cyclist who was tipped to win and who would, in theory, be supported throughout by his teammates. But things could easily change during the race, and pacts were not always adhered to. In 1982, the acknowledged leader of the Italian team was Giuseppe Saronni, as the course seemed ideal for him. Francesco Moser was also part of the team. Goodwood, in Sussex, was a former British motor-racing track, and the cyclists were to ride for eighteen laps, a total of 275 kilometres. The sting lay in the tail of each lap, with a steep climb up the South Downs.

Martini was anxious for his team not to repeat the mistakes of 1981, when Saronni was narrowly beaten in Prague. In interviews at the time and since, Saronni has appeared to blame Moser for that defeat, but he was not averse to a little *mea culpa*. As he later said, 'If we had not fought against each other, Moser and I would have won four world championships each.' He also confirmed that the climate within the Italian team was far from harmonious: 'In the national team it was different to nowadays, where everything is sweetness and light. In those days there were various clans. There were friendships and people had enemies. Different kinds of alliances were formed. We were divided. And I think that this damaged both of us.'

Goodwood was a tough race in front of a huge crowd. The Italian team rode to Martini's plan, chasing down all breaks. They were also given a hand towards the end by Greg Lemond, who actually helped defeat his American teammate Jonathan Boyer, who had burst away on the final ascent (thus confirming that it wasn't only the Italian team which had problems of unity). And then, with the camera peering through the crowds, came Saronni's decisive sprint. He picked up so much speed on the ascent that all the other riders were left in his wake. It was a spectacular piece of cycling, and it soon earned an extravagant nickname: *la fucilata di Goodwood*, the Goodwood rifle shot. Saronni's sprint stunned the crowd and the watching millions back in Italy, taking him five seconds ahead of Greg Lemond.

TV commentator Adriano De Zan, in typically ebullient fashion, aped the commentator from Italy's recent World Cup football triumph with a triple cry: *Saronni, campione del mondo, Saronni, campione del mondo, Saronni, campione del mondo*. *La Gazzetta* also celebrated an extraordinary summer for Italian sport: *Saronni Mondiale! Dopo il calcio trionfa il ciclismo* (Saronni world champion. After football we triumph in cycling). Bruno Raschi described the victory with a typical rhetorical flourish: 'Saronni broke from the race with an antelope-like leap!' *La Gazzetta* later called the sprint 'one of the most magnificent moments in the history of modern cycling'.

Saronni's rifle-shot sprint was an inspiration for at least two important cyclists of the 1990s and 2000s. In 1982 Lucio Petacchi saw the race live on TV with his sons in Castelnuovo di Magra, a small town near La Spezia in northern Tuscany. After Saronni's victory, Lucio picked up little Alessandro, eight years old at the time, and started dancing with him on their front-room sofa, which collapsed under their weight. A Saronni fan, Lucio told Alessandro that one day he would be as good as the cyclist they had just seen win the world championship. Alessandro Petacchi was to become one of the best Italian sprinters of the late twentieth and early twenty-first centuries, with more than 160 victories. That same day another eight-year-old also saw Saronni's win on a TV in a bar in a different part of Tuscany, before taking part in an impromptu bike race with friends: 'And I won: for myself, for Saronni and because I realised that winning came naturally to me.' That eight-year-old was Paolo Bettini, who would go on to win two consecutive world championships and on one occasion, in 2006, like Saronni in 1982, just after Italy had triumphed in the World Cup.

But it was also difficult for later riders to escape from the shadow of the Goodwood rifle shot. When Alessandro Ballan won the world championships in Varese in 2008, his sprint was immediately compared to Saronni's, twenty-six years earlier. In the end it was left to Saronni himself to try to make room for new stories and legends: 'Don't make comparisons with the Goodwood rifle shot,' he asked. 'This is the Varese rifle shot.' Colnago sold a lot of bikes on the back of Saronni's popularity, and the red cycle he rode at Goodwood became known as 'the Saronni red'. Gianni Brera wrote of that bike that 'Leonardo da Vinci invented the bicycle and now, 500 years later, Colnago perfected it.' The Colnago bike ridden at Goodwood is now on show in the national cycling museum on the Ghisallo peak.[8]

PART V

The Age of Doping

A Slow Death. Doping and
Italian Cycling, 1968–99

'As an experienced sporting journalist, my idea is that we should all put "DDTR" ("Dependent on Drug Test Results") at the end of every article which celebrates a victory, an important sporting event, a success, a person'

– *Gian Paolo Ormezzano*

'Revelation after revelation, scandal after scandal . . . the cycling of recent years has slowly lost any importance from a sporting point of view. It is empty and punctured'

– *Moser*[1]

'You cannot compete in the Tour de France on mineral water alone'

– *Jacques Anquetil*[2]

The Giro d'Italia of 1968 was the first to be won by Eddy Merckx, Gimondi's great rival, and the first in which doping was a major issue in the race from start to finish. The shadow of Tom Simpson's death in the 1967 Tour hung over the first Giro to be held since that tragedy. In banners and graffiti fans accused riders of taking drugs, and journalists made frequent reference to the problem throughout the race. Moreover, rumours circulated about results which were not made public, or alleged attempts to avoid testing altogether. For some obscure reason, it had been decided not to reveal the results of any tests until the race was over. As the Giro ended (in Naples) the shocking news broke in the press: a number of top cyclists had tested positive at various stages of the Giro. *L'Unità* led with this headline, '*Gimondi, Motta e Balmamion drogati!*' (Gimondi, Motta and Balmamion drugged!). This was therefore a scandal which affected the winners of the Giro in 1962, 1963, 1966 and 1967. Earlier in the same season Vittorio Adorni had been excluded from the Tour of Sardinia after testing positive during that race. In Milan, with the Giro over, a long list of positive tests was read out to awaiting journalists. The room went quiet. This was no small matter. Ten names were implicated in the scandal.

The list read as follows (the race had been run from 20 May to 11 June 1968).

> First test. 22 May. Positive. Motta, Delisle, Abt
> Second test. 25 May. Positive. Bodrero
> Fifth test. 2 June. Positive. Balmamion
> Seventh test. 9 June. Positive. Van Schil, Galera
> Eighth test. 12 June. Positive. Gimondi, Diaz, Di Toro.[3]

What conclusions were to be drawn from these tests? If they were correct, the only logical outcome was that nearly all of the top riders and many of the *gregari* were using drugs to help them ride. And how long had this been going on? Above all, the names of Gimondi, Motta and Balmamion meant that this scandal went to the very top. Another of those who tested positive had ridden as a *gregario* for Merckx. Many were surprised that Merckx's name was not on the list. In the short term, all the cyclists involved protested their innocence.[4] But Italy needed to choose its national team for the upcoming Tour. Would these riders be included?

The cyclists involved did not claim that they had not taken anything at all. Some took refuge in the classic 'dodgy bottle' theory, or argued that someone could have tampered with their food.

Other cyclists threatened to sue those papers that described them as '*drogati*' – drug addicts. Gimondi was described by journalists as 'a man whose life has been ruined', 'whose last hope lies in the outcome of tests on a sample held in a fridge in Rome . . . [he is like] a condemned man who believes that he is innocent'.

Not surprisingly, gossip had been rife throughout the Giro of positive tests (rumours which also included Merckx) and the result of the race was not seen as final. If the tests were confirmed, all the riders involved would be banned for a month and would miss the Tour. Their names would be removed from the Giro's history books and they would forever be footnotes marked by a shameful asterisk. More seriously, the credibility of the sport itself was on the line. The papers began to refer to the whole affair as 'Giro-Chaos'. 'The main subject of conversation,' one journalist wrote, 'was doping.'[5] In the meantime, elaborate preparations were made for the counter-analysis of the 'organic liquid' of the cyclists involved. The sealed test-tubes were to be reopened by Professor Montanaro (president of the control commission) in Rome with a notary present to check on procedures. The Giro organisers were horrified. They had created a monster which not only revealed how much drug-taking was going on (and thus undermined the Giro in the eyes of the fans), but also threatened to alienate the riders and, above all, the sponsors. The top cyclists employed expensive lawyers in order to challenge the validity of the whole testing procedure. Their careers were at stake. A lot of money was on the line.

For Gimondi, Motta and the other less famous cyclists involved, the case dragged on throughout June. Both Gimondi and Motta were excluded from the Tour team and Gimondi admitted that he was too ashamed even to go and train on the streets. In July, he confessed to having taken Reactivan during the Giro, a stimulant which he said had been recommended to him by the vice-president of the Italian cycling federation, and which was not among those substances officially banned.[6] The vice-president in question denied that he had 'recommended' the drug to Gimondi, but admitted that he had advised him that it was not a banned substance. Journalists grappled with the medical implications as the general public lost patience with the story's finer details.

Groups of riders threatened to strike, and protested against the anti-doping controls. The professional cyclists' association issued a statement which read 'we are not long-haired hippies . . . we reject the accusation that we are drug addicts'. A meeting of fifty-one professional cyclists saw three hours of debate and unanimous calls for the anti-doping tests and rules to be suspended and redrawn. In the end, many of the tests were not confirmed, as the various committees involved decided on their validity. The first rider to be cleared was two-time Giro winner Franco Balmamion (the substance found in his urine had not been officially banned). On 13 July, Gimondi's ban was overturned as well. He had managed to convince the authorities that the freely available Reactivan had caused his test to be positive. Doubts remained about how much the influence of Gimondi's fame and his ability to employ expensive lawyers and experts had on his case,[7] but his name thus remained in the official Giro rankings for 1968. Meanwhile, Gianni Motta's case ended up in court and, unlike Gimondi, he was never officially cleared. As a result, his name does not appear on the final classification for the race, and his stage win (and sixth place overall) was expunged from the record books. The same fate befell Franco Bodrero, a former Fiat-worker-turned-professional-cyclist, who was to die at the age of twenty-seven in 1970.[8] He only won one stage of the Giro, and that was taken away from him. But if the authorities thought the 1968 doping scandal was bad, they had not reckoned with the mayhem their testing programme would produce the following year.

The Giro d'Italia, 2 June 1969. Eddy Merckx, who had won in 1968, was in complete control of the race. The sixteenth stage had just ended, a flat and boring 'transition' stage from Parma to the nondescript industrial seaside town of Savona. Merckx had already won four stages, and finished second in a number of others. In the Parma–Savona stage he had ridden within himself, finishing thirty-sixth. He was wearing the pink jersey, and nobody looked like taking it off him before the end of the race in Milan, just eight stages away. More extensive anti-doping tests had been introduced that year, and testing was held after every stage for the Giro leader and stage winners, among others. After 1968's ended with a whole raft of positive tests on mainly top Italian riders, debate had raged on throughout the rest of the year. In 1968 the results of the tests were only announced once the Giro had finished. Things would be different in 1969.

For the 1969 Giro a special Hewlett-Packard-sponsored mobile laboratory followed the riders in order to carry out the required tests. Every day, the first two in every stage, the overall race leader and two cyclists chosen at random were tested. Merckx had been tested on nine occasions in the race and had passed every time. In fact, no rider had been found positive for anything in the entire Giro. It appeared to be a clean race. In Savona, the ritual was repeated. Dr Bogliolo, who was responsible for the testing programme, gave Merckx a plastic container. He urinated into it and then the mobile lab found a safe place in which to stop and carry out the tests, in this case in the car park of the local police station. The testers had to work late. It was 4 a.m. before the first results came through, and the counter-analysis wasn't confirmed until eight o'clock. By that time, the riders were already up and about.

Vincenzo Torriani, the undisputed patron of the Giro, took it upon himself to inform Merckx of the shocking news in his hotel: the cycling superstar and favourite for overall victory was to be disqualified after testing positive for a stimulant called Fencamfamina. This was the most serious doping scandal to hit the Giro when it was in full flow, and it was a dramatic moment, captured by TV cameras. Merckx (with his fantastic cyclist's tan) was interviewed by Sergio Zavoli crying on his bed in his hotel room in Albisola, near Savona. He protested his innocence, saying that he 'had taken nothing' and that his life was 'ruined'. Dark mutterings of conspiracy theories soon surfaced, with Merckx complaining that he had been excluded to allow the Italian Gimondi (in second place, 1.41 minutes behind at the time) to win. Next day, some of these conspiracy theories were already being aired in the press. *Il Corriere della Sera*'s headline read: 'A "doped" Merckx has been chucked out of the Giro. There are suspicions of sabotage against the Belgian'.[9] The year 1969 was marked by strikes, bombs and demonstrations in Italy, but cycling still mattered. On 3 June *L'Unità* carried a huge photograph of Merckx, in tears, on its front page. Its headline also summed up the various theories about what had happened: 'Merckx expelled. Was it drugs, a mistake or a plot?'

In a country in which the judicial system has always been highly politicised and often unreliable, it was not surprising that 'the Merckx case' divided Italians. Why, many fans asked, had Merckx tested positive after a flat stage which he had not even tried to win? Who had gained from his disqualification? Was anybody else involved? After all, Merckx had tested positive for a substance similar to the one Gimondi had admitted taking in 1968 and, that year, those found positive had not only ridden the whole race, but most had seen their bans overturned. Other sports had already become embroiled in doping controversies. In 1964 the Italian Serie A was decided amid allegations of doping and had similarly divided the country over the rights and wrongs of the case, spawning a raft of conspiracy theories and even causing street riots.[10]

The widespread practice of doping, by its very nature a secretive activity, and the use of complicated anti-doping tests (something of which few people had specialist knowledge) encouraged a culture of suspicion to envelop the sport. Victories began to be seen as evidence of doping in themselves, as were heavy defeats, unexpected moments of tiredness or the sudden loss of time and energy (known in Italian as *cotte*, being cooked). Anti-doping tests and discussions about them were marked by allegations of fixing and conspiracy. Had someone tampered with the samples? Whose urine had been used? It was said that the positive sample was not Merckx's at all, but came from the Italian cyclist Roberto Ballini. There were rumours that Merckx had found a special kind of drug in China.

Incredible stories did the rounds, such as that of a priest who claimed that Merckx's bottle had been switched while he was attending morning prayers. Had other positive tests been covered up in some way? Had Merckx been handed a dodgy water bottle? These doubts were reinforced by the fact that cyclists rarely confessed to having taken drugs, especially once anti-doping measures had been introduced. The *omertà* of the peloton was near-total in this realm for years and remains so today. Many fans either simply refused to accept that the Merckx tests were genuine, or saw him as a scapegoat. As another banner put it, 'The Giro has lost Merckx, but not its drugs'.

The press was highly critical of what had taken place – apart from *La Gazzetta dello Sport*, that is, which had a vested interest in defending decisions taken by the Giro governing body (and therefore in defending the reputation of the Giro, which provided huge revenues for the paper every year). In *La Gazzetta* Bruno Raschi wrote wistfully about the damage done to the race as a whole, and the way Merckx had 'lit up the race'.[11] For *Il Corriere della Sera* the race itself had no more value: 'The Giro is over, whoever wins now.'[12] Some cycling fans agreed. Graffiti reading 'Gimondi the thief' appeared on the Giro course, painted on the asphalt. Indro Montanelli, the venerable journalist and cycling enthusiast, was outraged by the Merckx incident. In a celebrated editorial-letter in *Il Corriere della Sera* entitled '*Tutti a casa*' (Everyone should go home), he wrote that the affair was 'something we should all be ashamed of'. Montanelli argued that the race should have been suspended, and the other cyclists should have pulled out in protest. 'This incident goes way beyond sport. It is a stain on our honour ... Gimondi and his colleagues should not just have threatened to withdraw from the Giro, they should have done so.' The journalist hinted at a conspiracy in favour of Italian riders and added that 'this type of patriotism only makes one more Belgian than Italian'. Another journalist commented on a banner which read 'Viva Gimondi, but what if Merckx was still here?' 'The writer of that graffiti was ill-informed. Merckx was still there. His shadow obscured Gimondi's pink jersey.'[13]

Merckx had effortlessly won the 1968 Giro and in 1969 he said, 'I have fallen into a trap. Somebody wants to do me in. My samples have been manipulated.' The whole event remained impressed on the memory of all those cycling fans who witnessed it. It was the first time a race leader had been thrown out of a Giro or a Tour and the story would dog Merckx for the rest of his career. Alongside his many victories, it was perhaps the most memorable moment of his cycling life, and it would be referred to constantly over the years that followed. In his hotel room, Zavoli was able to ask Merckx a direct question: 'Mr Merckx, you have always claimed that you have never taken part in doping. What have you got to say now that you have tested positive?' Anti-doping was in its infancy at the time. In 1965 Belgium had been the first country to pass an anti-doping law. Checks showed that drug-taking was extremely widespread. Of the 254 tests carried out that year in Merckx's Belgium, nearly a quarter were positive.

After the shock news in 1969, Gimondi refused to wear the pink jersey the next day, preferring that of the Italian national championship. This was partly out of respect for Merckx, but also because drug-taking was so common in professional cycling at that time. As Gimondi later admitted, all the cyclists knew that they had been lucky not to have been found positive – 'we all did it'.[14] During a debate on *Il processo alla tappa*, Gianni Brera said 'they all take drugs'.[15] For a short time the cyclists were undecided as to whether they should set off, and, when they did, the pace was almost sedentary. Merckx's Faema team withdrew altogether. Everyone was worried. *La Gazzetta* journalist Luigi Gianoli recalled that day's racing as 'a fraught, dishonourable, uncomfortable stage'.[16]

This was a controversy to rank with that of 1948, when Coppi pulled out because of the 'pushing' of Magni up the mountains.

But it was also a sign of something much worse. Doping stories and suspicions of doping would begin to dominate accounts of the race in the 1970s and 1980s, and by the 1990s doping was threatening the whole credibility of the sport. In 1969, cycling's age of innocence came to an end. After Savona, whenever a cyclist was banned, or tested positive, reference would be made to Merckx crying in his hotel room. After that hotel room hit the TV screens, cycling would never be the same again.

Far from uniting Italians around an Italian winner of the Giro, the Merckx incident in Savona split the nation down the middle. Merckx already had many admirers and fans in Italy, and he rode for an Italian team. Italian sporting fans often identify as much with sponsors and companies as they do with the nationality of riders or drivers. With Ferrari, for example, Italians support the car and the company, irrespective of the nationality of the driver. Michael Schumacher, a German who spoke little or no Italian, became a national hero in Italy after repeatedly winning for Ferrari in the 2000s. Merckx's nationality mattered little. He was a winner, his victories were spectacular and he concentrated much of his effort on the Italian Giro and the classics in Italy. When he was disqualified, many were dismayed and refused to accept the verdict of the Giro authorities. Through the Italian mindset, various conspiracy theories were unveiled (and these were backed by Merckx himself, as well as in Belgium). Fiorenzo Magni called the anti-doping tests 'a con' and Gino Bartali was even more explicit: 'I have never been a fan of anti-doping tests. I have always said that the Italians should try and win against the foreign riders, but this does not mean we should secretly dope them.' Banners on the course claimed that Merckx 'had been doped' and radical students made connections between the Merckx case and their own protests. A student interviewed in Savona said that 'what happened to Merckx has given us an opportunity to spread our ideas about what is wrong with this country, about the systems in place in Italy, the political cannibalism which we have here'.[17]

The scandal was huge and led to a diplomatic incident between Belgium and Italy, questions in both national parliaments and an Italian government enquiry. Cycling fans in Belgium were furious, as were many others. The entire country was united behind its greatest sporting superstar. Threats were made to sabotage the Tour if Merckx was not allowed to ride. The events in Savona became an international talking point, and not just among cycling fans. The Belgian government issued a statement which claimed that the accusations against their national hero were 'absolutely without foundation'. According to them, a conspiracy had not been organised by the sporting authorities, but Merckx was the 'sacrificial victim of a criminal plot'. Strong words indeed. Rumours had been doing the rounds throughout the Giro of positive tests, which were, it was said, being hidden from the public. Merckx's ban was lifted on 15 June at a meeting in Belgium, where it was decided that he hadn't intentionally taken drugs. This compromise meant that he would be allowed to ride the Tour. *La Gazzetta dello Sport* claimed, 'Belgium has won.'[18] In France, Merckx went on to destroy the opposition, including Gimondi. He won by a stunning 17.54 minutes overall. It was clearly the case that Merckx had no need of chemical substances in order to beat the other cyclists of the 1960s and 1970s.[19]

There is still a great deal of embarrassment surrounding stories of doping in the 1960s. This whole controversy is rarely mentioned in accounts of the race or in the biographies of the popular cyclists involved. In some cases, Motta's sixth place in 1968 has even slipped back into the record books. Gimondi's doping problems are often omitted from accounts of his career or articles written about him, but he would also test positive at the Tour in 1975. It is as if the widespread drug-taking of the 1960s (and since) should be hushed up. It is almost considered bad taste to bring up such issues, and the whole subject of doping is generally brushed under the carpet, laughed off. But this was no laughing matter, and the failure of both cyclists and authorities to deal with doping in the 1960s was to have disastrous consequences for the health of the riders, and for the sport as a whole, in the years to come.

After the 1968 scandal and the Merckx affair of 1969, 1970 saw a 'clean' Giro, at least officially. But the 1971 race was also marred by lengthy debates over doping. Gianni Motta was among the favourites for overall victory in that race, and his team (which now included his great rival Gimondi) seemed, on paper at least, extremely strong. Both men were pictured arm-wrestling in a parody of their famous rivalry. But things went badly wrong, right from the start. On the third stage, Gimondi lost nearly nine minutes. It seemed that the team leader was now Motta. Then disaster struck. After the sixth stage, it was announced that Motta had tested positive for doping earlier in the race. Under new rules, drawn up in the wake of the damage done to the Giro after Merckx was thrown out while leading in 1969, Motta was fined, given a ten-minute penalty and a conditional ban, but allowed, nonetheless, to ride on.[20]

Motta's first reaction was to claim that he had taken an *erba* (a herb) in the form of a kind of tea drink, but the tests detected ephedrine, a banned substance. For years Motta had taken advice from a certain Dr Di Donato who, it was said, was an expert in all kinds of scientific 'remedies' and new training regimes. Journalists concluded 'this really is a disastrous Giro'. Like Merckx, Motta cried in his hotel room on hearing the news. Unlike Merckx, however, his fate that year did not become part either of the memory or the history of the Giro. Motta told journalists that 'the people will see me as a drug addict now', apparently forgetting that he had already tested positive and been banned in 1968.

It was said that Motta had to take sleeping pills that night in order to get some rest. The next day, some fans hurled accusations of 'drug addict' at him before the start, as he had feared. Motta later admitted that he had taken a 'substance' containing ephedrine and that he had done so without realising he was doing anything wrong. There was no more talk of 'herbs' or 'tea'. At the end of the Giro, Gimondi was booed by the crowd, and Motta was held responsible for what journalists called 'the Italian disaster' in that particular race.[21]

Following the doping scandals of 1968, 1969 and 1971, which had threatened to derail the whole Giro, something strange happened. After 1971 and until the 1980s, very few riders tested positive. What was going on? Had riders simply stopped taking drugs? This is possible, but not very likely. Had they become experts in getting round the anti-doping tests? Again, this is highly possible, and there are many stories of the ruses used to avoid being caught. Absurd stories did the rounds, such as this apocryphal tale. A cyclist was riding the Giro in the 1970s. He was terrified of the anti-doping tests and decided to ask his wife to pass him a clean sample of pee. He then transferred this sample using a rubber tube. When the tests came back, the doctor said, 'I've got some good and bad news. The good news is that your sample is clean. The bad news is that you are pregnant.'

The real answer to what happened with the anti-doping crusade probably lay in the furore which surrounded the testing in 1968, 1969 and the early 1970s, when leading cyclists, including Merckx and Motta, had all tested positive. At that point, the organisers almost certainly realised that doping was widespread among professional cyclists, and they faced a stark choice. They could intensify the anti-doping crusade, and risk undermining the whole sport and alienating the big sponsors, or they could turn a blind eye to what was happening, and tone down the whole anti-doping programme. Perhaps they chose the latter route. We have no evidence either way. But the outcome was that doping became accepted practice for most of the 1970s and 1980s. When the international cycling authorities started to clamp down again in the late 1990s, they discovered that nearly every cyclist was using chemical help. Nobody was really clean any more. The disastrous result of this practice was that it did what the authorities had been afraid of in the 1970s: it damaged cycling, possibly for ever, as a credible sporting activity.

Something strange was certainly going on behind the scenes. As the historian Christopher Thompson has pointed out, 'significant procedural issues – both scientific and legal – plagued the issue of drug testing from the start, as well as the existence of powerful interest groups and institutions likely to oppose the punishments that ensued from a positive result'.[22] These pressure groups 'included the public and politicians responding to public pressure; courts determined to uphold the legal and procedural rights of professional racers, including the right to work and the right to medical care . . . commercial sponsors defending racers, organizations representing professional racers and race organizers'.[23] By refusing to meet the problem head-on, the authorities made sure that the whole issue of doping and the use of anti-doping tests would continue to plague the sport.

In January 1984 millions of Italians turned on their televisions to watch a thirty-two-year-old cyclist ride round and round a cement cycle track in Mexico City for an hour, on his own. That man was Francesco Moser and he was using a radical new space-age kind of bike (with filled-in disc wheels) to try to break the world one-hour record, set by Eddy Merckx in 1972 (also in Mexico City). Most experts had considered Merckx's record unbeatable, and Moser was thought to be at the end of his career. Nobody gave him much of a chance, but interest was high nonetheless.

Against all expectations, however, Moser succeeded in breaking the record twice in a week after a long build-up, and his future fame was guaranteed.[24] Three hundred loyal fans travelled to Mexico to watch the 'race' live and some had even chartered a plane. A particularly passionate Neapolitan fan took a taxi all the way from Naples to the airport in Milan after missing his train, spending 500,000 lire in the process. Enzo Bearzot, Italy's football manager, was also at the trackside, and he said 'this is more exciting than a World Cup final'. Back in Moser's home village in Trentino the wine cellars were opened up to celebrate his achievement and cars drove around honking their horns for hours.

Not everyone was convinced by the validity of what happened, however. Interviewed in the press, Eddy Merckx was bitter. He said that 'Moser was helped by medicines and by new technology . . . by new processes and a whole range of scientists.' There had been many hold-ups in the attempt at the record, and rumours of doping were already doing the rounds at the time. It was said that the constant postponements were due to delays in blood which was being delivered from Italy. Other gossip mentioned diplomatic bags full of new blood.

It was the first time that a cyclist had covered more than 50 kilometres in an hour during a record attempt, and the impact back home in Italy was enormous, earning Moser large sums of money through sponsorship deals. One of the advantages of the new aerodynamic wheels was that sponsors' names could be shown on them, and they were continually in view in a record attempt or during a time trial. *La Gazzetta dello Sport* carried a huge banner headline, '*Moserissimo!*',[25] and then led with '*Moser: fantastico bis*' (fantastic repeat performance) after his second successful attempt. Huge controversy followed the astonishing decision of television stations to cease live coverage nine minutes from the end of the hour (in order to show an episode of *The Streets of San Francisco* . . .), thus depriving fans of the moment when Moser broke his own, recently set, record. On the first occasion, Moser hadn't just beaten the previous record, he had smashed it, riding nearly two kilometres more than Merckx had in 1972.

Moser's hour record was a sign of things to come, in any number of ways. It showed the massive impact of technology on speed; for years, bikes had been more or less the same. After Moser in 1984, different kinds of bikes started to be used and developed for various kinds of races, and wind tunnels and advanced carbon technology transformed design, weight and speed. The position of the cyclists' hands also changed for time-trial races and sprints.[26] Moser's sponsor Enervit (manufacturers of an energy drink) helped finance the whole event, and they went to town in terms of advertising and publicity in the wake of the record being broken. Huge advertisements appeared in the press with the by-line '*Enervit e Moser insieme per un grande record*' (Enervit and Moser together for a great record). Candido Cannavò, writing in *La Gazzetta dello Sport*, also noted the medical aspects linked to the record attempt, calling the whole event a 'sporting [and] scientific adventure', although he claimed that it was 'the man' – Moser – who had really won a challenge against himself.[27]

Cycling was irrevocably changed in January 1984. At that moment, a sport was transformed into a purely televisual spectacle. Live coverage was introduced and dozens of journalists travelled to Mexico City to report on the event. Moser's success made headlines and it remains his most famous achievement in the sport, but his hour-record extravaganza transformed the sport in other, more sinister, ways. Moser employed an entire team with a number of doctors, who monitored his every heartbeat and gave him special blood transfusions, which were not banned at the time. These experts included the key figure of a doctor and researcher named Francesco Conconi. Finally, Moser's Mexican adventure revealed how manufacturers and designers had begun to dominate the human element of the sport.

In 1984 those television spectators back home in Italy were unaware that Moser had changed his blood in order to gain an advantage, something he only confessed to in 1999. These transfusions were organised by Conconi, a doctor with a list of rich and famous clients who had already become Italy's official medical sporting guru. Moser's record-breaking achievement made Conconi famous, and in the press the praise was evenly shared between doctor and cyclist. Later, Conconi would reach heady institutional heights as the 'Magnificent Rector' of the prestigious University of Ferrara. Less meritoriously, he would also stand trial for alleged crimes linked to sports doping.

Conconi's key role in the 1984 record was well documented and widely praised at the time, and an entire medical team followed Moser to Mexico. The journalist Leonardo Coen wrote at the time that 'Francesco Conconi, a bio-chemist from Ferrara University, is the man who created the Moser miracle. This Conconi seems to have the Midas touch. The athletes he looks after make huge progress.'[28] Reading between the lines, this was a barely disguised allusion to the practice of doping. The truth, however, only came out in 1999, thanks to extensive criminal enquiries.

This history should really end here, in January 1984, with the scientific concoctions being prepared by Francesco Moser and his team of doctors for his world hour-record attempt in Mexico City.

Or perhaps it should end in the mid-1990s, with the widespread use of EPO and blood doping among Italian cyclists.

It should almost certainly finish in 1999, as Marco Pantani smashed his hand into a mirror on hearing that he would be excluded from a race he had already won.

This history should end at some point in the 1980s and 1990s for one simple reason: from here on, this is no longer a book about cycling. Most of the rest of this volume will not deal with stories of great climbs, or sprints, or punctures, or breakaways. Rather, we enter a shadowy world of blood transfusions, hormones, testosterone, cocaine, arrests, protests, masking agents, police swoops and sacks of blood in Spanish fridges. This is the murky world of medically inspired cheating, with its tales of the extraordinary extent which people will go to win, or just to participate. Almost every cyclist after the mid-1980s needs an asterisk after his name, a footnote, a second glance. Maybe the whole sport requires an asterisk. Nearly everyone has been caught at it, at one time or another. This is not a case of one bad apple. The whole orchard is rotten. In fact, it is almost impossible to think of a major (or even a minor) Italian cyclist from the last thirty years who has not at some stage been banned for doping. Many of the names involved are unfamiliar, as doping reached deep into the peloton. After the 1980s cycling became a sideshow to the real story, a story of institutionalised fraud (of the public, the fans, the TV audience, the cyclists themselves) and mass chemical debauchery. A website dedicated entirely to doping cases over the last fifty years contains dozens of Italian names.[29]

A group of sportsmen, participants in one of the most popular sports in the world, have systematically resorted to a whole range of drugs in order to improve their performance. In this endeavour they have been aided and abetted by doctors, drugs companies, managers, trainers, fellow cyclists and the authorities who were meant to be running the sport, including those who should have been exposing the drug cheats. Journalists and the media failed to expose what was going on. After the 1980s, no result was final. On endless occasions (after yet another positive test and ban) journalists and fans pronounced cycling dead. They were right. What lived on was not a sport, but a grotesque and moribund farce, where riders pumped their bodies full of all sorts of dangerous substances in order to win, or simply to keep up.

Why was the sport not cleaned up? One problem was the sums of money involved. It was easier and safer simply to ignore the issue for years, as the coffers filled up with loot. Moreover, professional cycling is a small world, in which news travels fast. Group loyalty almost always takes precedence over individual morality in the group, and the peloton is difficult to penetrate or reform. Whistle-blowers got (and still get) short shrift, and were often forced to retract confessions, or retire from the sport altogether. Teams and sponsors craved victory, by any means. Forgiveness was swift. Doped cyclists returned as if nothing had happened, and the fans seemed to have the same blind spot. And it was the cyclists themselves who suffered the most. Some committed suicide, others turned to more recreational drugs. The side-effects of EPO and other doping agents also seemed to lead to a number of suspicious deaths. Others left the sport altogether, horrified by the damage they were doing to their bodies. Invariably cyclists denied that they had taken anything (from Merckx onwards), and resorted to conspiracy theories. Very few came clean, or admitted anything. Many carried on using drugs even after they returned from bans. But this only fuelled rumours about all cyclists.

This culture of suspicion damaged the sport in other ways. Rapid progress was frowned upon, or openly derided as chemically induced. Nobody was free from doubt. Not being found positive was seen as suspicious in itself. And as these suspicions were so often justified, the culture of mistrust only grew. Journalists claimed that they were open-minded, that they would give victorious cyclists the benefit of the doubt, but this was extremely difficult in a sport where winners were often unmasked, and very quickly, as cheats. On the other side of the coin, journalists and commentators could not afford to write off the whole sport. After all, their livelihoods depended on its survival. This was, of course, very true indeed of *La Gazzetta dello Sport*, sponsor and organiser of the Giro d'Italia. *La Gazzetta* was in an ambiguous position. On the one hand, some of its journalists led a brave and competent fight against doping – a battle for which they were often insulted by the fans, and risked cutting themselves off from the cyclists with whom they lived cheek by jowl during big races and often built up personal friendships. But on the other, *La Gazzetta* exalted many of those cyclists who had been intimately linked to doping or had been banned in the past. Given the extent of the doping issue, this was inevitable. Nonetheless, much of this selective forgetting jarred with official pronouncements about crackdowns and 'getting tough'.

Perhaps cycling was simply inhuman, a sport too difficult for the normal body to withstand? This idea had been around for years. Coppi had freely admitted to taking various chemical substances, and Jacques Anquetil had famously said, 'You cannot compete in the Tour on mineral water alone.' Tom Simpson died on Mont Ventoux in 1967 in part because of amphetamines in his body. Average speeds of races continued (suspiciously) to increase, year on year. There was less and less time to rest. Each stage was ridden to the limit. Was it impossible to keep up without artificial aids? In 1999 the sport reached the point of no return, fifteen years after Moser's world record in Mexico. But in order to tell this story in full, we need to concentrate on the career of a unique cyclist: Marco Pantani.

The Tragic Odyssey of Marco Pantani

'More than a cyclist, Pantani is an emotion'
– *Gianni Mura*[1]

Marco Pantani was born in 1970 in the central Italian city of Cesena, and grew up in the nearby resort town of Cesenatico. His early life was far from easy. His mother worked as a hotel cleaner for a time, after his father lost his job as a plumber. Pantani started losing his hair at the age of fifteen, something that perhaps contributed to his painful shyness. Some suggest that he might have been bipolar. He had a difficult relationship with his parents and tended to bond with a number of father figures – a neighbour called Guerrino Ciani, one of his first trainers, Vittorio Savini, his grandfather Sotero Pantani, and the former cyclist and sporting director Luciano Pezzi.

In the early 1980s Pantani began riding with the local 'Fausto Coppi sports club' and in 1983 his father and grandfather bought him a gleaming new racing bike. He quickly showed great promise, above all as a climber, but in 1985 he suffered the first of a terrible series of accidents which were to dog his career, when he fell and broke his collarbone. Five years later, in 1990, he slid on an oil patch and dislocated his shoulder. But despite these setbacks, he racked up a series of wins, and his reward was a professional contract with the Carrera team (and clothing company) in 1992. His first Giro, in 1993, was as *gregario* for Claudio Chiappucci, and he retired after the eighteenth stage. Yet he was still virtually unknown among the public as large, especially outside of his home region of Emilia-Romagna. All this was soon to change.

I first became interested in cycling in the early 1990s, thanks to the extensive coverage of the Giro and the Tour, every spring and summer, on Italian television. State channels would dedicate hours to each stage, especially when the racing reached the mountains, and cycling was a talking point in the national press, in bars and in front rooms. Watching a month of a big stage race live on television was an emotional experience. It was like going on holiday without leaving your sofa. You saw towns and cities, from the air and from the ground, and you almost literally climbed up and flew down mountains alongside the cyclists and on motorbikes. It was thrilling. I soon had my own favourites, and, like most budding fans, I chose those cyclists who stood out, the ones who attacked, the climbers and the aggressive riders.

My first hero was Claudio Chiappucci, who revelled in solo breaks and came close to winning the Tour. I watched Gianno Bugno take two world championships in a row in the early 1990s, and dominate a Giro d'Italia where he led from start to finish. But the most exciting rider of all, by far, was Marco Pantani. To watch Pantani climb was like seeing someone fly uphill. He was so light, so fragile, so obviously damaged, and yet so powerful when the mountains came around. Pantanimania took over Italy from the mid-1990s onwards, as the private and public life of this unique sportsman became intertwined in a sort of soap opera. At his peak, Pantani stopped Italy in its tracks, as Coppi and Bartali had in the 1940s and 1950s. He achieved record audiences for hours of live sport, which also made him into a very marketable commodity indeed.

The year 1994 saw Pantani become a star in Italy, after two thrilling stage victories during the Giro. He won two big mountain stages and the climbs included the Stelvio (one of the places Coppi had made his own) and the Mortirolo. That week, 'Marco entered the everyday lives of millions.'[2] On the 1995 Tour, Pantani first revealed himself to the rest of the world with two more stunning mountain finishes in the French Alps and the Pyrenees. Two years later, in the 1997 Tour, he only lost thanks to German rider Jan Ullrich's dominance in the time trials, but he provided fans with the most memorable moment of the whole race, on the Alpe d'Huez. Gianni Mura, who would become the most powerful creator of the Pantani myth, wrote that 'he broke like the cyclists of old, those we had in our sticker albums, on the marbles we played with, in our dreams'.[3] That day he scaled eighteen of the twenty-one hairpin bends alone, and covered the 14.5-kilometre climb in just 37.35 minutes, breaking his own record. But Pantani was also thrilling in descent, shifting his torso off the seat to a terrifying position with his crotch millimetres away from the back wheel.

In his prime, Marco Pantani was one of the most extraordinary cyclists of modern times. He was 'a fantastic, unrepeatable creator of emotions'.[4] A climbing specialist, he usually performed poorly in time trials and was apt to crash frequently. To win any race, Pantani had to attack on the mountain stages. When on form, he would perform a kind of ritual striptease before attacking. He would tear off his trademark bandana or hat (his self-styled nickname was 'the Pirate') and sometimes chuck aside his glasses (and on one occasion even his diamond stud earring) and then attack on the foothills or as a big climb was about to begin.[5] The gauntlet thrown down, he was away. Once he had broken, nobody could live with him. Pantani, like Coppi, appeared to fly up those huge mountains, his light body propelled by perfect timing, and time was taken from his rivals in great chunks.[6] It was a thrilling sight, and it made Pantani a hero among cycling fans, and not just in Italy. He had a short time at the top, and he won very little in comparison with other great riders. As Mura has written, Merckx won more races in a year than Pantani did in his whole career, but when he did win, his riding was memorable, spectacular, tear-inducing.

In 1998, with the retirement of five-time winner Miguel Indurain, Pantani's time had come, and he destroyed Ullrich in the French Alps, taking seven minutes out of him on one stage. After he had won the Tour – the first Italian to do so for thirty years – Pantani became a superstar. He had come back from two horrific accidents in the same year (in May 1995 and during the Milan–Turin race in October 1995), the second of which had threatened to derail his whole career. Fans flocked to Cesenatico just for a glimpse of their hero. It seemed the beginning of a long and glorious career. Like Fausto Coppi, Pantani had won the Giro and the Tour in the same season. But he would never complete another Tour.

Pantani's long agony had really begun in June 1999, when he was at the height of his fame. It was the third-last stage of the Giro d'Italia, and Pantani appeared unbeatable. On the ride up the mountains to the plush ski resort of Madonna di Campiglio in north-eastern Italy, Pantani had swept past the group and any potential challengers. He was solidly in the lead with only two days of the race to go. The Giro d'Italia was in the bag, or so it seemed.

On the morning after that stage, Pantani was woken at 7.15 by a knock on his hotel room door, as were the other nine top riders on the Giro. It was the anti-doping team, led by Antonio Coccioni, International Commissioner of the UCI, and they wanted blood. Pantani's sample was taken at around 7.46 a.m. and then the team checked the samples. They were looking for indirect signs of EPO, and the test was a fairly simple one. EPO (eritropoietina) is a genetically engineered protein found naturally in the kidneys. If injected regularly, EPO stimulates bone marrow to produce more red-blood cells. An increased number of red cells boosts stamina by producing more oxygen. It also cuts recovery time to a minimum. This drug was widely used by top cyclists in the 1990s and was at first extremely hard to identify as a drug – given that it is something produced naturally by the human body.

In the late 1990s, an 'indirect' test was introduced which used a fairly arbitrary dividing line of 50 per cent (of red-blood cells) to indicate the presence of EPO in the blood. Pantani's blood that day came in at 53 per cent and 1 per cent was then taken off the final figure. Under the federation rules then in place (which had been backed by Pantani) he was immediately disqualified from cycling for fifteen days, and was therefore out of the race. At 9.40 a.m. Pantani was informed of the results, and at 10.12 an official announcement was made to the world. The whole Mercatone Uno team withdrew from the Giro. Pantani, bare-headed and grim-faced, walked through the crowd of *carabinieri* and photographers to his car. He told reporters on leaving the hotel 'this time I will not get up again', a reference to his many comebacks from serious injury. His hand was bandaged. Later it emerged that he had smashed it into a mirror in his hotel room after the test results had been announced. He was clearly not superstitious by nature. On another famous occasion, he had been injured during a race after hitting a black cat.

The 50 per cent blood rule had been devised partly to protect the health of riders said to be using EPO, as artificially high red-blood cell levels can easily lead to heart attacks and strokes. Cyclists using EPO would sometimes have to keep their heart monitors on all night in order to wake themselves up if the rate got too low for their own good. But the test was also designed as a warning to all those who took EPO. Unshaven and extremely upset, Pantani drove off at high speed. He was never to be the same cyclist again, or the same man. The EPO 'test' has been refined since 1999, but at that time was based in part on guesswork and on the average red-blood cell levels among cyclists. A level above 50 per cent proved nothing in itself, but the rules had been set.[7] On 9 June, Pantani held a press conference, an event which was broadcast live on Italian state radio and, in full, on TV half an hour later. The 'Pantani case' was huge news. It was a strange press conference. As one journalist wrote, nobody asked the question which was on everybody's lips. 'Had Pantani taken EPO, or not?'[8] In 1997 top rider Claudio Chiappucci had been suspended for the same reason just before the race began and missed the whole Giro as a result, and in 1998 Pantani's *gregario* Riccardo Forconi had been forced out of the Giro (won by Pantani) after his test was also found to be over 50 per cent, but the impact of those tests was nothing compared to Pantani's blood result. Neither of these incidents led to many headlines. Marco Pantani's ban was world news.

Pantani had seemed invincible. And in 1999, he probably was. He had always been a spectacular rider in the mountains, someone who stopped conversation in bars as he flew around the curves, bald head gleaming in the sun, leaving all others in his wake. But in the 1999 Giro, there was more. He dominated the race from the start. When his chain slipped off, he fixed it and still managed to win, speeding past some forty riders including Laurent Jalabert, who said: 'If I hadn't got out of the way, he'd have ridden right over me.'

Nobody else was getting a look-in. It was a triumph. For *La Repubblica*, Pantani had 'literally dominated this edition of the pink race'. The papers dubbed him a 'vampire', but the blood analogy would end up being a disturbing one. The penultimate mountain stage was to be the coronation of the undisputed king of cycling. As he rode up the winding path to Madonna di Campiglio, past the spectacular peaks of the Dolomiti di Brenta mountain ranges, Pantani knew he had won his second Giro in a row, and was set to rewrite the history books. He was five and a half minutes ahead in the race, and also held the *ciclamino* points jersey (and the King of the Mountains jersey), having won four stages. On 5 June *La Gazzetta dello Sport* had led with this huge (and perhaps, in the end, prophetic headline): *'Inebriati da Pantani'* (Intoxicated by Pantani). The edition of that paper was just reaching Madonna di Campiglio as Pantani left his hotel.

But instead of getting on his bike the next day to ride over the Gavia and the Mortirolo peaks, among thousands of adoring fans, Pantani was driven home to Cesenatico, and could only watch on television as another man – the unremembered Ivan Gotti – took his crown. Paolo Savoldelli, like Gimondi with Merckx thirty years earlier, refused to wear the pink jersey the day after Marco's ban ('for me Pantani is clean', he said). Savoldelli's own test results had been high during the Giro. The headlines the next day were very different from those of 5 June. *La Stampa* spoke in apocalyptic terms: 'It is the end of cycling as we know it.' The Giro itself took backstage, as Pantani's fate became *the* story. For Gianni Minà the 'race went on like a headless chicken . . . at a funereal pace'.

The evening before, Pantani had dined with veteran journalist Candido Cannavò, who had become a personal friend. On 8 June Cannavò, a fervent Catholic, wrote an editorial directed at Pantani. Its argument was eloquent: '*Nessuno di noi è assente dal peccato*' (Nobody is free of sin).[9] Cannavò called on Pantani to confess. But Pantani felt betrayed, in the newspaper which had made his name and which organised the Giro. He never forgot that article, and neither did his fans. It was to be one of many. Soon, judicial enquiries would open in a number of cities concerning Pantani's 'sporting fraud'. The subsequent trials would drag on for years. From 1999 onwards, Pantani was besieged by the media, the cycling authorities, the press and a number of investigating magistrates. Felice Gimondi, who was involved with the Bianchi bike company as well as with Marco's sponsor, Mercatone Uno, was one of the few people admitted to Pantani's hotel room that day. On leaving the hotel Gimondi said, 'I encouraged him. I reminded him of Merckx in 1969 in Savona, who was banned after a doping test and went on to win the Tour a month later. I can see that it is a terrible time for him and the team but I am sure that he will react like the champion he is.'

But many of those close to Pantani were more pessimistic about the effect of the scandal on the cyclist's fragile psyche. Giuseppe Martinelli, his sporting director, was spot-on in his comment: 'If I know Marco, he will never recover from this disgrace.' Pantani had come back from horrific injuries and bad luck on more than one occasion in the past, but this public humiliation would be too much for him to bear. Magistrates seized all the material and blood used in the tests and the results were confirmed by a laboratory in Parma. Meanwhile, Pantani and his entourage began to organise a media counter-offensive. On his way home he stopped at a hospital in Imola to have his blood tested again. Not surprisingly, it came in way below the crucial 50 per cent limit. Furious groups of 'Pantani's People' (or the 'people of the Pirate' as some newspapers called them) took to the streets in protest (many had spent all night in their cars and camper vans to see their hero on the mountain stage, in vain). Most were in shock. Five hundred cyclists and fans rode through Cesenatico in protest. As with so many other events in Italian sporting history, the Pantani case would divide Italians into two separate camps. No real dialogue between the two would ever be possible.

In 1999, most fans and journalists found their minds going back thirty years. As with Eddy Merckx in 1969, an anonymous hotel room was the setting for a doping scandal of earth-shattering proportions. And, as in 1969 with Merckx, Pantani was leading the race at the time, and was the overwhelming favourite for overall victory. Pantani had become almost Merckx-like in that Giro, winning a number of stages and dominating the race from start to finish. Like Merckx, again, Pantani protested his innocence and began to mutter about conspiracy theories. However, Merckx was very different from Pantani in one crucial way – his strength of character. While the Belgian rider bounced back immediately to crush his rivals in the Tour just weeks later, Pantani never recovered from the events of the 1999 Giro. Merckx was made a stronger cyclist and a stronger man by the events of 1969, but 1999 broke Pantani. Today, Merckx is a well-respected figure, a national hero in Belgium, and train stations and stamps are dedicated to him. Pantani is no longer with us.

For Pantani, unlike Merckx in 1969, there was to be no immediate comeback. He went home to Cesenatico, complete with its security door, and 'cried for days', according to his girlfriend. His house was surrounded by two hundred journalists and it was around that time – again, according to his girlfriend – that he began to consume 'industrial quantities' of cocaine. Pantani did not even ride in the 1999 Tour, let alone win it. In fact, he never won another big stage race. In less than five years, he would be dead.

Much rhetoric surrounded (and still surrounds) the events at Madonna di Campiglio in 1999. It is seen as *the* tragic turning point in one man's life. Many have claimed that Pantani 'was killed', 'died' or 'started to die' on 5 June 1999 at Campiglio, and not in February 2004 in Rimini. Pantani, from that moment on (but in particular, in retrospect, after 2004), has become a victim, not a protagonist, a hero or a criminal. Pantani was first a living martyr, with all the classic traits of martyrdom – real physical injury (from his many falls), persecution and humiliation in the media and the courts (Campiglio, the trials) and decline (his sporting failures).

Similar rhetoric has been used for the whole sport of cycling, whose final demise is also often dated back to 5 June 1999. Both Pantani and cycling itself, it is said, died that day, although both actually lived on. The irony was that in 1998, at the Tour, many commentators, journalists and experts had seen Pantani as the 'saviour of his sport'.[10] How wrong they all were. Now, less than a year later, he was being seen as the very antithesis of a saviour, as the man who had fatally undermined the sport.

After the tests at Madonna di Campiglio and his disqualification, Pantani's first reaction was an extreme one. He wanted nothing more to do with cycling. He didn't even want to get on a bike again. 'I don't want to hear anything about cycling and bikes. This is too much. I am a clean rider. Do they want to ruin me, to trick me?'

Later, he tried to make a comeback on numerous occasions, with varying degrees of success. He won a few more stages at the Tour (but none at the Giro), but he never again made a serious challenge for a major race. Pantani also spent a long time in courtrooms and in discussion with lawyers. He was tried on charges of 'sporting fraud' associated with his supposed drug-taking on two occasions. The judges in one case concluded that 'the fact was not a crime' (at the time it took place) but also argued that it was very probable that Pantani had indeed taken EPO. They also ruled that the correct procedures had been followed in 1999 which had led to his ban. Pantani was innocent under Italian law, but serious doubts remained over his conduct. In any case, the damage to his career and reputation had been immense.

Over the years, numerous conspiracy theories have been aired to explain the events of June 1999. The most absurd was contained in a letter sent by a notorious criminal from prison to Pantani's mother in 2007. Renato Vallanzasca wrote that a friend of his told him before the 1999 tests that he should bet on Pantani losing the race 'because he would certainly not win'. As with many other cycling mysteries – the deaths of Bottecchia and Coppi, for example – these conspiracy theories multiplied over the years. They were and are a potent factor in the contemporary portrait of Marco Pantani as a victim of obscure and dark forces, a martyr, a scapegoat for the crimes of others. But a number of alternative conspiracy theories about Pantani do not paint him as a victim. During the 1998 Giro, Pantani's *gregario* Forconi was excluded from the race after a time trial following blood tests. Pavel Tonkov, Pantani's rival for the title that year, hinted at the possibility that samples had been switched.[11] That day, officially, Marco's result came in at 49.3 per cent. He was sailing close to the wind, very close, even then.

It was St Valentine's Day 2004 when the concierge broke down the door of an upmarket seafront hotel residence – Le Rose – in Rimini, a place which no longer exists. A small barricade of furniture was blocking the way in. That February there were only a few guests in the place. The concierge had become suspicious after failing to see one particular guest for some time. On entering the small apartment, the police were confronted with a vision of chaos. Clothes were strewn everywhere and a small, shaven-headed thirty-four-year-old man lay face down on the carpet. He was wearing only a pair of trousers, and, it transpired, had died some hours earlier of what the doctors described as 'acute cocaine poisoning'. In 1998 the man who was now lying on that floor in Rimini had ridden into Paris in triumph, wearing the yellow jersey. *L'Equipe* had hailed him as something new, the saviour of cycling: 'nobody like him has been seen for at least forty years in this sport'.

That man was Marco Pantani, who, only five years earlier, had won both the Tour and the Giro in the same season. Pantani had just 'celebrated' his thirty-fourth birthday and he had been holed up in Rimini for five days. He had made a few phone calls to various pushers and had accepted a fatal delivery of 30 grammes of coke from a 'worker' earlier that day. The same 'worker' was later arrested in Naples and sentenced to five years for drug-related offences. Pantani had also purchased some heroin during his stay by the sea. During the last year of his life he had lived a nomadic existence, moving between Cuba, Predappio (a small town in Emilia-Romagna), Cesenatico and the fleshpots of the Adriatic Riviera.

After a birthday party on 13 January 2004 in Predappio, Pantani withdrew the equivalent of £15,000 from his account and left for Milan. After ten days in his manager Manuela Ronchi's house there, Pantani packed his bags. Ronchi called Pantani's father, who arrived in Milan only to have a furious argument with his son on the stairs. For some time, Pantani's parents had been trying to convince the former cyclist to check into a clinic for his drug addiction. Pantani moved to a hotel close to the station. He then called his manager without revealing where he was. After arranging to meet him, Pantani fled to Rimini in a taxi.

Controversy still surrounds the cyclist's death, and Pantani's mother continues to maintain that her son was murdered. She also blamed the press and cycling's governing body for his death. 'I knew,' she said, 'that my son would end up like Coppi.' In 2006 *L'Équipe* journalist Phillipe Brunel published a book which exposed a series of contradictions and doubts about the precise way in which Pantani died.[12] Magistrates had carried out a long and detailed investigation, and contemplated exhuming Pantani's body for further tests. For years, Pantani had been depressed, confused and lonely, and addicted to a variety of drugs. There can be no doubt that his life was a tormented one. His inner demons were strong. He once said that he rode quickly up mountains in order to 'shorten the agony'.

But was Pantani doped? Matt Rendell writes that 'everything that Marco had achieved between May 1994 and August 1995 had been chemically assisted' and, 'There is incontrovertible evidence that Marco's entire career was based on r-EPO abuse, which was both effective and, until 2001, undetectable by tests used in professional cycling.'[13] If he was guilty of using EPO, Pantani was not alone in this practice. There had been 'massive r-EPO abuse by a large section of the international cycling community to manipulate athletic performance'.[14] In Pantani's case much of the focus has been on the well-publicised abnormal readings from 1995 (a massive and dangerous 60.1 per cent after his crash during the Milan–Turin race[15]), and the famous 53 per cent from Campiglio in 1999. But the really devastating proof lies with the variations in blood figures, over time and in conjunction with big races and training sessions. In 2001 Pantani was given a six-month ban after a syringe with insulin was found in his hotel room. There is quite a lot of evidence that his drug use contributed to his sense of despair. Many cyclists from the 1980s and 1990s have suffered from clinical depression, and some have committed or attempted suicide.

Why was Pantani never able to recover from the events of June 1999? After all, many other cyclists had been suspended or banned, had served their time (in his case, this was only fifteen days) and had returned to the sport. One answer lay with Pantani's personality, his paranoia, his 'obsessive-compulsive disorder'. But an analysis of Pantani's own conspiracy theories with regard to the events at Campiglio is also helpful in this context. Digging deeper (and beyond the paranoia) the 'conspiracy' was not to do with

being 'found positive' for any specific drug (he wasn't) or even with
being disqualified. It wasn't to do with what happened as much as
with when it happened. What really angered and depressed him
was his conviction that the test results had been 'timed' to coincide with his total domination of a big race – and to take that
victory away from him. He won very little in his entire career, and
he had fought back from a series of horrific accidents – and then
Campiglio ended everything, to his mind at least. In some ways,
this was paranoia. In others, it was not. Other conspiracy theories
were created or fuelled by Pantani's entourage. His agent's book
is an extended version of various conspiracy theories.[16] Pantani's
fans were also enthusiastic supporters of these theories. Perhaps
this is not so surprising in a society where official institutions lack
legitimacy and it often seems reasonable not to trust them, and to
assume that they don't act impartially. This applies to all parts of
the state machine, including drug-testing agencies.

After Pantani's death in 2004, Candido Cannavò's mind went back to
June 1999. 'Pantani the hero left the hotel escorted by two *carabinieri*.
And I felt that cycling was finished, for ever. One thing is certain, it
was the end of Pantani.' After that moment, according to Cannavò,
who knew Pantani well, he 'saw enemies everywhere' and 'his self-
destructive personality took over'. Cannavò was brutally honest about
Pantani's use of doping. 'We don't know what kind of champion
Pantani would have been without his poisoned and enhanced blood.'

Marco Pantani's funeral on 18 February 2004 was compared by
many to those linked to other great sporting tragedies in Italy – that
of the *Grande Torino* football team in 1949, that of Fausto Coppi in
1960 and that of the victims of the Heysel tragedy in 1985. It was
said that 'the whole of Italy came to a halt' and Cannavò wrote of
a 'lost hero who we all adored'.[17] Many cycling greats turned up,
including Gimondi, Motta, Gaul, Adorni, Moser and Bugno. His
coffin was carried by some of his faithful *gregari* as more than 20,000
people thronged the church.

Today, Marco Pantani is remembered in a number of ways. Hundreds of people visit his resting place in Cesenatico and there are at least twenty monuments dedicated to his memory across Italy (including a fairly hideous one on the Mortirolo). Every Giro now has its Pantani Pass and he has also been discussed and remembered in books, articles, films and special videos.[18] The most extraordinary monument of all stands near Imola, where a huge four-metre-high replica marble with an image of Pantani dominates the landscape next to the A14 motorway.[19] In the 1960s and 1970s children would often play on the beach or in the courtyard with plastic marbles with figures of cyclists inside, constructing complicated courses and little Giros for their heroes. Pantani's massive monument was a homage to this passion (which has died out) and to the myth of 'the Little Elephant' (l'Elefantino).

Cycling on Trial. Doping in the Italian Courts

'Clean cycling is an illusion'
— *Francesco Moser,* L'Équipe, *1999*

In 1999 Marco Pantani's very public humiliation forced the authorities into action. Some fifteen years after Moser's record in Mexico, Dr Francesco Conconi and some of his assistants were placed under investigation, their offices raided and their computers searched. Many of the files found on Conconi's computer contained evidence relating to the blood levels of famous athletes, including Claudio Chiappucci and Pantani. It seemed that a crackdown on doping in sport, and in cycling in particular, had finally begun in earnest. The widespread use of EPO, blood doping, growth hormones and testosterone had brought cycling to the edge of collapse, in particularly in the main cycling countries which ran their own important national races – Italy, Spain and France.

Preliminary investigations into the Conconi case closed in 2000, but the trial only began in October 2003, with far fewer athletes involved than expected and with a much weaker list of 'crimes' than had originally been anticipated. Procedural changes had led to frustrating delays and many journalists lost patience with the whole affair. The case slipped out of the media spotlight (as happens so often with interminable Italian trials). These delays helped Conconi and his associates, as the statute of limitations was fixed at seven and a half years from the most recent 'crime'. The legal process had to be completed within this period for a conviction to be valid. The start date was originally set as August 1995, the date of the most recent file found on Conconi's computer, with its blood values relating to various athletes.[1] Many of the results seemed to show consistent variations in blood values around the time of competitions – clear evidence of sophisticated doping systems. But despite this evidence it proved very difficult for the public prosecutor, Pierguido Soprani, to bring in his case. During the trial Soprani argued that 'state doping' had been organised via Conconi's lab, but the laws in place in the 1980s and 1990s had not defined doping as a crime. According to the public prosecutor, Conconi even experimented with EPO on himself.

The Conconi legal process dragged on for years, and was weighed down by technical and legal issues. In the end, the only charge to survive the lengthy legal process was that of 'sporting fraud'. The trial ended in an anti-climax, with a verdict which few understood. For the court, Conconi was guilty of doping-related offences, but these crimes had fallen under the statute of limitations. Too much time had passed between the original crimes and the final sentence. This was a familiar story. The painfully slow and inefficient justice system in Italy often brought the statute of limitations into play, and wealthy suspects could use the rules to their advantage through their well-paid lawyers.

Conconi, therefore, was technically 'not guilty' and had no criminal record. As the trial process finally came to an end, however, the judge took the unprecedented step of labelling Conconi, and his two colleagues, Ilario Casoni and Giovanni Grazzi, 'morally guilty' of the promotion of doping in sports. This statement betrayed frustration with the trial's outcome, and the lack of a clear-cut verdict allowed all those involved to claim that they had been cleared of all wrongdoing. When the sentence was pronounced in November 2003, there was a great deal of disappointment. Many felt that a great opportunity had been wasted. Claudio Gregori, one of the most outspoken critics of doping in cycling, wrote in *La Gazzetta dello Sport* that 'the cover-up is complete'. Conconi was overjoyed. 'I have helped sport, and not doped athletes.'[2]

This was the worst of all outcomes for those looking to clean up cycling, and Conconi continued his sparkling academic career, giving interviews to all the major papers as if nothing had happened. The trials had exposed a system of institutional doping, sponsored and paid for by the Italian sporting authorities in order to improve results, but nobody appeared to be guilty of anything. Conconi was not a maverick working outside the system, but a crucial cog in the wheel. He was also a powerful man, with influential friends. One of his associates was Romano Prodi, Prime Minister of Italy on various occasions in the 1990s and 2000s and former head of the huge state conglomerate IRI.

Despite the outcome of the Ferrara trial, the Conconi investigation opened up a can of worms which was difficult for the authorities (if not the general public) to ignore. In 1999, during questioning (by the *carabinieri*) in relation to the Conconi case, Moser made this shock confession: 'Yes, I was subject to blood transfusions . . . thanks to Conconi and Ferrari. Up until 1985. This was sporting medicine, but others would like to call it doping . . . In any case more dangerous substances are used today, like eritropoietina erythropoetine [EPO].'[3] The famous hour record had taken place in part thanks to blood manipulation; 1984 had seen the introduction of new forms of deceit for financial and sporting gain. By the 1990s, almost everyone would be at it.

Moser's confession brings into play another key figure in the story of doping and cycling in Italy in the 1990s and 2000s: Dr Michele Ferrari, who had also been part of the Conconi–Moser back-up team during the 1984 world record attempt in Mexico. Later, Ferrari became almost as infamous (and sought after) as Conconi himself and he acquired two nicknames, *testarossa* (red head) and *il mito* (the myth). Over the years, Ferrari worked with dozens of other top cyclists. Here are some of his declarations to the press: 'It is only doping when the tests say it is,' 'Ninety per cent of the drugs which are seen as doping don't help performance, they make it worse,' 'I don't prescribe eritropoietina [EPO], but I justify the use of it,' 'In the world of cycling doping is everywhere and many of these drugs have terrible side-effects, but doping is useless, it doesn't help,' 'Banning things doesn't work, it just exposes the athletes to more risks.'

What did this all mean? Were all those who had worked with Ferrari and Conconi using forms of blood-related doping, including USA star Lance Armstrong? According to the judge in Ferrara, the use of doping was widespread and institutionalised. And this did not apply to cycling alone.

Conconi had first started to work with CONI, the Italian Olympic Committee and central Italian sporting institution (funded directly by the government), in 1980. From his base in his laboratory in Ferrara he began to collaborate with a whole series of athletes in a wide variety of sports. Moser's record provided Conconi with a high level of media visibility, and other sporting stars, inspired by Moser's surprising and remunerative success, flocked to Ferrara. The list of names reads like a roll-call of Italian sporting victories in the 1980s and 1990s: Alberto Cova (10,000 metres world champion, 1984 Olympics), cyclists of the calibre of Pantani, Evgeni Berzin, Chiappucci, Stephen Roche, Gianni Bugno, the Olympic walking champion Maurizio Damilano as well as many of the cross-country skiers in the 1994 Winter Olympics (in which Italy did very well). Even minor sports like bowls and canoeing were involved. The suspicion was that, by the 1980s, it was not the best sportsmen or women who were winning, but those with the best doctors.

In its reporting on the investigations and trial, *La Repubblica* concluded that there had been a system of 'doping which was planned, researched, organised and carried out by those sporting authorities who were supposed to be carrying forward the struggle *against* doping'.[4] It was not surprising, perhaps, that so many tests over the years had proved to be negative, if the governing sports body was allegedly pursuing an official 'doping' policy for its own top athletes, and paying huge sums to finance that policy. Conconi's laboratory received some 170 million lire a year in the 1995–8 period. Only a few individuals stood up to this system, such as athletics coach Sandro Donati, who warned over the possible health risks of 'uncontrolled' EPO doping and later encouraged the anti-drugs programme under which Marco Pantani would be suspended 'for health reasons' in sensational circumstances in 1999.

In 2004, Ferrari, like Conconi (and Pantani himself), was put on trial by the Italian state. A court in Bologna later decided that he was guilty of 'sporting fraud . . . linked to pharmacological doping' and he was given a twelve-month prison sentence. But on appeal, in May 2006, the original sentence was overturned (largely for techni-cal and legalistic reasons). The appeal court found that the charge of sporting fraud had fallen under the statute of limitations while the issue of 'doping' was dropped altogether. Once again, as with Conconi, thanks to the inefficiency of the system Ferrari was able to claim that he had not committed any crime. After the first sentence, Lance Armstrong had issued a statement in support of Ferrari, call-ing him a 'friend'. The same statement added that Armstrong's team was suspending all links with Ferrari. Despite their verdicts, the Conconi, Ferrari and Pantani trials unearthed a wealth of evidence about doping practices in sport. By the end of the 1990s, it was clear that the problem of doping was not so much sporadic as endemic.

Neither Pantani's shock ban nor his death put a stop to the wave of doping. As testing improved, more and more cyclists tested positive. In recent years, doping scandals have led to bans for the winners of the Giro – in 2006 (Ivan Basso), 2007 (Danilo Di Luca) and the second-placed rider in the 2008 Giro (Riccardo Riccò). And these were just the most well-known cases. By the twenty-first century it was quite difficult to find Italian cyclists who had not, at one time or another, been tested positive and been suspended. Blood tests had first been brought in in 1997, and the testing programme has become more and more accurate and extensive in recent years. There is a wealth of evidence that doping was more or less common practice in the peloton throughout the whole of the 1990s.

Synthetically produced blood hormone drugs were the key to this hegemony. For a long time they were more or less impossible to test for directly (a test for synthetic EPO was only devised in the twenty-first century) as they are produced naturally in and by the body. For years, only rough indirect evidence could be used to 'locate' them (such as oxygen levels in the blood, the figure which led to Pantani's ban in 1999). Forms of blood doping were often combined with a whole series of strategies aimed at hiding the fact that doping had taken place – masking agents, fake blood, the corruption of the anti-doping agencies, financial and political pressure brought to bear on the cycling authorities. Top doctors and scientists worked as dopers, keeping themselves one step ahead of the testers. In the end, the authorities were forced to resort to police-state methods in order to clamp down on something in which almost everyone was involved. Tests became random, and common. 'Biological passports' were introduced, with constantly updated information from a whole series of tests. Cars, houses, hotel rooms and laboratories were searched, cyclists, doctors, team managers and even cyclists' wives were arrested and interrogated. Riders had to keep the cycling authorities informed of their every movement, every training session, every weekend away, and if they didn't suspicions were raised.

In the early period of cycling, drugs were taken to provide short-term energy boosts and little more (and the consequent 'down' after stimulant use could do as much harm as good). Early 'home-made' techniques were almost certainly not the difference between winning and losing. Doping became more and more sophisticated over time in line with medical progress. A lot of money was there to be made from helping top athletes to win. In the era of Coppi, it was said, the effect of stimulants was like that of a better kind of petrol (for a short time). But by the 1990s, doping was creating a whole new engine for its users. The best dopers won consistently, until, that is, they were caught. With scientifically based blood doping, which began to come in during the 1980s, the effects of the treatment were longer lasting and more balanced (and they could be turned on and off almost at will so as to avoid detection). Blood doping gave athletes more stamina, not necessarily more speed, and did not have the downside of stimulants (at least in the short run). Blood doping thus used natural elements or synthetic copies of substances produced by the body to create super-cyclists.

Vested interests also meant that penalties were too mild. Memories were short. Those caught doping were not ostracised. With time, they were rehabilitated. For all the talk of a 'war on doping', the rhetoric and the calls for instant justice after every case, the world of cycling could not and would not break with its heroes and its stars. In 2008 I attended the presentation of that year's Giro d'Italia in Milan. It was a glittering occasion, full of journalists and cycling stars from past and present. Felice Gimondi and Fiorenzo Magni were there, and Paolo Bettini was the star, having just won the world championship. The theatre was packed. But the contradictions were evident. Danilo Di Luca, for example, was actually on stage, despite a recent ban for doping. But the most contradictory moment of all involved Marco Pantani, and his memory. A special prize was awarded in his honour, and a film about him was shown. The beatification of Pantani was the worst way possible to carry forward the fight against doping, presenting him as a saint and conveniently excising the dark side of his career, and his life, from the record books. Wild applause greeted the Pantani section of the event, but I felt uneasy. If this was the official face of the Giro, what hope was there for this sport?[5]

Ever since the demise of Marco Pantani, the story of Italian and international cycling has developed into a long series of 'doping scandals'. To give a sense of the tragedy which has engulfed this 'sport', here are descriptions of some of the most important cases.

Ivan Basso was the golden boy of Italian cycling, and was tipped to take over from Lance Armstrong at the Tour. He was third at the Tour in 2004 behind Armstrong and second (again behind the American) in 2005. Alarm bells started to ring in June 2006, when he was barred from the Tour along with other top stars due to links with the colossal Fuentes scandal, which was also known as *Operación Puerto* (Operation Mountain Pass). A large quantity of blood (some one hundred or so 'portions') had been found at Dr Eufemiano Fuentes' house in Spain in May 2006, along with code names identifying the cyclists who had received transfusions. One of the sacks of blood was linked to the code name 'Birillo', which was the name of Ivan Basso's dog. Earlier in 2006 Basso had (easily) won the Giro. In 2007 he was given a two-year ban after his blood was discovered in a fridge in Dr Fuentes' clinic. Basso admitted donating his blood and a charge of 'attempted doping' (after an initial denial), but claimed that he had never actually used performance enhancing drugs or hormones. In the 2009 Giro, after returning from his ban, he finished fifth. Gilberto Simoni had aired his suspicions after Basso's dominance in 2006, calling his performances 'extraterrestrial'. Basso had won that Giro by over nine minutes, more than any rider since 1965. He would win again, much less impressively, in 2010.

Danilo Di Luca won the Giro in 2007 (the first rider from the south to do so) and was second in 2009. On 22 July 2009, it was announced that Di Luca had tested positive for CERA (a new form of EPO) on two occasions during the Giro. His positive tests were confirmed and he was also given a two-year ban. The winners of the Giro in 2006 and 2007 had thus both been caught on doping charges and been given long bans. The damage to the sport was immense.

But the whole of the 1990s and 2000s had been riddled with doping scandals. To cite just a few of these cases: Francesco Casagrande tested positive for testosterone in March 1998, as did Rodolfo Massi of Italy (cortisone) during the 1998 Tour de France.

Massi was kicked out of the Tour (and it was particularly embarrassing that he was King of the Mountains at the time) and arrested
by police. Some claimed that he was 'one of the peloton's drug deal-
ers'. In 2005 another Italian rider suffered the indignity of being
thrown out of the Tour during the race. Dario Frigo's wife's car
was stopped as it crossed a border and EPO was discovered. Both
husband and wife were taken into custody. Later, a French court
gave the couple a six-month suspended prison sentence. It was the
end of Frigo's cycling career. Another new 'golden boy', Riccardo
Riccò, was also thrown out of the Tour in 2008 (after a positive test
following the time trial), although by the time he was banned he
had won two stages. He admitted to taking a new form of EPO.
Riccò had finished second in the Giro that year, exciting a new
generation of fans. His ban was later reduced to twenty months,
and he returned to racing in 2010. In February 2011 he nearly died
after injecting himself with his own blood, kept in his fridge.[6] And
the list goes on. There is no point in laying out all the names here.
It becomes boring, like all lists. Everyone, or nearly everyone, has
been caught at it, at one time or another.[7]

Few of the winners of the Giro in the 1990s and 2000s were free
from doping scandals. Many had received bans. Nobody was actually stripped of a title they had won (although this is more or less
what happened to Pantani in 1999) but suspicion fell on all riders,
even those who were not actually convicted of doping crimes. The
courts had also got involved, creating confusion between sporting
justice and criminal justice. Lack of confidence in the doping testers, the authorities who were meant to be combating the doping and
the courts, meant two things. First, it was seen as acceptable simply
to dismiss the verdicts of any of these bodies as politically inspired
and/or part of conspiracies either within cycling or in a wider sense.
Second, a lack of confidence in the institutions designed to apply
laws, rules and regulations meant that suspicion fell on all riders, all
the time. Just because somebody had not been found positive for

performance-enhancing drugs, this did not mean that he had not taken them. Maybe they had just got lucky, perhaps they had friends in high places, or fewer enemies than some of the other riders; possibly they were better at hiding their doping, or avoiding testing, or they had found the right 'doper'.

Whatever the reason, the combination of widespread drug use and delegitimised institutions in Italy was catastrophic for the image of the sport. Nobody believed that cycling was clean any more, or that there was any hope that it ever would be: if this was a sport in which nearly everyone was cheating most of the time, what was the point of watching it, or getting excited about who was winning, or becoming a fan of one cyclist or another? The same could well have been said of Italian football in the 1990s, where an organised system of corruption and match-fixing had been uncovered, the likes of which had never been seen before in international sport.

Given the fact that cycling was in a deep crisis of its own making, but also that many fans still loved watching cycling and taking part in the sport, a compromise was needed. Thus, the history of cycling became more and more significant to its followers, who drank in the nostalgia of the past in order to quench their thirst for fan participation. Memories of a sporting golden age became more important than the present-day Giro, and sales of books and films about the past continued to grow. This was particularly true for *La Gazzetta*, which cleverly used history – of which it was both a protagonist and a custodian – to boost its income and popular interest in the Giro. A second way out of the dilemma created by the fact that nobody believed in the sport they were watching any more was to resort to endless chat and discussion. The race itself was marginalised in favour of argument, polemic and 'debates'. As with football, the sport mattered less and less, and certainly much less than the pronouncements of managers, pundits, journalists and cyclists. While the journalists of the 1950s and 1960s were experts in telling their readers what had happened, with TV this was no longer necessary. The viewers had seen everything already, repeated *ad nauseam*. So journalists wrote about other things to do with cycling: tactics, arguments, personalities, the cyclists' wives. By taking refuge in never-ending punditry, analysis and debate, the cycling itself could safely be ignored.[8]

Route of the centenary Giro d'Italia, 2009

FRANCE

GERMANY

SWITZERLAND

AUSTRIA

HUNGARY

Alpe di Siusi

Bressanone Brixen

San Martino di Castrozza

SLOVENIA

Morbegno

Valdobbiadene

Bergamo

Milan

Padua

Grado

Jesolo

CROATIA

Venice

Turin

Pinerolo

Arenzano

Sestri Levante

Bologna

Faenza

BOSNIA HERZEGOVINA

Cuneo

Riomaggiore

Forlì

Lido di Camaiore

Florence

Campi Bisenzio

Monte Petrano

CORSICA
(France)

Chieti

Rome

Sulmona

Blockhaus

Anagni

SARDINIA

Benevento

Bari

Naples

Avellino

Vesuvio

Cagliari

Stages

Finish ●◀——○ *Start*

●——○
Time trial

Palermo

● Reggio Calabria

SICILY

ALGERIA

TUNISIA

9–31 May 2009. The race started on the Lido in Venice and finished in Rome.

The Post-modern Age: Sprinters and Cowboys

As cycling entered the post-modern age, it was clear that this was not just a sport which had changed, but a different kind of sport altogether. After Marco Pantani, Italian cycling tended to give birth to riders capable of winning big one-day races. It also spawned a series of brilliant sprinters. One of these riders stood out from all the others, for his talent, his voracious appetite for victory, his glamorous image and his larger-than-life personality. 'Super Mario' Cipollini was from Lucca in Tuscany, an hour's drive from Fiorenzo Magni's birthplace and not too far from Gino Bartali's stamping ground outside Florence. Tall and powerfully built, he could do one thing extremely well: sprint. Cipollini came into his own in the very last part of every stage, perfectly set up by his teammates, who 'prepared the sprint for him'. The sight of him crossing the finish line first, his massively long arms high in the air in triumph, became a familiar one for cycling fans across the world.

'Super Mario' wasn't particularly interested in the other parts of the big races. He never finished a Tour de France, although he would sometimes crawl through the mountain stages in the Giro, waiting for more flat stages and more sprints. In a glittering career his striking outfits and enormous hair would cross the line first on numerous occasions (191 times, to be precise), and his victories included a world championship and a Milan–San Remo (both in his magnificent season of 2002). Even his nicknames were spectacular, 'the Lion King' (another reference to the big hair) and 'Super Mario' (after the video game character).

By the time he retired (after an ill-fated and short-lived come-back), Cipollini had won a record forty-two stages at the Giro (beating Binda), as well as twelve stages at the Tour.[1] He was the perfect rider for the post-modern, televisual sport cycling had become. With fewer and fewer successful breaks coming to frui-tion, and the dominance of the teams, more and more races ended up being decided at the sprint. Teams now had this down to a fine art, and specialist *gregari* were assigned the role of preparing the sprint, which required perfect timing and positional sense. In this brave new world, Cipollini was a superstar. He dressed eccentrically for the cameras (and was sometimes even fined for his increasingly absurd outfits) and played up to his film-star and playboy image. He would turn up in tight-fitting suits as a zebra or a tiger. The organisers of the Tour and the Vuelta lost patience with his antics after a while, and he was excluded from the Tour on a number of occasions. The governing body feared it was becoming a circus.

Yet for all its apparent frivolity, Cipollini's career was not with-out its dark side. Like almost all the cyclists of his generation he was associated with doping, and his name was linked to some of the documents in Spain which were unearthed in the infamous Fuentes scandal.[2] However, he did not test positive during his career. Officially, he was clean. In 2007 Cipollini was put on trial for tax evasion by the Italian state. The tax authorities argued that he had 'pretended' to live abroad (in Monaco) and had therefore avoided paying tax on millions of euros of earnings. In reality, it appears that Cipollini actually lived in Tuscany, where his two daughters went to school.[3] Although he appealed against the court's decision, Cipollini was in the end forced to pay up. In 2009 he was given a twenty-two-month sentence by a court in Lucca for 'failing to declare tax in 2003 and 2004'. The sums involved were enormous: nearly two million euros of earnings and half a million euros which should have been declared. The amount Cipollini would now have to pay, including interest and fines, would be almost a million euros.[4] In recent years, a similar fate has befallen other Italian celebrities such as motorcycle riders Valentino Rossi and Max Biaggi and the opera singer Luciano Pavarotti. However, in June 2010, Cipollini was cleared on appeal as the judges decided that he had been living in Monte Carlo after all, and thus 'should have been paying his taxes in that principality'.[5] Despite this legal process, Cipollini's popularity remains sky-high in Italy and abroad.

The cycling of Cipollini was also a sport played out on a global stage. Cyclists no longer emerged from the harsh poverty of rural Italy. That Italy was long gone. In a globalised world, the new stars were often from wealthy backgrounds, and from places never before associated with cycling – such as Texas.

Lance Armstrong has had a long and fruitful association with Italy, and Italian cycling. But his rapport with *il bel paese* has not always been easy, and it was marked by terrible tragedy on the Tour, in 1995. Marco Pantani had a particularly difficult relationship with Armstrong. Lance admired the Italian rider, and the two rode up Mont Ventoux together in 2000. Most commentators agree that Armstrong allowed Pantani to win that stage, out of respect. Gianni Mura wrote that 'Pantani won [the stage] because Armstrong is a true gentleman'. But Pantani himself was offended by the very idea that such a thing could have happened, and continued to criticise Armstrong without citing him by name. Pantani was also said to have been offended by Armstrong's references to his hated nick-name, '*l'Elefantino*'. He usually called him 'the American'. In the end, on that Tour, Pantani pulled out, and Armstrong went on to win again. But their rivalry was, to say the least, short-lived.

Lance Armstrong cut his cycling teeth in Italy. In 1992, after a strong performance in the Olympics, he won a contract with the Italian-based Motorola team. He then went on to win the world championships at the age of twenty-one in Oslo in 1993. Between

1992 and 1995 he lived for a time in a modest flat in Como and then stayed in a hotel in the lakeside town of Bellagio, close to the famous Ghisallo climb, the national cycling museum and the church dedicated to cyclists.[6] Neighbours in Como remembered Armstrong as being quiet and reserved. He did his own cleaning and spoke passable Italian. His training would often include a lap of the lake, 180 kilometres in all, after a cappuccino in the local bar. Local residents also remember him sunbathing on his fourth-floor balcony in the summer, or bumping into him, covered in sweat, in the corridor after his training sessions on the static bike (what Italians call *i rulli*) he had set up in the basement.

In 2009 Armstrong returned to cycling after retiring following his record seventh win in the 2005 Tour. He was thirty-seven years old and the big stage race in which he chose to make his comeback was the Giro d'Italia, partly as preparation for the Tour which followed. It was to be the first time he had ever ridden in the Giro. Armstrong's stated reason for returning to the sport was to raise awareness of cancer, but his competitive spirit had certainly not diminished. He was unpaid and his blood tests were due to be announced online. But things went wrong right from the start of that season. In a mass pile-up during the 2009 Vuelta a Castilla y León he crashed and broke his collarbone, a classic cycling injury which had also befallen Fausto Coppi. Yet, just four days after an operation in the USA, Armstrong was, in trademark fashion, back on his bike. He started the Giro on 9 May and rode solidly throughout, finishing in twelfth place overall (nearly sixteen minutes back from the winner, Denis Menchov of Russia) without winning a stage. Armstrong's decision to ride the Giro created a media circus the like of which had rarely been seen, and reawakened world interest in the Giro.

La Gazzetta, of course, was overjoyed at the publicity. A journalist was given a special mission – to follow Armstrong every day, and produce daily bulletins on everything he did, however mundane. In the race itself, Armstrong's lack of training prevented him from challenging for overall victory, even if he had wanted to do so. At times he reminded observers of the older Coppi, riding along in the group, a shadow of himself. Later it became more and more obvious that he was using the Giro to train himself up for the Tour. People, including fans, began to criticise the American: 'Why did he come here at all?'[7] He took few risks. All this showed a lack of respect for the Italian race, but at least he was there, for the first time, at nearly thirty-eight, back in the pack, carrying his own water bottles, riding for his teammate.[8] And he rode the whole race, at times looking very strong. He went on to finish third overall at the Tour that year. Armstrong had made some good friends as a young rider in Italy. One of these was a promising young rider, Fabio Casartelli.

A chirpy, dedicated cyclist, Fabio Casartelli's career took off at the 1992 Barcelona Olympics, where he won the gold medal, aged only twenty-two, in the road race category. Casartelli's medal caught the attention of the Motorola team, who offered the young rider a contract in the 1994 season. He was to start off as a supporting rider, a *gregario*. As a lowly member of his team, Casartelli's main job was to sustain the team's leading light, the promising young American Lance Armstrong. The two became firm friends in the lead-up to the 1995 tour, as Armstrong now lived and trained in Italy.

The fifteenth stage of the Tour – held on 18 July 1995 – was bathed in sunshine. That day's route consisted of a number of medium-sized climbs in the Pyrenees. It was a tough route, adapted to specialist climbers (and not, at that time, to Armstrong). Casartelli's main job that day, as usual, was to help his team captain limit any time losses to the overall leaders.

Road cycling is a dangerous sport. Riders move across slippery and bumpy roads at high speed. In the mountains, these dangers are multiplied. At speeds of up to 80 kilometres an hour, surrounded by other cyclists, cars, motorbikes and thousands of excited spectators, one slip can lead to major injury. Roads are usually unprotected, and there is the ever-present fear of shooting off the side of a steep mountain. On that day Casartelli was coming down a winding mountain road on the Col du Portet d'Aspet with a group of other cyclists. It was about 11.45 in the morning. As he made a left turn, someone slipped, bringing other riders down with him. Casartelli fell awkwardly, cracking his skull against one of the stone blocks erected to prevent cars going off the road. He was not wearing a helmet and, as the other cyclists came to his aid, they knew the injury was a serious one. The ambulance duly arrived, but nothing could be done.[9]

Fabio Casartelli was pronounced dead after suffering three heart attacks in the helicopter on the way to the hospital. He was only twenty-four, and had just become a father. Since his death, helmets have (after much prevarication) been made obligatory. Casartelli was the third cyclist to die on the Tour since it began in 1903, and the first Italian. His bicycle was later taken to the shrine dedicated to his memory at the cycle museum at Madonna del Ghisallo.

Out on the road, however, the race was still going on. The Tour organisers took the extremely controversial decision not to cancel that day's events, or to inform the riders on the road of the earlier crash (some, however, were told by their teams). French rider Richard Virenque duly won the stage, and celebrated as the usual victory ceremonies went ahead.

As the riders came off the course, many burst into tears on hearing the news of Casartelli's death. A meeting was held that night at which many argued that the next day's racing should be cancelled. In the end, financial pressures were too great, and the show went on. However, the riders had decided to honour the death of their colleague in a different way. First, all 130 of them held a minute's silence. Then, at each intermediate stage, a rider from Casartelli's team was allowed forward to win, and the final stage saw the riders in formation. Finally, at the finish line, Casartelli's only Italian teammate came forward to 'win' the stage as the rest of the peloton looked on. All the prize money from that day was donated to the Casartelli family. It was a moving tribute, and fitting testimony to the close-knit nature of the peloton. Gianni Mura called that stage 'a funeral which lasted for 237 km' as the riders decided to subvert the event, very simply, by not racing against each other. They merely covered the ground they had to cover, in order to get to the end of the stage.

Lance Armstrong was devastated by the news of the death of his friend. During a later stage at Limoges, two days after the accident, he burst from a small group eighteen miles from the finish line to win. As he crossed the line, Armstrong pointed to the sky with both hands, as a tribute to Casartelli. He later said: 'Today's win was not for me, or my sponsor or even for my country, it was simply for Fabio and his family . . . I rode so fast because I had four legs today, mine and Fabio's.' Gianni Mura wrote eloquently about this beautiful gesture: 'Today the heart of the Tour (and I suppose this is rhetoric) has started to beat again in a more normal way, on the road, under the sky.'[10] Mura, Italy's most distinguished sports journalist, has always had a soft spot for Armstrong and this affection derives from the events following Casartelli's death on the Tour, as well as Armstrong's own well-known return from illness to win the French race seven times, victories reported by Mura in *La Repubblica*.

Fabio Casartelli is now remembered by a monument at the spot where he died. Usually, whenever the Tour passes through there, the riders stop and stand in silence for a few minutes. Each year the Tour organisers hold a ceremony for the dead rider. Armstrong has made a point of helping Casartelli's young wife Annalisa and son, and has never forgotten the sacrifice of his teammate, even as he went on to recover from cancer to become one of the greatest cyclists of all time.

But Lance Armstrong's relationship with Italy and Italian cycling has also had repercussions arising from the issue which has dominated the sport since the 1990s: doping. In July 2004, he was the undisputed king of the Tour, the most powerful rider in the peloton, and well on his way to a sixth consecutive victory. Filippo Simeoni was a journeyman rider, born in the same year as Armstrong. He was good enough to become Italian champion in 2008 and to win a couple of stages at the Vuelta, but he was no threat to Armstrong as a cyclist. In that Tour a dispute between these two men became national news, and it was a disagreement that was played out in public, during the race itself, in front of the TV cameras.

It was the eighteenth stage and five riders had broken from the pack. Simeoni cycled out to join the break and then something extraordinary happened. Armstrong, the race leader, rode out on his own towards the small pack of cyclists up ahead. This was unusual to say the least, and commentators at the time were baffled. Armstrong's lone break caused chaos and confusion in the peloton. The break-away riders were equally nonplussed. With Armstrong among them they had no chance of succeeding in their break, and would soon be pulled back in. The five pleaded with Armstrong to go back to the group, but he refused, apparently saying that Simeoni had to come back with him as well.[11] This is what eventually happened. Simeoni openly criticised Armstrong, saying, 'he shouldn't worry about little cyclists like me', while Armstrong claimed he had been 'protecting the interests of the peloton', a phrase which could be interpreted in many different ways. The truth was that Armstrong had a bone to pick with Simeoni and he had publicly humiliated him, exhibiting his power over the group in a stark way. Later in the race, Simeoni took a kind of revenge on the Texan by forcing Armstrong's team to catch him on numerous occasions in the final stage of the race, which is usually seen as a wave-by for the winner. The two men were already at war in the courts, and now that struggle was being transposed on to the Tour itself, and being played out in a very public way.

The origins of the spat go back to the confessions and statements made by Filippo Simeoni with regard to Dr Michele Ferrari, who had been investigated and put on trial by the Italian judicial authorities. In 2002 Simeoni claimed that Ferrari had shown him how to use EPO and human growth hormones during 1996 and 1997. In court he repeated his allegations, and admitted that he had been involved in doping for a number of years. Armstrong, who had worked with Dr Ferrari for some time, accused Simeoni of being a 'liar' in an interview with *L'Equipe* in 2003. After this statement, Simeoni then cited Armstrong for defamation. Armstrong publicly defended Ferrari after he was found guilty in the first trial, but he also ended his professional relationship with the doctor, declaring his opposition to all forms of doping in sport. In the end, Ferrari was cleared on appeal.

This intricate quarrel led directly to the bizarre events during the 2004 Tour, where it appeared as if Armstrong was punishing Simeoni for things he had said to the press and the magistrates. None of this was without consequence back in Italy. For a time, it appeared as if Armstrong would be prosecuted for witness intimidation (which would have been one of the most extraordinary cases of 'witness intimidation' in legal history, taking place, as it did, during the Tour de France itself, on bikes). This charge was never brought, however. In the end, the defamation charges also came to nothing. Armstrong later regretted what he had done that day on the Tour, and the way it affected his relationship with Ferrari and Simeoni. But by then it was too late.

The furore would not die down. In 2009, in an unprecedented decision, Simeoni's team was not invited to participate in the Giro. In itself, this was not unusual, but what was strange was that Simeoni was the current national champion, the wearer of the Italian jersey (but he was also thirty-seven years old, a fact which may have played a part in this decision). Normally such riders are expected to ride the Giro. Some journalists argued that Simeoni had been excluded as a favour to Armstrong, who would be riding the Giro for the first time and had brought a huge publicity machine with him to the race. Simeoni handed back his Italian championship jersey in protest and Armstrong's ride in the Giro turned out to be something of a damp squib. He would not return in 2010.

The 2010 Giro encapsulated the contradictions of cycling, today, in Italy. The race was a rip-roaring success, especially its attempts to recreate the past with some stages on dirt tracks and non-asphalted roads. The faces of the cyclists after one such stage reminded some fans of cyclists in the 1950s and 1960s, when the sport was 'anti-quated, heroic, exhausting, and covered with sweat'.[12] On the last stage of the race the riders entered the Arena di Verona, an extraordi-nary setting. The place was packed to the rafters. Cycling, it seemed, had survived. The Giro still had the ability to move people. But the winner of that race was Ivan Basso, a talented rider who had just returned from a long ban following charges of doping. The crowd cheered him to the rafters, but his very presence underlined the problems still faced by the sport.

Conclusion: Bikes, Italy and the Sport of Cycling

'Goodbye, bicycle'
– Gianni Brera, 1964

'Coppi is still alive'
– Rino Negri, 2006

On the other side of Milan from Renzo Zanazzi's bar-shrine there is a potent symbol of the power cycling once held over the Italian popular imagination. Close to what was once the city's trade fair, an area currently undergoing controversial redevelopment, there is a covered, oval building which looks a little like a football stadium. As you walk around the outside, you can peer in through the gaps in the stands. A banked wooden track runs in front of numerous stands. It becomes apparent that this is not a football stadium at all, and for anyone who knows anything about cycling it is obviously a velodrome, a place built especially for track racing. In fact the Vigorelli, as it is known, was opened in 1935, when it replaced a previous cycling stadium nearby.[1] The wood of the track was so perfect that some compared it to a classic northern Italian violin, the Stradivarius.

For years, the Velodromo Vigorelli was a place of pilgrimage for cycling fans, a kind of Mecca, an exalted place: '*La Scala del ciclismo*'. Italy's biggest race of all, the Giro d'Italia, often finished here in spring, when the velodrome hosted the lap of honour and the winner's ceremonies. Track races were common, weekly events. Six-day (and night) racing packed out the stands, in a heady mixture of sweat and glamour, smoke and noise. Fausto Coppi broke the world one-hour record here, in 1942, in dramatic circumstances, as Allied bombs rained down on the city. One bomb later hit the track itself. Six new hour records were set on the 397-metre banked track between 1935 and 1958. After the war this was where cycling enthusiasts would come to see their heroes close up, either during the sprint finishes to great one-day races, such as the autumn Giro di Lombardia, or in special exhibition events. Coppi was at home here, as was Gino Bartali. In the 1960s and 1970s Antonio Maspes would train at the Vigorelli every morning, and then race there for money and in national and international competitions. The Vigorelli was also a celebrated concert venue, hosting a rare (for Italy) Beatles performance in 1965 and an infamous riot during and after a Led Zeppelin concert in 1971, as well as innumerable political meetings. This whole urban area is rich in cycling and sporting history. The nearby Arena stadium, built under the reign of Napoleon in the early nineteenth century, was often selected as the site for the end of the last stage of the Giro d'Italia, and also hosted the Italian football team's first ever game, in May 1910.

In the 1970s, almost invisibly, the Vigorelli went into steep decline. Suddenly, it seemed, as that decade came to an end, that nobody wanted to pay to watch track cycling any more, or any kind of cycling for that matter. Fewer and fewer races were held there, financial losses mounted, the track was expensive to maintain and the velodrome was closed. Heavy snowfall in 1985 did great damage to the sloping roof. Millions were then spent on a costly restoration programme, and the track was renamed and remarketed, but to no avail. After a time, the owners were forced to accept the truth: nobody wanted the velodrome, neither the spectators, nor the riders. A legendary sporting venue therefore simply shut its doors and began to rust and rot, slowly, in the open air.

It was as if Wembley or the Bernabéu were closed down, standing like abandoned monuments, in the centre of their respective cities, ignored even by passers-by. Today, the Vigorelli is almost always locked up, and it is very quiet.

The fate of Italy's velodromes, once the urban heartbeat of a national sport, is a potent reminder of how other activities (above all football and motorsport) have overtaken cycling for spectators and fans. All over Italy, similar stories could be told of beautiful and famous tracks that had been left to rot, or simply pulled down. This was the case in Mantua, where the track around the football stadium once used by 1930s champion and local hero Learco Guerra was quietly torn out, without a whimper of protest. In Rome, the cycling stadium from the 1960 Olympics in the EUR district lay overgrown and abandoned for years, and the same was true of an expensive velodrome built for the 1976 track world championships near Lecce in the south of Italy. From a Mecca for cyclists, the Velodromo Vigorelli (or the Velodromo Maspes Vigorelli as it was now officially called) became a kind of real Italian-based Mecca in July 2008. That summer a long-running dispute over the construction of a mosque in Milan was (briefly) resolved with the decision to allow Muslims in the city to pray inside the old cycling track area.

Once it had all been so different. Velodromes were arenas in which fans touched their heroes, covered them with kisses and awarded them garlands of flowers, and booed their rivals. It was in these places that this most democratic of sports paid homage to its followers. Today, such velodromes are no more than distant memories. Those that remain standing are testimony to a once great sport fallen on hard times, a religion lacking in followers, or even in preachers, a passion spent. They are monuments to the past, looking down like the Ozymandias of Shelley's poem: 'Nothing beside remains. Round the decay of that colossal wreck, boundless and bare, The lone and level sands stretch far away.' Today only a small specialist bike shop cut into the walls of the former stadium in Milan allows a glimpse into the sport's glorious past, with the stories told by its owner and the fading photographs of Coppi and Bartali on the walls.[2]

Cycling history is full of tales of epic feats, often involving individual riders breaking away and covering huge distances on their own. These moments have become the stuff of legend: as with Gino Bartali's mountain victories in the 1948 Tour de France, Fausto Coppi's lone 190-kilometre ride during the 1949 Giro d'Italia, Charly Gaul's snow-ridden break near Trento in 1956, Eddy Merckx in the driving rain in 1968, Lance Armstrong's triumphs in the French mountains. Cycling fans are obsessives, linking themselves (and their lives) to individual riders and celebrating mythical feats with plaques, monuments, stories and anniversaries.[3] The potent memory of cycling prowess – and of its many disasters – is an essential part of its appeal. The sport also has something intrinsically proletarian and democratic about it. Much of a race can still be seen for nothing. The Giro and the Tour come to the people, to their main streets or through their fields. It gives them a glimpse of their heroes, and their villains. All they have to do is step outside their front door to watch the peloton ride by. Then it has gone, but next year, at around the same time, the ritual will be repeated. It is one that has captured the imagination of millions of Italians, created an annual, month-long party. It is the Giro d'Italia, and the history of Italy should not be written without alluding to it.

Italians took to professional cycling almost from the very beginning, and the sport became a mass obsession in the inter-war years. They identified with bike racing for a number of reasons. Many Italians cycled to work right up to the 1960s and also worked on their bikes. The bicycle signified work. Moreover, the very terrain of Italy, with its mountains, foothills, plains, lakes and spectacular views, encouraged cyclists to take to their bikes and 'conquer' the same peaks as their heroes. The development of the Giro d'Italia made cycling into a national sport.

By the 1920s, cycling was already big business, and the fact that some of the key bike manufacturers were Italian was another reason for this development. Cycling soon had a regular season, running from March to September, and bounded by two one-day classics, both organised by *La Gazzetta dello Sport*, Italy's main sporting newspaper. The Milan–San Remo began the season and the Giro di Lombardia, 'the race of the falling leaves', ended it. In the middle were the Giro d'Italia, the Tour and the Vuelta, the three great national stage races. If you were a cycling fan, you could watch or follow races for seven months a year. Each local area began to promote its own races, and some even managed to organise stage-based competitions. In the sport's heyday, thousands of one-day races, little Giri and exhibition races sprung up all over Italy, but very few of these became part of the annual calendar for long. With the decline of cycling as a popular sport in the 1980s and 1990s, many of these races faded as viable entities. Other races with long traditions and histories died out over time, such as the Milan–Turin, which was too short and flat to work with the increased speed of the sport.

Italian cycling was organised around rituals which transformed it into a potent form of civil religion. Each Giro d'Italia stage and one-day classic had its own set of traditions and histories, with appropriate nods to the memory and achievements of past cyclists who had ridden the same route. Certain mountains became known for past valiant rides, and the highest mountain on the Giro every year is now dubbed the 'Coppi Pass', in honour of Fausto Coppi.

Cyclists taking part in the Giro were not just riding in an annual race; they were taking part in the creation and recreation of historical, national and regional narratives. These stories were embellished and transformed every year, becoming compelling myths, reinforced by nostalgia, commemoration and constant retelling. Following the Giro in person was a perfect way of understanding and experiencing Italy, and of writing about what 'Italy' was. Cycling journalists seized this opportunity with relish, filing articles which contained as much about the type of truffles and Barbaresco they had tasted on route as about the cyclists and races they were supposed to be covering. They saw the Giro as a sociological and cultural mirror, a powerful means of seeing and explaining a country which many regarded as being inexplicably and irrevocably divided. It was rare for a race not to be accompanied by personal, political and international debates which went way beyond cycling itself.

If cycling was a means of creating consent, it also had its own 'organic intellectuals'.[4] The mass of cycling fans were from the working class and the peasantry, but the sport attracted writers, journalists, artists, poets, photographers and film-makers. These intellectuals did not just follow cycling in an abstract fashion, they wrote about it and contributed to its popularity. Many dedicated weeks of their lives to the Giro, filing daily bulletins for their readers. No sport in Italy, before or since, has attracted such a wealth of words. Numerous novels have been dedicated to cyclists and cycling.[5] All the most celebrated Italian journalists – and not just sports journalists – wrote about the Giro. Often these articles became books. They are now regarded as literature.

In following the Giro, these writers became part of the Giro d'Italia itself. The race was not just about its riders. It was a collection of elements which created a show, a circus, an event which was then narrated, explained and debated through the media and via its fans. Journalists and writers were seen in cars, they followed the course, they mixed with cyclists, managers, fans and in turn had their own readers, followers and fans. Many of these intellectuals claimed that they 'knew nothing' about cycling itself, but others saw themselves as experts.

Il Corriere della Sera, Italy's most respected and high-quality daily newspaper, based in the cycling capital Milan, was home to the greatest of these writer journalists. Orio Vergani (later followed by his son Guido) set a precedent for the likes of Dino Buzzati (novelist, journalist, artist) and Indro Montanelli. Readers of *La Repubblica* from the 1970s onwards were lucky enough to be able to follow Mario Fossati's magisterial contributions on cycling and it continues to publish the elegant and caustic prose of Gianni Mura, who specialises in reporting from the Tour.[6] Mura's dispatches from France, with their mixture of gastronomy (Mura and his wife also write a regular food column for the newspaper), geography, history and cycling have become a model for new sports journalism. *La Gazzetta dello Sport* was always the first port of call for cycling fans, with Bruno Raschi as the prince of the cycling journalists. Gianni Brera, the most original and influential of Italy's sporting journalists, published the most lyrical study of the sport yet, based on his hero Fausto Coppi. His *Coppi e il diavolo* was years ahead of its time.

For some, the journalists themselves were a 'second peloton'. All had a strong sense of belonging, but were also rivals where scoops, interviews and stories were concerned. Each stage was reconstructed as a little story, a narrative, often with the journalists themselves at its centre. Cycling itself was not crucial to these articles, and they were often seen as pieces of pure literature, or as ways of informing readers about Italy itself, not just the outcome of a cycling race.

Sports journalists were also often seen as intellectuals, especially those with a grander, rhetorical style. Among these were *Gazzetta* writers such as Bruno Roghi, Bruno Raschi (so important that he travelled in the car of the patron of the Giro, Vincenzo Torriani), Luigi Gianoli and Gianni Brera. Claudio Gregori and Marco Pastonesi advanced this great tradition into the *Gazzetta* of the 1980s, 1990s and 2000s. Pastonesi specialised in the stories of the non-stars of the sport, the slaves, the lowly *gregari*.

Journalistic teams divided up their tasks. Some gave a purely technical account of the race, others did interviews. Yet others – the stars, those known as 'the big signatures' in Italy – were seen as being above such menial work. They were expected to provide an insight into the bigger picture, the context, an overall analysis of strategy and tactics, to write poetically about the decline of a once great champion, perhaps, or the struggles of a *gregario*, and, of course, to reflect on Italy itself.

Technology revolutionised the way the Giro was understood and organised. Radio reported on cycling from 1932 onwards. In 1951, a special radio car started to follow the race in order to transmit information back to the press room. TV began transmitting from the Giro in 1957. The medium for following the tour was important, as the familiar radio commentaries of Mario Ferretti were replaced in the early 1960s by the booming voice of Adriano De Zan, an evocative and technically competent commentator who would employ rhetoric (and burst into tears) with very little prompting. De Zan commentated on dozens of Giros until the 1990s. For a time, his son took over the commentary on a rival, commercial station.

New rituals were constructed in the television age. The astonishing success of the daily Giro programme *Il Processo alla tappa* in the 1960s, with its mix of technical analysis of each day's events, gossip, interviews and highlights, was crucial to this process. Fronted by Sergio Zavoli, *Il Processo alla tappa* reinvented the language used by television to understand sport, with interviews from motorbikes (which were later banned after accusations that the riders were being distracted), spectacular shots of races and contributions from intellectual fans such as Pier Paolo Pasolini, Dino Buzzati, Roland Barthes, Luciano Bianciardi and Vasco Pratolini. The programme also made a number of ex-cyclists into stars in their new roles as pundits, and brought the voices and faces of the riders themselves into Italy's homes. Cycling had always been spectacular. In the 1960s, it became part of the 'society of spectacle'.

Television made hills, towns and finish lines familiar to those who had not and never would visit them. All this was done at the pace of a bike journey, as Italy was viewed from cars, motorbikes and, later, helicopters. Cycling also created myriad opportunities for sponsorship and product placement. The 'caravan' of the early television age was aimed at the public on the streets and at home. Later, advertising became more subtle, offering brand identification. By the 1990s, Marco Pantani's shirt and hat were covered in a whole range of symbols and names.

Memories were linked to Italy itself. Many people found that the

Giro spoke to them of the past, envoking nostalgic memories of previous races and of the past in general. For the journalist and writer Marcello Venturi (famous above all for his book about the Cefalonia massacre of 1943, which would later form the basis of Louis de Bernières' *Captain Corelli's Mandolin*), who covered the 1955 Giro, 'sport and nostalgia are inextricably linked . . . the Giro d'Italia is also a way of going back into history'.[7] Another writer who followed the Giro in the 1990s made a similar point: 'The Giro is a land of memory.'[8] Gianni Brera looked back on past Giri as 'the epoch of the poor' and another great cycling journalist argued that 'Giro d'Italia is also a way of revisiting our own sense of poverty'. In the 1950s Brera had already written a book entitled *Addio bicicletta* (*Goodbye to the Bicycle*). Nostalgia for a golden age was embedded in the experience of the Giro. Cyclists were continually compared with their predecessors, whose epic feats were enveloped in myth.[9] As with the Tour, the Giro 'suggests "links", "memories" . . . via the memory of a country'.[10] It is a 'genuinely national institution . . . a *lieu de mémoire*, a generator and repository of popular national symbols and myths'.[11]

When they sat in those cars that followed the riders up and down the country, writers saw an Italy which, in the big cities anyway, had disappeared. They reported on an Italy of the provinces, a normal, working-class or peasant Italy that participated in and viewed the Giro as an opportunity to have a party. When Venturi's Giro passed through Viareggio in Tuscany in 1955 he saw crowds of 'workers in their work suits, who had just left the factory'.[12] Photographers picked up on this, with innumerable images of priests and nuns jostling for space alongside kids and the town mayor, as the Giro came through. In such towns, Giro time was carnival time. People ate cake in the open air by the sea and drank wine, waiting for the cyclists to speed by. Cycling was a people's sport, a sport for the working class and the peasantry. But was this a provincial Italy or a strong, unified nation? Some have argued that for a long time cycling was experienced above all as a local sport. It did 'not speak a national language'.[13]

For some writers, then, following the Giro was a way of rediscovering a 'true', provincial, rural Italy. Vasco Pratolini, the Florentine novelist who worked as a correspondent on the Giro in 1947 and then again in 1955, wrote: 'I will discover Italy, a country made up of fields, seas, mountains, land and skies, a young Italy . . . I will uncover our fatherland spread out as a set of fields and skies, seas, mountains, lands, different and surprising at every view from the motorway, at every turn in the road.' For Pratolini, following the Giro gave a better understanding of Italy than any analysis of an election or a referendum. The Italy which presented itself to him, from the caravan behind the cyclists, was an Italy of workers, peasants, cycling fans, 'a provincial people'. But Pratolini also saw the Giro as a kind of holiday, as well as a re-evocation of his childhood, an opportunity to wallow in nostalgia.[14] So the Giro revealed a 'true' Italy but it also unveiled an Italy which had been overtaken in the cities (where most of the journalists lived). Correspondents were often shocked at the poverty they came across while following the race.

Yet the Giro was never just a 'mirror', as Mario Fossati called it. The accounts of Italy told through the Giro were always representations, filtered through the imagination and the culture of the urban journalists, the cycling hacks and the fascinated intellectuals who followed the race.

Every year, the Giro route showed Italians where Italy was. It mapped out their own country for them, it 'made the Italians travel'.[15] Racers conquered hills (scollinare) but the hills also conquered them. Sometimes, the geography was too much, the weather too bad to carry on. Snow in Trentino forced half the field to pull out in 1956 and entire stages were abandoned in other years. Mountains and climbs took on their own personalities – they were 'terrible', a 'wall', 'mythical'. Amateur cyclists rode up these peaks and took photos at the top. Just covering the ground was enough for many. Geography was reinvented by great epic rides. Italy never created a myth to rival that of the Mont Ventoux, but it came close with the hairpins of the Stelvio climb.

Cycling also united Italians against 'foreigners'. Victories abroad created a sense of national pride, particularly at the Tour. The national rivalries with France, and the invasion of France by Italy in 1940 (as well as the subsequent participation of French troops in the war in Italy after 1943) gave a special edge to this sporting rivalry. In the immediate post-war years, things got quite nasty at the Tour. Yet cycling could also bring people together. Fausto Coppi has been seen as someone who helped to bring about 'at a popular level, something of a rapprochement between France and Italy' after the Second World War.[16] Cycling could be a forum in which a European ideal could be played out, moving beyond the nationalist divisions which had led to two world wars in thirty years.

For the Giro, rivalries between Italians split fans and led to bitter debate, but national sentiments re-emerged when foreign cyclists began to challenge for victory in the 1940s. In such cases, Italian fans would often put aside their personal differences to cheer for an Italian against a foreigner. Nonetheless, it was the cycling that really mattered, and the great foreign stars were hugely popular, and had their own fans in Italy – from the first foreigner to win the Giro, the Swiss rider Hugo Koblet in 1950, through a whole series of star riders such as Bobet, Gaul, Kübler, Anquetil, Merckx, Indurain, Hinault and Roche.

So the Giro both created and reflected Italy at the same time. Social and geographical change permeated and affected the race. From the dirt tracks of the early races, the riders increasingly had the luxury of asphalt roads, and even motorways to ride on. One third of the 1938 Giro was still not ridden on asphalt, and riders often complained that they were 'drowning in dust'. In early races, it was often impossible to see who was riding, and very difficult for the riders themselves to see where they were going. As Italy was modernised, so was the Giro. Developments in the manufacturing of clothing, bikes, motorbikes, TV cameras, cameras and cars changed the way the race was experienced and represented.

But the Giro only gave hints of an insight into Italy. It encouraged superficiality, as images flashed by – a priest, a man with a
dog, peasants working the field. It was thus perfect for the creative
journalistic poetry of writers like Pratolini or Buzzati, but hardly
encouraged (nor could it do so) any real, deep research into the
way Italy was changing. Rather, it tended to create a vast amount
of rhetoric. In this way, the Giro was a short cut to real investiga-
tive journalism or writing. It often appeared as if these writers
were writing about Italy, were saying something profound, but
this was not always the case. The Giro often provided a superficial
view, a postcard Italy, a set of clichés linked together – the provinces, the fields, the churches, the bell towers . . . and then the
next set of images. What the correspondents were watching was
a film, unedited, and not particularly well shot. It was, as Ortese
wrote 'walls, wind, memory'. After all, the Giro did not stay long
enough to make any lasting impact. It turned up, and the next day
it was on its way. In many studies, the link between real changes
and the Giro has often been hyped up and taken as read, just as
it was at the time. Journalists and writers liked to think that they
were analysing how Italy was changing, but this was not always
the case.

Cycling was Italy's most popular sport, in a country obsessed
with sport, for more than sixty years. Every year the Giro d'Italia
attracted millions of spectators. Cyclists became popular heroes.
Most came from grinding poverty, and many had learnt to ride
delivering bread, groceries or letters, or riding hundreds of kilometres to and from building sites or factories. Cycling and work
were inextricably linked. The bike was an everyday object, instantly
recognisable. Everyone understood what it meant to ride uphill,
and downhill.

Very quickly, the sport's stars became national figures, household
names – Ganna, Gerbi, Girardengo, Binda, Guerra, Bartali. In 1946,
Fausto Coppi's ride in the Milan–San Remo was so important that it

threatened to wipe out the memory of the war itself. It was through the Coppi–Bartali rivalry that cycling reached a popularity never seen before or since. Society, politics, culture, sexual mores, religious differences and ethnic divisions were played out through and exacerbated by a sporting rivalry which was never simply about sport. It is still widely believed that the victory of an Italian cyclist in 1948 in the Tour de France did much to prevent civil war in the country. Outdated adultery and divorce laws were discredited and reformed after the way they were used to harass Coppi and his married lover. And arguments rage, even today, about who passed who *that* bottle.

In the early sixties, a social and cultural revolution took place. Italians abandoned the rural lives that had been their lot for thousands of years. TV game shows had, as their top prize, not a Bianchi or a Legnano but a Fiat 500. Italy invented, produced and sold millions of Vespas and Lambrettas. Super-highways criss-crossed the country, carrying families on holiday with their bags piled on top of their tiny vehicles. Geography and landscape became less mysterious. There was no more need for the Giro to 'explain' Italy to the Italians. They could see their own country for themselves now, from the window of a car or from the back of a scooter. Other, more glamorous sports – football, motor racing, skiing – which were less exhausting and made you much more money, began to take over. Ferrari fans began to outnumber those following the great cycle races.

It was to take years for cycling as an activity to make a comeback, although bikes never went away in certain parts of Italy, in particular in the flat, small, cycle-friendly cities of the Po Valley – Ferrara, Parma, Forlì. By the 1980s, Italy's cities had become ecologically unsustainable. There were too many cars, too much traffic, too few parking spaces, too much movement, far too much pollution. Car ownership in northern Italy rivalled that of Los Angeles. Local councils in Italy, as in the rest of the world, struggled to find solutions to these problems. The car lobby was potent, and there was resistance to any restriction on motor-car activity. Steps were taken in the right direction in the 1980s. City centres were 'closed' to traffic (although this closure was at best partial) and some free cycle schemes were introduced. But these policies were half-hearted and met with bitter opposition. Milan's free 'yellow bike' scheme in the 1980s was such a farcical failure that all such similar schemes were scotched for the following thirty years, and cycling itself was discredited. Cyclists themselves did not help. Hardly anyone wore a helmet, or reflective clothing. Many regularly rode on pavements (often for self-preservation, admittedly) and jumped red lights.

Cycle lanes in the big cities were rare and, when they were to be found, absurdly planned. Milan was perhaps the most extreme example of an anti-cycling city, with its notional 23 kilometres of cycle lanes, as compared to over 900 kilometres in a similar city like Vienna, or 500 kilometres in Freiburg. Even in places (such as wide central boulevards) where a cycle lane would have been easy to create, they were notable by their absence, or blocked by parked cars, bollards or pedestrians. The problem went to the very heart of the way a city was managed and understood. When roads were rebuilt or planned, they were usually done so without cycle lanes even being considered as an option, despite a law which obliged councils to insert bike paths when restoring roads.

But cyclists were not taking all this lying down. At a number of levels, Italy's bike lovers fought back against motorised hegemony. In Milan and other cities, from the 1990s onwards, every Thursday night cyclists joined together to ride slowly and noisily through the middle of the city, infuriating car drivers stuck behind them. This was Milan's version of critical mass, an urban happening, a political statement and a physical activity, all at the same time. Politically, these groups were in part inspired by the Dutch Provos of the 1960s, who advocated free cycles in all cities and dreamt of white bicycles on motorways. These semi-spontaneous groups of bikers adopted a wide-ranging critique of consumer society, and used the bicycle as an ecological weapon in the daily battle against pollution and motor-car-based accidents. At last, local and national administrators were forced to act, especially as pollution reached record levels.

A number of popular 'car-free Sundays' were held in Italian cities, through which citizens rediscovered their streets, and were at last able (if only for a day) to cycle or walk through them without fear of accident or need to wear a face mask.

By the early twenty-first century there were an estimated thirty million bicycles in Italy (not far short of the thirty-two million motor vehicles) and annual national production was 3.2 million, with 1.7 million bikes sold in 2000 alone. The bike had become a statement of intent and of change, a way of transforming everyday life and the future of urban transport. Riding a bike thus became a political issue, a way of challenging the arrogance of motorists, who had constructed Italy in their own image, and entirely for their use. But this form of politics was relatively detached from the sport of cycling, which took place in privileged circumstances (roads without traffic) and in a rarefied world of sponsors and technological advances. The bike had made a comeback, but the sport of cycling remained stuck in its past (albeit a glorious one), and struggled to recover from a doping epidemic which had turned many fans away.

This fightback was not limited to cyclists on the streets. Manufacturers also attempted to deal with the perils of urban cycling. Milan's brilliant bike designer Cinelli produced something called the Bootleg. The very philosophy of this bike was one which promoted survival in the city. The tyres were too big to get caught in treacherous tramlines, and the frame and wheel design made the bike capable of nipping through traffic, but strong enough to withstand the stress of Milan's cobblestones. The capital of design and fashion was putting these qualities to good use in the daily battle for space on her mean streets, and for the hearts and minds of her residents. Unexpectedly, things started to change. When Milan's centre-right council introduced a free bike scheme (this time the bikes were orange, not yellow) in 2008, it was, against all expectations, a great success. Free orange bikes appeared everywhere, and the council was forced to install new parking points because of high demand. There was a future without cars, but the road towards it was still full of pitfalls.[17]

As I left Renzo Zanazzi's little basement bar in Milan some years ago, before I started to write this book, blinking in the harsh sunlight and struggling to make my voice heard above the roar of the traffic, the images dotted all around the walls of the bar remained with me. Fausto Coppi smiling, standing next to his brother Serse, his face caked in mud. Zanazzi himself, young and fresh-faced, with his own, less illustrious cycling brother, and Gino Bartali, the 'man of iron', powering up yet another mountainside on the way to yet another victory. The golden age of Italian cycling was short but glorious. At its peak, Italian cycling provided its millions of passionate fans with moments of joy and wonder but also times of heartbreak and huge disappointment. Today, that sport is no longer with us. Renzo Zanazzi's bar will one day be closed down, and its pictures will be removed from the walls and sold off or thrown away. Yet the memories of that golden age will live on, and, when histories of Italy are written, they should always find a place for cycling, the bike and those great sporting heroes of the past. Despite everything, now in his eighties, Renzo Zanazzi is still out there, riding his bike every day, whatever the weather. His passion survived through the years. *Pedalare! Pedalare!*

Appendix 1

Coppi on his bike. Life on two wheels – his daily training regime (Novi Ligure, late 1940s, early 1950s)

5 a.m.	Wake up (*gregari* woken by Cavanna banging his stick on the door)
	For the *gregari*, 60-kilometre time trial alone
6 a.m.	Breakfast. Tea, cakes, orange juice (other riders at that time filled up with rice and steak)
7.30 a.m.	Go to Novi Ligure or Tortona
9 a.m.	Wednesday and Friday mornings: long training runs of 180–220 kilometres, water, bread rolls
12.30 p.m.	Return, massage (by Cavanna), salt bath
2–4 p.m.	Siesta, followed by tea and biscuits
5 p.m.	Novi Ligure
7–7.30pm	Dinner (no alcohol)
9.30–10 p.m.	(at the latest) Bed (9 p.m. for *gregari*)

Other rules: no walking, ever.

Appendix 2

Tour de France, 1948
Palmiro Togliatti shot (Rome),
11.30, 14 July 1948

Stage date	Stage details	Winner	Second place	Overall leader
15 July	Cannes–Briançon (274 kilometres)	Gino Bartali (10 hours, 9 minutes, 38 seconds)	Briek Schotte (6.18 behind)	Louison Bobet (Bartali second at 1.06)
16 July	Briançon–Aix-les-Bains (263 kilometres)	Gino Bartali (9 hours, 30 minutes, 14 seconds)	Constant Ockers (5.53 behind)	Bartali (Bobet second at 8.03)
18 July	Aix-les-Bains–Lausanne (256 kilometres)	Gino Bartali (8 hours, 29 minutes, 55 seconds)	Briek Schotte (1.18 behind)	Bartali (Bobet second at 13.47)

Appendix 3

Luigi Malabrocca (1920–2006), record of defeat/victory in the battle for last place and the overall black jersey, 1946–9

1946 Giro d'Italia. Last: 4 hours, 9 minutes, 34 seconds behind the winner (Gino Bartali)

1947 Giro d'Italia. Last: 5 hours, 52 minutes, 50 seconds behind the winner (Fausto Coppi)

1949 Giro d'Italia. Second to last: 7 hours, 47 minutes, 26 seconds behind the winner (Fausto Coppi)

Other 'winners' of the black shirt:

1948 Aldo Bini
1949 Sante Carollo
1950 Mario Gestri
1951 Giovanni Pinarello

Renzo Zanazzi finished last in the Giro d'Italia in 1952, but by then the black shirt was no longer part of the race.

Appendix 4

Fiorenzo Magni's victories in the Tour of Flanders, 1949–51

Year	Winner	Second Place	Third Place	Distance
1949	Fiorenzo Magni 7 hours, 21 minutes	Valère Olivier @ same time	Briek Schotte @ same time	260 kilometres
1950	Fiorenzo Magni 8 hours, 15 minutes	Briek Schotte @ 2 minutes, 15 seconds	Louis Caput @ 9 minutes, 20 seconds	273 kilometres
1951	Fiorenzo Magni 7 hours, 43 minutes, 3 seconds	Barnard Gauthier @ 5 minutes, 35 seconds	Attilio Redolfi @ 10 minutes, 32 seconds	274 kilometres

Notes

INTRODUCTION

1 'Discorso di Sua Santità Pio XII per l'accensione della lampada votiva destinata alla celeste patrona dei ciclisti, Palazzo Pontificio di Castel Gandolfo – Mercoledì, 13 ottobre 1948', in *Discorsi e Radiomessaggi di Sua Santità Pio XII*, X, Decimo anno di Pontificato, 2 marzo 1948–1 marzo 1949, Tipografia Poliglotta Vaticana, Rome, p. 257.

2 The local priest at the time, Don Ermelindo Viganò, whose statue stands nearby, was the inspiration behind this unusual blessing of his church on the hill top. In 2009 this relay was repeated in order to celebrate the events of 1948–9.

CHAPTER 1

1 Italians sometimes claim, incorrectly, that Leonardo Da Vinci invented the bicycle.

2 See Stefano Pivato, 'Tour e Giro: una storia comparativa', and Saverio Battente, 'Biciclette e impresa economica', in Gianni Silei, ed., *Il Giro d'Italia e la società italiana*, Piero Laicata Editore, Manduria/Bari/Rome, 2010, pp. 31–44 and pp. 101–24. For the international history of the bicycle, see David Herlihy, *Bicycle. The History*, Yale University Press, New Haven, 2004. For Italy see Guido Vergani, ed., *L'uomo a due ruote. Avventura, storia e passione*, Electa, Milan, 1987.

3 Gaetano Bonetta, *Corpo e nazione. L'educazione ginnastica igienica e sessuale nell'Italia liberale*, Franco Angeli, Milan, 1990, p. 17.

4 See ibid., pp. 230–41.

5 The French newspaper was *l'Auto*, which later became *l'Équipe*.

6 *La punzonatura* also took place for the big one-day classics organised by *La Gazzetta*, the Milan–San Remo, the Milan–Turin and the Giro di Lombardia.

When the race began in another city, for example in Palermo in 1949, *la punzonatura* was moved to that city. After 1960, the starting stage has changed frequently and the ritual of *la punzonatura* fell into disuse.

7 Claudio Gregori, *Luigi Ganna. Il romanzo del vincitore del primo Giro d'Italia del 1909*, EditVallardi, Milan, 2009. See also Paolo Facchinetti, 'La grande avventura', in Gino Cervi and Paolo Facchinetti, *Il Giro d'Italia. Strade, storie, oggetti di un mito*, Bolis Edizioni, Azzano San Paolo, 2009, pp. 9–25, *Cronache del primo Giro d'Italia*, Otto/Novecento, Milan, 2010.

8 Gregori, *Luigi Ganna*, pp. 14–20. For the Milan–San Remo see Enzo Baroni and Cesare Pesenti, *Milano–San Remo. 100 anni leggendari*, RCS Sport, Milan, 2007.

9 Grant Jarvie and Joseph Maguire, *Sport and Leisure in Social Thought*, Routledge, London, 1994, p. 117.

10 Antonio Lorenzini, *I ciclisti rossi. I loro scopi e la loro organizzazione*, Ditta Fratelli Cesarani, Caravaggio, Bergamo, 1913, p. 7.

11 Massimiliano Boschi and Giuliana Zanelli, *Movimenti di masse. I funerali di Andrea Costa e il convegno dei Ciclisti Rossi in due filmati di inizio Novecento*, Bacchilega Editore, Imola, 2004 (this publication also contains a DVD of the congress), pp. 24–5.

12 For the 'red cycling' movement see Stefano Pivato, *La bicicletta e il sol dell'avvenire*, Florence, Ponte alle Grazie, 1992, pp. 143–80, 'The Bicycle as a Political Symbol: Italy 1885–1955', *International Journal of the History of Sport*, 7, 2, 1990, pp. 177–81.

13 Lorenzini, *I ciclisti rossi*, p. 9.

14 Cited in Guido Vergani ed., *L'Uomo . . .*, p. 67, 'Il ciclismo nel delitto', *Nuova Antologia di Lettere*, Scienze ed Arti, vol. LXXXVI, IV serie, vol. CLXX, Rome, 1900.

15 See Stefano Pivato, 'The Bicycle as a Political Symbol: Italy 1885–1955', p. 173.

16 Ivanoe Bonomi, 'Lo "sport" e i giovani', *Avanti!*, 29.9.1910.

17 For the 1903 Tour and the violence which marked the race see Philippe Gaboriau, 'The Tour de France and cycling's Belle Epoque', *International Journal of the History of Sport*, 20, 2, 2003, pp. 65–7. Gerbi was not the intended target of the attack, it seems.

18 For Gerbi see V. Varale, *Avventure su due ruote*, Editrice Italiana, Rome, 1964.

19 *I 12 Battaglioni Bersaglieri ciclisti della guerra 1915–1918*, Milan, Tipozin-cografia, 1966, p. 136.

20 See Oliver Janz, 'The Cult of the Fallen Soldiers in Italy after the First World War', in Olaf Farschid/Manfred Kropp/Stephan Dähne, eds, *The First World War as Remembered in the Countries of the Eastern Mediterranean*, Orient-Institut, Beirut, 2006, pp. 203–11; and his 'Death and Mourning in the Memory of World War I in Italy' in Elena Lamberti/Vita Fortunati, eds,

Memories and Representations of War in Europe. The Case of World War I and World War II, Amsterdam/ New York, Rodopi, 2009, pp. 272–286.

21 For a fine history of Italy in the First World War see Mark Thompson, *The White War. Life and Death on the Italian Front, 1915–1919*, Faber & Faber, London, 2009.

22 Lucio Fabi, *La vera storia di Enrico Toti*, Edizioni della Laguna, Gorizia, 1993, p. 40.

23 *Monfalcone, 6 agosto 1916 (Boll. Militare Uff. Disp. 84 del 1916)* http://www. fanfaralonate.net/Toti/Toti01.htm

24 For Misiano see John Foot, *Modern Italy*, Palgrave Macmillan, London, 2003, p. 29.

25 See John Foot, *Italy's Divided Memory*, Palgrave Macmillan, London, 2010, pp. 31–44.

26 *Lettere di Enrico Toti. Raccolte ed ordinate da Tommaso Sillani*, Edizioni Bemporad, Florence, 1924, p. 61, cited in Lucio Fabi, *Enrico Toti. Una storia tra mito e realtà*, Persico, Cremona, 2005, p. 37.

27 Fabi, *Enrico Toti*, p. 93.

28 Ibid., p. 8.

29 *Bella, non piangere*, directed by Davide Carbonari (1955). The film critic Morandini has called this film a 'patriotic tear-jerker, one of the most feeble B-movies of the 1950s'.

CHAPTER 2

1 '26 Giugno 1918. Ministero della Guerra. Bonomi', cited in Paolo Facchinetti, *Bottecchia. Il forzato della strada*, Ediciclo Editore, Portogruaro, 2005, p. 25.

2 Facchinetti, *Bottecchia*, p. 50.

3 Piero Stefanutti, *Ottavio Bottecchia: quel mattino a Peonis*, Comune di Trasaghis, Trasaghis, 2005, G. V. Fantuz, *Ottavio Bottecchia. Botescià: bicicletta e coraggio*, Libreria dello Sport, Milan, 2005, Giulio Crosti, *Bottecchia. Vita, viaggi, avventure e misteriosa morte del vincitore di due Tour de France (1924–1925)*, Comp. Editoriale, Vicenza, 1977, Enrico Spitaleri, *Il delitto Bottecchia*, Antonio Pellicani Editore, Rome, 1987, Giorgio Garatti, *Il leggendario Bottecchia, Tutta la verità sulla sua morte*, Trevigiana Editore, Treviso, 1974, Elio Bartolini, *Ottavio Bottecchia*, Studio Tesi, Pordenone, 1992, Roberto Fagiolo and Francesco Graziani, *Bottecchia l'inafferrabile*, Nutrimenti, Rome, 2005. See also the documentary *Bottecchia, l'ultima pedalata*, directed by Gloria De Antoni (2008) (Cineteca del Friuli).

4 Adriano De Zan with Pier Augusto Stagi, *Gentili signore e signori buongiorno. Cinquant'anni di ciclismo*, Baldini & Castoldi, Milàn, 1999, p. 59.

CHAPTER 3

1 *Il Tempo*, 10.2.1978, in Marco Pastonesi, ed., *Girardengo*, Ediciclo Editore, Portogruaro, 2005, p. 72.

2 Candido Cannavò, 'Innamorati di quel ciclismo', in Pastonesi, ed., *Girardengo*, pp. 9–10, Gian Luca Favetto, 'Costante, il participio presente', in *Girardengo*, p. 15. For Girardengo and Italian national identity see Anthony Cardoza, 'Making Italians? Cycling and National Identity in Italy, 1900–1950' in *Journal of Modern Italian Studies*, 15, 3, 2010, pp. 364–7.

3 Gian Luca Favetto, 'I cento sprint della corsa perfetta', *La Repubblica*, 11.3.2007.

4 Baroni and Pesenti, *Milano–San Remo. 100 anni leggendari*, p. 37.

5 Rino Negri, *Leggendari. Da Girardengo a Pantani. I grandissimi del ciclismo*, Presentato da Eddy Merckx, SEP Editrice, Milan, 2001, p. 21.

6 See Valerio Piccioni, *Quando giocava Pasolini. Calci, corse e parole di un poeta*, Limina, Arezzo, 1996, pp. 71–2.

7 Marco Pastonesi, 'Girardengo Bernardini', in Pastonesi, ed., *Girardengo*, pp. 101–13.

8 Marco Ventura, *Il campione e il bandito. La vera storia di Costante Girardengo e Sante Pollastro*, Il Saggiatore, Milan, 2006, p. 121.

9 In the 1990s singer-songwriter Francesco De Gregori dedicated a song to this story, called 'Il Bandito e il campione' (lyrics by Luigi Grechi).

10 Ventura, *Il campione e il bandito*.

11 In recent years Novi Ligure has also been associated in the public mind in Italy with a horrific double murder which took place in 2001. For a portrait of the town and the story of this event see Luca Fontana, 'Percossi e attoniti', *Diario della Settimana*, 2.3.2001, pp. 22–31.

CHAPTER 4

1 Cited in Marco Pastonesi, 'Per noi era l'extraterrestre', in Angelo Zomegnan, ed., *Alfredo Binda. Cento anni di un mito del ciclismo*, Editoriale Giorgio Mondadori, Milan, 2002, p. 45. Macchi was one of Binda's 'faithful *gregari*'.

2 See the comments of Gianni Mura, 'La leggenda del Re Leone', in Simone Barillari, ed., Gianni Mura, *La fiamma rossa. Storie e strade dei miei Tour*, Minimum Fax, Rome, 2008, pp. 293–5.

3 Vittorio Varale, *Binda: i suoi debutti, la sua carriera, le sue vittorie*, Varese, Istituto Editoriale Cisalpino, 1928, Guido Giardini, *Ciclismo per tutti: Manuale teorico-pratico per l'allenamento. Con la prefazione di Bruno Roghi ed il giudizio di Alfredo Binda e dei competenti più noti d'Italia. La bicicletta in tutti i tempi*, Milan, La Gazzetta dello Sport, 1938, Giancarlo Pauletto, ed., *La*

testa e i garun. Alfredo Binda si confessa a Duilio Chiaradia, Ediciclo Editore, Portogruaro, 1998.

4 Cited in Louis Nucera, *Le roi René*, Sagittaire, Paris, 1976, p. 15.

5 For Pavesi see Gianni Brera's marvellous account in *Addio bicicletta*, Longanesi, Milan, 1964.

6 Renzo Dall'Ara, *Locomotiva umana. Learco Guerra, l'avventura di un campione nella leggenda del ciclismo*, Tre Lune, Mantua, 2002, p. 119.

7 For Mussolini's body see Sergio Luzzatto, *Il corpo del Duce. Un cadavere tra immaginazione, storia e memoria*, Einaudi, Turin, 1998, and Luisa Passerini, *Mussolini immaginario. Storia di una biografia, 1915–1939*, Laterza, Bari, 1991, and for Silvio Berlusconi see Marco Belpoliti, *Il corpo del capo*, Guanda, Milan, 2009.

8 Carlo Levi, *Cristo si è fermato a Eboli*, Mondadori, Milan, 1958 (first published Einaudi, Turin, 1945), p. 120.

9 Carlo Longhini, *Le giornate rosse. 1919 a Mantova*, Sometti, Mantua, 2009.

10 For Guerra's life and career see Dall'Ara, *Locomotiva umana*.

11 Guerra twice won the special one-day race organised in honour of Mussolini, which started in his birthplace in Predappio and finished in Rome, and ran from 1928 to 1933.

12 For Binda's version see Pauletto, *La testa e i garun*, p. 83, see also Dall'Ara, *Locomotiva umana*, pp. 68–9.

13 Dall'Ara, *Locomotiva umana*, p. 74.

14 'Il Giro d'Italia', in Mario Isnenghi, ed., *I luoghi della memoria. Personaggi e date dell' Italia Unita*, Laterza, Bari, 1997, p. 341. But Pivato provides no evidence to back up this claim. See also Daniele Marchesini, *L'Italia del Giro d'Italia*, Il Mulino, Bologna, 2003, pp. 122–3.

15 See also the criticism of Binda's rationalism published in *Lo Sport Fascista* in 1928 cited by Simon Martin, *Football and Fascism. The National Game under Mussolini*, Berg, Oxford, 2004, p. 23.

16 'Binda è rimasto solo' (8.2.1963) now republished in Giuseppe Castelnovi and Marco Pastonesi, *Bella è la sera . . . Bruno Raschi*, EditVallardi, Milan, 2008, p. 85.

17 Enrico Landoni, 'Regime e ciclismo: ai margini o ai vertici dello sport nazionale', in Silei, ed., *Il Giro d'Italia e la società italiana*, pp. 142–3.

18 Pauletto, *La testa e i garun*, p. 73.

19 Dall'Ara, *Locomotiva umana*, pp. 57–62.

20 Chesi was shot by partisans on 15 August 1944.

21 For the relationship between cycling and fascism see Daniele Marchesini, 'Pedalare per il Duce? Ciclismo e fascismo', in Guido Conti, ed., *Biciclette. Lavoro, storie e vita quotidiana su due ruote*, Monte Università Parma, Parma, 2007, pp. 29–36, and *L'Italia del Giro d'Italia*, pp. 97–126.

326

22 Landoni, 'Regime e ciclismo', in Silei, ed., *Il Giro d'Italia e la società italiana*, pp. 150–54.

CHAPTER 5

1 'La promessa mantenuta', *La Gazzetta dello Sport*, 1.7.1946.

2 Franco Giannantoni and Ibio Paolucci, *La bicicletta nella Resistenza*, Edizioni Arterigere, Varese, 2008, p. 15.

3 Giovanni Pesce, 'Pedalavano i partigiani', in Vergani, ed., *L'uomo a due ruote*, p. 90.

4 For all these events, and how they were remembered, see my *Italy's Divided Memory*, pp. 71–183.

5 'In un Giro passato, a Chieti arrivo Bartali', *L'Unità*, 22.6.1946.

6 'Bartali maglia rosa', *L'Unita*, 3.7.1946.

7 'Cottur vincitore della Milano–Torino', *L'Unità*, 16.6.1946.

8 See the chapter on Fiorenzo Magni below.

9 'Parla Ortelli la "maglia rosa"', *L'Unità*, 24.6.1946, 'Spinazzi . . .', *L'Unità*, 29.6.1946.

10 Marchesini, *L'Italia del Giro d'Italia*, p. 197.

11 Orio Vergani and Guido Vergani, *Caro Coppi. La vita, le imprese, la malasorte, gli anni di Fausto e di quell'Italia*, Mondadori, Milan, 1995, p. 44.

12 Leo Turrini, *Bartali. L'uomo che salvò l'Italia pedalando*, Mondadori, Milan, 2005, p. 113.

13 *Il Corriere di Trieste*, cited in Paolo Facchinetti, *Quando spararono al Giro d'Italia. Storie dal Giro*, Limina, Arezzo, 2006, p. 17.

14 *La Gazzetto dello Sport*, 15.6.1946.

15 Daniele Marchesini, *Coppi e Bartali*, Il Mulino, Bologna, 1998, pp. 52–5.

16 A reference to the so-called 'unredeemed lands', which nationalists claimed were needed to fully unify Italy.

17 Facchinetti, *Quando spararono*, p. vii.

18 *Il Corriere della Sera*, 16.6.1946.

19 Facchinetti, *Quando spararono*, p. vii.

20 'Gli incidenti di Pieris scatenano a Trieste una pericolosa ondata di squadrismo fascista', *L'Unità*, 2.7.1946.

21 Marco Pastonesi, *Gli angeli di Coppi: Il campionissimo raccontato da chi si correva insieme contro e soprattutto dietro*, Ediciclo Editore, Portogruaro, 1999, p. 86.

22 Facchinetti, *Quando spararono*, p. 90, Marchesini, *L'Italia del Giro d'Italia*, pp. 232–3.

23 Facchinetti, *Quando spararono*, p. 81.

24 Ibid., p. 4.

25 Ibid., p. 83.

26 Beppe Conti and Gian Paolo Ormezzano, *Il Giro d'Italia. Una storia d'amore*, Diemme, Teramo, 2007, p. 186.

27 Davide Cassani, *Almanacco del ciclismo 2007*, Gianni Marchesini Editore, Bologna, 2007, p. 364.

CHAPTER 6

1 'Prefazione', Marco Pastonesi, ed., *Cavanna. L'uomo che inventò Coppi*, Ediciclo Editore, Portoguaro, 2006, p. 9. For Cavanna and the milieu of Novi Ligure see also Jean-Paul Ollivier, *Fausto Coppi. La tragedia della gloria con uno scritto di Giorgio Bocca*, Feltrinelli, Milan, 1980.

2 Cited in Carlo Delfino, 'Se la dolcissima campagna novese (gli esordi di Biagio Cavanna)', in Pastonesi, ed., *Cavanna*, p. 33.

3 Pierre Chany, *Les rendez-vous du cyclisme ou Arriva Coppi*, La Table Ronde, Paris, 1960; see also John Marks, 'Se faire naturaliser cycliste: The tour and its Non-French competitors', *International Journal of the History of Sport*, 20, 2, 2003, pp. 211–12.

4 Conti and Ormezzano, *Il Giro e l'Italia*, p. 7.

5 Cited in Giuseppe Pignatelli, 'Fausto Coppi', *Dizionario Biografico degli Italiani*, Istituto della Enciclopedia Italiana, Treccani, Rome, 1983, vol. 28, *Conforto–Cordero*, p. 604.

6 Riccardo Filippi cited in Marco Pastonesi, 'Il cieco (il meglio di BC)', in Pastonesi, ed., *Cavanna*, p. 78.

7 Negri, *Leggendari*, p. 144.

CHAPTER 7

1 Gianni Mura, 'Fausto Coppi. Novant'anni in fuga il mito perfetto di un uomo al comando', *La Repubblica*, 15.9.2009.

2 Cited in Orio Vergani and Guido Vergani, *Caro Coppi*, p. 82.

3 Mary McCarthy, *The Stones of Florence and Venice Observed*, Penguin, London, 2006, p. 180.

4 Until recently, much of this material was not available to an English-speaking public, but with the publication of William Fotheringham's definitive biography in 2009, this is no longer the case, *Fallen Angel. The Passion of Fausto Coppi*, Yellow Jersey Press, London, 2009.

5 Gianni Brera, *Coppi e il diavolo*, Baldini & Castoldi, 2008 (Rizzoli, 1981), p. 154.

6 Fotheringham, *Fallen Angel*, pp. 260, 265.

7 Mura, 'Fausto Coppi', *La Repubblica*, 15.9.2009.

8 Bruno Raschi cited in Rino Negri, *Bartali Coppi mai nessuno come loro*, Reverdito Edizioni, Trento, 2001, p. 70.

9 For a powerful satire of these attitudes see director Pietro Germi's dissection of small-town hypocrisy in the 1960s, *Signore e signori* (1965).

10 Mura, 'Fausto Coppi', *La Repubblica*, 15.9.2009.

11 Brera, *Coppi e il diavolo*.

12 See the collection of pieces in Orio Vergani and Guido Vergani, *Caro Coppi*.

13 Ollivier, *Fausto Coppi*.

14 Coppi's myth, perhaps, can only be compared with the stories linked to the life of the Italian national hero Giuseppe Garibaldi. For Garibaldi's myth see Lucy Riall, *Garibaldi: Invention of a Hero*, Yale University Press, New Haven, 2007.

15 Brera, *Coppi e il diavolo*, p. 13. Brera's depiction of Castellania is the best we have. See pp. 11–29.

16 For the details see Fotheringham, *Fallen Angel*, pp. 20–21.

17 Coppi came first in the Giro in 1940, 1947, 1949, 1952, 1953 and won the Tour in 1949 and 1952. He also won the world championships in 1953.

18 As calculated by the great journalist Rino Negri, see Fotheringham, *Fallen Angel*, p. 165.

19 Orio Vergani cited in Turrini, *Bartali*, pp. 103–4. See also Fotheringham, *Fallen Angel*, pp. 33–4.

20 The next time they were to ride the same Giro together – after six years of war – Bartali was first, by 47 seconds.

21 Cited in Ollivier, *Fausto Coppi*, p. 59.

22 Brera, *Coppi e il diavolo*, p. 69.

23 Gian Franco Venè, *Vola Colomba. Vita quotidiana degli italiani negli anni del dopoguerra: 1945–1960*, Mondadori, Milan, 1990, pp. 5–107. This long account is entitled Giro d'Italia.

24 We should also include here the events at the 1946 Giro in Trieste, see pp. 80–91.

25 See also Marchesini, *Coppi e Bartali*, pp. 9–11, Marks, 'Se faire naturaliser cycliste', p. 211, Chany, *Les rendez-vous du cyclisme ou Arriva Coppi*, p. 12.

26 Gian Paolo Ormezzano, *Storia del ciclismo*, Longanesi & Co., Milan, 1985, p. 92.

27 Venè, *Vola Colomba*, pp. 120–42.

28 For the Superga tragedy and the *Grande Torino* football team see John Foot, *Calcio: A History of Italian Football*, HarperPerennial, London, 2007, pp. 89–100.

29 For a critique of the association between heroic and mythical language and

cycling from the golden age see Pivato, 'Tour e Giro: una storia comparativa', in Silei, ed., *Il Giro d'Italia e la società italiana*, pp. 36–8.

30 Giuseppe Castelnovi, *Cuneo–Pinerolo. Il Giro sulle Alpi piemontesi a 60 anni dall'impresa di Coppi*, EditVallardi, Milan, 2009.

31 Fotheringham, *Fallen Angel*, pp. 175–8.

32 *Fausto Coppi. An Italian Story*, Jean Christophe Rosé, 1996. Coppi was helped at the start of the climb by the break made by his teammate Nino Defilippis, a popular and talented cyclist from Turin known as 'Cit' ('the Little One'), thanks to his size and the fact that he was the youngest rider to win a stage and wear the pink jersey at the Giro, in 1952, when he was just twenty years old. For the life and career of Defilippis see Gian Paolo Ormezzano, 'Defilippis, il torinese che "sgridava" Coppi e poi lo aiutava a vincere', *La Stampa*, 14.7.2010.

33 'Papà solo al comando oggi rivivrò la leggenda', *La Stampa*, 19.5.2009 (interview with Faustino Coppi).

34 Cited in Pastonesi, *Gli angeli di Coppi*, p. 73.

35 See Fotheringham, *Fallen Angel*, p. 149.

36 And Ottavio Bottecchia's brother Giovanni died after being hit by a car in 1927.

37 Dino Buzzati, *The Giro d'Italia. Coppi versus Bartali at the 1949 Tour of Italy*, Velopress, Boulder, 1999, pp. 87–93 (original edition: Dino Buzzati, *Dino Buzzati al Giro d'Italia*, preface by Claudio Marabini, Arnoldo Mondadori editore, Milan, 1981).

38 Orio Vergani and Guido Vergani, *Caro Coppi*, p. 130.

39 See also Mauro Gorrino, *Serse e la bestia*, Limina, Arezzo, 2005.

40 For Coppi's *gregari* see Pastonesi's study, *Gi angeli di Coppi*, Fotheringham, *Fallen Angel*, pp. 130–35.

41 For Carrea see Fotheringham, *Fallen Angel*, pp. 128–30, and Pastonesi, *Gli angeli di Coppi*, pp. 52–7, Marco Pastonesi, *Vai che sei solo. Storie di gregari (e non solo)*, Libreria dello Sport, Milan, 1996, pp. 15–18.

42 Ermanno Paccagnini, ed., *Marcello Venturi sulle strade del Giro (14 Maggio–5 Giugno 1955)*, De Ferrari, Genoa, 2004, p. 50.

43 Gianni Brera, *L'anticavallo. Sulle strade del Tour e del Giro*, Baldini & Castoldi, Milan, 1997, pp. 102–5.

44 Ormezzano, *Storia del ciclismo*, p. 94.

45 Cited in Ollivier, *Fausto Coppi*, p. 197.

46 Curzio Malaparte, *Coppi e Bartali. Con una Nota di Gianni Mura*, Adelphi, Milan, 2009, pp. 25, 31.

47 Giorgio Bocca, in Ollivier, *Fausto Coppi*, p. 10.

48 Ibid.

49 'Quegli ultimi giorni di Fausto tra febbri e diagnosi sbagliate', *La Repubblica*, 6.1.2002.

50 William Fotheringham's *Fallen Angel*, pp. 264–7, closes with a description of a gathering of 'old men' at Coppi's graveside.

CHAPTER 8

1 Carlo Maria Lomartire, *Insurrezione. 14 Luglio 1948: L'attentato a Togliatti e la tentazione rivoluzionaria*, Mondadori, Milan, 2007, p. 166.

2 Paul Thompson, *The Voice of the Past. Oral History*, Oxford University Press, Oxford, 2000, p. 161.

3 The bibliography on Bartali is vast. The most elegant account is Turrini, *Bartali*, but see also the recent work of Paolo Alberati, *Gino Bartali. "Mille diavoli in corpo"*, Giunti, Florence, 2006, Sandro Picchi, ed., *Quanta strada ha fatto Bartali*, Giunti, Florence, 2006, and Giancarlo Brocci, *Bartali. Il mito oscurato: Il duello sportivo del secolo non lo vinse Coppi*, Protagon Editori Toscani, Florence, 2000.

4 For Gaetano Pilati see P. Costantini, *Gaetano Pilati, vita di un socialista*, a cura della Sezione 'Gaetano Pilati' di Firenze del Psi, Firenze, 1978, and http://www.pertini.it/turati/a_pilati.html

5 Bartali was awarded a posthumous gold medal by the Italian state. The first writer to carry out research into this story was the cyclist Paolo Alberati, *Gino Bartali. Mille diavoli in corpo*.

6 For the relationship between cycling and fascism, and the role of Bartali in that period, see Marchesini, 'Pedalare per il Duce? Ciclismo e fascismo', in Conti, ed., *Biciclette. Lavoro, storie e vita quotidiana su due ruote*, pp. 29–39, and 'Fascismo a due ruote', in Maria Canella and Sergio Giuntini eds, *Sport e fascismo*, Franco Angeli, Milan, 2009, pp. 85–98.

7 See also the comments of Patrick McCarthy in 'Itinerary 3: Cycling: Politics and Mythology', *Journal of Modern Italian Studies*, 5, 3, 2001, pp. 345–7.

8 Patrick McCarthy, 'Itinerary 2: Two Fascist Champions', *Journal of Modern Italian Studies*, 5, 3, 2001, p. 345.

9 Papa Pio XII, 'Discorso di sua santità Pio XII agli uomini dell'Azione Cattolica, Piazza San Pietro – Domenica, 7 settembre 1947' in *Discorsi e Radiomessaggi di Sua Santità Pio XII*, IX, Nono anno di Pontificato, 2 marzo 1947–1 marzo 1948, Tipografia Poliglotta Vaticana, pp. 213–220. http://www.vatican.va/holy_father/pius_xii/speeches/1947/documents/hf_p-xii_spe_19470907_uomini-azione-cattolica_it.html. See also Stefano Pivato, *Sia lodato Bartali. Ideologia, cultura e miti dello sport cattolico (1936/1948)*, Edizioni Lavoro, Rome, 1996, p. 43.

10 A poster was produced which read as follows: 'BARTALI ha inviato all'On. De Gasperi il seguente telegramma: "Con la più viva gratitudine accolga i sensi della più profonda devozione e gli auguri fervidissimi per la grande vittoria

della democrazia" GINO BARTALI.' 'Bartali has sent the Honourable De Gasperi a telegram: "With sincere thanks I underline my devotion to you and send deep wishes of good luck for the great victory of democracy".'

11 For the Coppi and Bartali story as a national unifying myth see Marchesini, *Coppi and Bartali*, and my short article, 'The good, the bad and the ugly. Reflections on the adverts for the new 500' published in Italian as 'L'auto cattocomunista', *Diario della settimana*, 27.7.2007, pp. 22–4.

12 Emilio De Martino, *Bartali al Giro di Francia 1948*, Edizioni Sportive, Baldini & Castoldi, Milan, 1948, p. 50.

13 See Tom Behan, '"Going Further". The Aborted Italian Insurrection of July 1948', *Left History*, vol. 3, no. 2–vol. 4, no.1 (1996), pp. 169–70. This article and the book from which it is adapted represent one of the few pieces of serious research into the events of July 1948, Tom Behan, *The Long-Awaited Moment: The Working Class and the Italian Communist Party in Milan, 1943–1948*, Peter Lang, New York, 1997. See also Walter Tobagi, *La rivoluzione impossibile. Politica e reazione popolare*, Il Saggiatore, Milan, 1978, and M. Caprara, *L'attentato a Togliatti. Il 14 Luglio 1948: Il PCI tra insurrezione e Programma democratica*, Marsilio, Venice, 1978. Both books were published to coincide with the thirtieth anniversary of the strikes. A further general study appeared on the fiftieth anniversary – Gigi Speroni, *L'attentato a Togliatti. I giorni della paura*, Mursia, Milan, 1998. There are good local studies of events at Livorno (Andrea Grillo, *Livorno: una rivolta tra mito e memoria. 14 Luglio 1948, lo sciopero generale per l'attentato a Togliatti*, Bfs Edizioni, Pisa, 1994), Monte Amiata (Gino Serafini, *I ribelli della montagna. Amiata 1948: anatomia di una rivolta*, Edizioni del Grifo, Montepulciano, 1981) and Siena (S. Orlandini, *Luglio 1948. L'insurrezione proletaria nella provincia di Siena in risposta all'attentato a Togliatti*, Clusf, Florence, 1976). In 2007, a further synthesis appeared – with ample space dedicated to Bartali – by the journalist Carlo Maria Lomartire, *Insurrezione*. For a good account of the question of *doppiezza* and the debates within the PCI leadership around the time of the strike, see Di Loreto, *Togliatti e la "doppiezza"*. July 1948 was a powerful source of leftist myths about 'betrayal' and 'defeated revolution' – some of which re-emerged in the 1960s and 1970s. For an analysis of the idea of history 'as it might have been' see Alessandro Portelli, 'Uchronic dreams: working-class memory and possible worlds', in Samuel and Thompson, eds., *The Myths We Live By*, Routledge, London, 1990, pp. 143–160. Finally, of course, the DC and the anti-communist forces in Italy used the events of July 1948 to propagate the myth that the PCI had prepared a plan for revolution to overturn the results of the April election – the famous combination of a 'plan K' and an 'hour X'.

14 Cited in Lomartire, *Insurrezione*, p. 98; see also Behan, *The Long-Awaited Moment*, Behan, '"Going Further". The Aborted Italian Insurrection of July 1948', pp. 169–203.

15 Lomartire, *Insurrezione*, p. 236.

16 De Martino, *Bartali al Giro di Francia 1948*, p. 73.

17 Ibid., p. 89.

18 Pauletto, ed., *La testa e i garun. Alfredo Binda si confessa a Duilio Chiaradia*, p. 140.

19 This version is also repeated in histories of the Tour; see Bill and Carol McGann, *The Story of the Tour de France*, vol. 1, *1903–1964*, Dog Ear Publishing, Indianapolis, 2006, p. 158, Matt Rendell, *Blazing Saddles. The Cruel and Unusual History of the Tour De France*, Quercus, London, 2007, p. 102, Geoffrey Wheatcroft, *Le Tour. A History of the Tour De France*, Pocket Books, London, 2004, pp. 146–7.

20 See also the elaborate account of the phone conversation in Paolo Alberti, *Gino Bartali*, p. 115

21 Pino Ricci, ed., Gino Bartali, *Tutto sbagliato, tutto da rifare*, Arnoldo Mondadori Editore, Milan, 1979, p. 154.

22 Romano Beghelli and Marcello Lazzerini, *La Leggenda di Bartali. Raccontata da Gino Bartali, raccolta e narrata da Marcello Lazzerini Ricostruzione storica a cura di Romeno Beghelli*, Ponte alle grazie, Florence, 1992, p. 198. According to other versions, it was Paschetta who brought the news about the Togliatti events to Bartali and the other riders on the afternoon of 14 July; see Alberati, *Gino Bartali*, pp. 113–15.

23 Ricci ed., Gino Bartali, *Tutto sbagliato, tutto da rifare*, p. 125. Giulio Andreotti confirms this version in his *1948. L'anno dello scampato pericolo*, Rizzoli, Milan, 2005, pp. 102–3, although he adds that this moment was 'exploited' afterwards by commentators (and its importance exaggerated). There is also a similar version in Andreotti's *De Gasperi visto da vicino*, Rizzoli, Milan, 1986, p. 143, where he describes the idea that the news of Bartali's victory reaching Parliament prevented a massacre as 'a legend'.

24 Andreotti, *De Gasperi*, p. 143. There is no record of the interruption in the official Italian parliamentary records.

25 Pivato, *Sia lodato Bartali*, p. 50.

26 For example, Lomartire refers back to Turrini as a source, *Insurrezione*, p. 254.

27 Pivato, *Sia lodato Bartali*, pp. 49–55. In any case, this was a stage that Bartali had to win to have any chance of taking the overall Tour victory.

28 Carlo Trabucco, *Il Popolo*, 18.8.1948.

29 *Gioventù*, 1.8.1948.

30 All these and other such pieces can also be found in Pivato, *Sia lodato Bartali*, pp. 137–50.

31 De Martino, *Bartali al Giro di Francia 1948*, p. 10. There were even popular stories which linked Bartali directly to the idea of religious miracles, as with the peasant who claimed to have seen two angels flanking Bartali on a mountain stage on the Pordoi.

32 Paolo Facchinetti wrote in his study of the famous events surrounding the 1946 Giro and Trieste that the Bartali 1948 myth is 'perhaps an exaggeration' but that 'there is no doubt, . . . that the arrival of 17 riders at [Trieste] prevented an ethnic and political conflict between Italians and Slavs', Paolo Facchinetti, *Quando spararono al Giro d'Italia. Storie dal Giro*, Limina, Arezzo, 2006, p. 4.

33 Gino Bartali, *La mia storia*, narrata da Gino Bartali con la collaborazione di Mario Pancera, Soc. Editrice Stampa Sportiva, *La Gazzetta dello sport*, 2nd edn, Milan, 1963, p. 85.

34 There is no mention of the De Gasperi phone call here, and Bartali states that he heard the news from the radio and via phone. He has this to say on the 'myth': 'I never gave much weight to the stories that I had "saved the fatherland", in the day of my victory at Briançon with the attempt on Togliatti's life which had paralysed the nation. Moreover, that happy period soon turned sour,' Ricci, ed., Gino Bartali, *Tutto sbagliato, tutto da rifare*, p. 154. Bartali is still telling essentially a story about *cycling* here.

35 Beghelli and Lazzerini, *La Leggenda di Bartali*, p. 187. In the same volume there is an extended comparison between the historical figures of Garibaldi and Bartali. This book also contains the first published version about the activities of Bartali during the war, which would later form the basis of Paolo Alberti's *Gino Bartali* of 2006 and the popular film transmitted in two parts on national television in the same year, *Gino Bartali. L'intramontabile*.

36 Raimondo Manzini cited in Pivato, *Sia lodato Bartali*, p. 126.

37 Lomartire, *Insurrezione*, p. 192, which helped 'free the hearts and minds of Italians from the spectre of fratricidal conflict which had hung over the nation for just over forty-eight hours', ibid.

38 Cited in Orio Vergani and Guido Vergani, *Caro Coppi*, p. 72.

39 Pivato, *Sia lodato Bartali*, p. 50.

40 As in the title of Turrini's book, *Bartali. L'uomo che salvò l'Italia pedalando*.

41 De Martino, *Bartali e il Giro di Francia 1948*, p. 101.

42 Franco Quercioli, 'Quella volta che Ginetaccio . . . Il 14 Luglio di 56 anni fa Pallante sparava a Togliatti e Bartali vinceva il Tour', *L'Unità*, 14.7.2004. See also Daniele Marchesini, who claims that 'without doubt Bartali's triumph . . . was a factor in the lessening of tensions at that time', *Coppi e Bartali*, p. 92.

43 Marchesini, *Coppi e Bartali*, p. 93.

44 Picchi, ed., *Quanta strada ha fatto Bartali*, p.122.

45 Ibid., p. 125.

46 See for example the work by Riall, *Garibaldi. Invention of a Hero*, and Robert Gerwarth, *The Bismarck Myth. Weimar Germany and the Legacy of the Iron Chancellor*, OUP, Oxford, 2007.

47 John Dickie, 'Imagined Italies', in D. Forgacs and R. Lumley, eds, *Italian Cultural Studies. An Introduction*, OUP, Oxford, pp. 19–33.

48 The term *doppiezza*, which translates literally as duplicity or double-dealing, here refers to the tendency of the Communist leadership at this time in Italy to allow its base to believe that they believed in revolution, while preaching moderation in public, see Pietro di Loreto, *Togliatti e la "doppiezza": il Pci tra democrazia e insurrezione (1944-49)*, Il Mulino, Bologna, 1991.

49 There is a growing literature in this area, after years of near silence. See for example Davide Bidussa, *Il mito del bravo italiano*, Milan, Saggiatore, 1994, Filippo Focardi, 'La memoria della guerra e il mito del "bravo italiano". Origine e affermazione di un autoritratto collettivo', *Italia Contemporanea*, 220–221, September–December 2000, pp. 393–399.

CHAPTER 9

1 E. Paccagnini, ed., *Marcello Venturi sulle strade del Giro*, pp. 60–61. For the history of the *gregari* see above all the work of Marco Pastonesi, who has conducted interviews and written about many of the 'ordinary' cyclists in Italy from the golden age to the present day: *Vai che sei solo, Gli angeli di Coppi* and *Il diario del gregario, ovvero Scarponi, Bruseghin e Noè al Giro d'Italia*, Ediciclo Editore, Portogruaro, 2004, Giuseppe Castelnovi and Marco Pastonesi, *Una vita da gregario. Storie e aneddotti di protagonisti all'ombra dei campioni*, SEP Editrice, Milan, 2004.

2 Pastonesi, *Gli angeli di Coppi*, p. 9.

3 Ibid.

4 http://www.ugotognazzi.com/pezzi_memorabili.htm

5 See Benito Mazzi, *Coppi, Bartali e Malabrocca. Le avventure della Maglia Nera*, Conti, Bologna, 1993, republished in a new edition with a slightly different title, *Coppi, Bartali Carollo e Malabrocca. Le avventure della Maglia Nera*, Ediciclo Editore, Portogruaro, 2005. Paolo Colombo, Gioachino Lanotte, *La corsa del secolo. Cent'anni di storia italiana attraverso il Giro*, Mondadori, Milan, 2009, pp. 94–5, Marchesini, *Coppi e Bartali*, pp. 112–14, Castelnovi and Pastonesi, *Una vita de gregario*, pp. 78–81, Pastonesi, *Gli angeli di Coppi*, pp. 147–9, Pastonesi, *Vai che sei solo*, pp. 61–4, Dino Buzzati, *The Giro d'Italia*, pp. 87–93, Alberto Brambilla, *La coda del drago. Il Giro d'Italia raccontato dagli scrittori*, Ediciclo Editore, Portoguaro, 2007, pp. 165–72.

6 Folco Portinari, 'Addio a Malabrocca, grande mito della . . . maglia nera', *L'Unità*, 4.10.2006.

7 Mazzi, *Coppi, Bartali, Carollo e Malabrocca.*
8 Matteo Caccia, *La maglia nera, divertente epopea di un campione molto anomalo*, Filodrammatico, 10.3.2009. Another play, *Malabrocca al giro d'Italia*, was also put on in Turin in 2010, directed and interpreted by Alberto Barbi. The first issue of *Slow*, the Slow Food movement's official magazine, carried an article by Dario Ceccarelli dedicated in part to Malabrocca which was entitled 'L'arte di arrivare ultimo' ('The Art of Arriving Last') in *Slow. Messaggero di gusto e cultura*, 1, 1, 1996, Slow Food Editore, Bra, pp. 42–45.

CHAPTER 10

1 La pista del passato', in Giordano Cioli and Mirella Meloni, *Ferdinando Terruzzi, Il Re delle Seigiorni: da Sesto San Giovanni per conquistare il mondo*, Blu Edizioni, Turin, 2005, p. 9.
2 Cioli and Meloni, *Ferdinando Terruzzi*, p. 13.
3 Camilla Cederna, 'La "Sei Giorni" (February 1961), in *Il meglio di* [Camilla Cederna], Mondadori, Milan, 1987, p. 215.
4 Cioli and Meloni, *Ferdinando Terruzzi*, p. 54.
5 For the full story see Cioli and Meloni, *Ferdinando Terruzzi*.
6 Luciano Bianciardi *L'antimeridiano. Opere complete. Volume secondo*, Luciana Bianciardi et al eds., *Scritti giornalistici* ISBN Edizioni, Excogita Editore, Milan, 2008, p. 1745 (18.10.1971).

CHAPTER 11

1 Fotheringham, *Fallen Angel*, p. 75.
2 Marchesini, *Coppi e Bartali*, pp. 103–116
3 Pier Bergonzi, 'La verità sullo scambio della borraccia', in Pier Bergonzi et al., eds, *Chiedi chi era Coppi. Il Grande Fausto come non l'avete mai visto*, La Gazzetta dello Sport, Milan, 2009, p. 147.
4 See for example the front page and caption to the special supplement to *Lo Sport Illustrato*, 2, 8 January 1953 reproduced in Bergonzi, ibid., p. 146.
5 Ibid., p. 149.
6 Marchesini, *Coppi e Bartali*, p. 110.
7 Ibid, p. 114.
8 Fotheringham, *Fallen Angel*, p. 262.
9 Rino Negri, *Bartali Coppi: mai nessuno come loro*, Reverdito edizioni, Trento, 2001, p. 48.
10 See Foot, *Calcio*, pp. 42–81, for a discussion of the Italian concept of fair play in relation to football.

11 David Forgacs and Stephen Gundle, *Mass Culture and Italian Society from Fascism to the Cold War*, Indiana University Press, Bloomington, 2007, pp. 175–7.

12 In Ollivier, *Fausto Coppi*, p. 8.

13 Marchesini, *Coppi e Bartali*, p. 80.

14 Orio Vergani and Guido Vergani, *Caro Coppi*, p. 110.

15 In Ollivier, *Fausto Coppi*, p. 12.

16 Giancarlo Brocci cited in Fotheringham, *Fallen Angel*, p. 91.

17 And there was a very good chance of victory in 1950 before the Italian team withdrew in protest.

18 Turrini, *Bartali. L'uomo che salvò l'Italia pedalando*, p. 156.

19 Alessandro Dall'Aglio, *Emigrazione italiana e sport a Nizza nel secondo dopoguerra (1945–1960)* (unpublished thesis, University of Parma, 2002–3), p. 209.

20 Cited in Dall'Aglio, *Emigrazione italiana e sport a Nizza nel secondo dopoguerra*, p. 209.

21 *Il Corriere della Sera*, 20.7.1949. Binda was the national team coach until 1962 and he also presided over the unexpected Tour victory of the young Tuscan rider Gastone Nencini in 1960, which was interpreted as a tactical triumph and was without a single stage win for the overall victor.

22 1949, *Sports Digest*. Later published in Italian as *Coppi e Bartali*. Con una nota di Gianni Mura, Adelphi, Milan, 2009.

23 Malaparte, *Coppi e Bartali*, p. 29.

24 In Ollivier, *Fausto Coppi*, p. 29.

25 Curzio Malaparte, *Maladetti Toscani*, Mondadori, Milan, 1997.

26 In Ollivier, *Fausto Coppi*, p. 7.

27 Rino Negri, *Bartali Coppi*.

28 For a recent discussion of Italian national identity see Silvana Patriarca, *Italian Vices. Nation and Character from the Risorgimento to the Republic*, CUP, Cambridge, 2010.

29 Malaparte, *Coppi e Bartali*, pp. 83, 85.

30 Gianni Mura, 'Fausto Coppi', *La Repubblica*, 15.9.2009.

31 Orio Vergani and Guido Vergani, *Caro Coppi*, p. 29.

32 Brocci, *Bartali, Il mito oscurato*, p. 20.

33 Orio Vergani and Guido Vergani, *Caro Coppi*, p. 8.

34 Ormezzano, *Storia del ciclismo*, p. 150.

35 Ibid., p. 94.

36 Malaparte, *Coppi e Bartali*, p. 27

37 Fotheringham, *Fallen Angel*, pp. 106–7.

38 Orio Vergani and Guido Vergani, *Caro Coppi*, p. 72.

39 Ormezzano, *Storia del ciclismo*, p. 95.

40 See also Fotheringham, *Fallen Angel*, p. 125.

41 The 1950 withdrawal of the Italian team took place in a year when Coppi was not riding.

42 http://www.ciclomuseo-bartali.it/web/

CHAPTER 12

1 Cited in Pastonesi, *Vai che sei solo*, p. 60.

2 Gian Maria Dossena, *Il Leone delle Fiandre*, Compagnia Editoriale, Rome, 1991.

3 For a taste of these debates see Foot, *Italy's Divided Memory*, chapter 7.

4 'Memoirs of the Italian resistance', *International Socialism*, 89, winter 2000. Ballerini had also been a cycling fan, and it is said that he was particularly fond of Aldo Bini, who was also born in the Prato area.

5 Here, again, numbers vary. According to the Fondazione della RSI, Istituto Storico Onlus, *Albo caduti e dispersi della Repubblica Sociale Italiana*, edited by Alberto Conti, 2003, the following seven fascists died at Valibona (or soon afterwards due to the injuries they received in the battle there): Mauro Calenzo, Pietro Incalza, Emilio Introvigne, Alfredo Pierantozzi, Carlo Rossi, Duilio Sanesi, Giovanni Tomini.

6 Stuart Hood, *Pebbles from My Skull*, Quartet Books, London, 1973, p. 46.

7 M. Rosaria Bassi ed., *I nonni raccontano. La guerra, il fascismo, la resistenza. Lavoro di ricerca degli alunni della scuola elementare di Calenzano nel 1995*, Giunti, Florence, 1996, pp. 110–13.

8 *I nonni raccontano*, p. 110.

9 Mauro Canali, *Le spie del regime*, Il Mulino, Bologna, 2004, p. 529.

10 CLNAI, Corpo Volontari della Libertà, Comando Formazioni 'Giustizia e Libertà', Ufficio Stralcio, Milan, 14.6.1945.

11 Sentenza (Sentence), Corte D'Assise di Firenze, 24 Febbraio 1947.

12 Fotheringham writes, however, that 'Magni was tried after the war on a charge of collaboration, but was cleared,' *Fallen Angel*, p. 66. See for more details, Michele de Sabato, *In margine alla battaglia di Valibona. Documenti e immagini*, Pentalinea, Prato, 2000.

13 See Franco Quercioli, 'Magni, il terzo uomo che divideva', *L'Unità*, 28.7.2004.

14 There are many anecdotes to this effect among cycling fans.

15 Marchesini, *Coppi e Bartali*, p. 64.

16 See the covers of *diSegnocomune*, March 2003 and May 2003.

17 Fotheringham, *Fallen Angel*, p. 99. After an appeal from Magni's team the jury

produced a second version, removing the offending claim that there had been 'spinte con evidente carattere preordinato' in Magni's favour.

18 *La Gazzetta dello Sport* was very unhappy with Coppi himself for devaluing 'their' race and the cycling authorities banned Coppi for a month (a ban which was later rescinded).

19 'Magni ha ucciso il Giro?', *L'Unità*, 6.6.1948.

20 'Viva Coppi campione della bicicletta, abbasso Magni campione della spinta' (cited in Turrini), striscione, 1948. Another analysis claims that Magni was 'seen as being guilty of holding retrogade political views', Daniele Marchesini et al., *Pàlmer, borraccia e via!*, p. 190.

21 Other articles also made reference to Magni's past; see for example 'Cecchi ha epurato Fiorenzo Magni', *L'Unità*, 2.6.1948. See also 'Fiorenzo Magni ha barato in salita', *L'Unità*, 5.6.1948.

22 For a fuller citation see Marchesini, *Coppi e Bartali*, p. 65.

23 Magni was also a symbol of a changing Italy in other ways, with his Nivea sponsorship (he was the first rider to use shirt sponsorship, partly as a response to the huge economic power of the teams led by Coppi and Bartali) and with his new job as a car salesman in the rich north, Marchesini et al., *Pàlmer, borraccia e via!*, pp. 92–5.

24 Aldo Capanni and Franco Cervellati, eds, *Gli anni d'oro del ciclismo pratese*, Comune di Prato, Provincia di Prato, Pentalinea, Prato, 2000, p. 102.

25 Ibid., p. 102.

26 Sandrino Carrea cited in Pastonesi, *Gli angeli di Coppi*, p. 56.

27 'FIORENZO MAGNI vince irresistibilmente nella più difficile corsa straniera su strada', *La Gazzetta dello Sport*, 11.4.1949. Guido Giardini, 'Col cuore in tumulto'. See also the account in Dossena, *Il Leone delle Fiandre*, pp. 25–47.

28 Emilio De Martino, 'La rivincita', *Gazzetta dello Sport*, 12.4.1949.

29 See also Fotheringham, *Fallen Angel*, p. 87.

30 Mario Fossati, 'Il Cio premia il leone Magni ultimo dei grandi', *La Repubblica*, 4.7.2001. For other portraits of Magni see Cesare Fiumi, 'Magni: "Bartali, il mio nemico il Diavolo"', *Il Corriere della Sera*, 22 .1.1994, Claudio Gregori, Angelo Zomegnan and Rino Negri, 'Magni, un ruggito lungo 80 anni', *La Gazzetta dello Sport*, 7.12.2000.

31 Gianfranco Josti, 'Fiorenzo Magni, "terzo uomo" taglia il traguardo degli ottanta', *Il Corriere della Sera*, 3.12.2000.

32 For the events during the 1950 Tour see Wheatcroft, *Le Tour*, pp. 151–2, and Marchesini, *Coppi e Bartali*, p. 66.

33 Now in Paolo Brera and Claudio Rinaldi, *Giôann Brera. Vita e scritti di un Gran Lombardo*, Boroli Editore, Milan, 2004, p. 156.

34 He also came second twice and he wore the pink jersey for a grand total of twenty-four days.

35 Marchesini, *Coppi and Bartali*, pp. 103-5.

36 Magni actually owned two car showrooms and he also ran a business selling heating fuel, Marchesini, *L'Italia*, p. 206.

CHAPTER 13

1 Roland Barthes described Gaul as the 'new archangel of the mountain' in 'The Tour de France as Epic', now in *The Eiffel Tower and Other Mythologies*, University of California Press, Los Angeles, 1997 p. 89.

2 Fantini died in 1961 after a fall during the Tour of Germany.

3 Cited in Paolo Facchinetti, *L'apocalisse sul Bondone, Storie dal Giro*, Limina, Arezzo, 2006, p. 42.

4 Many of these citations are to be found in the most complete account of that days' events and the way they have been told, Facchinetti, *L'apocalisse sul Bondone*.

5 All quotes from *La Gazzetta dello Sport*, 8-9.6.1956. See also Pietro Dotti, *La lunga corsa di Ercole. Inseguendo Charly Gaul*, Limina, Arezzo, 1997.

6 The huge bicycle parking area provided for Pirelli workers in Milan can be seen in the film *La Vita Agra*, released in 1964 (directed by Carlo Lizzani).

7 Gianni Clerici, *Il Giorno*, 30.7.1966, cited in Aldo Grasso, *Storia della Televisione Italiana*, Garzanti, Milan, 1992, p. 150. For the history of this programme see ibid., pp. 150-52.

8 For an analysis of this development and its affects see John Foot, *Milan since the Miracle. City, Culture and Identity*, Berg, Oxford, 2001, pp. 85-107, and 'Television and the city. The impact of television in Milan, 1954-1960', *Contemporary European History*, 9, 3, 1999, pp. 379-94.

9 On this change see the comments by Luigi Tomassini, 'L'immagine fotografica del campione', in Silei, ed., *Il Giro d'Italia e la società italiana*, pp. 46-77.

10 For the film and the role of bicycles in it see Robert Gordon, *Bicycle Thieves*, Palgrave Macmillan, London, 2008, pp. 37-46, and Forgacs and Gundle, *Mass Culture and Italian Society*, p. 15.

11 Silvio Lanaro, *Storia dell'Italia repubblicana. Dalla fine della guerra agli Anni Novanta*, Marsilio, Venice, 1992, p. 224.

CHAPTER 14

1 Cited in Riccardo Nencini, *Il giallo e la rosa. Gastone Nencini e il ciclismo negli anni della leggenda*, Giunti, Florence, 1998, p. 228.

2 *Lettera a una professoressa*, Libreria Editrice Fiorentina, Florence, 1967.

3 Nencini, *Il giallo e la rosa*, p. 24.

4 Franco Quercioli, 'Nencini, un mugellano solo al comando', *L'Unità*, 21.7.2004.

5 Pauletto, ed., *La testa e i garun*, p. 177.

6 Raschi, 'Pianse una sola volta', *La Gazzetta dello Sport*, 2.2.1980, now in Castelnovi and Pastonesi, *Bella è la sera*, p. 146.

7 Raschi, 'Pianse una sola volta', in Castelnovi and Pastonesi, *Bella è la sera*, p. 147.

8 'Il Leone del Mugello pianse una sola volta', *La Gazzetta dello Sport*, 2.2.1980.

9 Adriano De Zan, *Gentili signore e signori buongiorno*, p. 103; for the 'Tuscan character' see also Malaparte, *Maladetti Toscani*.

10 Anna Maria Ortese, 'Il bravo ragazzo che fu a un passo della vittoria', *L'Europeo*, 1995, 4, reprinted in 'Giro d'autore', *L'Europeo*, 30.04.209, pp. 86–89.

11 Rendell, *Blazing Saddles*, p. 137

12 Bill and Carol McGann, *The Story of the Tour de France*, vol. 2, *1965–2007*, Dog Ear Publishing, Indianopolis, 2008, p. 14.

13 Raschi, 'Pianse una sola volta', in Castelnovi and Pastonesi, *Bella è la sera*, p. 147.

14 See Pauletto, ed., *La testa e i garun*, pp. 176–8.

15 Quercioli, 'Nencini, un mugellano solo al comano', *L'Unità*, 21.7.2004.

16 Rino Negri, 'L'elogio di De Gaulle che commosse Nencini', *La Gazzetta dello Sport*, 23.7.2000.

17 Paul Dimeo, *A History of Drug Use in Sport. 1876–1976. Beyond Good and Evil*, Routledge, London and New York, 2007, p. 59, William Fotheringham, *Put Me Back on the Bike. In Search of Tom Simpson*, Yellow Jersey Press, London, 2003, p. 160.

18 Owen Mulholland, *Cycling's Golden Age, Heroes of the Postwar Era 1946–1967*, Velo, Boulder, Colorado, 2006, p. 125.

19 For this incident see also Louis Malle's famous documentary film about the Tour, *Vive le Tour* (1962) which shows cyclists collapsing, seemingly under the influence of drugs.

20 Riccardo Nencini, *In giallo al Parco dei Principi*, Florence Press, Florence, 1988, Gianni Cerri, *Nencini*, Comp. Editoriale, Vicenza, 1978, Pietro Cipollaro, *Pellaccia da Discesa. Gastone Nencini. L'incompreso Leone del Mugello*, Geo Edizioni, Empoli, 2009.

CHAPTER 15

1 Colombo, *La corsa del secolo*, p. 135.

2 Eugenio Capodacqua, 'Io e Merckx, che grandi sfide allora la bici emozionava i tifosi', *La Repubblica*, 18.1.2003.

3 Mario Fossati, 'La corsa di primavera e i rimpianti di Gimondi', *La Repubblica*, 20.3.1999.

4 Christopher Thompson, *The Tour de France: A Cultural History*, University of California Press, Los Angeles, 2006, p. 2.

5 Colombo, *La corsa del secolo*, p. 127. To get an idea of Merckx's dominance in this period, let's just take the Giro and the Tour. In the 1968 Giro, Gimondi was third, just over nine minutes behind Merckx. In 1969, as we have seen, Merckx was disqualified while in the lead and Gimondi went on to win. In 1970 Merckx beat Gimondi into second place by over three minutes and in 1972 Gimondi trailed in eighth, over fourteen minutes behind the Belgian. A year later, the gap was nearly eight minutes, as Gimondi stood next to Merkcx on the podium again. In 1974 Merckx won again, with Gimondi third, a mere thirty-three seconds behind. Finally, in 1976, with Merckx in decline, Gimondi finished ahead of him in his last, victorious Giro. If we move on to the Tour, in 1969 (after the drugs scandal at the Giro), Merckx finished twenty-nine minutes ahead of Gimondi (in fourth place). In 1972, Gimondi was second (to Merckx, of course), over ten minutes behind. The time either rider finished behind the other is given in brackets. DNE denotes 'did not enter the race'.

Giro d'Italia, 1967–76

	1967	1968	1969	1970	1971	1972	1973	1974	1975	1976
Gimondi	1	3 (9.05)	1	2 (3.14)	7 (7.30)	8 (14.05)	2 (7.42)	3 (33)	3	1
Merckx	9 (11.41)	1	DISQ	1	DNE	1	1	1	DNE	8 (7.40)

Tour de France, 1969–75

	1969	1970	1971	1972	1973	1974	1975
Gimondi	4 (29.24)	DNE	DNE	2 (10.41)	DNE	DNE	6 (20.58)
Merckx	1	1	1	1	DNE	1	2

6 Raschi, in Castelnovi and Pastonesi, *Bella è la sera*, p. 116. The fact that there were two Belgians in the group of four was seen as a disadvantage for Gimondi, but Maerteens later said that Merckx had wanted Gimondi to win, and that they didn't work together. Graeme Fife, *Tour de France. The History, the Legend, the Riders*, Mainstream, Edinburgh, 1999, p. 34.

7 Nicola Montella, 'Il primo amore di Felice Gimondi', *Diario della Settimana*, 15.6.2007, pp. 32–4.

8 Brera, *L'Anticavallo*, p. 118.

9 Ibid., p. 238.

10 Bruno Raschi, in Castelnovi and Pastonesi, *Bella è la sera*, p. 122.

11 Brera, *L'Anticavallo*, pp. 239-40.

12 Marchesini, *L'Italia del Giro d'Italia*, p. 261.

13 'Gianoli, la cronaca si fa poesia', *La Gazzetta dello Sport*, 17.9.1998.

14 Mario Fossati, 'La corsa di primavera e i rimpianti di Gimondi', *La Repubblica*, 20.3.1999. Gimondi was philosophical about Merckx's habit of winning every stage possible. See Maurizio Crosetti, 'quello là', *La Repubblica*, 20.5.2007.

15 Rendell, *Blazing Saddles*, p. 169.

16 In 1969, as this chapter details, he was thrown out of the race because of alleged doping when in the lead, and in 1971 he did not enter the Giro.

17 Wheatcroft, *Le Tour*, p. 216.

18 Nino Nutrizio, 'Un semidio sui pedali', *L'Europeo*, 1969, 31, 1971, nn.13–37. Republished in 'Campioni indimenticalbili', *L'Europeo*, III, 1, 2004, p. 162.

19 Or even entire books: Antonio Rondina, *E' o non è Merckx il più in gamba di tutti i tempi?*, Economica, Jesi, 1976, and Pietro Cipollaro, *Bartali e Coppi meglio di Merckx*, Il Fiorino, Modena, 2002.

20 Pier Paolo Pasolini, 'La faccia di Merckx', *Il Tempo*, 10.5.1969.

21 Leonardo Coen, 'Tanti auguri, Merckx i 60 anni del più forte', *La Repubblica*, 17.6.2005.

22 Favetto, 'I cento sprint della corsa perfetta', *La Repubblica*, 11.3.2007.

23 Wheatcroft, *Le Tour*, p. 218.

24 Pasolini, 'La faccia di Merckx', *Il Tempo*, 10.5.1969.

25 Brera, *L'anticavallo*, p. 264.

CHAPTER 16

1 Interview in the excellent documentary film about the 1968 championships, *Con la maglia iridata. I campionati del mondo di ciclismo su strada. Imola, 1968*, Giangiacomo De Stefano, Macine Film, 2008.

2 Bruno Raschi, 'Un arcobaleno immenso', *La Gazzetta dello Sport*, 1.9.1968.

3 'Le vittorie di Merckx sono scandali', 'Il caos', *Tempo*, 7.6.1969, in Piccioni, *Quando giocava Pasolini*, p. 77.

4 A bike was later manufactured bearing the name the Basso Gap in honour of the 1972 victory.

5 Bruni Raschi, 'Il pronostico sbagliato', *La Gazzetta dello Sport*, 7.8.1972, in Castelnovi and Pastonesi, *Bella è la sera*, p. 111.

6 Mario Fossati, 'Fortunati voi, tutti bici e scuola', *La Repubblica*, 16.3.1990.

CHAPTER 17

1 Pivato, 'Il Giro d'Italia', in Isnenghi, ed., *I luoghi della memoria*, p. 344.

2 Bianciardi in *L'antimeridiano*, pp. 1710, 1786, 1880.

3 In the post-war period Italian riders won the world championship track race in 1958, 1968, 1972, 1973, 1977, 1982, 1986, 1988, 1991, 1992, 2002, 2006, 2007 and 2008.

4 Pivato, 'Il Giro d'Italia', in Isnenghi, ed., *I luoghi della memoria*, p. 343.

5 Cited in Pastonesi, *Vai che sei solo*, p. 5.

6 Paccagnini, ed., *Marcello Venturi sulle strade del Giro*, p. 109.

7 Ignazio Moser won the Italian national pursuit championships in August 2010, 'Sono un Moser e non mi pento', *La Gazzetta dello Sport*, 26.8.2010.

8 For more details see Gianni Marchesini, *La fucilata di Goodwood. Storia dell'agguato di Saronni alla maglia di campione del mondo 1982 in Inghilterra*, Compagnia Editoriale, Rome, 1983.

CHAPTER 18

1 'Moser: Illusione il ciclismo pulito', *La Repubblica*, 10.4.1999. For Moser see C. Andreotti and R. Mosca, *Francesco Moser, Storia di un campione*, Publilux, Trento, 1984, Enervit, *Il record dell'ora di F. Moser a Città del Messico, Relazioni e documenti dell'Equipe Enervit*, Also, 1984, Beppe Conti, *La vita segreta di Moser, I retroscena di una carriera raccontati da Giorgio Vannucci*, Landoni, Legnano, 1984.

2 Cited in Jeremy Whittle, *Le Tour. A Century of the Tour de France*, Collins, London, 2003, p. 145.

3 Di Toro failed to give a sample, but he had been hospitalised after a fall.

4 Gino Sala, 'I corridori respingono sdegnati l'accusa doping', *L'Unità*, 17.6.1968.

5 Gino Sala, *L'Unità*, 18.6.1968.

6 It was just about to be included in the list, and would be the substance found in Merckx's positive sample in 1969.

7 'Gimondi: squalifica sospesa', *L'Unità*, 13.7.1968.

8 'Bodrero morto a 27 anni', *La Stampa*, 16.7.1970.

9 *Il Corriere della Sera*, 3.6.1969.

10 For the details see Foot, *Calcio*, pp. 275–7.

11 Bruno Raschi, 'Merckx costretto al palo (positivo al controllo medico)', *La Gazzetta dello Sport*, 3.6.1969.

12 *Il Corriere della Sera*, 4.6.1969.

13 Paolo Bugialli, 'La corsa è finita a Savona. Poi pedalavano i ragionieri', *Il Corriere della Sera*, 9.6.1969. For the whole story from Zavoli's point of

view see Sergio Zavoli, *Diario di un cronista. Lungo viaggio nella memoria*, Mondadori, Milan, 2002, pp. 386–91.

14 Angelo de Lorenzi, *E non chiamatemi (più) cannibale. Vita e imprese di Eddy Merckx*, Limina, Arezzo, 2003, p. 125.

15 Zavoli, *Diario di un cronista*, p. 390.

16 'Un lapillo forte come un vulcano', *La Gazzetta dello Sport*, 3.6.1969.

17 *La Gazzetta dello Sport*, 3.6.1969.

18 Odilio Ghinolfi, 'Decisione a Bruxelles. Potrà correre il Tour Merckx ritenuto colpevole forse involontario graziato', *La Gazzetta dello Sport*, 15.6.1969. For more on this story see Beppe Conti, *Ciclismo. Inganni e tradimenti*, Ecosport, Milan, 2010, pp. 97–103.

19 Mauro Melani, 2003. http://www.ilciclismo.it/dev/index.php/app/ilciclismo/ilciclismoID/session/mod/pages_news_details/page_id/6859/chapter_id/4

20 'Motta penalizzato. Doping!', *L'Unità*, 27.5.1971.

21 Gino Sala, 'I motivi del disastro degli italiani', *L'Unità*, 11.6.1971.

22 Thompson, *The Tour De France*, p. 244.

23 Ibid.

24 Rule changes brought in were to wipe Moser's time from the record books because of the special bike he used, and meant that – officially – Merckx's record was not broken until 1993. The hour record became an incomprehensible mess, with continual debates over what a bicycle actually was and what shape it should take, as well as where and how the rider should be sitting when racing. Over time, the whole history of the record was rewritten, and the roll-call of times now makes complicated reading. The mystique of the record, so celebrated with Coppi's wartime attempt and then with Moser, was lost, to be replaced by endless and rather boring debates (and rulings) over the shape of the wheels, sitting and hand positions, and the advantages of funny-shaped helmets.

25 *La Gazzetta dello Sport*, 20.1.1984.

26 Moser tried again in his forties after new bikes had seen both Graham Obree and Chris Boardman break the record in the early 1990s.

27 'Moser fantastico bis!', *La Gazzetta dello Sport*, 24.1.1984.

28 'Il colpo magico dei soliti noti', *La Repubblica*, 7.8.1984.

29 http://www.cycling4fans.de

CHAPTER 19

1 Barillari, ed., Mura, *La fiamma rossa*, p. 209.

2 Matt Rendell, *The Death of Marco Pantani. A Biography*, Weidenfeld & Nicolson, London, 2006, p. 69.

3 Barillari, ed., Mura, *La fiamma rossa*, p. 209.

4 Ibid., p. 286.

5 Ibid., p. 285.

6 Not suprisingly, Pantani was often compared to Coppi – for the way he rode, for his cycling style, for his victories and because of his early death, see these two headlines from 28.7.1998, 'Pantani come Coppi, vola in vetta al Tour', *Il Corriere della Sera*, 'Pantani come Coppi, una leggenda al Tour', *La Repubblica*. However, Pantani was probably closer in character and style to Charly Gaul, with whom he struck up a friendship. See Rendell, *The Death of Marco Pantani*, pp. 89–90.

7 For a critique of the 50 per cent test, which some have described as sending out a message that 'stealing was OK, but you can only steal £1000', see Jeremy Whittle, *Bad Blood. The Secret Life of the Tour de France*, Yellow Jersey Press, London, 2008, pp. 171–3.

8 Marco Pastonesi, 'La voce pacata e le domande inespresse', *La Gazzetta dello Sport*, 10.6.1999.

9 Candido Cannavò, 'Il peccato si cancella con un gesto di umiltà', *La Gazzetta dello Sport*, 8.6.1999.

10 Rendell, *The Death of Marco Pantani*, p. 5.

11 For the Forconi incident see Rendell, *The Death of Marco Pantani*, pp. 113–14, 134–5, 204, and Barillari, ed., Mura, *La fiamma rossa*, p. 273.

12 Phillipe Brunel, *Gli ultimi giorni di Marco Pantani*, Rizzoli, Milan, 2008.

13 Rendell, *The Death of Marco Pantani*, pp. 283, 290.

14 Ibid., p. 283.

15 '18 October 1995, the values found in his blood were very unhealthy, after tests following the crash where he had broken his left leg. In short, the solid part of his blood had reached dangerous levels. It was as if a blood sample had been taken from an old man with problems of circulation, not a young 25-year-old athlete. The levels worried the doctors in Turin,' Pietro Cheli, *Diario della Settimana*, 20.2.2004.

16 Manuela Ronchi, *Man on the Run. The Life and Death of Marco Pantani*, Robson Books, London, 2005. Pantani's mother has also published a book, Tonina Pantani and Enzo Vicennati, *Era mio figlio*, Mondadori, Milan, 2008. For a number of these conspiracy theories see the site http://www.nessunotocchipantani.splinder.com/

17 'Choc, sgomento, incredulità, dolore: il mondo lo piange'. 'Se n'è andato', *La Gazzetta dello Sport*, 15.2.2004.

18 Pier Bergonzi, Davide Cassani and Ivan Zazzaroni, *Vai Pantani!*, Mondadori, Milan, 2006.

19 The marble is close to the Mercatone Uno HQ, Pantani's former sponsors.

CHAPTER 20

1 Later the prosecutor tried to shift this date forward in order to avoid the case falling under the statute of limitations, in line with statements made by cyclists later in the 1990s.

2 'Conconi, è troppo tardi', *La Gazzetta dello Sport*, 20.11.2003.

3 'Moser ai Nas è vero, ho fatto emotrasfusione', *La Repubblica*, 25.4.1999.

4 'Ecco il doping di Conconi', *La Repubblica*, 27.10.2000.

5 It is interesting to note that Matt Rendell's forensic analysis of Pantani's career and his involvement in blood doping has never been published in Italy.

6 After Ferrari and Conconi, another doctor also made the headlines, for the wrong reasons, in 2003. Carlo Santuccione was at the heart of what became known as the Oil for Drugs scandal.

7 Luigi Perna, Riccò mi ha detto di aver fatto un'autotrasfuzione', *La Gazzetta dello Sport*, 8.2.2011.

8 But for an optimistic analysis of the 2010 Giro, won by Basso, see Gianni Mura, 'Il campione timido e il Giro ritrovato', *La Repubblica*, 31.5.2010.

CHAPTER 21

1 Gianni Mura wrote a melancholic piece comparing Cipollini with these giants of the past, Barillari, ed., Mura, *La fiamma rossa*, pp. 293–5.

2 Eugenio Capodacqua, 'Nome in codice: Pavarotti Cipollini nel dossier doping', *La Repubblica*, 24.8.2006.

3 'Ha evaso 5 milioni, Cipollini processato', *La Repubblica*, 12.1.2007.

4 'Evasione fiscale: Cipollini condannato', *La Repubblica*, 17.4.2009.

5 'Cipollini assolto "Non c' è stata evasione fiscale"', *La Gazzetta dello Sport*, 9.6.2010.

6 Dario Ceccarelli, 'Il Texano pedala ancora', *Diario della Settimana*, 30.6.1999.

7 Maurizio Crosetti, *Armstrong. Il ritorno del sopravvissuto*, Baldini & Castoldi, Milan, 2009, p. 198.

8 For the full story and more details see Crosetti, *Armstrong*.

9 For a series of articles on the Casartelli tragedy see Barillari, ed., Mura, *La fiamma rossa*, pp. 156–70.

10 Barillari, ed., Mura, *La fiamma rossa*, p. 169. For the Limoges stage see also Crosetti, *Armstrong*, pp. 158–65.

11 According to Jeremy Whittle, however, the breakaway riders blamed Simeoni directly, and were too scared to talk to Armstrong. For Whittle's account of the incident and its aftermath see *Bad Blood*, pp. 133–8 and 153–6.

12 Francesco Moser, 'Prefazione', in Pastonesi, *Vai che sei solo*, p. 5.

CONCLUSION

1 This was a fascist building, and the date chosen for its inauguaration was the anniversary of Mussolini's rise to power in 1922, the 'March on Rome': 28 October.

2 Richard Williams, 'A golden era of cycling revealed through an open door', *Guardian*, 10.11.2009.

3 They are also adept at reciting the numerous statistics which emerge from this sport, even though cycling statistics are notoriously unreliable and variable.

4 A term first coined by Antonio Gramsci. For an application of Gramsci's ideas to studies of sport see David Rowe, 'Antonio Gramsci: Sport, Hegemony and the National-Popular', in Richard Giulianotti, ed., *Sport and Modern Social Theorists*, Macmillan, London, 2004, pp. 97–110.

5 See the stories in Stefano Pivato, Loretta Veri and Natalia Cangi, eds, *In bicicletta. Memorie sull'Italia a due ruote*, Il Mulino, Bologna, 2009.

6 Barillari, ed., Mura, *La fiamma rossa*.

7 Paccagnini, ed., *Marcello Venturi sulle strade del Giro*, pp. 14, 22.

8 Gian Luca Favetto, *Italia, provincia del Giro. Storie di eroi, strade e inutili fughe*, Mondadori, Milan, 2006, p. 39.

9 The classic mythological (and highly influential) analysis of the Tour can be found in Barthes, 'The Tour de France as Epic', and see also his *What is Sport?*, Yale University Press, New Haven, 2007, pp. 27–43.

10 Georges Vigarello, 'Il Tour de France. Memoria, territorio, racconto', in Antonio Roversi and Giorgio Triani, *Sociologia dello Sport*, Edizioni Scientifiche Italiane, Naples, 1995, p. 249.

11 Marks, 'Se faire naturaliser cycliste', p. 208.

12 Paccagnini, ed., *Marcello Venturi sulle strade del Giro*, p. 61.

13 Pivato, *Sia lodato Bartali*, p. 14.

14 Vasco Pratolini, *Al Giro d'Italia. Vasco Pratolini al 38 Giro d'Italia (14 maggio–5 giugno 1955)*, Ermanno Paccagnini ed., Edizioni La Vita Felice, Milan, 2001.

15 Marchesini, *L'Italia del Giro d'Italia*, p. 95.

16 Marks, 'Se faire naturaliser cycliste', p. 210.

17 Luigi Offeddu and Ferruccio Sansa, *Milano da morire*, BUR, Milan, 2007, Guido Viale, *Vita e morte dell'automobile. La mobilità che viene*, Bollati Boringhieri, Turin, 2007, http://www.bicimilano.it/, http://www.critical-massmilano.it/

Bibliography

Alberati, Paolo, *Gino Bartali. "Mille diavoli in corpo"*, Giunti, Florence, 2006.

Andreotti, C. and Mosca, R., *Francesco Moser, Storia di un campione*, Publilux, Trento, 1984.

Andreotti, Giulio, *De Gasperi visto da vicino*, Rizzoli, Milan, 1986.

— *1948. L'anno dello scampato pericolo*, Rizzoli, Milan, 2005.

Barillari, Simone, ed., Gianni Mura, *La fiamma rossa. Storie e strade dei miei Tour*, Minimum Fax, Rome, 2008.

— ed., *Eroi, pirati e altre storie su due ruote. Un secolo di ciclismo*, BUR, Milan, 2010.

Baroni, Enzo and Pesenti, Cesare, *Il Lombardia. Una corsa, 100 storie*, RCS Sport, Milan, 2006.

— *Milano–San Remo. 100 anni leggendari*, RCS Sport, Milan, 2007.

Bartali, Gino, *La mia storia*, narrata da Gino Bartali con la collaborazione di Mario Pancera, Soc. Editrice Stampa Sportiva, *La Gazzetta dello Sport*, 2nd edn, Milan, 1963.

Barthes, Roland, *Miti d'oggi*, Einaudi, Turin, 1994.

— 'The Tour de France as Epic', in *The Eiffel Tower and Other Mythologies*, University of California Press, Los Angeles, 1997.

— *What is Sport?*, Yale University Press, New Haven, 2007.

Bartolini, Elio, *Ottavio Bottecchia*, Studio Tesi, Pordenone, 1992.

Battente, Saverio, 'Biciclette e impresa economica', in Silei, ed., *Il Giro d'Italia*, pp. 101–24.

Beghelli, Romano, and Lazzerini, Marcello, *La leggenda di Bartali. Raccontata da Gino Bartali, raccolta e narrata da Marcello Lazzerini, Ricostruzione storica a cura di Romeno Beghelli*, Ponte alle Grazie, Florence, 1992.

Behan, Tom, '"Going Further". The Aborted Italian Insurrection of July 1948', *Left History*, vol. 3, no. 2–vol. 4, no. 1.

— *The Long-Awaited Moment: The Working Class and the Italian Communist Party in Milan, 1943–1948*, Peter Lang, New York, 1997.

Bergonzi, Pier, 'La verità sullo scambio della borraccia', in Pier Bergonzi et al., eds, *Chiedi chi era Coppi. Il Grande Fausto come non l'avete mai visto*, La Gazzetta dello Sport, Milan, 2009.

— and Trifari, Elio, eds, *Un secolo di passioni. Giro d'Italia 1909–2009*, Rizzoli, Milan, 2009.

Bergonzi, Pier, Cassani, Davide and Zazzaroni, Ivan, *Vai Pantani!*, Mondadori, Milan, 2006.

Bianciardi, Luciano, *L'antimeridiano. Opere complete*, volume secondo, Luciana Bianciardi et al., eds, *Scritti giornalistici*, ISBN Edizioni, Excogita Editore, Milan, 2008.

Bonetta, Gaetano, *Corpo e nazione. L'educazione ginnastica igienica e sessuale nell'Italia liberale*, Franco Angeli, Milan, 1990.

Bonomi, Ivanoe, 'Lo "sport" e i giovani', *Avanti!*, 29.9.1910.

Boschi, Massimiliano and Zanelli, Giuliana, *Movimenti di masse. I funerali di Andrea Costa e il convegno dei Ciclisti Rossi in due filmati di inizio Novecento*, Bacchilega Editore, Imola, 2004.

Bottecchia, l'ultima pedalata, directed by Gloria De Antoni (2008) (Cineteca del Friuli) (documentary).

Brambilla, Alberto, *La coda del drago. Il Giro d'Italia raccontato dagli scrittori*, Ediciclo Editore, Portogruaro, 2007.

— *Biciclette di carta. Un'antologia poetica del ciclismo*, Limina, Arezzo, 2009.

Brera, Gianni, *Addio bicicletta*, Longanesi, Milan, 1964.

— *L'Arcimatto 1960–1966*, Andrea Maietti, ed., Baldini & Castoldi, Milan, 1993.

— *L'Anticavallo. Sulle strade del Tour e del Giro*, Andrea Maietti, ed., Baldini & Castoldi, Milan, 1997.

— *Coppi e il diavolo*, Baldini & Castoldi, Milan, 2008.

Brera, Paolo and Rinaldi, Claudio, *Gioannnfucarlo. La vita e gli scritti inediti di Gianni Brera*, Edizione Selecta, Pavia, 2001.

— *Giôann Brera. Vita e scritti di un Gran Lombardo*, Boroli Editore, Milan, 2004.

Brocci, Giancarlo, *Bartali, Il mito oscurato. Il duello sportivo del secolo non lo vinse Coppi*, Protagon Editori Toscani, Florence, 2000.

Brunel, Phillipe, *Gli ultimi giorni di Marco Pantani*, Rizzoli, Milan, 2008.

Buzzati, Dino, *The Giro d'Italia. Coppi versus Bartali at the 1949 Tour of Italy*, Velopress, Boulder, 1999 (original edition Dino Buzzati, *Dino Buzzati al Giro d'Italia*, Preface by Claudio Marabini, Arnoldo Mondadori Editore, Milan, 1981).

Canali, Mauro, *Le spie del regime*, Il Mulino, Bologna, 2004.

Capanni, Aldo, and Cervellati, Franco, eds, *Gli anni d'oro del ciclismo pratese*, Comune di Prato, Provincia di Prato, Pentalinea, Prato, 2000.

Caprara, M., *L'attentato a Togliatti. Il 14 Luglio 1948: Il PCI tra insurrezione e Programma democratica*, Marsilio, Venice, 1978.

Cardoza, Anthony, '"Making Italians?". Cycling and national identity in Italy: 1900–1950', *Journal of Modern Italian Studies*, 15, 3, 2010, pp. 354–77.

Cassani, Davide, *Almanacco del ciclismo 2007*, Gianni Marchesini Editore, Bologna, 2007.

Castelnovi, Giuseppe, *Cuneo–Pinerolo. Il Giro sulle Alpi piemontesi a 60 anni dall'impresa di Coppi*, EditVallardi, Milan, 2009.

Castelnovi, Giuseppe and Pastonesi, Marco, *Una vita da gregario. Storie e aneddotti di protagonisti all'ombra dei campioni*, SEP Editrice, Milan, 2004.

— *Bella è la sera . . . Bruno Raschi*, EditVallardi, Milan, 2008.

Ceccarelli, Dario, 'L'arte di arrivare ultimo', in *Slow. Messaggero di gusto e cultura*, 1, 1, 1996, Slow Food Editore, Bra, pp. 42–5.

Cederna, Camilla, 'La "Sei Giorni"' (February 1961), in *Il meglio di* [Camilla Cederna], Mondadori, Milan, 1987.

Cerri, Gianni, *Nencini*, Comp. Editoriale, Vicenza, 1978.

Chany, Pierre, *Les rendez-vous du cyclisme ou Arriva Coppi*, La Table Ronde, Paris, 1960.

Cioli, Giordano and Meloni, Mirella, *Ferdinando Terruzzi, Il Re delle Seigiorni: da Sesto San Giovanni per conquistare il mondo*, Blu Edizioni, Turin, 2005.

Cipollaro, Pietro, *Bartali e Coppi meglio di Merckx*, Il Fiorino, Modena, 2002.

— *Pellaccia da Discesa. Gastone Nencini. L'incompreso Leone del Mugello*, Geo Edizioni, Empoli, 2009.

Coen, Leonardo, 'Tanti auguri, Merckx i 60 anni del più forte', *La Repubblica*, 17.6.2005.

Colombo, Paolo, and Lanotte, Gioachino, *La corsa del secolo. Cent'anni di storia italiana attraverso il Giro*, Mondadori, Milan, 2009.

Con la maglia iridata. I campionati del mondo di ciclismo su strada. Imola, 1968, Giangiacomo De Stefano, Macine Film, 2008 (documentary).

Conti, Beppe and Ormezzano, Gian Paolo, *Il Giro d'Italia. Una storia d'amore*, Diemme, Ancarano, 2007.

Conti, Beppe, *La vita segreta di Moser, I retroscena di una carriera raccontati da Giorgio Vannucci*, Landoni, Legnano, 1984.

— *Ciclismo. Inganni e tradimenti*, Ecosport, Milan, 2010.

Cordelli, Franco, *L'Italia di mattina. Il romanzo del Giro d'Italia*, Giulio Perrone Editore, Rome, 2009.

Cronache del primo Giro d'Italia, introduzione di Ermanno Paccagnini, presentazione di Umberto Colombo, Otto/Novecento, Milan, 2010.

Crosetti, Maurizio, *Armstrong. Il ritorno del sopravvissuto*, Baldini & Castoldi, Milan, 2009.

Crosti, Giulio, *Bottecchia. Vita, viaggi, avventure e misteriosa morte del vincitore di due Tour de France (1924–1925)*, Comp. Editoriale, Vicenza, 1977.

Dall'Aglio, Alessandro, *Emigrazione italiana e sport a Nizza nel secondo dopoguerra (1945–1960)* (unpublished thesis, University of Parma, 2002–3).

Dall'Ara, Renzo, *Locomotiva umana. Learco Guerra, l'avventura di un campione nella leggenda del ciclismo*, Tre Lune, Mantua, 2002.

De Lorenzi, Angelo, *E non chiamatemi (più) cannibale. Vita e imprese di Eddy Merckx*, Limina, Arezzo, 2003.

De Martino, Emilio, *Bartali al Giro di Francia 1948*, Edizioni Sportive, Baldini & Castoldi, Milan, 1948.

— 'La rivincita', *Gazzetta dello Sport*, 12.4.1949.

De Zan, Adriano with Stagi, Pier Augusto, *Gentili signore e signori buongiorno. Cinquant'anni di ciclismo*, Baldini & Castoldi, Milan, 1999.

Di Loreto, Pietro, *Togliatti e la "doppiezza". Il PCI tra democrazia e insurrezione 1944–49*, Il Mulino, Bologna, 1991.

Dimeo, Paul, *A History of Drug Use in Sport. 1876–1976. Beyond Good and Evil*, Routledge, London and New York, 2007.

Dossena, Gian Maria, *Il Leone delle Fiandre*, Compagnia Editoriale, Rome, 1991.

Dotti, Pietro, *La lunga corsa di Ercole: inseguendo Charly Gaul*, Limina, Arezzo, 1997.

Enervit, *Il record dell'ora di F. Moser a Città del Messico, Relazioni e documenti dell'Equipe Enervit*, Also, 1984.

Fabi, Lucio, *La vera storia di Enrico Toti*, Edizioni della Laguna, Gorizia, 1993.

— *Enrico Toti. Una storia tra mito e realtà*, Persico, Cremona, 2005.

Facchinetti, Paolo, *Bartali e Togliatti. Un grande trionfo al Tour de France e un attentato politico: due storie intrecciate nella storia d'Italia*, Compagnia Editoriale, Rome, 1981.

— *L'Italia di Coppi e Bartali*, Compagnia Editoriale, Rome, 1981.

— *Gli anni ruggenti di Alfonsina Strada. Il romanzo dell'unica donna che ha corso il Giro d'Italia assieme agli uomini*, Ediciclo Editore, Portogruaro, 2004.

— *Bottecchia. Il forzato della strada*, Ediciclo Editore, Portogruaro, 2005.

— *L'apocalisse sul Bondone, Storie dal Giro*, Limina, Arezzo, 2006.

— *Quando spararono al Giro d'Italia. Storie dal Giro*, Limina, Arezzo, 2006.

— 'La grande avventura', in Gino Cervi and Paolo Facchinetti, *Il Giro d'Italia. Strade, storie, oggetti di un mito*, Bolis Edizioni, Azzano San Paolo, 2009.

Fagiolo, Roberto and Graziani, Francesco, *Bottecchia l'inafferrabile*, Nutrimenti, Rome, 2005.

Fantuz, G. V., *Ottavio Bottecchia. Botescià: bicicletta e coraggio*, Libreria dello Sport, Milan, 2005.

Fausto Coppi. An Italian Story, Jean Christophe Rosé, 1996 (documentary).

Favetto, Gian Luca, *Italia, provincia del Giro. Storie di eroi, strade e inutili fughe*, Mondadori, Milan, 2006.

Fife, Graeme, *Tour de France. The History, the Legend, the Riders*, Mainstream, Edinburgh, 1999.

Fiumi, Cesare, 'Magni: "Bartali, il mio nemico il Diavolo"', *Il Corriere della Sera*, 22.1.1994.

Fontana, Luca, 'Percossi e attoniti', *Diario della Settimana*, 2.3.2001.

Foot, John, *Milan since the Miracle. City, Culture and Identity*, Berg, Oxford, 2001.

— *Modern Italy*, Palgrave Macmillan, London, 2003.

— *Calcio: A History of Italian Football*, Fourth Estate, London, 2006.

— *Italy's Divided Memory*, Palgrave, New York, 2010.

Forgacs, David and Gundle, Stephen, *Mass Culture and Italian Society from Fascism to the Cold War*, Indiana University Press, Bloomington, 2007.

Fossati, Mario, 'Il Cio premia il leone Magni ultimo dei grandi', *La Repubblica*, 4.7.2001.

Fotheringham, William, *Put Me Back on the Bike. In Search of Tom Simpson*, Yellow Jersey Press, London, 2003.

— *Fallen Angel. The Passion of Fausto Coppi*, Yellow Jersey Press, London, 2009.

— *Cyclopedia. It's All About the Bike*, Yellow Jersey Press, London, 2010.

Gaboriau, Philippe, 'The Tour de France and cycling's Belle Epoque', *International Journal of the History of Sport*, 20, 2, 2003.

Garatti, Giorgio, *Il leggendario Bottecchia, Tutta la verità sulla sua morte*, Trevigiana Editore, Treviso, 1974.

Giannantoni, Franco and Paolucci, Ibio, *La bicicletta nella Resistenza*, Edizioni Arterigere, Varese, 2008.

Giardini, Guido, *Ciclismo per tutti: Manuale teorico-pratico per l'allenamento. Con la prefazione di Bruno Roghi ed il giudizio di Alfredo Binda e dei competenti più noti d'Italia. La bicicletta in tutti i tempi*, La Gazzetta dello Sport, Milan, 1938.

Gordon, Robert, *Bicycle Thieves*, Palgrave Macmillan, London, 2008.

Gorrino, Mauro, *Serse e la bestia*, Limina, Arezzo, 2005.

Governi, Giancarlo, *Il grande airone. Il romanzo di Fausto Coppi*, Nuova ERI, Turin, 1994.

Grasso, Aldo, *Storia della Televisione Italiana*, Garzanti, Milan, 1992.

Gregori, Claudio, *Labron. La vita e le avventure di Toni Bevilacqua*, Alta Quota, S. Maria di sala (VE), 2002.

— *Luigi Ganna. Il romanzo del vincitore del primo Giro d'Italia del 1909*, EditVallardi, Milan, 2009.

— *ABiCi. L'alfabeto e la storia della bicicletta. Museo Toni Bevilacqua di Sergio Sanvido*, EditVallardi, Milan, 2010.

Gregori, Claudio, Zomegnan, Angelo and Negri, Rino, 'Magni, un ruggito lungo 80 anni', *La Gazzetta dello Sport*, 7.12.2000.

Grillo, Andrea, *Livorno: una rivolta tra mito e memoria. 14 Luglio 1948, lo sciopero generale per l'attentato a Togliatti*, Bfs Edizioni, Pisa, 1994.

Herlihy, David, *Bicycle. The History*, Yale University Press, New Haven, 2004.

'History as it really wasn't: the myths of Italian historiography. A roundtable', with Ruth Ben-Ghiat, Luciano Cafagna, Ernesto Galli della Loggia, Carl Ipsen and David I. Kertzer. Introduction by Mark Gilbert in *Journal of Modern Italian Studies*, 6, 3, 2001.

Hood, Stuart, *Pebbles from My Skull*, Quartet Books, London, 1973.

I 12 Battaglioni Bersaglieri ciclisti della guerra 1915–1918, Tipozincografia, Milan, 1966.

International Journal of the History of Sport, 2003, 20, 2. Special issue on the Tour de France.

Isnenghi, M., ed., *I luoghi della memoria. Personaggi e date dell'Italia unita*, Laterza, Bari, 1997.

Janz, Oliver, 'Death and Mourning in the Memory of World War I in Italy', in Elena Lamberti and Vita Fortunati, eds, *Memories and Representations of War in Europe. The Case of World War I and World War II*, Rodopi, Amsterdam/New York, 2009.

Janz, Oliver, 'The Cult of the Fallen Soldiers in Italy after the First World War', in Olaf Farschid, Manfred Kropp and Stephan Dähne, eds, *The First World War as Remembered in the Countries of the Eastern Mediterranean*, Orient-Institut, Beirut, 2006.

Jarvie, Grant, and Maguire, Joseph, *Sport and Leisure in Social Thought*, Routledge, London, 1994.

Josti, Gianfranco, 'Fiorenzo Magni, "terzo uomo" taglia il traguardo degli ottanta', *Il Corriere della Sera*, 3.12.2000.

Lanaro, Silvio, *Storia dell'Italia repubblicana. Dalla fine della guerra agli Anni Novanta*, Marsilio, Venice, 1992.

Landoni, Enrico, 'Regime e ciclismo: ai margini o ai vertici dello sport nazionale', in Silei, ed., *Il Giro d'Italia e la società italiana*.

Lettere di Enrico Toti. Raccolte ed ordinate da Tommaso Sillani, Edizioni Bemporad, Florence, 1924.

Levi, Carlo, *Cristo si è fermato a Eboli*, Mondadori, Milan, 1958 (first published Einaudi, Turin, 1945).

Lomartire, Carlo Maria, *Insurrezione. 14 Luglio 1948: L'attentato a Togliatti e la tentazione rivoluzionaria*, Mondadori, Milan, 2007.

Lorenzini, Antonio, *I ciclisti rossi. I loro scopi e la loro organizzazione*, Ditta Fratelli Cesarani, Caravaggio, Bergamo, 1913.

Malaparte, Curzio, *Maladetti Toscani*, Mondadori, Milan, 1997.

— *Coppi e Bartali. Con una Nota di Gianni Mura*, Adelphi, Milan, 2009.

Marchesini, Daniele, *Coppi e Bartali*, Il Mulino, Bologna, 1998.

— et al., *Pàlmer, borraccia e via! Storia e leggende della bicicletta e del ciclismo*, Ediciclo Editore, Portogruaro, 2001.

— *L'Italia del Giro d'Italia*, Il Mulino, Bologna, 2003.

— 'Pedalare per il Duce? Ciclismo e fascismo', in Guido Conti, ed., *Biciclette. Lavoro, storie e vita quotidiana su due ruote*, Monte Università Parma, Parma, 2007.

— 'Fascismo a due ruote', in Maria Canella and Sergio Giuntini eds, *Sport e fascismo*, Franco Angeli, Milan, 2009.

Marchesini, Gianni, *La fucilata di Goodwood. Storia dell'agguato di Saronni alla maglia di campione del mondo 1982 in Inghilterra*, Compagnia Editoriale, Rome, 1983.

Marks, John, 'Se faire naturaliser cycliste: The tour and its Non-French competitors', *International Journal of the History of Sport*, 20, 2, 2003, pp. 203–26.

Martin, Simon, *Football and Fascism. The National Game under Mussolini*, Berg, Oxford, 2004.

Mazzi, Benito, *Coppi, Bartali e Malabrocca. Le avventure della Maglia Nera*, Conti, Bologna, 1993.

— *Coppi, Bartali, Carollo e Malabrocca. Le avventure della Maglia Nera*, Ediciclo Editore, Portogruaro, 2005,

McCarthy, Patrick, 'Itinerary 2: Two Fascist Champions', *Journal of Modern Italian Studies*, 5, 3, 2001, p. 343–5.

— 'Itinerary 3: Cycling: Politics and Mythology', *Journal of Modern Italian Studies*, 5, 3, 2001, pp. 345–7.

McGann, Bill and Carol, *The Story of the Tour de France*, vol. 1, *1903–1964*, Dog Ear Publishing, Indianapolis, 2006.

— *The Story of the Tour de France*, vol. 2, *1965–2007*, Dog Ear Publishing, Indianapolis, 2008.

Montella, Nicola, 'Il primo amore di Felice Gimondi', *Diario della Settimana*, 15.6.2007.

Mulholland, Owen, *Cycling's Golden Age. Heroes of the Postwar Era, 1946–1967*, Velo, Boulder, 2006.

Mura, Gianni, 'Fausto Coppi. Novant'anni in fuga il mito perfetto di un uomo al comando', *La Repubblica*, 15.9.2009.

Negri, Rino, *Un uomo solo. Fausto Coppi nella vita, nella storia, nella leggenda*, Reverdito Edizioni, Trento, 1996.

— 'L'elogio di De Gaulle che commosse Nencini', *La Gazzetta dello Sport*, 23.7.2000.

— *Bartali Coppi: mai nessuno come loro*, Reverdito Edizioni, Trento, 2001.

— *Leggendari. Da Girardengo a Pantani. I grandissimi del ciclismo*, Presentato da Eddy Merckx, SEP Editrice, Milan, 2001.

Nencini, Riccardo, *In giallo al Parco dei Principi*, Florence Press, Florence, 1988.

— *Il giallo e la rosa. Gastone Nencini e il ciclismo negli anni della leggenda*, Giunti, Florence, 1998.

Neri, Sergio, *Coppi vivo*, Compagnia Editoriale, Rome, 1979.

Nutrizio, Nino, 'Un semidio sui pedali'. *L'Europeo*, 1969, 31, 1971, nn. 13–37. Republished in 'Campioni indimenticabili', *L'Europeo*, III, 1, 2004.

Offeddu, Luigi, and Sansa, Ferruccio, *Milano da morire*, BUR, Milan, 2007.

Ollivier, Jean-Paul, *Fausto Coppi. La tragedia della gloria con uno scritto di Giorgio Bocca*, Feltrinelli, Milan, 1980.

Orlandini, S., *Luglio 1948. L'insurrezione proletaria nella provincia di Siena in risposta all'attentato a Togliatti*, Clusf, Florence, 1976.

Ormezzano, Gian Paolo, *Storia del ciclismo*, Longanesi and Co., Milan, 1985.

Ortese, Anna Maria, *La lente scura: scritti di viaggio*, Luca Clerici, ed., Milan, Adelphi, 2004.

— 'Il bravo ragazzo che fu a un passo dalla vittoria', *L'Europeo*, 1955, 4, reprinted in *L'Europeo*, 'Giro d'autore', 30.4.2009.

Paccagnini, Ermanno, ed., *Marcello Venturi sulle strade del Giro (14 Maggio–5 Giugno 1955)*, De Ferrari, Genoa, 2004.

Pantani, Tonina and Vicennati, Enzo, *Era mio figlio*, Mondadori, Milan, 2008.

Pasolini, Pier Paolo, 'La faccia di Merckx', *Il Tempo*, 10.5.1969.

Pastonesi, Marco, *Vai che sei solo. Storie di gregari (e non solo)*, Libreria dello Sport, Milan, 1996.

— *Gli angeli di Coppi. Il Campionissimo raccontato da chi ci correva insieme, contro e soprattutto dietro*, Ediciclo Editore, Portogruaro, 1999.

— 'Per noi era l'extraterrestre', in *Alfredo Binda. Cento anni di un mito del ciclismo*, Zomegnan, Angelo, ed., Editoriale Giorgio Mondadori, Milan, 2002.

— *Il diario del gregario, ovvero Scarponi, Bruseghin e Noè al Giro d'Italia*, Ediciclo Editore, Portogruaro, 2004

— ed., *Girardengo*, Ediciclo Editore, Portogruaro, 2005.

— ed., *Cavanna. L'uomo che inventò Coppi*, Ediciclo Editore, Portoguaro, 2006.

Patriarca, Silvana, *Italian Vices. Nation and Character from the Risorgimento to the Republic*, CUP, Cambridge, 2010.

Pauletto, Giancarlo, ed., *La testa e i garun. Alfredo Binda si confessa a Duilio Chiaradia*, Ediciclo Editore, Portogruaro, 1998.

Penn, Robert, *It's All About the Bike. The Pursuit of Happiness on Two Wheels*, Particular Books, Penguin, 2010.

Pesce, Giovanni, 'Pedalavano i partigiani', in Guido Vergani, ed., *L'uomo a due ruote. Avventura, storia e passione*, Electa, Milan, 1987.

Petrucci, Giampiero, *Dizionario del ciclismo italiano*, Bradipolibri, Turin, 2003.

Picchi, Sandro, ed., *Quanta strada ha fatto Bartali*, Giunti, Florence, 2006.

Piccioni, Valerio, *Quando giocava Pasolini. Calci, corse e parole di un poeta*, Limina, Arezzo, 1996.

Pignatelli, Giuseppe, 'Fausto Coppi', *Dizionario Biografico degli Italiani*, Istituto della Enciclopedia Italiana, Treccani, Rome, 1983, vol. 28, *Conforto–Cordero*.

Pius XII, Pope, 'Discorso di Sua Santità Pio XII agli uomini di Azione Cattolica', *Piazza San Pietro – Domenica, 7 settembre 1947, Discorsi e Radiomessaggi di Sua Santità Pio XII*, IX, Nono anno di Pontificato, 2 marzo 1947–1 marzo 1948, Tipografia Poliglotta Vaticana, Rome, pp. 213–20.

— 'Discorso di Sua Santità Pio XII per l'accensione della lampada votiva destinata alla celeste patrona dei ciclisti, Palazzo Pontificio di Castel Gandolfo – Mercoledì, 13 ottobre 1948', in *Discorsi e Radiomessaggi di Sua Santità Pio XII*, X, Decimo anno di Pontificato, 2 marzo 1948–1 marzo 1949, Tipografia Poliglotta Vaticana, Rome, p. 257.

Pivato, Stefano, 'The Bicycle as a Political Symbol: Italy 1885–1955', *International Journal of the History of Sport*, 7, 2, 1990, pp. 173–87.

— *La bicicletta e il sol dell'avvenire*, Florence, Ponte alle Grazie, 1992.

— *Sia lodato Bartali. Ideologia, cultura e miti dello sport cattolico (1936/1948)*, Edizioni Lavoro, Rome, 1996.

— 'Italian Cycling and the Creation of a Catholic Hero: the Bartali Myth', in Richard Holt, J. A. Mangan and Pierre Lanfranchi eds., *European Heros: Myth, Identity, Sport*, Frank Cass, London, 1996.

Pivato, Stefano, Veri, Loretta, and Cangi, Natalia, eds, *In bicicletta. Memorie sull'Italia a due ruote*, Il Mulino, Bologna, 2009.

Portelli, Alessandro, 'Uchronic dreams: working-class memory and possible worlds', in Raphael Samuel and Paul Thompson, eds, *The Myths We Live By*, Routledge, London, 1990.

Portinari, Folco, 'Addio a Malabrocca, grande mito della . . . maglia nera', *L'Unità*, 4.10.2006.

Pratolini, Vasco, *Al Giro d'Italia. Vasco Pratolini al 38 Giro d'Italia (14 maggio–5 giugno 1955)*, Ermanno Paccagnini, ed., Edizioni La Vita Felice, Milan, 2001.

Quercioli, Franco, 'Quella volta che Ginetaccio . . . Il 14 Luglio di 56 anni fa Pallante sparava a Togliatti e Bartali vinceva il Tour', *L'Unità*, 14.7.2004.

— 'Nencini, un mugellano solo al comando', *L'Unità*, 21.7.2004.

Rendell, Matt, *The Death of Marco Pantani. A Biography*, Weidenfeld & Nicolson, London, 2006.

— *Blazing Saddles. The Cruel and Unusual History of the Tour de France*, Quercus, London, 2007.

Ricci, Francesco, *Il '68 a pedali. Al Giro con Eddy Merckx*, Limina, Arezzo, 2008.

Ricci, Pino, ed., Gino Bartali, *Tutto sbagliato, tutto da rifare*, Arnoldo Mondadori Editore, Milan, 1979.

Ronchi, Manuela, *Man on the Run. The Life and Death of Marco Pantani*, Robson Books, London, 2005.

Rondina, Antonio, *E' o non è Merckx il più in gamba di tutti i tempi?*, Economica, Jesi, 1976.

Rosaria Bassi, M., ed., *I nonni raccontano. La guerra, il fascismo, la resistenza. Lavoro di ricerca degli alunni della scuola elementare di Calenzano nel 1995*, Giunti, Florence, 1996.

Rowe, David, 'Antonio Gramsci: Sport, Hegemony and the National-Popular', in Richard Giulianotti, ed., *Sport and Modern Social Theorists*, Macmillan, London, 2004.

Sabato, Michele de, *In margine alla battaglia di Valibona. Documenti e immagini*, Pentalinea, Prato, 2000.

Seaton, Matt, *Two Wheels*, Guardian Books, London, 2007.

Serafini, Gino, *I ribelli della montagna. Amiata 1948: anatomia di una rivolta*, Edizioni del Grifo, Montepulciano, 1981.

Silei, Gianni, ed., *Il Giro d'Italia e la società italiana*, Piero Laicata Editore, Manduria/Bari/Rome, 2010.

Speroni, Gigi, *L'attentato a Togliatti. I giorni della paura*, Mursia, Milan, 1998.

Spitaleri, Enrico, *Il delitto Bottecchia*, Antonio Pellicani Editore, Rome, 1987.

Stefanutti, Piero, *Ottavio Bottecchia: quel mattino a Peonis*, Comune di Trasaghis, Trasaghis, 2005.

Thompson, Christopher, *The Tour de France. A Cultural History*, University of California Press, Los Angeles, 2006.

Thompson, Mark, *The White War. Life and Death on the Italian Front, 1915–1919*, Faber & Faber, London, 2009.

Thompson, Paul, *The Voice of the Past. Oral History*, Oxford University Press, Oxford, 2000.

Tobagi, Walter, *La rivoluzione impossibile. Politica e reazione popolare*, Il Saggiatore, Milan, 1978.

Tomassini, Luigi, 'L'immagine fotografica del campione', in Silei, ed., *Il Giro d'Italia e la società italiana*.

Turrini, Leo, *Bartali. L'uomo che salvò l'Italia pedalando*, Mondadori, Milan, 2004.

Varale, Vittorio, *Binda: i suoi debutti, la sua carriera, le sue vittorie*, Varese, Istituto Editoriale Cisalpino, 1928.

— *Avventure su due ruote*, Editrice Italiana, Rome, 1964.

Venè, Gian Franco, *Vola Colomba. Vita quotidiana degli italiani negli anni del dopoguerra: 1945–1960*, Mondadori, Milan, 1990.

Ventura, Marco, *Il campione e il bandito. La vera storia di Costante Girardengo e Sante Pollastro*, Il Saggiatore, Milan, 2006.

Vergani, Guido, ed., *L'uomo a due ruote. Avventura, storia e passione*, Electa, Milan, 1987.

Vergani, Orio and Guido, *Caro Coppi. La vita, le imprese, la malasorte, gli anni di Fausto e di quell'Italia*, Mondadori, Milan, 1995.

Viale, Guido, *Vita e morte dell'automobile. La mobilità che viene*, Bollati Boringhieri, Turin, 2007

Viberti, Paolo, *Coppi segreto. Il racconto di Marina la figlia del Campionissimo*, SEI, Turin, 2009.

Vigarello, Georges, 'Le Tour de France', in Pierre Nora, ed., *Les Lieux de mémoire*, vol. II, *Les Traditions* (Gallimard, Paris, 1992, pp. 887–925, translated into English as 'The Tour of France', in Nora, ed., *Realms of Memory: Rethinking the French Past*, Columbia University Press, New York, 1997, vol. 2, and into Italian as 'Il Tour de France. Memoria, territorio, racconto', in Antonio Roversi and Giorgio Triani, *Sociologia dello Sport*, Edizioni Scientifiche Italiane, Naples, 1995, pp. 249–79

Wheatcroft, Geoffrey, *Le Tour. A History of the Tour De France*, Pocket Books, London, 2004.

Whittle, Jeremy, *Le Tour. A Century of the Tour de France*, Collins, London, 2003.

— *Bad Blood. The Secret life of the Tour de France*, Yellow Jersey Press, London, 2008.

Williams, Richard, 'A golden era of cycling revealed through an open door', *Guardian*, 10.11.2009.

Zavoli, Sergio, *Diario di un cronista. Lungo viaggio nella memoria*, Mondadori, Milan, 2002.

Index